AFFIRMATIVE ACTION NOW

AFFIRMATIVE ACTION NOW

A Guide for Students, Families, and Counselors

James A. Beckman

ELIHU BURRITT LIBRARY
C.C.S.U.
NEW BRITAIN, CONNECTICUT

Greenwood Press
Westport, Connecticut • London

Ref
KF
4155
Z9
B43
2006

Library of Congress Cataloging-in-Publication Data

Beckman, James A.
    Affirmative action now : a guide for students, families, and counselors / James A. Beckman.
      p. cm.
    Includes bibliographical references and index.
    ISBN 0–313–33415–3 (alk. paper)
    1. Affirmative action programs in education—Law and legislation—United States.   2. Universities and colleges—Admission—Law and legislation—United States.   3. Affirmative action programs in education—United States—Handbooks, manuals, etc.   4. Universities and colleges—United States—Admission—Handbooks, manuals, etc.   I. Title.
KF4155.Z9B43   2006
342.7308'7—dc22   2005033545

British Library Cataloguing in Publication Data is available.

Copyright © 2006 by James A. Beckman

All rights reserved. No portion of this book may be reproduced, by any process or technique, without the express written consent of the publisher.

Library of Congress Catalog Card Number: 2005033545
ISBN: 0–313–33415–3

First published in 2006

Greenwood Press, 88 Post Road West, Westport, CT 06881
An imprint of Greenwood Publishing Group, Inc.
www.greenwood.com

Printed in the United States of America

The paper used in this book complies with the
Permanent Paper Standard issued by the National
Information Standards Organization (Z39.48–1984).

10 9 8 7 6 5 4 3 2 1

This book is dedicated to every student who has struggled to overcome adversity and hardship in the pursuit of education and the "good life" for themselves and their loved ones.

Contents

Preface		ix
Acknowledgments		xv
	Introduction: An Overview on the Ever-Changing Notion of Affirmative Action in Higher Education	1
1	How Did We Get to This Point? A Brief History of the Usage of Affirmative Action in Higher Education from the Tumultuous Civil Rights Era to *Gratz* and *Grutter* in 2003	13
2	*Gratz v. Bollinger* and *Grutter v. Bollinger*: The Changing Affirmative Action Analysis	25
3	How Colleges and Universities Revised or Eliminated Affirmative Action Programs in the Immediate Aftermath of the *Gratz* and *Grutter* Decisions	33
4	What about Affirmative Action in "Percentage Plan" States? The Unsettled Status of Affirmative Action in Higher Education in California, Texas, and Florida after *Gratz* and *Grutter*	41
5	General Advice to Students and Parents in Navigating the Maze	59
6	Six Steps to Completing the Compelling Application Essay	83
7	Consideration of Historically Black Colleges and Universities: Admittedly a "Different World"	97
8	Congratulations: You've Been Accepted to College, but Now Need to Pay for It: Financial Aid and Student Aid in the Post–*Gratz* and *Grutter* World	103
9	Veterans and Affirmative Action	119
10	Affirmative Action in the Coming Years	129

Appendix A	Four-Year Degree-Granting Colleges and Universities, The Use of Affirmative Action (or Lack Thereof), and Minority Enrollment Data	133
Appendix B	Department of Education Guidelines on Use of Race in Financial Aid Decisions/Awards	375
Appendix C	Recommended Resources and Internet Sites	397
Appendix D	The College Application Checklist	401
Notes		405
Index		419

Preface

This book addresses the state of affirmative action in higher education after the landmark decisions *Gratz v. Bollinger* and *Grutter v. Bollinger* in 2003, and explains and demystifies the use of affirmative action in admissions and financial aid decisions at the college and university level since then. While the Supreme Court settled several "big picture" issues in 2003 in *Gratz* and *Grutter* regarding the use of race as part of a university's affirmative action plan in admissions, numerous questions remain, from the perspective of prospective students, their parents, and even college administrators. Thus, the paramount goal of this book is to successfully guide the reader through the maze of the status of affirmative action in higher education since the summer of 2003—hopefully to point out to students and parents how best to maximize the potential benefits of universities and colleges that employ affirmative action, and to point out to college administrators how best to minimize the risks while administering such programs (if the college or university decides to employ affirmative action at all). I have endeavored to make this book a valuable resource for any person trying to make sense of the issue and practice of affirmative action in higher education in the twenty-first century—especially college-age students and their parents, as well as the counselors and teachers who provide advice and guidance to these students and parents.

For the general reader who is broadly interested in the topic of affirmative action in higher education, this book covers the field from the famous *Regents of the University of California v. Bakke* decision in 1978, through the *Gratz* and *Grutter* decisions in 2003, and especially examines the current status of affirmative action in the terrain of higher education. Also discussed is the issue of how much race and gender are to be considered in the admissions and scholarship context, and in what fashion. For the college administrator, this book analyzes the guidelines set forth by the Supreme Court in *Grutter* for a permissible affirmative action plan or program. For prospective students (and their parents), this book doubles as a handbook, enabling them to understand how affirmative action is implemented at the college, graduate, or professional school level, as well as how to tailor an application for admission to an institution utilizing an affirmative action program. The book also surveys colleges and universities around the country that continue to employ affirmative action, and states that have restricted the use of affirmative action by virtue of state laws (for example, Florida, California, Texas, and Washington), as well as other states that are contemplating such an approach.

A few words are in order about the structure and layout of this book. Largely in order to set the stage and context, Chapters 1 and 2 contain background material on the issue of affirmative action in higher education. It is virtually impossible to understand the current status of affirmative action in higher education without knowing at least a little of the historical context. Thus, specifically, Chapter 1 briefly explains the history of affirmative action in higher education in the modern era, from *Bakke* to *Gratz* and *Grutter*. Contrary to popular belief, affirmative action today does not mean the use of quotas or set-aside seats for minority candidates or candidates from other historically underrepresented groups. The U.S. Supreme Court made it clear over a quarter century ago, in the landmark *Bakke* case, that the use of rigid quotas or set-asides is not permissible under either Title VI of the Civil Rights Act of 1964 (which prohibits any discrimination based upon race at any public or private institution that receives federal funds) or the Equal Protection Clause of the Fourteenth Amendment. Rather, since 1978, when "affirmative action" is used in discussions about higher education, the term correctly connotes the use of special recruiting efforts, or the use of race as a "plus factor," or one of many separate components that might be consulted or considered in evaluating the candidate's worthiness for admission. Of course, as readers are probably aware, many questions arose in the ensuing years, between 1978 and 2003, regarding the proper implementation and use of affirmative action in higher education. Thus, Chapter 1 will also briefly delineate these problems, which developed over the quarter century after *Bakke*.

Chapter 2 contains an in-depth analysis of the *Gratz* and *Grutter* decisions of June 2003, with particular attention being paid to the guidance the Court gives in *Grutter* on how to permissibly utilize race-conscious admissions plans at the college and university level. While I have struggled to keep the use of legal jargon to a minimum, the complete avoidance of the legal requirements of affirmative action in a book of this nature would be a grave mistake and would also do the reader a great disservice. For good or bad, modern affirmative action is a legal creation and a social policy program that has been largely defined, refined, and crafted in the crucible of Supreme Court decisions and lower court determinations. As such, a basic understanding of the legal perimeters and dimensions is necessary in comprehending the overall practice (or lack thereof) of affirmative action today. As Harvard Law Professor Christopher Edley once aptly commented, in the area of affirmative action, "many individuals think that shooting from the hip should suffice. This is not rocket science; this is harder than rocket science."[1] Thus, while a discussion of certain legal concepts and principles is unavoidable in order to understand the practice of affirmative action, I have tried my best to explain them in the most straightforward manner possible, hopefully without oversimplifying the legal analysis and requirements.

After discussing the legal requirements for affirmative action in higher education set forth by the Supreme Court in the Michigan decisions of 2003, Chapter 3 then analyzes how colleges and universities reacted to the *Gratz* and *Grutter* decisions in the months and years after the decisions were handed down by the Court. Chapter 3 also addresses how race-conscious programs are being administered and developed in the post–*Gratz* and *Grutter* era. In Chapter 4, issues of affirmative action and higher education at the state level are discussed, with particular focus on those states that have passed laws prohibiting the use of affirmative action in their higher education systems, namely, Texas (Ten Percent Plan), Washington (Initiative 200), California (Proposition 209), and Florida (the One Florida Plan). This chapter also delineates current changes in the above percentage plan programs, and other states that are contemplating local laws that seek to avoid the use of race-conscious plans in higher education, such as Michigan's Civil Rights Initiative.

Perhaps most important to college applicants and their parents, the second half of this book (Chapters 5–10) provides concrete and specific advice on, among other things, on how to navigate the affirmative action maze in admissions, how to construct an effective application essay, and how to locate and apply for financial aid and scholarships that continue to employ race, gender, veteran status, or other factors as selection criteria. Specifically, Chapter 5 sets forth fifteen specially created rules for students (and parents) to consider in navigating the affirmative action maze in the admissions process. Then, a whole chapter, Chapter 6, is dedicated to offering advice to students on how to effectively and persuasively prepare the application essays, which, after *Gratz* and *Grutter*, is one of the chief ways in which universities and colleges consider diversifying factors under affirmative action plans. Chapter 7 addresses Historically Black Colleges and Universities (HBCUs), often overlooked by students, and not only covers the background and tradition of these institutions, but also addresses positive and negative aspects of attending an HBCU and whether HBCUs utilize affirmative action in their admissions or financial aid programs. This chapter further deals with how HBCUs approach the issue of diversity in higher education, and how they attempt to achieve diversity in student bodies that are predominantly and traditionally composed of African American students.

After this thorough coverage of affirmative action and admissions, Chapter 8 turns to the issue of financial aid and how a student might pay for the college of his or her dreams. Specifically, this chapter analyzes minority scholarship and financial aid programs in the wake of *Gratz* and *Grutter*, especially in light of how interpretation of these decisions may impact the way colleges and universities view the still-valid federal case *Podberesky v. Kirwan*, the 1994 Fourth Circuit decision that limited the use of exclusive minority-based scholarships and programs. Chapter 8 also discusses the current U.S. Department of Education Guidelines on the permissibility of minority-based scholarship programs, and instructs students on how to obtain additional institution-by-institution information on the continuing availability of these funds. Chapter 9 delineates affirmative action programs geared toward veterans and service members of the U.S. armed forces. Finally, Chapter 10 delineates the likely path of affirmative action in higher education in the coming years, and offers conclusions for the reader.

At the end of the text, readers will find general research aids and resources to further help in their search for information on the implementation of affirmative action in higher education since 2003. Of particular importance is Appendix A, which lists all four-year degree-granting institutions in the United States and the extent (if at all) to which race is considered in the admissions process, along with 2005–2006 data on the level of minority enrollment at each institution among those groups that are typically the beneficiaries of affirmative action plans (i.e., African Americans, Asian Americans, Hispanic Americans, and Native Americans). This appendix is designed to serve as a quick reference to determine the degree of racial diversity at the colleges and universities of interest to the reader (student or parent), at least to the degree reported by the college. Other appendixes include the U.S. Department of Education Final Policy Guidance Regarding Race and National Origin Based Financial Aid, and a list of Internet sites and resources, and a checklist of issues to consider for the college applicant.

The aim of this book is to ambitiously offer relevant information to readers from a variety of perspectives, from the prospective student to the college administrator. Depending on the individual reader's perspective, some chapters of the book will be more valuable than others. For example, those studying the broad history of affirmative action as a social policy to compensate for prior societal discrimination and to eradicate lingering current discrimination might find Chapters 1–4 to be of special interest. The college administrator, trying to make sense of the current requirements for utilizing race or other factors in decisions regarding admissions and financial aid, might find Chapters 1–3 and Chapter 8 to be of particular value. Prospective college applicants and their parents, will likely find the concrete advice section on financial aid and admissions to be of particular relevancy and value. For prospective students who live in a state that has passed laws prohibiting affirmative action or is creating alternatives to affirmative action at the state level, Chapter 4 will be of particular relevance. If you are interested in an HBCU, then Chapter 7 is clearly for you. The admissions and financial aid practices of hundreds of individual institutions are cited in the pages that follow, and the reader can find particular institutions by consulting the detailed index at the end of this book. I hope that, whatever the perspective, the reader will find this work to be of great value in ascertaining and demystifying the current status of affirmative action, which is often a difficult proposition in light of the constantly changing law and practice. This book should provide accurate, up-to-date information on both the current law and the practice of affirmative action at the college/university level, regardless of whether the reader is interested in a private or public institution, a community college or an Ivy League college, an HBCU or a land-grant institution, or whether the institution is in California, Florida, Texas, Virginia, New York, Ohio, or any other state.

James A. Beckman
Tampa, Florida

Acknowledgments

There are many people who were, directly or indirectly, helpful in the writing of this book and recognized its importance. First and foremost, I have been fortunate to have worked with Senior Editor Marie Ellen Larcada of Greenwood Press during the last five years, both on this project and a previous one. Not only has her technical knowledge of the world of publishing been of great service to me, but her sage advice and guidance also have been indispensable. She offered early support and should be credited with recognizing the value of a book of this nature to thousands of students and parents who are seeking timely and accurate information on how affirmative action really works in the admissions process in higher education The original idea and genesis of this book are as much Ms. Larcada's as they are mine. Second, my profound thanks are extended to Greenwood Press, and the countless individuals there who have assisted me in a major or minor way in the completion of this book. I feel privileged to have worked on two book projects with this excellent publishing company, and have been incredibly impressed with the professionalism of several Greenwood Press representatives who I have come into contact with these last several years. I would also like to extend a special thanks to the Production Editor for this book, Ms. Carla L. Talmadge, whose meticulous attention to detail in editing the manuscript has vastly improved the ultimate readability and clarity of this book.

I am also fortunate to have many excellent colleagues at the University of Tampa who have supported me, offered guidance from time to time, and recognized that scholarship is an indispensable part of being an effective teacher. I would like to thank *all* of the members of the Government and World Affairs Department at the University of Tampa, who offered their good will and support for this project. In particular, I would like to acknowledge the support of Professor Robert Kerstein, chair of the Government and World Affairs Department, for his constant support, and leadership to the junior members of the department. I am also indebted to Professor Richard Piper, who was an inspiration to me as one of my former teachers, and now as a colleague at UT. Finally, I would like to acknowledge the support and friendship of Assistant Professor Paulina Ruf during my last six years at the University of Tampa. Also, I would like to thank Associate Professor Christopher Capsambelis, chair of the Criminology Department, and Professor Tom Hickey and Assistant Professor Anthony LaRose for their constant support and encouragement during the course of this project. I would also like to extend a special note of thanks to University of Tampa vice president for enrollment Barbara Strickler, who provided background information for this project through an informational interview conducted in September 2004 and a myriad of forwarded articles that she thought might be relevant.

In addition to the strong support of colleagues noted above, I was fortunate to have the assistance of several incredibly bright University of Tampa Honors Program students (now graduates) who helped in the research and writing of this book. First and foremost, I would like to thank Ms. Liza Lugo-Clark, who helped me in conducting the research needed to complete this book in the fall semester of 2004. Ms. Clark, now a law student at the University of Florida, conducted weekly research in newspaper databases and journals during a time when institutional implementation of affirmative action in higher education appeared to be changing on a daily basis. For her sound research and weekly reports on the research, I am grateful. Ms. Clark also has graciously provided consent for the reproduction of her application essay for law school, which appears in Chapter 8. Second, I would like to extend my thanks to two other graduates of the University of Tampa Honors Program, Ms. Leslie Moreira, who is now a graduate student in history at Florida State University, and Ms. Iyandra Smith, who is pending matriculation to law school. Ms. Moreira and Ms. Smith graciously allowed reproduction of their application essays for graduate school and law school, respectively, both of which appear in Chapter 8.

I would also like to acknowledge the very strong institutional support provided by the University of Tampa, which included a generous award of a faculty grant to help in the researching and writing of this work, namely, the David Delo Faculty Research Grant, in 2005–2006. The grant allowed me to purchase many books and supplies needed to work on this important project. I am grateful for receiving this faculty research grant for the second time, having previously been awarded the same in 2002–2003 (for work on *Affirmative Action: An Encyclopedia*).

This acknowledgment would not be complete without noting the constant love and support of my wife, Maria D. Beckman, during the researching and writing of this book. Regardless of the complexity of the project undertaken and the hurdles to be overcome, her support has been unwavering, her encouragement constant, and her good humor and patience in tolerating me during the completion of this project almost Herculean.

Lastly, any errors or omissions found in this work are solely attributable to the author. I have done my best to delineate the state of affirmative action in higher education in such a way as to make it applicable to the broadest group of readers with different perspectives, from different walks of life, and from different regions and states within the United States. I have also strived to explain the legal requirements of affirmative action in as straightforward a manner as possible—without oversimplifying or watering down the legal requirements and standards. My fervent hope is that this book will help readers make sense of how universities and colleges currently approach the issue of affirmative action, and that it will play a positive role in many a student's application and admission to the college or university of their dreams.

Introduction:
An Overview on the Ever-Changing Notion of Affirmative Action in Higher Education

Today, students and college administrators alike may be confused about the role race may (or should) play in the college admissions process. In the 1960s, "relatively few students of color pursued a higher education in the United States. Today, however, about one in five U.S. college students is a minority."[1] As more and more students from historically underrepresented backgrounds and groups enter mainstream colleges and universities, many of these institutions are struggling to become "inclusive universities"[2] as is possible under the circumstances. This may involve the recruitment of minority students or students from underrepresented groups, conducting race-conscious admissions programs, and providing financial aid. However, as much as administrators desire to make their institutions as "inclusive" as possible, a great amount of confusion exists as to the legal perimeters or rules of inclusiveness, especially when race is considered as a factor in promoting inclusiveness. Indeed, a review of the latest comprehensive institution-by-institution guides to colleges and universities in the United States illustrates this confusion. As one flips through the pages of books like *Peterson's Guide to Four Year Colleges and Universities* and the Princeton Review's *Complete Book of Colleges*, it quickly becomes apparent that there are no national standards as to the use or relevancy of race or minority status as a factor in the admissions process. In fact, as one moves from institution to institution within such guides and reads the admissions requirements and/or procedures for each institution, a whole array of different approaches to the use of race and minority status is evident.

Currently, only a small number of the more than 1,500 four-year degree-granting institutions list the minority status of the applicant as a "very important factor" or "important factor" in the admissions process.[3] One report from 2005 indicated that only 2.2 percent of the institutions responding to the collection of this data deemed the applicant's race or ethnicity to be a factor of "considerable importance," and only 16.4 percent deemed it to be of "moderate importance."[4] However, a much larger number and majority of the institutions fail to list the minority status of the applicant as an important or very important factor in the admissions process. Some of these institutions list one's racial group or minority status as "a factor" or "other factor" that might be relevant (or might not be) in the decision-making process, along with factors such as one's prior work experience, performance in a campus interview, and relation to other alumni/ alumnae (called a "legacy"), among others. According to the above report, 24 percent of the responding institutions listed the applicant's race or ethnicity as a factor of "limited importance." However, many institutions do not consider race at all in admissions and scholarship determinations, or have done away with race-conscious affirmative action programs within the last several years. Admission trends from 2004 indicate that close to 60 percent of the responding institutions indicated that the applicant's race or ethnicity had no importance in the admissions process.[5] One report from 2003 noted that "only 33% of colleges and universities [at the undergraduate level] consider race or ethnicity as a factor in the admission decision."[6] Data from a 2005 report indicates that the use of race and ethnicity is now again on the rise—up to 42.6 percent of colleges and universities employed race or ethnicity as a factor in admissions in the 2004–2005 admissions cycle. Another expert has estimated that of the 1,500-plus four-year degree-granting institutions in the United States today, only 300 to 400 actually employ race as a criterion in the admissions process.[7] Furthermore, many of the institutions that claim on their web pages or admissions brochures that they consider race may not do so, or may do so in a manner different from that stated in outdated recruitment materials.[8]

Thus, understandably and unfortunately, much confusion and many mistaken beliefs surround the use and practice of affirmative action in higher education. If you ask twenty different admissions counselors what are the important factors in admissions, you are likely to get twenty different responses. Today, to be sure, many universities and colleges, in the effort to be labeled as an "inclusive university," consider a plethora of factors in granting or denying admittance, including, conservatively, such things as overall high school transcript, application essay, extracurricular activities, and personal interviews. Colleges and universities today often consider other factors such as whether the applicant is an athlete, an artist, or a musician, has shown an aptitude for volunteer work, is a close relative of alumni, is a veteran, or has overcome serious obstacles in life. Is an applicant who has a higher grade point average (GPA) or standardized test score more meritorious or qualified for admissions than one who has maintained respectable grades and performed well on the standardized tests, but also has an attribute (like those listed above) that makes the applicant more well rounded? Is a student who has a 3.8 GPA, but comes from a privileged background, more meritorious than a student with a 3.4 GPA, but who has overcome significant prior obstacles in life? Most admissions counselors would answer these questions by saying that admissions should not be as narrowly and rigidly defined as simply performance on a standardized test, and the overall GPA. As will be delineated in the following pages, this book takes the same position as many admissions officials who specify that merit and "qualifications" relevant to selection for admissions or financial aid are subjective factors that should be only minimally defined as one's GPA or standardized test scores. A plethora of other factors—such as race, ethnicity, gender, veteran status, and physically handicapped status—are also relevant in selecting the right student for the right college, in making that elusive "right fit" between the institution and the student.

Of course, when we use the term "affirmative action," a whole host of preconceived notions and ideas often race to the forefront of our mind, only some of which are likely to be correct. One of the purposes of this book is to dispel these erroneous notions regarding affirmative action in higher education. One myth, or misconception, is that affirmative action only applies to African American students. While this was true historically, and black Americans were (and still are) one of the primary beneficiaries of affirmative action programs, today the list of potential beneficiaries to a properly implemented affirmative action plan comprises any group that might have been historically unrepresented in higher education, including African Americans, Hispanic Americans, Alaskans, Native Hawaiians, Asian Americans, women, veterans of the U.S. armed forces, applicants from low socioeconomic classes, and people with disabilities. Arguably, affirmative action even applies to white male students at the HBCUs. While the focus of this book will be on affirmative action programs that employ race or ethnicity as a factor, many sections of this book will make reference to how affirmative action applies to other disadvantaged groups as well.

Another misnomer is that, to the extent that an affirmative action plan is in place, it permits "less qualified" individuals to take the admissions or financial slots of those who are "more qualified." Of course, as the subsequent pages of this book will explore, this is not the case if the affirmative action plan is correctly implemented and works the way it was intended to. Under a properly operating affirmative action program, all students considered for admissions are basically qualified. Whether one applicant is more worthy than another depends on how you define merit, and what factors the university or college considers in defining merit and in making an educated, reasonable, and principled decision regarding admissions and/or financial aid. According to one report, "The more selective institutions were likely to attribute a higher degree of importance to a student's race or ethnicity than less selective institutions." Furthermore, according to the same report, "The fewer students an institution accepts, the more likely it is to place emphasis on the 'tip' factors in the admissions process. Since grades and test scores for the top competitors for selective college admission are often similarly high, these colleges must dig deeper for information with which to evaluate each applicant."[9]

For example, some readers of this book might be familiar with the story of Brooke Ellison, either through her book, *Miracles Happen: One Mother, One*

Daughter, One Journey, or through the made-for-television movie (the last film directed by Christopher Reeve before his death), *The Brooke Ellison Story*. Ms. Ellison was struck by a car when she was eleven, rendering her a quadriplegic. Yet, despite this physical handicap, she went on to ultimately finish grade school and high school with her original class, attend the Harvard University, excel, and graduate from there—all amazing accomplishments given the gravity of her injuries. By all accounts, Ms. Ellison's grades and standardized test scores were such that she would have been a competitive applicant for any university in the country, and she was recruited by Harvard based upon these alone, and *not* because of her disability. In fact, she wrote in her autobiography that "despite my A plus average and 1510 on my SAT, some people thought I was selected only because I was in a wheelchair. They thought I wouldn't succeed if I went." She went and graduated in four years, summa cum laude.

Her story raises many valid points in regard to college admissions and affirmative action in general—whether Harvard did or did not consider secondary factors in her application such as the personal essay, life experiences, gender, letters of recommendation, and the like. The point is also not to debate whether Harvard did or did not consider the obstacles she had to overcome in being selected over other applicants with roughly the same GPA or test scores. First, Ms. Ellison's story poignantly illustrates that a candidate with a high GPA who has overcome incredible obstacles in life is more impressive than one with the same GPA but no other diversifying factors from their background. Second, her case illustrates the perfect example of how affirmative action should work today. Ms. Ellison was obviously qualified to attend Harvard, in terms of both her GPA and standardized test scores, as most beneficiaries under affirmative action plans are, whether or not such factors played a role in admissions. In comparing her accomplishments with those of other candidates with the same superior test scores and grades (but without serious life obstacles to overcome), she outshines them all. Her example proves the value of considering life experiences, obstacles, and accomplishments. Third, according to her book, and the movie, the family had precious little to spend for an Ivy League education, in light of the medical treatment needed over the years for Ms. Ellison. This predicament Harvard University solved by being "extremely generous with financial aid" and by providing a van to take Ms. Ellison around the campus to classes and campus events, and even "renovated a dorm room to accommodate all her medical and physical needs, including space for Jean [her mother and caretaker]." According to Ms. Ellison, "I was so flattered and so stunned that—that they would really go to the—the lengths that they had gone to in order to get me here."[10] This case is not only the perfect example of how some people's life experiences and the obstacles they have overcome make their accomplishments all the more impressive and worthy of consideration by a college or university, but also shows that it is appropriate for colleges and universities to award financial aid to students based upon such factors—even if not called "affirmative action" per se.

Considering the above, why do certain affirmative action programs, for example, affirmative action based upon race, garner attention in the media, in litigation, and also garner such vociferous debate among various segments of our population? Part of the response stems from the original history of affirmative action, which was implemented initially not out of concerns for diversity or cultivating the "well-rounded" college applicant, but rather as a remedial program to compensate members of minority groups for previous societal or institutional discrimination. However, in the last quarter century, rightly or wrongly, modern affirmative action programs have focused more on the good to society and educational experience (under such rationales as "diversity in the classroom contributes to the overall educational value for collective society"), and less on remedial compensation for individuals. Another reason why race-conscious programs garner considerable attention and controversy stems from constitutional and statutory provisions that prohibit discrimination (good or bad, benign or invidious) on account of race. The Fourteenth Amendment's Equal Protection Clause guarantees that all citizens, regardless of race, will be treated equally under the law. Furthermore, Title VI of the Civil Rights Act of 1964 prohibits discrimination on account of race in public or private universities or colleges that receive federal funds. Affirmative action plans that utilize factors other than race (i.e., socioeconomic status, veteran status, legacies, etc.) are not subject to the same limitations under federal constitutional and statutory law, and thus, are also not subject to the same level of controversy. Finally, in terms of controversy, the reader must remember that one of the basic definitions of political science is, "The study of who gets what government resources, when, where, and why." The allocation of societal benefits also causes dissatisfaction to those who did not get the resources, or are upset with the allocation. The same holds true for affirmative action plans.

After a quarter century of relative uncertainty and lack of national uniformity, from 1978 to 2003, the Supreme Court was predicted to put some of the confusion to rest when it announced that it would review the Michigan cases *Gratz v. Bollinger*, 123 S. Ct. 2411, and *Grutter v. Bollinger*, 123 S. Ct. 2325, in 2003. However, as will be discussed later, the two cases actually came to different results, upholding affirmative action in one case, and rejecting it in the other. Hence, the results appeared "complicated for the public to digest," and it was left to "college lawyers [to] comb through the decisions trying to figure out what kind of admissions systems would pass legal muster."[11] As Julie Peterson, the associate vice president for media relations at the University of Michigan, stated, "There is a misconception Michigan had to do away with considering race [because of the decisions], but the reality is the court basically said affirmative action should remain."[12] While it is correct to say that the Court did answer some larger issues regarding affirmative action and higher education, the "Court hardly ended the debate over race-conscious college admission policies in its two landmark rulings."[13] This confusion and misconception stems from two different opinions. In *Gratz*, the Supreme Court held that the University of

Michigan's undergraduate admissions program violated the Constitution, and the Court struck down the race-conscious admissions program as illegal under the Fourteenth Amendment to the U.S. Constitution. However, in *Grutter*, the Supreme Court upheld the constitutionality of a race-conscious admissions program at the University of Michigan Law School. While, on the surface, the two resulting decisions are conflicting, a reading of both decisions together gives the college administrator a blueprint for how to permissibly construct a race-conscious admissions plan on either the undergraduate or graduate/professional school level. Taken together, the decisions also allow the continued use of narrowly tailored and properly drafted race-conscious affirmative action plans in higher education—in public and private colleges alike—at least for the next quarter century.[14] Very importantly, for the first time, the Supreme Court sanctioned the justification of "diversity" in the classroom as being a sufficient rationale to allow for the implementation of affirmative action plans. As a result, as one author and law professor has suggested, a "new generation of affirmative action programs in the wake of *Grutter* and *Gratz*" may be developing and there now exist potential benefits (for students) that are great "for a number of groups whose members have historically been unable to avail themselves of the opportunities and benefits associated with a higher education."[15] At the same time, there are many pitfalls for colleges and universities that, in their zeal to implement an affirmative action plan, might actually lead the school astray and into a myriad of legal problems and lawsuits claiming reverse institutional discrimination.

Some of those unversed in affirmative action history may ask why a book of this nature is needed. It is relevant, therefore, to discuss at this point the general need for a guidebook. For approximately a quarter century, from 1978 through 2003, there existed no uniform national standard for the utilization of racial criteria and preferences in decisions pertaining to admissions and scholarship availability under affirmative action programs at colleges and universities. Indeed, prior to 2003, the Supreme Court had decided on only one case that dealt with the issue of affirmative action in higher education—*Regents of the University of California v. Bakke*, 438 U.S. 265 (1978). It is true that the Supreme Court offered some basic guidance to the courts, colleges, and students in the *Bakke* case when it held that fixed racial quotas in higher education were unconstitutional. But the Court was extremely fractured in its decision (resulting in six separate opinions in the case) and, ultimately, implicitly approved the continued use of race as a factor in determining which students ultimately gained entrance into schools, but failed to offer any further definitive guidance. Phrased another way, so long as the institution was not employing a quota to reserve seats in a class based exclusively upon one's racial group, the institution's use of race might otherwise be permissible. Over the subsequent years, the amount of deference or weight given to racial characteristics of an applicant widely varied.

As will be discussed in Chapter 1, the Supreme Court's failure in *Bakke* to delineate the exact standards in which race may be utilized in higher education eventually ushered in a quarter century of confusion and ambiguity as to how aggressively an institution might use race in determining eligibility for admissions or scholarship programs. According to one scholar, "Rather than providing a definitive answer on affirmative action, *Bakke* nibbled at the question, settling only the narrower issue of racial quotas in admissions to state-supported schools and leaving later cases to test the propriety of affirmative action in other realms."[16] Theodore Shaw, head of the National Association for the Advancement of Colored People's Legal and Educational Defense Fund (NAACP-LEDF), has stated that the *Bakke* decision was "a significant loss" for students of color, as it did not recognize the need for aggressive race-conscious programs to compensate minority groups for the hundreds of years of racism and societal discrimination. Rather, according to Shaw, *Bakke* decision (especially in the Powell opinion, discussed extensively in Chapter 1), framed the issue in terms of what could be gained by black and white students alike in fostering diversity in the classroom, and not as a remedial compensation program. Hence, the *Bakke* decision was as much a decision about maximizing the learning experiences of white students, as it was about advancing students of color.[17]

The lack of Supreme Court guidance on this question during this period also correlated with a general movement among select tier-one colleges and universities to promote minority students as a remedy for their prior discrimination and underrepresentation in school, as well as to achieve diversity in the overall school body. During this period of relative confusion, how a college or university utilized race in its admissions decisions obviously varied from state to state, from region to region (based upon differences in federal circuit court jurisprudence that developed in the 1990s), and institution to institution. Between the *Bakke* and the *Gratz* and *Grutter* decisions, four U.S. Court of Appeals cases also analyzed the constitutionality of affirmative action in higher education, to differing results and conclusions. During this period, some institutions employed race in almost a mathematical manner, whereby the racial characteristic of the applicant would be assigned a point value, and plugged into an equation that would ultimately yield a point total dictating whether or not the applicant gained admission. Other institutions utilized race as a "plus factor," in essence a tie-breaker mechanism between equally situated candidates, based loosely upon the "Harvard Plan," which Justice Powell cited with approval in the *Bakke* case. In describing how the Harvard Plan works, Justice Powell wrote in *Bakke* that "the race of an applicant may tip the balance in favor just as geographic order or a life spent on a farm may tip the balance in other candidates' cases."[18] Still other schools utilized race along with a plethora of other life experience and background details of the candidate. Finally, many institutions were less than completely forthcoming in describing to what degree characteristics of race were utilized in the decision-making process. Students were forced to largely guess the degree to which they should make reference to their race, ethnicity, gender, or other special characteristics in putting together their applications to college.

Then, in 2002, the Supreme Court granted review in two cases (which were consolidated for Supreme Court review), entitled *Gratz v. Bollinger* and *Grutter v. Bollinger*, which were supposed to finally and conclusively decide the legality and propriety of affirmative action programs in higher education. As such, the *Gratz* and *Grutter* cases were heralded as the "Alamo of affirmative action,"[19] and the public waited anxiously for the fate of race-conscious affirmative action usage in higher education. Yet, as Michael Nettles has written, "In the end, the fragility of affirmative action was never more apparent than in a divided decision that left college and university leaders, faculty, students and prospective students, and plaintiffs and defendants alike continuing the discourse toward understanding the Court's decision."[20] On the morning of June 23, 2003, after almost twenty-five years of silence, the U.S. Supreme Court again weighed in on the issue of the operation and availability of race-based admissions and scholarship programs in higher education for the next several decades. On that day, the Supreme Court released its much-anticipated rulings in *Gratz v. Bollinger* and *Grutter v. Bollinger*. In its opinions, which will be discussed in more detail in Chapter 2, the Court addressed the issue of whether the University of Michigan's race-conscious admissions programs at its undergraduate and law schools were unconstitutional. While a majority of the Court, with a six to three split, found the University of Michigan's undergraduate admissions program unconstitutional in *Gratz*, the Court upheld the University of Michigan Law School's admissions program with a five to four majority vote in *Grutter*, stating that the "Equal Protection Clause does not prohibit the Law School's narrowly tailored use of race in admissions decisions to further a compelling interest in obtaining the educational benefits that flow from a diverse student body." The common point in both decisions, however, was that race may be used in admissions decisions (so long as done properly), and that concerns of racial diversity in the classroom do constitute a compelling government interest in allowing the implementation of such plans without constitutional objections. It should be noted that the Court also acknowledged that affirmative action is a temporary measure to achieve racial and gender equality, that affirmative action "must have a logical end point," and "25 years from now, the use of racial preferences will no longer be necessary to further the interest approved today." This has prompted at least one commentator to wonder whether, in light of the fact that the Court expects affirmative action practices to discontinue within the next twenty-five years, the *Grutter* decision is largely a Pyrrhic victory.[21] As of the publication of this book, only twenty-two years now remain, assuming that the Court, in 2028, honors Justice O'Connor's statement made two decades before.

Ultimately, taken together, both rulings permit undergraduate, graduate, and professional school programs to take into consideration the factor of race, along with other factors, unless otherwise prohibited by state law, and at least for the next decade or two. However, an admissions policy that takes race into account must be carefully designed to comply with the Court's guidelines, which were delineated in the majority opinion of the *Grutter* case. Additionally, for the first time since *Bakke*, the Court expanded the type of institutional justification acceptable to it in implementing affirmative action programs in the higher education context, thus expanding the permissible list of justifications to include the need to promote diversity within the classroom, in order to enhance the educational environment for both minority and nonminority students alike.

Under modern Equal Protection Clause jurisprudence, in order for a government-sponsored program to properly and legally utilize discriminatory racial practices (even in the benign discrimination context), the justification for the program should be based upon a compelling governmental interest. Prior to the *Gratz* and *Grutter* decisions, the Supreme Court had only definitively sanctioned one legitimate justification for implementing preferential affirmative action programs at the university and college level—to remedy prior institutional discrimination at the institution in question. Many of the other theories behind affirmative action programs, such as the role model theory, increasing diversity in society, increasing diversity in certain professions,[22] among other rationales/justifications, had all been previously rejected by the Supreme Court in cases pertaining to affirmative action outside of the higher education realm. However, the other chief justification, the diversity rationale, while often utilized by colleges and discussed in lower federal circuit court rulings from 1979 onward, never enjoyed the imprimatur of the Supreme Court prior to the *Gratz* and *Grutter* rulings. The diversity rationale, based upon Justice Powell's opinion in *Bakke*, had never received the approval of a majority of members of the Supreme Court, and therefore, had never become the law of the land, until the Supreme Court's acceptance of this rationale/justification in *Gratz* and *Grutter*.

The decisions of June 2003 amounted to a bombshell for many groups around the country. Conservative groups such as the Center for Equal Opportunity and the American Civil Rights Institute denounced the decisions that sanctioned "reverse discrimination" in higher education and prolonged the intense national debate over affirmative action for another twenty-five years. This view was embodied by Supreme Court Justice Antonin Scalia's position in the case. In his dissent, Scalia argued that the Court was putting forth no intelligible standard for institutions to follow, and the allowance of affirmative action in the *Grutter* decision seemed "perversely designed to prolong the controversy and the litigation." In closing his dissent, Scalia again made clear his long-standing opposition to race-conscious affirmative action, commenting that "the Constitution proscribes government discrimination on the basis of race, and state-provided education is no exception."

In the immediate aftermath of the decisions, groups opposed to affirmative action promised a continued war against the practice of affirmative action in higher education. For example, the Center for Individual Rights (CIR), the organization that sponsored the lawsuit against the University of Michigan and represented the white plaintiffs in that case, promised to continue bringing lawsuits challenging institutions that utilized affirmative action plans whose criteria went beyond those approved by the Court in *Grutter*. As such, the president of CIR, Terry Pell, said that the decision represented "the beginning of the end of race preferences."[23] As will be discussed in detail in Chapter 4, the groups also promised to continue to wage the war at the state level and to encourage individual states to discontinue the practice of affirmative action, as had previously been done in Florida, Washington, Texas, and California. For instance, Ward Connerly, one of the architects of California's law abolishing affirmative action in the state as of 1997, California Proposition 209, promised to rally for a similar law in Michigan, as well as three or four other states whose populace might support such laws on the state level.[24] These anti–affirmative action groups have also threatened the Department of Education's Office for Civil Rights (OCR) with lawsuits and complaints for unlawfully discriminating against white applicants in administering affirmative action programs. In 2004 alone, for example, the OCR opened investigations involving alleged reverse discrimination against white applicants at the University of Virginia (both in undergraduate admissions and at the law school), North Carolina State University, University of Maryland (at Baltimore) School of Medicine, and the College of William and Mary School of Law.[25]

Thus, despite the predictions that the *Gratz* and *Grutter* cases would once and for all answer the question of whether affirmative action programs that employed racial preferences would be permissible in higher education, they turned out to be anything but "the Alamo of affirmative action," as they were called at the time by one major magazine. Rather, the decisions were a compromise, forged by an extremely fractioned Court, much like the *Bakke* decision from a quarter century ago. Thus, the decisions in *Gratz* and *Grutter* have been described as compromise decisions that attempted to "split the baby," and left the practice of affirmative action in higher education alive, but battered. The decisions also left many individuals (students, parents, and administrators alike) and institutions uncertain about how to proceed with race-conscious admissions programs. Some institutions simply declared that they would discontinue racially conscious programs, while others said that they would study the decisions, and then determine how their practices needed to be revised. Still other groups promised to export the findings and justifications in *Grutter* to "other types of race-conscious policies in higher education—such as recruitment and outreach, financial aid, and retention programs."[26] The resulting ambiguity of the rulings was reflected in the *Chronicle of Higher Education* in its two chief articles following the decision, namely, "Affirmative Action Survives, and So Does the Debate: The Supreme Court Upholds Race-Conscious Admissions in Principle, But Not Always as Practiced" and "Friends and Foes of Affirmative Action Claim Victory in Rulings on Michigan Cases." Other papers around the country reported on the same ambiguity. For example, on the day following the decision, the *Cleveland Plain Dealer's* front page read, "Divided Supreme Court Upholds Affirmative Action—With Limits."

In the three years since the ruling, there exists a good deal of confusion as to what exactly are those limits. How are universities and colleges able to utilize race-conscious preferences without running afoul of the laws and the U.S. Constitution? How many colleges and universities attempt to do so? What factors and criteria may schools consider? Should schools consider phasing out affirmative action plans consistent with Justice O'Connor's statement that affirmative action in higher education should not be an issue in society by 2028? Moreover, many smaller colleges began to report that they simply would not consider race for fear of being sued and challenged in Court for not following the guidance set forth in the *Grutter* decision. In the words of Terry Pell, the decision actually "heightens the risk for universities that want to continue to use racial preferences in college admissions."[27] The CIR has promised that it will play a role in monitoring compliance/implementation and "testing both the continuing validity of the principles embraced in *Grutter* and the means employed to implement them."[28] Furthermore, many colleges and universities then began to remove all racial considerations pertaining to many scholarship programs. This trend is illustrated in a front-page *Chronicle of Higher Education*, dated March 19, 2004, entitled "Colleges Open Up Minority Programs to All: Institutions Fear Legal Action by Opponents of Affirmative Action." The article delineated prominent scholarship programs (historically, only offered to minority or female applicants) and how the scholarship criteria have changed since the Court's rulings of June 2003. Thus, it appears that a significant number of colleges and universities are moving away from, and not closer to, the practice of affirmative action because of the Court's rulings. Justice Blackmun once famously remarked, as part of his separate opinion in *Bakke,* that "in order to get beyond racism, we must first take account of race ... [a]nd in order to treat some persons equally, we must treat them differently. We cannot—we dare not—let the Equal Protection Clause perpetuate racial supremacy." Has Blackmun's admonition now come to fruition, or are universities and colleges taking account of race, and treating applicants differently, in order to ultimately get beyond racism? It is this question, among many other related questions of interest to students, parents, and administrators, which will be addressed and answered in the subsequent pages of this book.

1
How Did We Get to This Point? A Brief History of the Usage of Affirmative Action in Higher Education from the Tumultuous Civil Rights Era to *Gratz* and *Grutter* in 2003

THE EARLY HISTORY OF AFFIRMATIVE ACTION IN HIGHER EDUCATION

Depending on how broadly one defines the term "affirmative action," the idea or practice of granting racial preferences to achieve equality can be traced back hundreds of years, well before the modern era. One author in his book on the history of affirmative action began his study in the year 1619, when twenty Africans first arrived off the coast of the Jamestown Colony in Virginia. Thurgood Marshall, the first African American to serve as U.S. solicitor general and later as an associate justice of the U.S. Supreme Court, also believed that the idea of affirmative action had existed for over a century in the United States, and once commented that America had "several affirmative action programs" in the years immediately following the Civil War. For example, the Freedmen's Bureau (more completely named the Bureau of Refugees, Freedmen, and Abandoned Lands) was a temporary agency set up in 1865 to help newly freed black citizens in their transition from bondage to freedom. One of its greatest achievements was in the field of education, albeit providing only the rudiments of learning in such areas as reading and writing. Thus, the student or scholar wishing to trace the broad history of giving preferences or benefits in education can find some historical antecedents going back to the earliest days of the Republic. However, the reader should also note that any race-conscious program in American history (like the Freedmen's Bureau) that might have rendered some benefits to African Americans was the exception, rather than the norm.

Furthermore, outside of the racial preference context, colleges and universities did offer preferential treatment to certain groups, such as veterans, athletes, and descendants of graduates, well before the modern era. For example, following World War II, veterans of the armed forces were provided a year of readjustment benefits under the Servicemen's Readjustment Act of 1944 (G.I. Bill). While the legislation covered an array of benefits ranging from housing to medical and dental care, a notable portion dealt with education, and allowed for aid to cover tuition, fees, and room and board for veterans at institutions of higher learning. This type of preference or benefit was designed to increase the representation of veterans in school as a means of improving domestic opportunities for those returning from World War II, as well as to help the overall economy. Another example can be found in the original practice of legacy preference in higher education. This refers to the practice of granting preference to children or other relatives of a graduate of the institution in question. Ironically, the legacy preference was originally born not out of a desire to increase the representation of a disadvantaged group, but rather as a means of excluding Jews from elite institutions. The idea was that "if college admission was solely based on merit, the number of Jewish students would rapidly increase and they would be disproportionately represented among the student body."[1]

Despite the fact that there is some historical precedent for providing special benefits or preferences to disadvantaged groups, it was not until the latter half of the twentieth century that African Americans and members of other minority groups were able to attend white colleges and universities in significant numbers. Indeed, these minority groups were largely precluded from attending college before World War II by virtue of racist segregationist laws and practices. According to William Bowen and Derek Bok in their influential 1998 book, *The Shape of the River: Long-Term Consequences of Considering Race in College and University Admissions*, African Americans fell woefully behind in education prior to 1940. Bowen and Bok recount the dismal status of education for blacks:

> The median amount of education received by blacks aged 25–29 was about seven years. Only 12 percent of blacks aged 25–29 had completed high school; less than 2 percent could claim a college degree. Very few blacks managed to enter the higher-paying occupations. Only 1.8 percent of all male professionals were black, and only 1.3 percent of all male managers and proprietors. Blacks made up 2.8 percent of physicians, 0.5 percent of attorneys, and 0.5 percent of engineers.[2]

They further reported that in 1965 "only 4.8 percent of all U.S. college students were African American,"[3] "barely 1 percent of all law students in America were black," and "barely 2 percent of all medical students were African American, and more than three-fourths of them attended two all black institutions."[4]

The idea of using affirmative action in higher education originated roughly around the time that President Lyndon Johnson gave his famous commencement speech at Howard University in June 1965. Johnson called for some sort of preferential treatment in order to bring about true equality in society, stating, "You do not take a person who for years has been hobbled by chains and liberate him, bring him up to the starting line of a race and then say, 'you're free to compete with all the others,' and still justly believe that you have been completely fair."[5] It was about the time of Johnson's speech that many colleges and universities began to experiment with the idea of achieving racial equality by giving temporary preferences to minority students. For example, at Harvard Law School, starting in 1966, "black students with test scores far below those of their white classmates" were admitted.[6] Again, according to Bowen and Bok, "[I]n the years that followed, almost all leading colleges and professional schools came to believe that they had a role to play in educating minority students."[7]

Colleges and universities would then have a full decade to begin implementing various remedial means of achieving diversity in higher education and making up for previous institutional discrimination. While the Supreme Court did take up a case in 1974 that would have analyzed the constitutionality of affirmative action in higher education, the white student's claim of reverse discrimination was dismissed by the Court as moot, as the student was subsequently admitted to the school before the Court's review of the merits of the case.[8] Thus, it would be another four years, and roughly a decade and a half after President Johnson's Howard University speech, before the Supreme Court would finally weigh in on the legality of race-conscious affirmative action programs in higher education in *Bakke*.

REGENTS OF THE UNIVERSITY OF CALIFORNIA V. BAKKE

The origins of *Bakke* go back to 1968, a full decade before the Supreme Court actually ruled in the case, and about the time that many colleges and universities around the country were aggressively implementing new race-conscious programs that would benefit certain minority groups. In addition to lending a more complete understanding to the Supreme Court's ultimate ruling in *Bakke*, the facts surrounding the *Bakke* case are also worthy of review, as they will give the reader an idea of how typical race-conscious affirmative action plans operated during this era. In 1968, the University of California at Davis opened its medical school, and from the outset, the administrators were concerned about low minority enrollment at the school. Thus, in 1969, in the second year of its operation, a goal was set to recruit 8 minority students out of the 50 new entering students. By 1972, a plan was instituted to set aside 16 of 100 seats for applicants from nontraditional backgrounds. However, the definition of a "nontraditional background" was left open to interpretation and did not preclude, at least in theory, white applicants who had unique life experiences or backgrounds. In fact, by 1973, the application materials advised candidates that "nontraditional backgrounds" included applicants who were "economically and/or educationally disadvantaged." However, by 1974, the University of California at Davis had revised the definition, and the application materials specified that students from nontraditional backgrounds included "Blacks," "Chicanos," "Asians," and "Native Americans." Thus, from 1968 to 1974, the school went from an arguable race-neutral affirmative action program, which (like some modern affirmative action plans) utilized race as one of many possible factors in determining if a student had a nontraditional background, to a specifically race-conscious program, and no longer allowed for special consideration for the reserved sixteen seats unless the applicant came from a specified minority group.

As sixteen out of the total 100 seats were reserved exclusively for minority students, and white students had to compete for the remaining eighty-four seats, a dual admissions system developed. For white students, the application process was roughly as follows: First, any applicant with a grade point average (GPA) of less than 2.5 was rejected. Second, the remaining applicants were interviewed and awarded a score of 1–100 (which included points for the interview, as well as other information in the applicant's file, such as GPA, standardized test scores, letters of recommendation, etc.). Third, once all applicants received the score, all of the aggregate numbers were added together, and then divided by the number of applicants, yielding an average applicant score (which was used as a benchmark). Finally, the applicants were ranked and offers made based on each applicant's overall ranking and his or her individual composite score.

However, students from nontraditional backgrounds were handled in a different fashion. First, these applicants were routed to a different interview panel, whose members were sensitive to the need to improve minority enrollment. Second, each minority applicant was rated on the same 1–100 scale delineated above and allowed to compete for any of the 100 available seats (either the sixteen seats specifically reserved for minorities, or one of the remaining eighty-four non-reserved seats). Conversely, however, white applicants were competing for one of eighty-four seats, and could not gain admittance through one of the sixteen special set-aside seats, even if one of those slots remained vacant during any admissions year. Finally, the minimum GPA requirement of 2.5 was waived for minority students, allowing them to compete for the special set-aside seats.

During the years at issue in the *Bakke* case, the admissions process was very competitive: 2,464 applications were received for the 100 available seats in 1973, and 3,737 in 1974. Allan Bakke, a white male of Jewish ethnicity, applied for admission in 1973. He has been described as "an overly qualified applicant, having a standardized test score (Medical College Admission Test, MCAT) that put him in the top percentile of all test takers, as well as an above average 3.46 grade point average."[9] He was denied admission; some have speculated that he was rejected because he was an older applicant and because he applied late in the admissions year (and many of the eighty-four seats were already allocated on a rolling admissions basis). After being rejected, Bakke wrote to the dean of the admissions department, George H. Lowrey, and questioned his denial, and especially the use of race and ethnicity as selection factors. The following year, 1974, Allan Bakke applied again for admission, and was again rejected.

After the second rejection, Bakke filed a lawsuit in the state court system of California, where he sought judicial relief that would force the University of California to admit him immediately to the medical school. After he had filed suit, Bakke learned that four of the sixteen nontraditional background seats had not even been filled the first year he had been rejected. Bakke's lawsuit was based on several arguments. First, he claimed that the medical school's system, which reserved sixteen seats exclusively for members of racial minority groups, constituted a racial quota. Furthermore, according to Bakke's lawyers, the use of such a quota violated Title VI of the Civil Rights Act of 1964 (a federal statute that prohibits discrimination on account of race in public educational institutions or institutions receiving federal funds), as well as the Equal Protection Clause of the Fourteenth Amendment (a constitutional provision that prohibits states from denying citizens the "equal protection of the laws"). The University of California responded by positing several justifications for its racially restrictive affirmative action plan. First, the school argued that the plan was needed to compensate for "past and continuing racial injustice."[10] The school also argued that the special set-aside program was needed to ensure sufficient minority representation in the medical profession, to improve the chances that medical care would spread in traditionally lower-income minority communities, and to provide doctors who would become role models to disadvantaged youths; and that by increasing the diversity of the entering class, the overall education experience would improve.

The California courts were unsympathetic to the arguments of the University of California, and both the California state trial court and the California Supreme Court held that the medical school's racially conscious program violated the Equal Protection Clause of the Fourteenth Amendment. Specifically, the courts held that racial quotas or exclusionary racial preferences could not be utilized, absent a specific finding that the institution had a prior history of racial discrimination, and that the plan was adopted specifically to remedy the effects of prior institutional discrimination. The case was then appealed by the University of California to the U.S. Supreme Court, which heard the case during the 1977–1978 term.

Similar to the timing of the *Gratz* and *Grutter* decisions a quarter century later, the Supreme Court issued its much-anticipated ruling in the *Bakke* case on June 28, 1978, just before the beginning of the Court's traditional summer break. The Court decided the case by a narrow five to four vote, holding that the use of restrictive racial quotas was impermissible under the Equal Protection Clause of the Fourteenth Amendment. However, the undercurrents of the decision (and the resulting six separate opinions issued in the case) presented a much more complex picture. There were, in fact, three major coalitions, or blocs, in the decision, representing differing opinions on the viability and constitutionality of affirmative action plans in higher education. One bloc of four justices believed that the use of race as a preferential factor in any admissions decision was not only unconstitutional under the Fourteenth Amendment, but also violated Title VI of the Civil Rights Act of 1964. Specifically, Title VI of the Civil Rights Act stated that "no person in the United States shall, on the ground of race, color, or national origin, be excluded from participation in, be denied the benefits of, or be subjected to discrimination under any program or activity receiving federal financial assistance." A second bloc of four justices, sometimes described as the "anti-discrimination four," saw no Title VI problems and believed that racially conscious admissions plans should be permissible in many contexts, for example, to remedy prior institutional discrimination, to improve diversity, or to further any other important government reason for implementing the preferential plan.[11]

Justice Lewis Powell served as the crucial swing vote, joining both the four-justice blocs on different points. Justice Powell joined the first bloc of justices in holding that the affirmative action plan at issue in the *Bakke* case was unconstitutional under the Fourteenth Amendment. Powell believed that the medical school's plan allowing sixteen set-aside seats was too inflexible, and "totally foreclosed" nonminorities from competing for those seats. However, Justice Powell joined the second bloc of justices in holding that better-drafted, more narrowly tailored, and less-exclusionary affirmative action plans might be permissible in future cases. Furthermore, Justice Powell wrote a plurality opinion in the case, which, while not speaking for a majority of justices, articulated what has been called "the diversity rationale" of the *Bakke* case. In essence, Powell argued in his opinion that race and ethnicity could be factors that are considered in "the attainment of a diverse student body" and heterogeneity in higher education. Justice Powell cited with approval the Harvard Plan, which permitted race to be considered, along with other factors such as diverse geographical representation of students, travel experiences, and so on. In arguing that colleges and universities ought to be able to consider race to achieve diversity in the classroom, Powell wrote as follows in one of the key passages of his opinion:

> It is not an interest in simple ethnic diversity, in which a specified percentage of the student body is in effect guaranteed to be members of selected ethnic groups, with the remaining percentage an undifferentiated aggregation of students. The diversity that furthers a compelling state interest encompasses a far broader array of qualifications and characteristics of which racial or ethnic origin is but a single though important decision.

The above quotation and Powell's diversity rationale would eventually be cited by the Supreme Court with approval in *Gratz v. Bollinger* and be accepted by a majority of Supreme Court justices as being a binding rule under constitutional law in dealing with the issue of affirmative action in higher education. That is, in 2003, the Supreme Court would finally come around to Justice Powell's rationale in *Bakke* and affirm that a concern for diversity in higher education was a compelling governmental interest that would justify the implementation of an affirmative action plan. However, in 1979, Powell's diversity rationale was not binding on the rest of the Court, or the country, and he largely spoke for himself. It would take an additional twenty-five years before the majority of the Court would come around to his way of thinking about race and affirmative action in higher education.

IMPLEMENTATION OF THE *BAKKE* DECISION BETWEEN 1978 AND 2003

In the twenty-five years between *Bakke* and the *Gratz* and *Grutter* decisions, lower courts as well as colleges and universities around the country grappled with ways to interpret the exact perimeters of what was permissible under the *Bakke* ruling, and how to implement affirmative action and when it was appropriate, if at all, to use an applicant's race in college admissions decisions. Thus, in the two decades subsequent to the *Bakke* decision, race-conscious affirmative action was employed by a majority of the institutions of higher learning, and implemented to one degree or another by most elite universities and colleges in the country. Largely the result of the *Bakke* decision, race-conscious affirmative action programs "proliferated in academic institutions, ranging from informal preference-granting to formally race-normed admissions lists to specifically reserved scholarships."[12] For roughly two decades, "the *Bakke* decision...led the way for educational institutions to begin redressing the past wrongs of racial and ethnic discrimination."[13] Also, "a sizable and influential segment of higher education...maintained vigorously" that Justice Powell was correct in stating that diversity is a compelling educational interest worthy of being promoted to enhance the educational experience for all, and not only to address past wrongs and prior institutional discrimination. This became "an article of faith in the higher education community."[14]

The practice of affirmative action during this period was generally considered a success, both in terms of creating diversity on college campuses and in terms of how the beneficiaries of affirmative action programs fared after graduation. Indeed, Bowen and Bok's *Shape of the River* concluded that the use of affirmative action at elite institutions was advantageous to minority beneficiaries, that it did not unduly restrict opportunities for majority white candidates, and that the beneficiaries of affirmative action programs achieved notable success after graduation, either in the workforce or in graduate or professional schools. Bowen and Bok also concluded that the elimination of affirmative action in higher education would reduce minority enrollment by as much as 50 percent across the country. However, it is important to note that most of Bowen and Bok's findings focused on elite institutions in America, and that "the vast majority of undergraduate institutions accept all qualified candidates and thus do not award special status to any group of applicants, defined by race or on the basis of any other criterion."[15]

Thus, while differing approaches certainly existed for the use of race during this period, in one sense, race-conscious programs were more widespread and generally accepted than at any other time during the history of affirmative action in higher education. Indeed, despite the varying approaches to affirmative action from institution to institution, there was relative calm for about a decade and a half in terms of what the law provided on the subject of affirmative action. Then, from 1995 to 2003, the use of race-conscious affirmative action in higher education came under intense criticism and attack in the federal court system, as well as at the state level in California, Texas, Washington, and Florida. This extremely chaotic eight-year period, which ended with the Supreme Court's pronouncements in *Gratz* and *Grutter* in 2003, started with a case entitled *Hopwood v. Texas*, 78 F.3d 932 (5th Cir. 1996).

The facts surrounding the *Hopwood* case stem from the early 1990s, when the state of Texas attempted to increase minority enrollment in perceived adherence to the standards of the *Bakke* decision. Specifically, the University of Texas Law School, one of the elite law schools in the country and the institution at issue in the *Hopwood* case, implemented an affirmative action program whose goal was "to admit an entering class that contained 5 percent black and 10 percent Mexican American students."[16] The law school's admissions decisions were based upon an overall Texas Index (TI) number, which comprised the applicant's undergraduate GPA and his or her performance on the Law School Admission Test (LSAT). Based upon an applicant's TI number, his or her application would be placed in one of three categories: "presumptive admit," "presumptive deny," and a middle "discretionary" category. Generally, those applications placed in the "presumptive admit" category ultimately received letters of admission to the following year's entering class, while those in the "presumptive deny" category were almost always denied admission, although an exceptional candidate (i.e., a candidate whose TI score was viewed as an inadequate predictor of the student's potential success in law school—based upon other factors in the applicant's file) might still gain admissions in the rare case. The middle "discretionary" category meant that the applicant was competitive for admissions based upon GPA and LSAT scores alone, and that the admissions committee would fully consider the application in light of all other factors. However, in the attempt to achieve the goal of 5 percent minority representation of African Americans and 10 percent Mexican American enrollment, the school employed different cutoff numbers for each of the three categories, depending largely on race or ethnicity. In the "presumptive admit" category, for example, "In March 1992, the presumptive TI score for resident whites and nonpreferred minorities was 199, while the presumptive TI score for blacks and Mexican Americans was 189." The "presumptive deny" category employed different numbers as well; the presumptive TI "score for nonminorities was 192, while the denial score for those preferred minorities (blacks and Mexican Americans) was 179."[17]

Four white applicants (three male, one female—the lead plaintiff, Cheryl Hopwood) who were denied admission filed suit in the U.S. District Court, alleging that the University of Texas's affirmative action plan engaged in reverse discrimination in violation of the Equal Protection Clause of the Fourteenth Amendment and Title VI of the 1964 Civil Rights Act. At the district court level, however, the state of Texas prevailed on the argument that race could be employed. While the court noted that the four white applicants were disadvantaged during the admissions process (because of the benign institutional discrimination in favor of blacks and Mexican Americans), the court nonetheless found that the University of Texas Law School was correct in considering race in the admissions process. Specifically, the court found that the long history of discrimination against blacks and Mexican Americans, as well as the lack of diversity on campus, justified the employment of a race-conscious affirmative action plan by the University of Texas.

The case was then appealed to the U.S. Court of Appeals for the Fifth Circuit, which handles appeals from federal cases in Texas, Louisiana, and Mississippi. In a famous decision, the Fifth Circuit declared the University of Texas Law School's admissions plan to be unconstitutional under the Fourteenth Amendment. In response to the state of Texas's argument that the plan was needed because of the long history of discrimination and segregation in the state, the Fifth Circuit held that there must be a prior showing of discrimination at the institution in question that wishes to implement the program as a means of remedial compensation. Further, the court declared that Justice Powell's "diversity rationale" in *Bakke* was not binding on the court as he did not speak for the majority of the Supreme Court in the *Bakke* case. The court also thought it unlikely that most of the Justices on the Supreme Court in *Bakke* did not intend to make the concern for diversity in higher education a compelling government interest (i.e., a legitimate justification for the state, or its institutions, to employ affirmative action) in the ruling. In fact, the Fifth Circuit stated in the resulting *Hopwood* decision that considerations of race in order to achieve diversity on campus "contradicted, rather than furthered, the aims of equal protection" under the Constitution.

The resulting decision was the first shot across the bow of institutions that employed race-conscious affirmative action programs. Admissions departments and enrollment officers around the country were understandably shocked and confused by the ruling. As the Supreme Court declined to review the Fifth Circuit ruling on subsequent occasions, *Hopwood* was the law on affirmative action and higher education within that circuit. Thus, until June 2003, the decision ended the lawful practice of race-conscious affirmative action in higher education in the states that comprised the Fifth Circuit, namely, Texas, Mississippi, and Louisiana, unless the affirmative action plan was remedially instituted to compensate for prior discrimination by the institution in question. The decision practically meant that the affirmative use of race as a factor in higher education (in order to achieve diversity) was prohibited under the Constitution within the Fifth Circuit. In response to the *Hopwood* decision, Texas soon thereafter adopted a percentage plan (which will be discussed in more detail in Chapter 7) in lieu of affirmative action. Thus, with the *Hopwood* decision, one of the thirteen federal circuits would not allow the use of affirmative action to achieve diversity within its boundaries—three of the fifty states. As Professor Janis Judson has written on the subject, the *Hopwood* decision "specifically ended affirmative action in higher education in the state of Texas, but in a broader sense the decision highlighted the trend of dismantling affirmative action plans as inappropriate remedies for the nation's past injustices."[18]

After several additional years, a significant rift developed in the federal circuits as to the interpretation of the permissibility of utilizing race in admissions decisions. In 2000, the Ninth Circuit Court of Appeals, in *Smith v. University of Washington Law School*, 233 F.3d 1188, held that the use of race as a factor in public higher education in order to achieve a diverse student body was permissible under both Title VI of the Civil Rights Act and the Equal Protection Clause of the Fourteenth Amendment if the plan was "properly designed and operated." This decision accepted Justice Powell's diversity rationale as a legitimate "compelling governmental interest" in the adoption of a race-conscious affirmative action plan in higher education. Notably, the Ninth Circuit ruling was important in that it was the first federal circuit court decision that "approved the use of racial classification for a purpose other than to remedy demonstrated past discrimination."[19] This decision also put the Ninth Circuit at odds with the interpretation of the law in the Fifth Circuit. As the Ninth Circuit comprised nine western states (Washington, Oregon, California, Montana, Idaho, Nevada, Arizona, Alaska, and Hawaii) and two U.S. territories (Guam and the Northern Mariana Islands), the use of race in admissions decisions to improve diversity was now permissible in the nine western states, while prohibited in the three states within the Fifth Circuit. It should be noted, as will be discussed in Chapter 7, that two of the states (California and Washington) within the Ninth Circuit eliminated the use of affirmative action through state referendums.

Then, a year later, the Eleventh Circuit Court of Appeals (comprising Florida, Georgia, and Alabama), in *Johnson v. Board of Regents of the University of Georgia*, 263 F.3d 1234, struck down a University of Georgia admissions program that gave a point bonus to minority applicants. However, the Eleventh Circuit never decided if concern for diversity in higher education was a sufficient justification (i.e., a "compelling governmental interest") to implement an affirmative action plan, as the plan at issue was not narrowly tailored. According to the court, the plan, which gave a fixed number of points to every minority applicant regardless of the applicant's potential to contribute to diversity on campus, was too inflexible. In words that would mirror the language of the Supreme Court in the *Gratz* decision (and that would serve as advice to college administrators in the post-*Gratz* era), the court stated, "If UGA wants to ensure diversity through its admission decisions, and wants race to be a part of that calculus, then it must be prepared to shoulder the burden of fully and fairly analyzing applicants as individuals and not merely as members of groups when deciding their likely contribution to student body diversity."

The Eleventh Circuit decision highlighted the conflict between the circuits. Now the Fifth Circuit and the Eleventh Circuit, combined, put affirmative action in higher education into serious doubt in six southern states, and conflicted with the nine states of the Ninth Circuit. Florida, by this time, had joined Washington and California in eliminating the use of affirmative action in the state through Governor Jeb Bush's One Florida Plan. The conflict between the federal circuits was further intensified in 2002, when, in *Grutter v. Bollinger*, the Sixth Circuit (encompassing Michigan, Ohio, Kentucky, and Tennessee) validated a race-conscious affirmative action plan being utilized by the University of Michigan law school. This decision put the Sixth Circuit in alignment with the Ninth Circuit (in supporting affirmative action plans), and in conflict with the Fifth and the Eleventh Circuits (who had invalidated such plans). However, before the Sixth Circuit could rule in a second case involving the use of affirmative action at the University of Michigan's undergraduate level (*Gratz v. Bollinger*), which the Sixth Circuit explained it would do at a later time, the Supreme Court announced that it would take the rare step of consolidating and reviewing both cases together.

The stage was set for Supreme Court review in *Gratz* and *Grutter*, the first cases dealing with affirmative action and higher education heard by the Court since the *Bakke* decision in 1979. In the months leading up to the Supreme Court's review, the eyes of the nation were upon the cases and the Court. Even President George W. Bush became involved. On January 15, 2003, Bush gave a nationally aired speech declaring his opposition to the University of Michigan's affirmative action plans, stating that they were "divisive, unfair and impossible to square with the Constitution." To understand the current state of affirmative action and how it is implemented at the college level, we now turn to an analysis of the *Gratz* and *Grutter* decisions.

2

Gratz v. Bollinger and *Grutter v. Bollinger*: The Changing Affirmative Action Analysis

BACKGROUND AND PROCEDURAL HISTORY OF THE MICHIGAN CASES

In both the *Gratz* and *Grutter* cases, as in the other leading federal circuit cases discussed in Chapter 1, the plaintiffs challenged the use of race in the admissions process, claiming that the process discriminated against white applicants. Specifically at issue in *Gratz* and *Grutter* was whether race could be considered (and to what degree) in the college admissions process (*Gratz*) and in the graduate/ law school admissions process (*Grutter*). The undergraduate admissions program at issue employed the use of race not "as a 'plus' factor or as one of many factors to attain a diverse student body. Rather, race was one of the predominant factors...used for determining admissions."[1] At the undergraduate level, the University of Michigan utilized a mathematical formula that awarded African American, Hispanic American, and Native American applicants a twenty-point bonus, on a 150-point scale. This award of points had the tendency of skewing the formula in favor of minority candidates in almost every case, as the automatic twenty-point award was one-fifth of the points needed to guarantee admission. The minority-class point bonus was "the equivalent of an advantage a high-school student with a 4.0 grade point average would enjoy over a high-school student with a 3.0 grade point average."[2] The University of Michigan Law School, however, approached the use of race in a different fashion. The law school did not employ a point system and award points based upon race of the applicant. Rather, the law school's goal was to try to enroll a "critical mass" of traditionally underrepresented minority students, and would evaluate the candidate not based upon race alone, but preferably under a more holistic review of the applicant's life experiences, although the race of the applicant was an admittedly important factor in the review.

Despite the differing approaches to using race in the admissions process, the goal of both the undergraduate and law school admissions plans was, according to the University of Michigan, driven primarily by concerns regarding diversity and the overall educational experiences of its students, both white and black. In a 1999 report entitled *The Compelling Need for Diversity in Higher Education*, the University of Michigan put forward the defense that "the last Supreme Court decision addressing the use of race in admissions to institutions of higher education, *Regents of the University of California v. Bakke*, 438 U.S. 265 (1978), affirmed that the role of diversity in colleges and universities is both essential and compelling."[3] The University of Michigan also relied on a wide array of expert studies and reports that showed, in the words of Justice O'Connor, "that student body diversity promotes learning outcomes and 'better prepares students for an increasingly diverse workforce and society, and better prepares them as professionals.' "[4] The plaintiffs in both cases, who had been denied admission at the undergraduate or law school level, claimed that these plans reversely discriminated against white applicants, and improperly weighed race as too significant a factor in the process. The plaintiffs also argued that concerns over diversity in the classroom were not sufficient reasons to violate the Equal Protection Clause of the Fourteenth Amendment, which generally prohibits racial discrimination by states and their public institutions.

After an extensive trial and approximately three years of litigation, conflicting decisions were rendered by the U.S. District Court for the Eastern District of Michigan. On December 13, 2000, in the *Gratz* case, a district court judge upheld the admissions procedure then in place, maintaining that concern for diversity in higher education was a sufficient justification for implementing a race-conscious plan. Additionally, the judge, while ruling that a previous plan in effect from 1995 to 1998 was unconstitutional in "reserving" seats for minority students, generally approved the university's practice of awarding points based upon race in the decision-making process. However, on March 27, 2001, in the *Grutter* case, another judge ruled against the University of Michigan Law School and held that the school relied too heavily on race. The judge who decided the case in *Grutter*, unlike the one who decided the *Gratz* case, held that race should not be considered and promoted based upon concerns over diversity in the classroom. The disagreement over the proper role and scope of affirmative action in higher education between these two district court judges in the Eastern District of Michigan is emblematic of the division on the issue throughout the country. Both cases were then appealed to the U.S. Court of Appeals for the Sixth Circuit in 2001.

On May 14, 2002, the Sixth Circuit issued an opinion reversing the district court decision in *Grutter*, and approved the use of race in the law school admissions process. However, before the Sixth Circuit could issue a decision in *Gratz*, the Center for Individual Rights petitioned the Supreme Court to review both the cases. Many at the time thought that this motion was, at best, premature. The Supreme Court grants review in only the smallest fraction of cases; further, the Sixth Circuit had not even rendered a decision regarding the appeal for the

Gratz decision, which was still pending with the court. Nonetheless, in a very rare announcement, on December 2, 2002, the Supreme Court declared that it would consolidate and hear both cases in the spring of the following year.

SUPREME COURT REVIEW AND DECISIONS IN THE MICHIGAN CASES

Under intense public scrutiny and debate, oral arguments were held on April 1, 2003. In an unprecedented amount of interest, more than 300 organizations assisted in filing over sixty friends-of-the-court (amicus curiae) briefs with the Supreme Court, espousing the virtues of affirmative action in higher education. These included dozens of colleges and universities, over fifty Fortune 500 companies, and many high-ranking military members, including many prior superintendents/presidents from the service academies at Annapolis, Maryland; and West Point, New York. Then, on June 23, 2003, almost twenty-five years from the very day that the Supreme Court issued its *Bakke* decision (the only previous Supreme Court decision dealing with affirmative action and higher education), the Court announced its decisions on the Michigan cases. Prior to that, many media outlets reported that these cases would be the "Alamo of affirmative action" and would end the debate (and confusion) regarding affirmative action in higher education. However, the decisions in *Gratz* and *Grutter*, taken together, might be accurately described as a compromise decision worthy of Solomon—splitting the metaphoric affirmative action baby in two.

In a six to three vote in the *Gratz* decision, and in an opinion authored by then–Chief Justice William Rehnquist, the Supreme Court held that the University of Michigan's undergraduate admissions process of awarding points to underrepresented minority applicants was unconstitutional. The Court held that awarding points "solely because of their race, is not narrowly tailored to achieve the interest in educational diversity." Further, according to the Court, awarding points to all minority applicants made race the de facto decisive factor in the admissions process, and would be akin to a rigid mechanical formula, or a rigid racial quota—practices that are prohibited both under the *Bakke* ruling and under Title VI of the Civil Rights Act of 1964. In illustrating how impermissibly broad the University of Michigan formula was weighed in favor of race, Chief Justice Rehnquist pointed out that "even if [a student's] 'extraordinary artistic talent' rivaled that of Monet or Picasso, the applicant would receive, at most, five points," while "every single underrepresented minority applicant... would automatically receive 20 points for submitting an application."[5] It was this mechanical approach that fated the plan at issue in the *Gratz* case. The skewed point system in favor of race illustrated that at the undergraduate level (unlike the law school plan), there was a lack of individualized consideration and analysis of applications. This amounted to the unconstitutional use of race—the plan was not narrowly tailored to achieve diversity, as not all factors important to diversity were weighted equally.

However, in a narrow five to four majority in the *Grutter* decision, and in an opinion authored by Associate Justice Sandra Day O'Connor, the Supreme Court upheld the use of race in the University of Michigan's Law School admissions process, stating that "we endorse Justice Powell's view that student body diversity is a compelling state interest that can justify the use of race in the university admissions."[6] The Court concluded that "diversity [in higher education] will, in fact, yield educational benefits." The Court appeared confident in the conclusion that the benefits that will be created via diversity are "real" and "substantial," as " 'classroom discussion is livelier, more spirited, and simply more enlightening and interesting' when the students have 'the greatest possible variety of backgrounds.' "[7] Finally, diversity in the classroom "promotes 'cross-racial understanding,' helps to break down racial stereotypes, and 'enables [students] to better understand persons of different races.' "[8]

However, holding that diversity constitutes a compelling governmental interest that authorizes a public institution to benignly discriminate based upon race is only one-half of the analysis in determining whether or not the law school's plan survives Court review. The plan also needs to be narrowly tailored to achieve its goals. In the words of the Court, this means that the plan must " 'fit...the compelling goal so closely that there is little to no possibility that the motive for classification was illegitimate racial prejudice or stereotypes.' "[9] The Court was satisfied that the law school's plan was narrowly tailored in that it considered race "in a flexible, nonmechanical way" and that it "engages in a highly individualized, holistic review of each applicant's file, giving serious consideration to all the ways an applicant might contribute to a diverse educational environment."[10]

It should be noted that much disagreement among the justices existed below the surface of both decisions, and like the *Bakke* decision twenty-five years before, there are strong undercurrents suggesting that the surface may not stay calm for long. First, the actual votes in the cases were very close; five to four and six to three splits in *Grutter* and *Gratz*, respectively. Second, the authors of the *Gratz* and *Grutter* majority decisions (Rehnquist and O'Connor, respectively) are no longer on the Court. Third, there were multiple concurring and dissenting opinions in both cases. In *Grutter*, there were a total of six separate opinions, including very extensive and strongly worded dissents by Justices Scalia, Thomas, and Kennedy. *Gratz* was equally divisive, eliciting seven separate opinions. It is often said and taught in law schools that law students should read the dissenting and concurring opinions in the cases, as those opinions are important in that, sometimes, the positions articulated become the trend in the law in the future.

Taken collectively, the decisions established, or, as to certain issues, reaffirmed, the following ideas regarding affirmative action and higher education:

1. Quotas and rigid mechanical formulas are impermissible under both Title VI of the Civil Rights Act of 1964 and the Equal Protection Clause of the Fourteenth Amendment.

2. Justice Powell's "diversity rationale" from the *Bakke* decision is a legitimate consideration and one that survives constitutional scrutiny under the compelling governmental interest analysis.
3. In promoting diversity, race may be used as a "plus factor," so long as such a consideration is narrowly tailored and flexible, and applicants receive individual considerations (in part to preclude the possibility of a de facto quota system).
4. The Fourteenth Amendment does not yet impose a color-blind approach to issues of race in higher education, at least for the next twenty-five years.
5. Affirmative action plans may be used by both private and public universities.
6. In states like California, Florida, and Washington that preclude the use of race in education as a matter of state law, such prohibition is only applicable to public institutions, and not private universities and colleges within the states (and, therefore, race may be considered by private institutions).

IMPLEMENTATION OF *GRATZ* AND *GRUTTER*: WHAT DOES IT MEAN TO SAY THAT THE ADMISSIONS PROCESS MUST BE "FLEXIBLE," "HOLISTIC," AND "INDIVIDUALIZED"?

As affirmative action proponents had hoped, and as described above, the Court held that the benefits of diversity in the classroom are "substantial" and "not theoretical but real." In holding that "race unfortunately still matters," the promotion of diversity will help make classroom discussions and debates more lively, will break down stereotypes under the socialization theory of equality,[11] and will prepare students for the diverse melting pot—the real world. However, as the Court made very clear, if the admissions program seeks minority candidates under the diversity rationale, the individualized, nonmechanical, full-file review of applicants is "paramount." According to the Court, "In other words, an admissions program must be 'flexible enough to consider all pertinent elements of diversity in light of the particular qualifications of each applicant, and to place them on the same footing for consideration, although not necessarily according them the same weight.' "[12] In the words of Justice O'Connor, "context matters." As the director of admissions of a university has stated, in describing the institution's new affirmative action plan (implemented after *Gratz* and *Grutter*), "Race neither helps nor hurts applicants. We consider it a factor, just like we consider socioeconomic status, first-generation college attendance, new immigrant status, interests, talents, and of course, the academic issues of course preparation, test scores, grades" and other factors.[13]

Additionally, while the Supreme Court ultimately approved the practice of colleges and universities pursuing a goal of admitting a "critical mass" of minority applicants in order to amass a diverse student body, the decision does not give these institutions carte blanche authority to immediately begin considering race without some careful study. Rather, the use of race characteristics in admissions decisions continues to be constitutionally suspect, and if college administrators wish to utilize race, they should first meet and then develop a narrowly tailored affirmative action plan. The plan should delineate exactly what objectives are to be achieved, why the objectives are best accomplished through this plan, and what campus benefits will be derived from the program (e.g., the recruitment of more veterans on campus in order to have viewpoints in the classroom more favorable to U.S. military activities abroad). Above all, the plan of enrolling a "critical mass" should not simply be "some specified percentage of a particular group merely because of race or ethnic origin."[14]

Also, if affirmative action plans are implemented, pursuant to the Fourteenth Amendment and consistent with the requirements for the use of race in other fields, they must be "limited in time" and reviewed periodically. As the Supreme Court stated in *Grutter*, "In the context of higher education, the durational requirement can be met by sunset provisions in race-conscious admissions policies and periodic reviews to determine whether racial preferences are still necessary to achieve student body diversity."[15] Again, according to the Court, any "deviation from the norm of equal treatment" would only be "a temporary matter, a measure taken in the service of the goal of equality itself."[16]

Finally, Mark Killenbeck, a constitutional law scholar and professor of law at the University of Arkansas, has promoted an idea that he characterizes as "principled affirmative action."

> [A] diversity policy cannot and should not focus on a single group, either in theory or in practice... this is instead a debate about educational opportunity for all individuals, and it is important to remember that the policies at issue are as much about the needs and interests of, for example, Latinos and Native Americans, as they are of African Americans.[17]

This means that women, veterans, the handicapped, socioeconomically disadvantaged, and maybe even white males in some contexts, might be declared to be beneficiaries of affirmative action plans that are implemented to promote diversity in the classroom.[18] Indeed, under these other categories, many have pushed very hard for "class-based affirmative action," whereby preferences are given to students from low-income families. Harvard University has implemented socioeconomic status in its recruitment of students. Harvard utilizes "geodemographic data—which can estimate the income of a family by its ZIP code—in conjunction with test score information to identify high school juniors from low-income families who might be eligible for admission."[19] Of course, as will be discussed in Chapter 8, being granted admission to an elite institution means little if the applicant is unable to afford the tuition.

Thus, affirmative action, if implemented, should be carefully planned, narrowly tailored, done in good faith, temporary in nature, inclusive, and subject to periodic review. Again, according to Professor Killenbeck,

> [A]n institution wishing to take race into account must do so with care, mindful of each of the four hallmarks stressed by the Court. It cannot proceed in a

thoughtless or mechanical fashion... the willingness to expend the time, energy, and money necessary to create an admissions program within which consideration of race is simply one facet of a truly individualized decision.[20]

Truly, the "devil is in the detail," as the old saying goes, and administrators should be prepared to put their plan into writing and create a record of why race is being utilized as a factor. Indeed, one planning manual states that "because the use of race... inevitably raises questions of federal (and frequently state) legal compliance, lawyers with an understanding of these issues should be included in the process."[21] Otherwise, the school might be dragged into litigation for not being in compliance with the guidance of the Supreme Court in *Gratz* and *Grutter*. The degree to which institutions have expressed a willingness to spend additional resources in the implementation of an individualized, holistic review will be addressed in the following chapter.

3

How Colleges and Universities Revised or Eliminated Affirmative Action Programs in the Immediate Aftermath of the *Gratz* and *Grutter* Decisions

One month after the *Gratz* and *Grutter* decisions, in July 2003, the Civil Rights Project at Harvard University issued a report entitled *Reaffirming Diversity: A Legal Analysis of the University of Michigan Affirmative Action Cases*, authored and signed by eleven nationally prominent constitutional law scholars.[1] In this report, the authors recommended that universities and colleges not panic, and carefully review and revise their admissions plans in light of the Supreme Court's guidance. The report specifically recommended the following:

> Universities that employ systems which lack sufficient individualized review will need to re-examine their current admissions policies to determine whether their policies require adjustment or revision.... Institutions that have adopted more restrictive policies than the Court's decisions allow may wish to re-examine their policies to ensure that they are not "overcorrecting" out of a misplaced fear of being held legally liable.[2]

Furthermore, even those colleges and universities that already had plans in place that considered the race of an applicant in a way apparently sanctioned by the Supreme Court in *Grutter* might need to make revisions, if only to "add time limits to their whole-file review policies and to better document their consideration of race-neutral alternatives."[3] However, the report also warned that "other institutions, particularly those that have employed numerical systems with automatic point assignments for race, will have to undertake major reviews and revisions of their policies."[4]

Thus, college administrators knew that they now had the authorization to use race in admissions decisions, but were nonetheless hesitant about moving forward. Universities were reluctant, not in making a commitment for diversity on campus, but rather in view of the costs to implement an admissions process that takes an individualized, holistic approach to each applicant, especially at the large institutions that receive thousands of applications. With that many applications each year, schools such as the University of Michigan and the Ohio State University had employed a point system in the past, in part as a quick means of considering ethnicity or race in the decision-making process. Yet, in the months following the *Gratz* and *Grutter* decisions, the University of Michigan and Ohio State University both took the lead in scrapping their old approaches and spending considerable capital and resources in revising their respective approaches to continue to promote diversity in their classrooms. In explaining this transition, Martha Garland, vice provost and dean of undergraduate studies at Ohio State University, said, "The courts made it very clear that large size was no excuse to depersonalize the process. But Ohio State still has every right to seek educational diversity, be it from ethnic or racial minorities, students from different geographic areas, first generation college students or any number of identifying factors."[5]

The University of Michigan announced its revisions first, in August 2003, and decided that it could best conduct the holistic, individual review mandated by the Court by employing an essay-driven application for admissions, as opposed to the point-based system struck down in *Gratz*. While "academic criteria will continue to be the most important factors in considering a student for admission," admission counselors also look to see how well the applicant would contribute to the "intellectual vibrancy and diversity" of the university.[6] The applications in 2004 called for one 500-word essay and two 250-word essays, and applicants were instructed to address diversity. Specifically, one essay question read, "At the University of Michigan, we are committed to building an academically superb and widely diverse educational community. What would you as an individual bring to our campus community?" A second essay question asked the applicant to "describe an experience you've had where cultural diversity—or a lack thereof—has made a difference to you."[7] Applications also required a statement from the applicant's high school guidance counselor or principal on "any socio-economic, personal, or educational circumstance that may have affected this student's academic achievement, either positively or negatively." Other institutions pose similar questions to the applicant. For example, the University of Tampa asks applicants to

> write a carefully constructed essay on one of the following topics: (1) The University of Tampa takes pride in the contributions made by all members of our community. Briefly describe what you believe other students could learn from you, both in and out of the classroom; (2) Identify one person who has had a significant influence on you and briefly describe that influence; (3) Briefly describe a significant event or circumstance and how it has impacted your personal and academic development.

However, in deciding to place additional weight on these open-ended narrative portions of the application, universities are faced with the problem that their subjective review and evaluation becomes much more labor intensive (if they are using the essays as a crucial factor in the decision-making process). Thus, the University of Michigan announced that to read and review these applications, it would need to hire dozens of admissions officers, new full- and part-time application "readers," additionally. In the process put into place in 2004, the University of Michigan assigns two admissions counselors to review each application. If both officials agree as to admission or rejection, the file can be finalized. However, if the two reviewers cannot agree after both make a holistic, individualized review of the application, then the application is reviewed by another group of counselors. For undergraduate admissions alone, the University of Michigan receives approximately 25,000 applications each year for the roughly 5,000 available seats. This amounts to 75,000 essays that will have to be read and analyzed by admissions counselors. Some have argued that this might be too costly a process, especially in light of a large, basically qualified candidate pool.[8] In 2003–2004 alone, the University of Michigan would end up spending $1.8 million more, reportedly a 40 percent increase from 2002 to 2003.[9] It should also be pointed out that at public land-grant institutions like the University of Michigan and the Ohio State University, this is a cost that might ultimately be dictated by the allocation of funds by state legislatures.[10] Conversely, private institutions not subsidized by public funds might lack the resources to beef up the admissions department in such a fashion.

In addressing this issue, the College Resource Group, which specializes in advising colleges and universities, sent out a flyer to many of these institutions in the spring of 2004 that posed the following questions: "Do you have the admissions staff and resources to review applications? Have you allocated the resources needed to not only expand outreach to special populations, but also give the individual attention to applications that the Supreme Court decision requires?" It is clear that institutions need to increase the funding and resources if they wish to continue to consider race in the admissions and financial aid contexts as per the Court's guidance in *Gratz* and *Grutter*.

As mentioned before, the Ohio State University also employed a statistical formula similar to that of the University of Michigan prior to the *Gratz* and *Grutter* decisions. In fact, Ohio State was noted throughout the country for its commitment to diversity in the years prior to *Gratz* and *Grutter*. Ohio State initiated the Diversity Action Plan, which stated that the university's chief guiding principle was "the diversity of the student body and the success of all students." Among other features, the Diversity Action Plan led to the creation of a Diversity Council to monitor university progress, created the Institute for the Study of Race and Ethnicity, and authorized one-half million dollars in scholarship programs designed to increase diversity. When the Supreme Court ruled in June 2003 that the undergraduate admissions plan at Michigan was unconstitutional, the Ohio State University scrapped its previous affirmative action plan and, heeding the Court's guidance in *Grutter*, began drafting a new admissions plan that took a holistic, individualized approach to evaluating the applicants. In so doing, Ohio State also added an essay section to each application (initially four short-essay questions for the undergraduate admissions application, which was reduced to just two essays in 2005) as a vehicle to evaluate each candidate's ability to contribute to diversity on campus. Dean Garland has claimed that the new essay section of the application gives "the students a chance to shine," and students are encouraged "to write about anything that sets them apart or has affected their lives to this point as they apply to Ohio State."[11] According to an assistant director of undergraduate admissions at Ohio State, in reviewing the applications, the focus is still primarily on academic qualifications by way of college placement tests (ACT, SAT) and high school grades, but now also "factoring in such things as class standing, leadership roles, race, geography, community involvement or special circumstances."[12] The 2004–2005 application at Ohio State advises applicants that they "may be given additional consideration if you provide cultural, economic, racial or geographic diversity."[13]

However, just as with the University of Michigan, the revisions came with a cost. Ohio State spent an additional $250,000 on the admissions process to ensure compliance with *Grutter*, and hired an additional thirty-five individuals to read applicant essays and evaluate them.[14] After a year, the results were only modestly successful. At the University of Michigan, the new process, which involved a great influx of funds and personnel, resulted in a minority enrollment of 1 percentage point less than in 2003[15] and resulted in the lowest enrollment of African Americans in its freshman class in fifteen years.[16] However, after another year, the University of Michigan announced that its work has paid off, and that preliminary commitments of African Americans went up 20.1 percent between 2004 and 2005.[17] At Ohio State, minority enrollment dropped to 10 percent of the entering class in 2003, from 12 percent the year before,[18] and, in addition to the decline in the number of black freshmen, the number of Hispanics in the entering freshman class plummeted by 8.3 percent.[19] Further, unlike the University of Michigan's great improvement from 2004 to 2005, Ohio State had an increase of only an estimated 1 percent during the same period.[20] However, Ohio State officials, like those at Michigan, expressed confidence that in time, the new affirmative action plan would increase enrollment. In 2004, the President of Ohio State, Karen A. Holbrook, said that she would be "very surprised if we don't see an increase this [upcoming] year."[21] While 1 percent is not a great increase, officials remain confident that enrollment of minority students will improve.

The University of Massachusetts at Amherst, another high-profile institution that has "vowed to continue affirmative action," has moved from a process based upon numerical formulas to a holistic review, which has also involved the hiring of extra staff and additional expenses.[22] The University of Massachusetts acceptance rate for minority applicants remained the same, despite the change in process.[23] However, the number of overall applications actually dropped by 19 percent in the year following the *Gratz* and *Grutter* decisions, which, according to an associate director of undergraduate admissions at the University of Massachusetts, is attributable to the more lengthy and detailed applications now required in order to assess the applicant's potential to contribute positively to the campus life and classroom learning experiences.[24] Officials at Ohio State and Michigan also attribute the decline in the number of applications to the lengthy applications and the work required to complete the application essays.[25] As mentioned before, Ohio State even reduced the number of application essays from four in 2003 to two in 2005 due to the adverse impact on applicants.[26]

In addition to the more individualized, holistic approach mandated by the Supreme Court, several schools have turned to aggressive recruitment of minority applicants as a means of increasing minority enrollment on campus. For example, Dartmouth College also takes "an open-minded and flexible approach [in the] review process" by placing emphasis on applicant essays, letters of recommendation, and an applicant interview. According to Karl Furstenberg, the dean of admissions, Dartmouth also "recruits minority populations aggressively, producing 'a very well cultivated applicant pool.'"[27] The University of Illinois at Urbana-Champaign, after a sharp decline in minority enrollment in 2003, was up an estimated 25 percent in 2005 due to "aggressive recruiting, including calls to prospective students by more than 200 alumni and online chat sessions."[28] According to the University of Illinois's Chancellor Richard Herman, the university is "doing a better job of telling our story and marketing the institution."[29]

Two institutions in particular illustrate how enrollment numbers can be increased by aggressive recruitment alone. In fact, these institutions, the University of Texas and the University of Georgia, both were involved in famous federal court–based renunciations of affirmative action in 1996 and 2001, respectively. The University of Georgia and the University of Texas at Austin both publicly announced within a year of the *Gratz* and *Grutter* decisions that they also would be revising their admissions processes to improve minority enrollment. As discussed in Chapter 1, the University of Texas had been prohibited by a federal court order from utilizing race in admissions since 1996 as a result of the *Hopwood* decision. The University of Georgia's use of race was likewise held unconstitutional in 2001 by the federal Eleventh Circuit Court of Appeals in *Johnson v. Board of Regents of the University of Georgia*, which was accompanied by a decline in minority enrollment from 5.3 percent in 2003 to 4.5 percent in 2004. Cognizant of this decline, the University of Georgia announced that it had decided to "revise race in the admissions process," a decision that was hailed "as [a] sound educational policy."[30] While revisions to the process were still being debated and studied, Nancy McDuff, the admissions director, predicted that the University of Georgia "could again include using race, among other criteria, as a factor in admissions."[31] However, given the pace of the debates and studies, it is estimated that the earliest that the university could again utilize race in admissions would be in the fall of 2006.[32] As one University of Georgia professor on the task force commented, "I think we'd all like to see this done this year, but there is no point in doing something that won't hold up in court."[33]

In the interim, however, the University of Georgia is aggressively recruiting students, including using "faculty and administrators [to make] personal calls to students who had been accepted, urging them to enroll...and [using] Black students at UGA" for this purpose,[34] as well as waiving application fees in some cases.[35] This focus on recruitment of nontraditional minority students has been heralded as being extremely successful, and has resulted in a reported 73 percent increase in African American applicants from 2004. It was reported in May 2005 that "more than 1,110 black students applied to UGA this year, up from 883 in 2004. UGA offered admissions to 570 African American students, compared with 418 in 2004."[36] The University of Texas moved much quicker, with the then president of UT, Larry Faulkner, announcing within several hours of the *Gratz* and *Grutter* decisions that the university would move "fairly quickly" to return to the use of race in their admissions decisions.[37] The University of Texas began to again utilize race as a factor (among many factors) in admissions, commencing with the fall 2005 freshman class, for the first time since 1996. The University of Texas at Austin also continues to adhere to its percentage plan, whereby 10 percent of each high school class is guaranteed admission. For more information on the University of Texas's affirmative action and percentage plans, see Chapter 4, which discusses these issues in depth, and the University of Texas at Austin's specific admissions practices since 2003.

Yet, although many schools are revising their programs to include race in the admissions process, an equal number have decided to discontinue the use of race as a factor. Additionally, for many schools that historically eliminated affirmative action programs or never experimented with such programs to begin with, many of these schools have decided not to reinstitute affirmative action—either because the institution wishes to promote diversity in racially neutral ways, or to insulate themselves from potential lawsuits by "watchdog" groups like the Center for Individual Rights. This has prompted one writer to comment that "a few college leaders wonder just why it is that so many institutions are acting as if they lost the Michigan cases—indeed, as if the Supreme Court had actually banned affirmative action."[38] Arizona State University, in Tempe, for example, does not ask the applicants any questions regarding race or ethnicity on the application, or consider these factors during the admissions process. Rather, the university officials believe that a diverse class is best accomplished working with local high schools. As Arizona State's director of admissions, Tim Desch, stated in 2004, "We aim to help students aspire to higher education [by recruitment and outreach efforts] and make the pool more diverse well in advance of applying."[39] Yet, since 2003, "outreach" efforts to help students from underrepresented minority groups have declined substantially. According to the survey report from the National Association for College Admission Counseling, the number of institutions that claim to be "providing outreach" has declined from 63 percent of all responding schools (in 2003) to 47 percent (in 2004).[40]

Furthermore, this discontinuation of the use of race applies not only to admissions decisions, but in many cases has also been expanded to scholarship programs. (This will be more fully addressed in Chapter 8.) Colleges around the nation "are quietly opening up scholarships previously restricted to Black students. Programs aimed at recruiting and retaining minorities have been scrapped or broadened to include White students."[41] In a trend disappointing to many affirmative action supporters, institutions such as Harvard, Yale, Carnegie Mellon, Indiana University, Virginia Tech, and the College of William and Mary have discontinued race-specific scholarship programs. In addressing this trend, Theodore Shaw, president of the NAACP's Legal Defense Fund, stated, "I've been struck by the irony that, in the year since [the] Michigan [cases]... some institutions have retreated from affirmative action even though we won the case. They have not taken full advantage of what happened."[42] The former provost of the University of Michigan, Nancy Cantor, echoed this point by saying that "higher education has not taken up the victory that I believe we won in the Supreme Court."[43]

To what extent institutions have "taken up the victory" or have "retreated from affirmative action" since 2003 is still debatable, and many institutions (like the University of Georgia, cited above) are still studying the issue with plans to reintroduce the use of race in the near future. Furthermore, early studies have been inconclusive as to what effect (if any) the termination or revamping of affirmative action programs has had on minority enrollment. For example, in January 2005, the *Chronicle of Higher Education* announced that its survey of twenty-nine of the country's top institutions in the first year of admissions following *Gratz* and *Grutter* resulted in a "mixed enrollment picture."[44] Approximately 25 percent, or seven of the institutions, witnessed a decline in the number of black and Hispanic freshmen (including both Michigan and Georgia, as discussed above) from 2002 through 2004. However, the *Chronicle* also found that at eleven schools minority enrollment had increased from the year preceding the *Gratz* and *Grutter* decisions. The remaining eleven schools surveyed reported an increase in enrollment for either blacks or Hispanics (but not both), with a drop in the other racial group.[45] For example, the University of North Carolina at Chapel Hill witnessed a 5.8 percent decrease in the number of black freshmen enrolled between 2002 and 2004, while enjoying a 78.1 percent increase in the number of Hispanic freshmen enrolled in the same period.

This negative trend in minority enrollment has not been limited to race-conscious programs alone, but has been extended to legacy practices as well—at least at the mainstream public institutions. The legacy practice refers to the custom of giving advantages to the children or other relatives of alumni in the admissions process. The idea is that, ultimately, this will result in increased fund-raising, loyalty, and continued interest in the institution long beyond the years of attendance as a student. While there is nothing that legally prohibits colleges and universities from utilizing legacies, the practice has nonetheless also come under attack since 2003. According to Barmak Nassirian, an official at the American Association of College Registrars and Admissions Officers, "There's no question that the whole debate surrounding affirmative action opened the entire admissions process to public scrutiny—not just about minorities, but athletes, cello players, donors ... and there's no question that there's something about legacies that rubs people the wrong way."[46] Officials at many universities have been aware of this scrutiny of and distaste for legacies. Allowing for legacies has a ring of hypocrisy to it if the same institutions are not allowing other types of affirmative action for disadvantaged students. Institutions like the University of Georgia and Texas A&M announced the discontinuation of the legacy practice at about the same time that affirmative action plans/practices were halted, either through litigation or through the institution's own choosing.

While legacies are likely to continue at the prestigious private schools, like many of the Ivy League institutions, having legacy status no longer guarantees admission. For example, at the University of Notre Dame, which "accepts 23 percent of its legacy applicants, more than any other school in the country," applicants are advised that the university does not have a guaranteed legacy admissions practice.[47] According to one admissions department official at Notre Dame, legacies are now "at best, ... a nudge, not a push."[48] This is illustrated by a 2005 survey on the state of college admissions, which reported that while only 1.4 percent of colleges believed that "alumni relations" was of considerable importance in the admissions process, 63.3 percent did specify that the factor was of moderate or limited importance.

Appendix A is a comprehensive listing of all four-year-degree granting institutions in the United States, and the degree to which each school considers race, alumni prefaces, or other factors in its admissions process. Thus, for the college applicant who might wish to target schools with affirmative action plans, it would be prudent to first verify that the school in question considers race, legacies, or other factors of traditional affirmative action programs, before putting together the best possible application to improve your odds of admission in light of the plan (a topic that will be addressed in detail in Chapter 5).

4

What about Affirmative Action in "Percentage Plan" States? The Unsettled Status of Affirmative Action in Higher Education in California, Texas, and Florida after *Gratz* and *Grutter*

In the late 1990s, "percentage plans" were put forward in several states as a race-neutral, or color-blind, alternative to race-conscious affirmative action in higher education. The basic idea behind percentage plans was to guarantee students admissions to one of the public institutions of higher learning in the state based upon their academic performance in high school vis-à-vis the performance of other students in the class. Specifically, the percentage plan would guarantee that all students who graduated from high school above a certain percentile/percentage in regards to their standing in the class would be admitted to one of the institutions within that state's university system—either the flagship institution of the state or one of the other publicly operated universities. These plans were put into place in states that had abandoned their race-conscious affirmative action plans in higher education, the three leading and most well-known examples being the states of Texas (Texas Ten Percent Plan), Florida (One Florida Twenty Percent Plan), and California (California Proposition 209). The Supreme Court has seemingly approved of these plans, as Justice O'Connor, writing for the majority in *Grutter*, stated that the "... 'percentage plans,' recently adopted by public undergraduate institutions in Texas, Florida and California ... are currently engaged in experimenting with a wide variety of alternative approaches. Universities in other States can and should draw on the most promising aspects of these race-neutral alternatives as they develop."[1] Additionally, the state of Washington has eliminated the use of race as a factor in higher education by public referenda, as will be discussed below. At a minimum, students should be aware that minority enrollment in some of the flagship institutions (for example, the University of California at Berkeley and the University of Texas at Austin) has declined since the advent of these percentage plan schemes.

THE STATE OF TEXAS—AFFIRMATIVE ACTION AND THE TEXAS TEN PERCENT PLAN

Texas enacted its plan in 1997 after the use of race-conscious affirmative action was held to be unconstitutional in *Hopwood v. Texas*, as discussed in Chapter 1. This is the plan that George W. Bush helped pass as the then governor of Texas, and is heralded as an example of his belief in "affirmative access," and not affirmative action. As Bush announced in the presidential debates of 2000, "I signed legislation in Texas requiring [that] the top 10 percent of graduates from Texas high schools be automatically accepted in any public university in Texas. As a result of this policy minority enrollment in Texas universities is at an all-time high." After Bush became president, the Texas percentage plan in its brief was cited by his legal advisers, opposing affirmative action in the *Gratz* and *Grutter* cases. In 2004, Bush commented that he "supports affirmative access, which aggressively reaches out to minorities, is inclusive of all races, provides equal opportunity, and promotes diversity. I do not support racial quotas, preferences, or set-asides, which perpetuate divisions and can lead people to question the accomplishments of successful minorities."[2] President Bush's involvement has strengthened the supporters of the program who have beaten back attempts at changing the law during the last several years. As one Texas state senator commented, "If the president of the United States says this is the way to go, then why dismantle it?"[3]

The Texas plan does admit any high school student who graduates in the top 10 percent of his or her class to the public institution of choice in the state. Furthermore, unlike the percentage plans subsequently adopted in California and Florida, which guarantee top-ranked students a spot at only *one* of the public institutions within the state, the Texas plan guarantees admission to the school of the student's choice, usually the University of Texas at Austin (the state's flagship institution) or Texas A&M. In fact, in 2004, 66 percent of all freshmen at the University of Texas at Austin were automatically accepted by way of the Texas percentage plan (up from 41 percent in 1998).[4] Similarly, one-half of all freshmen at Texas A&M come to the school by way of automatic acceptance via the Texas plan. The president of the University of Texas at Austin, Larry Faulkner, has said that unless the law is modified, the campus will be "run over" by automatic-admit students under the percentage plan. One critic of the Texas law, Houston businessman Lee Moncrief, has said that the effect of the law "is a cancer on UT and Texas A&M."[5] However, students from rural and urban schools that had rarely sent their students to the state's prestigious flagship institutions are now able to secure admission if they land in the top 10 percent of their high school class. The law has provided motivation to a whole generation of nontraditional students who otherwise never would have considered the University of Texas or Texas A&M. As one high school student is reported as saying in a *Chronicle of Higher Education* article, "If it wasn't for the top-10-percent law, I would have stayed [ranked] 32...I wouldn't have fought as hard."[6]

Proponents of this plan argue that since race-conscious affirmative action plans were held to be unconstitutional after *Hopwood*, this approach is the next best alternative in ensuring diversity within the Texas public university system. One supporter of the law has said that the "top 10 percent is another tool to achieve diversity."[7] Specifically, in high schools that are densely populated with minority students, the plan ensures that the top 10 percent of the students will be guaranteed admission to the Texas higher education system. This approach, it is argued, avoids placing too much emphasis on standardized testing, performance on which is in part dictated by one's socioeconomic status. Furthermore, supporters argue that the law is still needed today, as, while the *Hopwood* decision has been overturned, the Supreme Court still does not permit widespread consideration of race as a factor in admissions decisions.

However, critics argue that this plan, while perhaps well intentioned, actually does considerable harm at the high school level, in essence acting as a force to ensure that the high schools remain in a state of de facto segregation. Otherwise, if high schools are truly integrated, the number of minority students gaining admission as part of the top 10 percent will decrease. Thus, the percentage plan in Texas actually is reliant upon segregated high schools in order to achieve the same levels of minority enrollment as before *Hopwood*. A report by a Princeton sociology professor on the impact of the Texas plan concludes that the enrollment of minority students at the University of Texas at Austin will decrease if students attend racially integrated high schools.[8] Thus, if pre-1996 minority enrollment numbers are to be maintained, the plan requires segregated high schools, so that most of the schools' top 10 percent is minority. Critics further argue that these percentage plans simply do not ensure adequate numbers of minority students in higher education. According to Gary Orfield, director of the Civil Rights Project at Harvard, the plans are not really concerned with remedial compensation or diversity, and are "a return to an old method... the evaluation of high school grades and class standing."[9] Recent enrollment data provide some supports for these arguments. For example, black students made up only 5 percent of the applicants automatically admitted under the Ten Percent Plan in 2004, when roughly 14 percent of the high school graduates were black. Finally, critics also point out that the law discriminates against graduates from academically challenging high schools who may be very well qualified, but not rank in the top 10 percent of their respective schools. The argument goes that a graduate from a competitive high school graduating in the top 20 or 30 percent of the class, or with superior SAT scores, "loses" his or her seat to a graduate from a less rigorous high school who graduates in the top 10 percent of that school's senior class, and often with lower SAT scores. In other words, according to Texas State Senator Jeff Wentworth, "There is great concern expressed to me by alumni about dumbing down of the University of Texas."[10] For example, a student who attended a selective high school graduated in 2005 just three spots outside the top 10 percent of her school. Despite a 4.4 weighted GPA and a 1380 on her SAT, she was told she would not be admitted to the University of Texas unless she first attended summer school.[11] Texas A&M attempts to cure this problem by offering automatic admission to any applicant who has an SAT score of at least 1300 and falls within the top 50 percent of their high school graduating class.

Yet, as discussed in Chapters 1 and 2, the *Hopwood* decision no longer represents a valid statement of law, and it has been replaced by the guidance rendered by the Supreme Court in *Gratz* and *Grutter*. This means that as a matter of federal law, affirmative action can be utilized within the federal Fifth Circuit (including Texas, Louisiana, and Mississippi) and is permissible under the Fourteenth Amendment, so long as the affirmative action plan is consistent with the guidance of the Court in *Gratz* and *Grutter*. However, the Texas Ten Percent Plan is also still in effect as a matter of state law, despite ongoing debates and efforts in the Texas legislature to change the often-cited Texas admissions process.

During the 2004–2005 legislative session of the Texas House of Representatives and Senate, considerable time was spent in debating whether to revise or to eliminate the Texas Ten Percent Plan. There were at least twelve different pieces of legislation pending that would either outright abolish the law or alter the current plan in material respects. The substance of these various amendments and/or revisions to the Texas plan is telling as to the controversy that surrounds the current law and, again, the many divergent viewpoints regarding the efficacy and propriety of the policy. For example, two of the proposed bills would have eliminated the plan altogether, on the grounds that the plan forces students to take easier classes in high school or transfer to a less academically rigorous school (in order to make it into the top 10 percent). Two other proposed bills would have changed the 10 percent plan to a 5 percent plan, making it more restrictive, with the only difference between the two bills being that one would call for implementation by 2006, and the other by 2010. Still another proposed bill/approach would have allowed the University of Texas and Texas A&M systems to decide where to place students accepted under the 10 percent plan, meaning that a student would not be guaranteed admission to a particular college, but only *one* of the public universities within the state. This approach would have been consistent with the approach of the state of Florida, which is delineated more fully beginning on page 52. Another proposed bill would have required students to complete a specific set of courses in order to gain automatic admission to a public university. A fifth approach proposed to increase the eligibility for minority students by allowing exemptions for those who have not met all of the admissions requirements. Finally, perhaps somewhat sarcastically, a bill was introduced that would have exempted any public college or university within the state from complying with the Ten Percent law if the incoming freshman class is as diverse (racially and ethnically) as its football team. All of these bills were ultimately defeated in May–June 2005, and the Texas legislature adjourned for the year without taking any action on the Ten Percent law, thus guaranteeing its unaltered existence until at least 2006–2007. In the meantime, debates will continue to rage on whether the plan is fair. In the words of Larry Faulkner, "I think there will be more to come."[12]

Furthermore, since 2003, different public institutions within the state have articulated that they will follow differing practices regarding the use of race, despite the fact that all of these institutions remain a part of the Texas state system. This has caused a fair amount of confusion as to what the future will hold for the state of Texas in this area. "No matter what the legislature decides, says Ms. Tienda, [a] Princeton professor, the top-10-percent debate is likely to be only the first act in a continuing drama."[13] First, as a general matter at present, while the reintroduction of race as a factor in admissions in Texas is now possible, the potential utilization of race as a factor by some institutions does not supplant or eliminate the Texas Ten Percent Plan and will only impact those students who would not have otherwise been admitted under the existing percentage plan.[14] Second, a disparity now exists among public institutions in Texas (just as with the rest of the country) on the use of race as a factor in admissions. The Board of Regents for the University of Texas system approved a measure to allow schools to petition the Board and request approval to utilize race as a factor in the admissions process, again so long as it was consistent with the Supreme Court's 2003 guidance in *Gratz* and *Grutter*. Yet, between 2003 and 2005, only the University of Texas at Austin submitted a proposal (which was subsequently approved) to allow for the use of race in its admissions practice. This was not a surprise, as the university president, Larry Faulkner, announced within hours of the Supreme Court's rulings in *Gratz* and *Grutter* that the University of Texas would move "fairly quickly" to reinstate race-conscious admissions plans. However, what was a surprise was that other public institutions in Texas (Texas A&M, for example, as described more fully below) did not immediately follow suit. The University of Texas began to consider race (above and beyond those automatically accepted under the percentage plan) along with socioeconomic factors, extracurricular activities, and standardized test scores, in 2003–2004.[15] The university also announced that it will spend $5.5 million in 2005 on scholarships for students from disadvantaged socioeconomic classes and from certain minority groups. The scholarship program, known as the Longhorn Opportunity Scholars Program, provides funds not only for tuition, but also to meet expenses for tutoring, internships, and other advantageous collegiate experiences.

The extent to which other schools in the system will utilize race (if at all) in the coming years is still unclear.[16] Texas A&M has already refused to revise its practices to reintroduce race as a factor. In December 2003, the university's president, Robert Gates, pointedly remarked that "students at Texas A&M should be admitted as individuals, on personal merit—and no other basis." At the same time, in 2004, Texas A&M also discontinued the practice of legacy preferences, saying that to consider legacies, but not race, would be "fundamentally inconsistent and unfair."[17]

Texas A&M has instead decided to pursue "expand[ed] outreach and financial aid," which will in turn lead to "expect[ed] increases" in the enrollment of African Americans and Hispanics.[18] As part of the outreach, an additional $3 million was earmarked in 2004 for recruiting minority students, and an additional $8 million for new scholarships geared toward minority students accepted at the institution. Curiously, however, the special recruitment and scholarships are directed toward blacks and Hispanics, and not other minority groups. The college specifically decided not to make similar recruitment and enrollment efforts for Native Americans, Native Hawaiians or Alaskans, or Asian Americans. Under the school's current approach, it is only the decision regarding admissions that is color blind and race neutral; its practices both before and after that point are racially conscious. According to Texas A&M officials, this approach of placing more attention on recruiting, and simultaneously not considering race in admissions, has led to a 36 percent increase in black enrollment from 2003 to 2004, and an increase of nearly 26 percent in enrollment for Hispanic applicants.[19] However, critics have argued that the increases touted by Texas A&M are deceptive, as the school had very few minority students before 2003, making the percentage increases appear substantial even when only a few more applicants are accepted. For example, the 36 percent increase in black enrollment corresponds to only an additional 55 students, from 158 black freshmen in 2003 to 213 in 2004. (Indeed, women and blacks were forbidden altogether from attending Texas A&M until 1961.) Furthermore, according to critics, if you look at the total percentage of college-age students in Texas who are African American and Hispanic, very few actually are admitted to one of the public institutions in Texas. According to *The Chronicle of Higher Education*, "Its [Texas's] total undergraduate enrollment is about 2.3 percent black and about 10.1 percent Hispanic. Blacks account for about 11.6 of the state's population and 11.2 percent of its college students, while Hispanics account for about 33.6 percent of the population and 23.7 of students."[20]

In light of these statistics, some critics say that colleges in Texas without race-conscious admissions plans maintain this poor status quo of lack of adequate representation of minority students. For example, a preliminary analysis of the University of Texas's entering class for the fall of 2005 indicates that approximately 5 percent is black (compared with 11.6 percent of state's population) and 19 percent is Hispanic (compared with 33.6 percent of the state's population). Furthermore, a year or two of positive increase in enrollment should not be the endgame or desired goal. As one critic (a state representative in Texas) has stated, "These are people [Texas A&M officials] who just got a first down on the kickoff, and are celebrating like they just won the Super Bowl."[21]

As if this disparity in practice was not sufficiently confusing, in February 2005, the University of Houston announced a third approach within the Texas system—that it will change its admissions policy to admit the top 20 percent of high school graduates—which, the officials believe, will further broaden a diverse applicant pool.[22] Furthermore, the college will accept some applicants from outside the 20 percent who have standardized test scores above a certain level. These applicants will also be reviewed with an eye toward the rigor of the student's high school, as well as the student's socioeconomic and family backgrounds. The University of Houston has indicated that it will follow this new "20 percent" approach commencing in the fall semester of 2006.

So, the applicant may be wondering what exactly is the current status of race at each of these institutions. As this is all in a state of flux, it is vital to verify institution by institution practices within the state. First, the applicant should recognize that the Texas Ten Percent Plan applies only to the public colleges and universities within the state. Private institutions in Texas are not precluded from employing race-conscious affirmative action plans in higher education, so long as the plans are consistent with both Title VI of the Civil Rights Act of 1964 and the Supreme Court's latest guidance in *Gratz* and *Grutter* (described in Chapter 2). The reader may also need to verify the extent to which the university or college in question has revised its process since June 2003. As of 2005, there are only 300 to 400 institutions that seriously consider race (of the more than 1,000 four-year degree-awarding institutions within the United States). As Theodore Shaw stated at a conference on affirmative action in February 2005, "Some institutions don't believe in this stuff."

THE STATE OF CALIFORNIA—AFFIRMATIVE ACTION AND PERCENTAGE PLANS

Like Texas, California initiated its percentage plan approach after the use of race-conscious affirmative action as a legitimate practice was first rejected within the state. In Texas, as discussed, race-conscious affirmative action was discontinued as a result of the *Hopwood* decision, which was itself invalidated by the Supreme Court's rulings in *Gratz* and *Grutter*. In California, however, the use of race-conscious affirmative action was rejected in a 1996 public referendum known as California Proposition 209 (also known as the California Civil Rights Initiative). Proposition 209 was a ballot measure that amended the California Constitution and banned any preferential treatment or discrimination based on race, gender, color, ethnicity, or national origin in public employment, contracting, and education.[23] Despite being challenged in the federal court system, California's Proposition 209 was upheld by the Court of Appeals for the Ninth Circuit as constitutional in *Coalition for Economic Equity v. Wilson*, 110 F.3d 1431 (9th Cir. 1997), *cert. denied*, 118 S. Ct. 397 (1997). The Supreme Court ultimately refused to grant review of the Ninth Circuit decision. Thus, unlike Texas, which may now consider race (if the institution so chooses) along with the percentage plan, California has a state constitutional law prohibition on the utilization of race in state institutions. As will be explained more thoroughly below, California Proposition 209 has had a devastating effect on the enrollment of African American and Hispanic American students at public institutions in the state. As the author of one reference book dealing with college admissions has admonished, "Black students should be cautioned that California Proposition 209 and the affirmative action controversy are still playing themselves out. Black enrollment at UCLA [for example] has dropped precipitously over the past year as a result."[24]

According to Robert Dynes, president of the University of California system, "Race is not on the application form...[and] they [the admissions committee] don't see it."[25] Students should therefore be aware that public institutions in California are under an obligation under state law not to utilize race, and hence will not consider it, in the admissions process. Also, if an applicant is interested in attending a public institution within the state and is a resident of the state, the most important factor will be the applicant's performance in high school and on standardized tests. Many students are admitted simply based upon their GPAs and SATs. According to President Dynes, "We have conventionally and continued to offer a place in the University of California for every student above that bright line who applies."[26] For those below that bright line, a comprehensive review is conducted by admissions personnel, where a variety of factors are considered, with the notable absent ones being race and ethnicity. Again, according to Dynes, the comprehensive review entails "GPAs, SATs, are you the first generation that's gone to college, do you come from a low income family, have you shown an ability to win, are you excellent at something, have you shown an ability to overcome difficulties?...the strongest weight in that are GPAs and SATs, and then there's about eight or ten other issues that show character or strength."[27]

Additionally, since the passage of Proposition 209, the state of California has been utilizing a percentage plan of sorts within the University of California system, guaranteeing admission into the system to any student who graduates in the top 4 percent of his/her high school class. This approach was implemented in July 2001. According to a report in *The Chronicle of Higher Education*, "The 4 percent policy plays a limited role in admitting students to the most-selective campuses, Berkeley and Los Angeles," while relying "more heavily on other programs, including public school outreach and financial aid, to encourage diversity."[28] Similarly, a former president of the University of California at Berkeley, Bob Laird, has commented that "the 4 percent plan in California is such a small figure that it has basically very little effect...[and] African-American students and Native American students haven't benefited at all."[29]

Furthermore, in a study conducted by the Civil Rights Project at Harvard, entitled "Percent Plans in College Admissions: A Comparative Analysis of Three States' Experiences," the authors conclude that these percentage plans "seem to have the least impact on the most competitive campuses, which have persisting losses in spite of many levels of efforts to make up for affirmative action."[30] This is most poignantly illustrated by looking at recent enrollment figures for the University of California at Berkeley, arguably one of the most prestigious universities not only in California, but also in the nation and in the world. In 2005, the University of California at Berkeley was named by the *Times Educational Supplement* as the second-best university in the world, after Harvard. However, the low percentage of blacks and Latinos on the campus is deplorable and recently at an all-time low. Within approximately two years of the passage of California Proposition 209, by 1998, the number of admitted

African American applicants drastically decreased, from 562 to 191. While this number spiked upward in 2000 to 338, it again dropped to 211 by 2003. In 2003–2004, only 98 African American students were actually enrolled in a class of 3,821, dismally constituting approximately two and one-half percent.[31] For the 2004–2005 class, there are only 108 black students (of which fewer than 40 are males) in an incoming freshman class of 3,671 students,[32] a situation that the University of California at Berkeley's new chancellor, Robert J. Birgeneau, has described as "a crisis,"[33] "shocking," and "appalling."[34] Bob Laird, the former president of Berkeley who presided over the college both before and after Proposition 209, has commented that the before and after images at the college are like night and day. Prior to Proposition 209, race "was a fairly strong consideration within the range of factors..."[35] However, according to Laird, the discontinuation of racial considerations has had "a devastating effect on the admission and subsequent enrollment of African-American, Latino and Native American students."[36] In the entering class of 800 students to the well-respected engineering program, there is not even one African American.[37]

Indeed, since the implementation of California Proposition 209, enrollment of minority students has declined 30 percent.[38] In both 2004 and 2005, across all of the nine schools that constitute the University of California statewide system, African American enrollment stood at about 3 percent.[39] This can be compared and contrasted with the higher enrollments for Asian Americans (37 percent), Latinos (13 percent), and non-Hispanic whites (38 percent).[40] These figures have remained consistent for fall 2005 enrollment data, whereby Asian Americans constitute 40 percent (an increase of 3 percent), white students, roughly 34 percent (a 4 percent decrease), Latinos, 16 percent (a 3 percent increase), and blacks comprising 3 percent more. The combined number of African American, Native American, and Latino students offered admission for the fall of 2005 across all nine institutions was 20.6 percent, only a .6 percent increase from 2004.[41] This marginal increase in the acceptance of minority students is largely due to increased enrollment of Latinos on campus. At the same time that Latinos are making progress, "the news is 'dire' for African Americans who remain a tiny fraction of the total number of students admitted."[42] This is illustrated by comparing the 1997 offers of admission, by race, for freshmen at the University of California system with the 2005 data. The number of offers drastically increased for Asian Americans (13,084 offers in 1997; 17,297 in 2005) and Latinos (5,570 offers in 1997; 8,438 in 2005), while for all intents and purposes staying roughly the same for African Americans (1,503 offers in 1997; 1,593 in 2005).[43] The stagnancy of African American admissions opportunity is further illustrated by the fact that, overall, offers of admission have increased by 10,401, from 39,616 in 1997 to 50,017 in 2005. Finally, perhaps an indication of how minority students have been discouraged in the likelihood of being successfully admitted in the wake of Proposition 209, the percentage of African American applications received by the University of California at Berkeley, which averages 20,000–30,000 applications a year, was never higher than 5.8 percent between the years 1996 and 2001.[44]

Likewise, minority enrollment figures (for black and Hispanic students) at the other prestigious public institutions in California, namely, California Institute of Technology (CalTech) and the University of California at Los Angeles (UCLA), are equally dismaying. CalTech, in Pasadena, California, is considered one of the most prestigious and academically challenging institutions in the country and is particularly known for its rigorous course work in the sciences and engineering. Many Nobel Prize winners serve on the faculty, and the teacher to student ratio is, incredibly, one to three. Yet, in the wake of Proposition 209, CalTech's enrollment figures were more racially exclusive than the dismal figures from the University of California at Berkeley. In 1996 and 1997, CalTech only enrolled two African American freshmen. This prompted one magazine, *The Journal of Blacks in Higher Education*, to report that "the lowest percentage of black students was at CalTech. At CalTech, only 5 of 882 students, or 0.6 percent, are black." In the same issue, the magazine further reported that "over the years, California Institute of Technology has shown little or no interest in student or faculty diversity" and that "the only black student or alumni organization is the CalTech National Society of Black Engineers. Probably its membership list can be maintained on the back of a matchbook cover."[45] The publicity for CalTech did not improve the following year, as CalTech earned the very dubious distinction of being labeled "The Whitest of the Nation's 25 Highest-Ranked Universities" by *The Journal of Blacks in Higher Education* in its spring 1998 issue. In describing the "whiteness" of CalTech, the magazine reported as follows:

> Yet measured by standard statistics CalTech has been unable, or unwilling, to take steps to diversify its faculty and student body. Today, black students make up only 0.9 percent of the student body at CalTech. In 1995 there were no black students in the freshman class. For the current freshman class there were 30 black applicants to CalTech, 9 of whom were accepted. Two black applicants enrolled. There are only 2 African Americans on CalTech's 285-member faculty. This is by far the lowest total number and lowest percentage of black faculty at any of the nation's 25 highest-ranked universities.... There are 18 full-time faculty members at MIT, nine times the number at CalTech. Princeton University has two black faculty members in its mathematics department alone, the same number of black professors on the entire CalTech faculty.[46]

CalTech has attempted to make inroads into this problem of having no racial diversity on campus, but the improvements have been quite modest. Critics argue that "despite the administration's lip service to the goal of further student and faculty diversity, the results are insignificant."[47] The University of California at Los Angeles (UCLA) has also had troubles in recruiting and maintaining minority students. UCLA has long had a reputation as representing the "epitome of diversity," where Asian Americans account for roughly 40 percent of the student body, and Hispanic Americans, another 15–20 percent.[48]

Yet, black applicants have represented only a fraction of the student body, and the UCLA experience mirrors that of the University of California at Berkeley in recent years. In 1997, 221 African American students enrolled at UCLA (similar to 260 at Berkeley that year). However, by 2004, enrollment had plummeted at UCLA, where only 110 black students were admitted in a class of 3,723 students (similar to 108 black students admitted to Berkeley in 2004). UCLA has announced, however, that it has made slight improvement from 2004 to 2005, in that the number of admitted black students has increased from 196 offers of admission in 2004 to 247 in 2005.

Yet, despite the prohibition by Proposition 209 on the use of race as a "preference," some California lawmakers, like their counterparts in Texas, have tried to implement legislation that would allow the kind of race-conscious considerations approved of in *Gratz* and *Grutter*. For example, in 2004, California Assembly Bill 2387 was introduced in the California General Assembly. This bill would have allowed for the use of race in higher-education decisions, not as a preference or quota, but as part of an individualized, holistic review of the kind approved by the Supreme Court in *Grutter*. In defending this proposed legislation (which ultimately failed), Ricardo Lara, director of communications for State Assemblyman Marco Firebaugh, stated that "the purpose of the bill is to give the admissions office a tool...where everything is taken into consideration" because "race and ethnicity all play a role as a precursor of the student's talent."[49] The proposed legislation read, in relevant part, as follows:

> [It] would add to the [existing Donahoe Higher Education Act] a provision authorizing the University of California and the California State University, until January 1, 2015, to consider culture, race, gender, ethnicity, national origin, geographic origin, and household income, along with other relevant factors, in undergraduate and graduate admissions, so long as no preferences is given, if and when the university, campus, college, school, or program is attempting to obtain educational benefit through the recruitment of a multifactored, diverse student body.

By the language (which is representative of several attempts at legislatively tinkering with California Proposition 209), the bill would have allowed, in theory, the kind of individualized and holistic review of candidates approved of in the *Gratz* and *Grutter* decisions, while not held to be an outright "preference" in violation of Proposition 209. However, several critics at the time pointed out that the bill would be unconstitutional, as Proposition 209 is enshrined as a constitutional provision, and can only be overturned by a constitutional amendment, and certainly not by a state statute. Further, while a final version of this bill was approved by the state senate and assembly, it was vetoed by Republican governor Arnold Schwarzenegger.[50] Though this bill was vetoed, it has served as a model for other attempts to reintroduce affirmative action in higher education in California. For example, a new bill, Assembly Bill 1452, was submitted in 2004–2005 and was almost identical to the language of Assembly Bill 2387. Critics of these efforts have discounted the legality/constitutionality of this approach and argue that the bill will be vetoed if passed by the legislature, and if not vetoed, it will be held by the courts to be unconstitutional under Proposition 209.[51]

At a minimum, however, many in the state are vowing to improve diversity as well as they can, despite Proposition 209. For example, Robert Birgeneau, in his inaugural address as the new chancellor of UC Berkeley, effective April 15, 2005, called for greater diversity on campus, stating that "our student body at Cal must reflect the majestic tapestry of cultures and peoples that constitute California."[52] He also pledged to study (and perhaps propose changes to) Proposition 209, which, he has claimed, has brought about the "unintended consequences" of "egregiously" low minority enrollment at Berkeley.[53] This has also prompted Chancellor Birgeneau to make as his number one goal the boosting of extremely low minority enrollment. In his address, he "stopped short of advocating voter action to reverse Proposition 209, although he has said he believes eventual rollback or reform of the law is inevitable."[54] Critics of Chancellor Birgeneau's policies said that allowing admissions officers to consider personal, nonacademic factors such as life experiences, musical talents, and so on, "was an attempt to sidestep the state's ban on the use of race in admissions decisions,"[55] an allegation vehemently denied by admissions officers in the University of California system.

THE STATE OF FLORIDA—AFFIRMATIVE ACTION AND THE ONE FLORIDA PLAN

In July 2000, Governor Jeb Bush of Florida oversaw the dismemberment of the use of race-conscious admissions policies within the public university system and replaced race-based admissions with a percentage plan approach. That is, under the One Florida Plan, any high school student who graduates in the top 20 percent of his or her class and has completed the college preparatory credits is guaranteed a seat in one of the eleven public institutions in the state. The plan does not guarantee admission to a particular university (e.g., the flagship University of Florida at Gainesville), but only into the state system, and one of the state schools.

Governor Bush has touted this plan as a way to eliminate the arguably divisive use of race as a factor in admissions, while still promoting diversity. In an editorial in the *Washington Post*, he claimed that Florida's elimination of affirmative action has been successful:

> In a news article on November 22 [2004], The Post reported on a drop in admissions of black students at several flagship universities nationwide. I am proud to report that Florida is not among those affected. We are having notable success in higher education for minorities... in university admission decisions

and in state government contracts, Florida has, under this program, become race-neutral. And, contrary to gloomy predictions in some quarters, the state university system has not suffered, nor have minority students.[56]

Again, according to the Office of the Governor, the "Talented 20 program" (as it is sometimes called) does not require that a student score well on standardized tests such as the SAT (Scholastic Assessment Test) and ACT (American College Test). According to the Florida plan, eliminating these tests from consideration will level the playing field for two reasons. First, minority applicants do not tend to perform as well on these standardized tests as white applicants. Second, and interrelated, test scores can be manipulated by resources, namely, the applicant's ability to take a private preparatory course for the SAT or ACT and his or her general socioeconomic status. Thus, according to Governor Bush, the plan eliminates the use of race as a factor, yet, at the same time, leads to diversity in the public institutions within the state.

Governor Bush has repeatedly claimed that the program is successful. In 2003, he stated that "we've got four years under our belt, and we can say that this [is] working, we're on the right track, and it's a far cry from what was predicted. One Florida is achieving its mission of more minority students having opportunity in higher education."[57] In the December 31, 2004, editorial in the *Washington Post*, Governor Bush wrote that minority enrollment "on Florida campuses has risen to 34 percent..."[58] While minority enrollment is increasing in Florida, critics argue that this reflects the overall enlargement in size of the applicant pool in Florida, and drastic increases among one minority class in particular (Hispanic Americans) and not the overall effectiveness of the One Florida Plan.[59] For example, according to Florida's Department of Education, overall student enrollment at all of Florida's eleven public institutions increased by 2.3 percent in 2004. However, minority enrollment increased only slightly, from 34.4 percent to 35 percent. Furthermore, while the overall percentage of black students at all eleven institutions marginally increased from 14.4 to 14.5 percent from 2003 to 2004, the enrollment of African Americans as freshmen actually dropped in 2004 from 17.5 to 16 percent, a trend that continued in 2005, again despite the overall increase in enrollment for all students in the state. Critics point out that this negative trend regarding enrollment of black students appears to be continuing unabated. In July 2005, for example, a preliminary report from the Florida State Board of Governors announced that the "number of black students admitted as freshmen in state universities has dropped by 1,400" since 2002, a reported 11 percent decrease over three years.[60]

Furthermore, according to the critics of Florida's anti-affirmative action stance, this negative trend among African American enrollees is easily obscured by Governor Bush's administration in Florida, by focusing on total minority figures instead of African American enrollment. According to the Florida State Board of Governors, while African American freshman enrollment appears to have decreased by 11 percent from 2002 to 2005, Hispanic American enrollment, conversely, has increased by roughly 20 percent during the same period.[61] Thus, by virtue of significant increases in Hispanic enrollment, the state can claim slight improvement in overall minority enrollment, despite the fact that black enrollment declines or stays the same (despite larger student/applicant pools). Critics argue that the "roughly 730 black freshmen [enrolled in fall 2004] are still fewer in number—and a smaller share of the first-year class—than in 2000, before the race-influenced admissions ban took full effect."[62] Critics further argue that the statewide minority enrollment numbers at all the state universities are skewed by the disproportionately high enrollment of minorities in two of the eleven schools, namely, Florida Atlantic University in Boca Raton where almost three of every four students are minorities, and Florida International University in Miami, where one of every three students are minorities.[63] Hence, in the words of one critic, "Gov. Bush lowers the bar by claiming credit for minority enrollment not plummeting since he enacted One Florida."[64] And according to Patricia Marin, an expert with Harvard University's Civil Rights Project, "One Florida may be credited with something it has nothing to do with."[65]

Putting aside the public institutions within the state and the One Florida plan, students should not overlook Bethune-Cookman College, in Daytona Beach, and Florida A&M University, in Tallahassee. Both these institutions have a long history of reaching out to minority student applicants. Key factors for admissions to Bethune-Cookman College are the "character and personality" of the applicant,[66] while Florida A&M prides itself on recruiting students who " 'ordinarily would not qualify' (but who are still above average), because that's part of the mission of our schools—to reach out, to lay down a path." Indeed, advice to minority applicants regarding Florida A&M is to "apply when you can 'bring to the university other important attributes or special talents' that might not be reflected in your transcript."[67]

These two institutions are also worthy of consideration for applicants who desire to attend a college in Florida with a strong representation of minority students on campus and services/resources directed specifically toward them. Bethune-Cookman College was founded by civil rights leader Dr. Mary McLeod Bethune in 1904, as a school that would provide an opportunity for African American women to pursue education. Dr. Bethune "has been described as 'the most influential African-American woman in the twentieth century, whose legacy is found in the fields of education, government, politics, economics, social activism, and women's rights."[68] In 1923, the school became coeducational after merging Cookman Institute. Today, the school has a student body of roughly 3,000, and is one of the largest of the approximately forty members of the United Negro College Fund. The school also has a plethora of clubs and chapters that focus on African American heritage, including chapters of the NAACP, the Thurgood Marshall Society, and the National Council of Negro Women (which, incidentally, had Dr. Bethune as its first national president).

Florida A&M, likewise, has a very high minority enrollment, where approximately 89 percent of the student body is black, only about 7 percent being white. Florida A&M also has a plethora of organizations such as chapters of the NAACP, the Pan-African Cultural Club, and the FAMU Gospel Choir (which has sold many albums to the public since 1985). Furthermore, the school has received its share of prestigious accolades. For example, *Time/Princeton Review* named FAMU its "College of the Year" in its 1998 edition. In 1999, FAMU ranked behind only two very famous HBCUs (Spelman College and Morehouse College) among the nation's "top fifty colleges for African Americans." Also, it was listed as one of the top colleges in the country for African American students in Isaac Black's, *African American Student's College Guide*, published in 2000.

THE STATE OF WASHINGTON—AFFIRMATIVE ACTION AND THE INITIATIVE 200

Finally, while not a "percentage plan" state, Washington has eliminated the use of racial preferences in public activities within the state. That is, Washington State adopted its Initiative 200 in 1998, which, like Proposition 209 in California, abolishes the use of race at the state level in education, employment, and contracting. The language of Washington Initiative 200 specifies that "the state shall not... grant preferential treatment to any individual or group on the basis of race, sex, color, ethnicity, or national origin in the operation of public employment, public education, or public contracting."[69] However, unlike California Proposition 209 (which amended the California Constitution to prohibit the use of race-conscious measures), the Washington State initiative did not amend the state constitution, and has the force of statutory law within the state, meaning that it could be changed by passing another statute or public ballot initiative. Indeed, as with Texas and California, there is legislation pending in the Washington state senate that would allow schools to consider race to diversify their student bodies, so long as race is utilized in a way consistent with the guidance of *Gratz* and *Grutter*. In essence, this law would exempt higher education from the current prohibitions contained in Washington Initiative 200, and allow for the individualized, holistic review based upon a myriad of factors including race.[70]

THE STATE OF LOUISIANA

Louisiana is another state in which the use of affirmative action has been banned. First, being part of the federal Fifth Circuit, Louisiana, along with Mississippi and Texas, was prohibited from 1996 to 2003 from using affirmative action under *Hopwood v. Texas* (discussed in Chapter 1), which was invalidated by the Supreme Court's decisions in 2003. Even though the "federal ban" within the Fifth Circuit was lifted in June 2003, it could be argued that the state constitution also appears to ban the use of race in decisions involving admissions and financial aid at public institutions of higher education within the state. Specifically, Article I, Section 3 of the Louisiana Constitution of 1974 prohibits the use of affirmative action, providing that "no person shall be denied the equal protection of the laws. No law shall arbitrarily, capriciously, or unreasonably discriminate against a person because of birth, age, sex, culture, physical condition, or political ideas or affiliations." Attempts at using affirmative action in contracting and public employment have met with court challenges and have resulted in their being held unconstitutional in light of the above prohibition in the Louisiana state constitution.[71] In fact, the Louisiana Supreme Court held that this provision "absolutely prohibits any state law which discriminates on account of race."

Furthermore, in 1996, then governor Murphy "Mike" Foster, Jr., in his first executive order, declared that there would be a prohibition on all state agencies (presumably including public educational institutions within the state) from employing race-conscious measures, such as quotas or set-asides. However, after national groups threatened to boycott tourism and travel in New Orleans and other areas within the state, he issued a new executive order, indicating that race and gender may be utilized in state decisions so long as they were not the primary or predominant factors in the decision-making process.

It is fair to say that the second executive order is consistent with what the Supreme Court said is permissible under the Fourteenth Amendment in the *Gratz* and *Grutter* decisions. Nonetheless, the leading public institution within the state, namely, Louisiana State University, has not altered its prohibition on the use of race in admissions after 2003. In fact, after the *Gratz* and *Grutter* decisions were announced, Dr. Marie Hamilton, assistant dean of the graduate school at LSU, stated point-blank that "affirmative action does not impact admittance" and that "everybody who applies is admitted on the same criteria."[72]

OTHER STATES

As alluded to in Chapters 1 and 2, opponents of race-conscious affirmative action have promised to continue to wage war at the state level against the use of race in any manner in higher education. In 2003 alone, seven significant anti-affirmative action bills were proposed in six different states.[73] In particular, according to the organization Americans for a Fair Chance, the states of Michigan, Colorado, Massachusetts, New York, Arizona, Missouri, and New Hampshire had been specifically targeted for action. In 2004, for example, Colorado narrowly defeated a bill in its senate (by one vote) that would have eliminated the use of race-conscious measures in Colorado schools. A similar law was proposed that would have prohibited affirmative action in universities and regional and technical colleges, but it was defeated in the state house and senate.

The State of Michigan

In spite of the threat of legal action and lawsuits against those schools that do not comply with the Supreme Court's rulings in *Gratz* and *Grutter*, one of the chief architects of California's Proposition 209, Ward Connerly, announced that he would take the affirmative action battle to the heart of affirmative action, the state of Michigan, where the *Gratz* and *Grutter* cases began. In the two years since the Supreme Court's ruling and Connerly's promise to wage the fight at the state level, he was successful in leading the effort to collect close to a million dollars for this purpose. Ward Connerly and his supporters obtained 500,000 signatures in order to have the Michigan Civil Rights Initiative placed on the Michigan ballot for voters to consider in November 2006. The Michigan Civil Rights Initiative intentionally mirrors the California Civil Rights Initiative. Early public opinion polls indicate that the law would have the support of a majority of voters in Michigan.

The Michigan Civil Rights Initiative would amend Michigan's Equal Protection Clause, which is found in Article I, Section 2 of the Michigan Constitution, and specifies that "[n]o person shall be denied the equal protection of the laws; nor shall any person be denied the enjoyment of his civil or political rights or be discriminated against in the exercise thereof because of religion, race, color, or national origin." The article would be amended as follows by the pending initiative:

> The University of Michigan, Michigan State University, Wayne State University, and any other public college or university, community college or school district shall not discriminate against, or grant preferential treatment to, any individual or group on the basis of race, sex, color, ethnicity, or national origin in the operation of public employment, public education, or public contracting.

As noted above, the language is nearly the same as California's Proposition 209, except for the fact that the Michigan Initiative, in addition to specifying three specific state-school systems, says the prohibition also covers "any other public college or university, community college or school district." Also, considering that the prohibition of race-conscious measures would extend to any "operation of public employment...education...contracting," some have argued that this would expand the prohibition on using affirmative action to recruitment efforts or scholarships offered within the state (arguably a broader prohibition than that currently in place with California Proposition 209).[74]

The State of Colorado

As was briefly mentioned at the beginning of this section, Colorado has defeated two bills in recent years that would have limited the use of race-conscious measures and affirmative action in education. Colorado is also on the list of potential battleground states for state-level public initiatives like California Proposition 209. However, while not removing outright the consideration of race in admissions and financial aid decisions at colleges and universities within Colorado, the University of Colorado system has made a step in that direction by announcing in 2005 its aim to adopt a plan similar to those in place in Texas, California, and Florida. This plan, negotiated over several months by various officials within the University of Colorado system as well as the Colorado General Assembly and the Colorado Commission on Higher Education, would guarantee admissions to one of the three campuses (Boulder, Colorado Springs, or Denver) that constitute the University of Colorado, so long as the applicant is in the top 10 percent of his/her class. Similar to Florida and California, but unlike Texas, the percentage plan would not guarantee admission to a student's number one selection in terms of campus, but rather just guarantees a seat at one of the three campuses.

However, administrators at the University of Colorado, cognizant of the problems and criticisms levied against the percentage plans in place in Texas, Florida, and California, have made class rank only one of the ways in which automatic admissions might be obtained. That is, in addition to being in the top 10 percent of your graduating class, there are two ways to earn an automatic admittance to the system. First, students are guaranteed a spot in the freshman class within the system, even if not ranked in the top 10 percent of their class, if they have a GPA of 3.8 or higher. Second, under this plan, students are also guaranteed a spot in the freshman class if they are in the top 25 percent of their graduating class, and have maintained a GPA of at least 3.5. A University of Colorado spokesperson estimated that "of 9,230 state residents who entered the University of Colorado last fall [2004], about 3,507, or 38 percent, would have qualified under the automatic-admission policy."[75]

Of all the percentage plans, the Colorado plan alone was put forth under no pretense that the plan would, or would not, impact diversity and result in the increase of minority enrollment on campus. Rather, the plan is part of the broader University of Colorado operating plan, mandated by the state of Colorado, which delineates how the university meets "certain goals of quality, access, and efficiency" in how it operates. Ex-president of the University of Colorado Elizabeth Hoffman commented that "the guaranteed admissions proposal is really a statement to the people of Colorado: If you meet certain standards, you'll be guaranteed admissions to the University of Colorado."[76] This plan becomes operational in 2006, meaning that students applying for admission in the fall of 2006 will be considered and admitted under this new approach.

5

General Advice to Students and Parents in Navigating the Maze

The first four chapters of this book delineate the current state of affirmative action, both in the legal requirements and in the practices of universities and colleges in administering such programs. The remaining chapters focus on what students and parents can do to maximize chances of success in admissions for the potential student. At a minimum, the applicant/student can make use of tips in relying, at least in part, on universities and colleges that might still utilize race as a factor in admissions or financial aid decisions. Following this, Chapter 6 will offer specific advice to students on how to approach the application essays, which are, after *Gratz* and *Grutter*, now the chief way in which universities and colleges make decisions based upon diversity and race in admissions.

RULE ONE: THERE ARE NO QUICK FIXES

Of course, at the beginning of this chapter, the reader should realize that there is no "quick fix" or simple solution for getting accepted or selected under a program based, in part, upon affirmative action considerations. As one author has written, "Affirmative action is neither out to hurt you nor out to give you something you don't deserve."[1] There is no substitute for the strongest possible grades and standardized placement test scores, which, according to recent reports and surveys, are by far the most important factors in admissions. For example, the National Association for College Admission Counseling (NACAC), in a report entitled *State of College Admission*, has stated that "since 1993, grades in college prep courses (a proxy for strength of curriculum) have remained the number one factor in the decision about whom to admit to college."[2] Of all colleges responding to the 2005 NACAC survey, 80.3 percent indicated that "grades in college prep courses" were of "considerable importance" and headed the list of factors by percentage of importance.[3] Further, according to the admissions department at Penn State University, two-thirds of their evaluation is based upon GPA alone, and only one-third is based upon other factors, such as test scores, class rank, and the applicant's personal statement.

Next, in terms of factors of considerable importance in the NACAC survey, were the applicant's performance on standardized admission tests and grades in all courses. While 60.3 percent of the colleges and universities responding indicated that "standardized admission tests" were of "considerable importance," 56.9 percent responded that "grades in all courses" were of "considerable importance." Thus, the student who is reading this book early in the admissions process (i.e., sophomore or junior year of high school or graduate/professional school) should first focus on keeping as strong a GPA as possible, as this continues to be one of the most important factors in the admissions process at virtually every school in the country. To the extent you can pick your schedule, select college preparatory courses, as this has remained the number one factor in evaluating you as a viable candidate. Also, select classes that you find to be of interest or about what you are passionate, as this will usually translate into a strong academic performance in the course.

The next most important factor is performance on standardized placement tests. Unfortunately, there are many articles and studies that suggest that a strong correlation exists between performance on these tests and the socioeconomic status of the test-taker. The likely reason is that the more resources a student has at his or her disposal, the better the student can prepare for standardized tests if the student so desires. For this reason, the idea that standardized testing is a neutral way to determine merit is a myth. Poorer students who attend substandard secondary schools, or cannot afford to enroll in an expensive prep course like Princeton Review or Kaplan, are not on a level playing field in terms of competition with others (based upon test score comparisons alone). Nevertheless, it goes without saying that any preparation that the student can undertake for these tests is highly recommended. Despite the unequal competition, standardized test score performance remains a chief component in most admissions programs. According to one expert, "Do not rely on affirmative action programs to give you an advantage. Remember that even with affirmative action, you are competing with other students of color who may have similar or better academic records than you."[4] Furthermore, only a third or so of all colleges and universities in the country claim to have affirmative action plans in place.

At best, affirmative action "factors" will be consulted to tip the scale if two or more candidates are equally situated and are competitive for the remaining seats in the entering class. Class rank historically was one of the chief "tip" factors after GPA and standardized test scores. However, as will be discussed more fully, since the *Gratz* and *Grutter* decisions, essays are now considered the most important tip factor, and will surpass class rank in the coming years. According to the 2005 NACAC survey (as the reader can see in Tables 1 and 2), the factors of considerable importance to admissions departments in 2004 at

Table 1
Factors in the College Admission Decision: Percent of All Colleges Attributing Levels of Importance, 2004

Factor	Considerable Importance	Moderate Importance	Limited Importance	No Importance
Grades in College Prep Courses	80.3	10.2	3.0	6.4
Standardized Admission Tests	60.3	27.5	5.4	6.8
Grades in All Courses	56.9	27.6	8.5	7.1
Class Rank	28.2	36.9	20.2	14.7
Essay or writing sample	25.2	35.4	20.3	19.1
Counselor Recommendation	18.4	43.5	25.7	12.3
Teacher Recommendation	18.1	40.9	28.4	12.5
Interview	8.7	28.9	32.6	29.8
Work/Extracurricular Activities	7.5	42.1	35.4	15.0
Student's Demonstrated Interest	6.9	15.8	30.1	47.3
State Graduation Exam Scores	6.4	9.8	24.0	57.4
Subject Tests (SAT II, AP, IB)	4.9	20.0	31.8	43.4
Race/Ethnicity	2.2	16.4	24.0	57.4
Ability to Pay	1.6	4.0	12.7	81.6
State or County of Residence	1.6	6.7	22.0	69.7
Alumni Relations	1.4	19.0	44.3	35.2

Reprinted with permission. Copyright 2004 National Association for College Admission Counseling. NACAC Admission Trends Survey, 2004.

colleges and universities, in descending order, were as follows: grades in college prep courses (80.3 percent), standardized admissions tests (60.3 percent), grades in all courses (56.9 percent), class rank (28.2 percent), essay or writing sample (25.2 percent), counselor recommendation (18.4 percent), teacher recommendation (18.1 percent), interview (8.7 percent), work/extracurricular activities (7.5 percent), student's demonstrated interest (6.9 percent), state graduation exam scores (6.4 percent), subject tests (SAT II, AP, IB) (4.9 percent); race/ethnicity (2.2 percent), ability to pay (1.6 percent), state or county of residence (1.6 percent), and alumni relations (1.4 percent).[5] The above factors from class rank to alumni relations become increasingly important as secondary, or plus,

Table 2
Factors in Admission, 1993–2004 (Percent of Institutions Reporting "Considerable Importance" Assigned to Factor)

	1993	1994	1995	1996	1997	1998	1999	2000	2001	2002	2003	2004
Grades/College Prep	82	83	80	78	81	79	84	78	80	76	78	80
Class Rank	42	40	39	36	34	32	32	34	31	35	33	28
Admission Tests	46	43	47	46	50	51	54	58	52	57	61	60
Grades/All Courses	39	37	41	38	41	44	42	43	45	50	54	57
Counselor Recomm.	22	20	19	17	20	16	16	16	17	16	17	18
Teacher Recomm.	21	19	18	19	19	16	14	14	16	14	18	18
Essay	14	17	21	20	18	19	19	20	20	19	23	25
Interview	12	12	15	13	11	11	9	11	11	10	9	9
Work/Activities	6	6	7	6	6	4	5	7	6	7	7	6
Ability to Pay	NA	NA	3	2	1	2	2	1	3	3	2	2
State Exams	NA	NA	NA	NA	NA	NA	NA	NA	NA	6	7	6
Subject Exams	NA	NA	NA	NA	NA	NA	NA	NA	NA	6	7	5
Residence	NA	NA	NA	NA	NA	NA	NA	NA	NA	2	2	2
Race/Ethnicity	NA	NA	NA	NA	NA	NA	NA	NA	NA	NA	3	2
Demonstrated Interest	NA	NA	NA	NA	NA	NA	NA	NA	NA	NA	7	7
Alumni Relations	NA	NA	NA	NA	NA	NA	NA	NA	NA	NA	NA	1

Reprinted with permission. Copyright 2004 National Association for College Admission Counseling. NACAC Admission Trends Surveys, 1993–2004.

factors. For example, while only 2.2 percent of colleges stated that race was of "considerable importance," 40.4 percent did indicate that an applicant's race/ethnicity was of "moderate importance" or "limited importance." Similarly, while only 1.4 percent of colleges stated that having relatives who were alumni was of considerable importance, 63.3 percent did specify that the factor was of moderate or limited importance. The same is true of virtually all of the other secondary factors listed Table 1. The first table delineates the levels of importance of various factors in admissions. The second table shows how colleges and universities have evolved regarding their views on the level of importance for each factor between 1993 and 2004.

RULE TWO: GET INVOLVED!

While one's GPA and standardized test scores are of obvious importance, there are other ways students can make themselves more marketable for college or graduate school. Put simply, students should get involved in extracurricular activities, sports, community service, and other activities of similar character. While the Supreme Court has specified that the recruitment and retention of underrepresented minority candidates is important for diversity, the Court was clear in also stating that colleges may not rely on race alone. That is, according to the Court, there are a variety of factors that go into the recruitment and retention of a diverse entering class beyond race. So, students should get involved in any activity that interests them. If you enjoy sports, play on a sports team. If you enjoy music, consider joining the school band or concert performances. If you are a member of an underrepresented student group, and are also an athlete, musician, or chess player, or display another unique skill, you double or triple the "plus" factors in your favor, and are a double or triple threat in terms of diversity! According to the NACAC survey referenced above, while only 7.5 percent of the colleges polled indicated that the student's work/extracurricular activities constituted a factor of considerable importance, a greater percentage indicated that this factor was of moderate importance (42.1 percent) or limited importance (35.4 percent).

RULE THREE: INVESTIGATE INSTITUTIONS THAT UTILIZE RACE IN THE PROCESS

Once you are in your last year of school and are considering education at the next level, it is time to start the admissions process. Standard initial advice for any prospective college student is to research various institutions and compile a list of potential schools based upon factors that are important to the applicant, including geography, academic reputation, and chances of admission (based upon the academic quality of the previous year's entering class), among other factors. However, those who hope to maximize their chances of admissions based upon affirmative action will want to verify to what extent the school is concerned with diversity and whether or not the institution has an affirmative action plan in place. Applicants should know the schools well before applying, as different schools look for different things in candidates (including differing approaches to considering diversity as part of merit). For example, Robin Mamlet, dean of admissions at several very prominent schools, has commented as follows:

> College admissions officers look for a good match. That's why, at Sarah Lawrence College, we sought students who desired to work closely with professorial mentors in one-to-one tutorials and who were creative and independently motivated; why at Swarthmore College we looked for students who were intellectually driven and would thrive in an academically intense environment; and why at Stanford we seek bright, engaged students who possess high energy, drive, and a desire to affect the world in positive ways... [w]e look to fill the various roles that students need to play in order to keep our community vital: as members of an orchestra or an athletic team, participants in a classics program, math geniuses, and more. Diversity is critical—from within the United States and, now more than ever, from around the world.[6]

This book is a good start in the process. However, the reader should also gather as much additional information about the schools in question by perusing college directory books, visiting the institutions online, and conducting other similar research. There are many books and other resources available that rank and discuss colleges and universities from different angles and viewpoints (i.e., based upon curriculum, size, student services, demographics, graduate school placement, etc.). A high school guidance counselor can help the applicant identify these resources. Counselors can also help the applicant with the completion of the application, and in identifying questions that the applicant might wish to raise to admissions officials at the school during the admissions process.

At a minimum, however, prospective students should request from all schools of interest a college catalogue and a viewbook. The catalogue will give detailed information on the college's mission, academic requirements and degree programs (i.e., majors, minors, certificate programs, etc.), extracurricular clubs and activities, and, of course, the cost of attendance. The viewbook will offer some of this information in a summarized format, and is much more concise and easier to read. A word of caution, however, is that you should not become too enamored with a particular institution based upon this information alone. Keep in mind that the viewbooks, and to a lesser extent the catalogues, are put together with advertisement in mind. That is, the schools are trying to put forward the "best sell" for prospective applicants. You might notice that the sun is always shining in viewbook photos, and the students and professors are always smiling. This, of course, is not the case in reality; people have bad days even at good institutions. This was perhaps most poignantly illustrated by a major faux pas by a prominent university in 2000, when a brochure photo was altered by digitally adding the image of an African American student to the center of the photo, which otherwise depicted an all-white group of students at a football game. The altered photo seemed to suggest that the campus was replete with racial harmony among students, even at football games. The photo also seemed to imply that the college was racially diverse and that minority students were at the center of the action at the university. This incident is a reminder not to take the glossy pages too seriously. Remember, viewbooks, catalogues, and brochures are, in essence, advertisements by the college designed to sell you the institution as a good place to spend four years.

As part of your research, in addition to verifying whether or not a school claims to have an affirmative action program in place, it might be wise to also investigate minority enrollment rates and figures at the institutions of choice because differing conclusions might be drawn as to the commitment to diversity on campus. High minority enrollment numbers that are above the national or regional averages would reflect that the institution is serious about its affirmative action plan (and diversity) and the school's success in recruitment and retention is reflected in its student demographic data. As two admissions officials have recommended,

> [M]inority students looking at particular college campuses may inquire about vestiges of discrimination or racism. Students and their family members may be aware of previous exclusionary admission policies, hate crimes or racially motivated incidents, low retention and graduation rates for minority students, and exclusion of content related to minority history, culture, and accomplishments from the college curriculum.[7]

Again, this book, and in particular Appendix A, will serve as a good starting point. Beginning in 2004, the *U.S. News & World Report* rankings have begun including information on certain schools that have notable initiatives in improving/increasing racial and/or ethnic diversity on campus. This information allows students to quickly identify a handful of selective schools based upon the school's noteworthy enrollment of above-average numbers of students from the following racial/ethnic backgrounds: African Americans, Hispanic Americans, American Indians, Alaskan natives, Asian Americans, and Pacific Islanders. For example, the report listed Georgia State University as one of the top nineteen schools in the country in terms of their clearly illustrated devotion to bringing in a diverse freshman class. The magazine reported that Georgia State University made the list with a 36 percent enrollment of African American students in 2003.

However, what if a university has an affirmative action program in place and low minority enrollment? On one hand, it is great that the institution now has a program in place to recruit and retain underrepresented students. On the other hand, however, the low minority enrollment figures, in conjunction with the existence of an affirmative action plan, may raise a red flag. At least two negative conclusions might be drawn from this data. First, it could indicate that the institution is not serious about its implementation of an affirmative action plan, as reflected or evidenced by low enrollment figures. Second, it could indicate that the institution is still struggling with the vestiges of institutional discrimination on campus. As the reader may recall from the previous chapter, the Department of Education's Office for Civil Rights, in its 1994 policy guidelines, has indicated that it is permissible to implement affirmative action plans when it is necessary to overcome the present effects of past racial discrimination at the institution. That is not to say that one eliminates that particular school from consideration, or that the institution does not educate students well. Rather, it is more a factor of whether the student would feel comfortable at the institution, or whether the school is "a good fit."

Whether the school is a good fit depends on your perspective as a student. As discussed in Chapter 4, the University of California at Berkeley, one of the leading and most well-respected institutions in the country, does not have any affirmative action programs in place (because of a state law prohibition stemming from California Proposition 209) and, in recent years, has a woefully low enrollment of African American students, currently less than 3 percent of the entering freshman class. As a student, you should ask yourself whether you will feel comfortable attending an institution of this type. Are you the type of student who needs to feel a part of a larger group of students from the same ethnic or racial background? For example, a student who graduated in May 2005 from UC Berkeley, when interviewed on the impact of the lack of diversity on campus, stated that he was usually the only black student in his classes and that "people always turn[ed] to me for the 'black American view,' as if I could speak for everyone. It's pretty weird."[8] Another black student at a predominantly white university in the South commented, "And so a lot of times I felt out of place, because you see all white faces. You know I'm only a fly in the buttermilk, so that took some getting used to...."[9] Yet another applicant (from the applying student's perspective) commented, "I got my packet from UC Santa Cruz, and they kept sending me stuff that was black-student oriented. I just felt like they just had to meet some quota. I didn't want to be one of the very few."[10] Would this fact even matter to you as a student? Would you feel comfortable being the sole black or Hispanic voice in the class? Would you feel more (or less) comfortable attending a university with a tradition of excellence (e.g., University of Michigan), with a demonstrated commitment to diversity as evidenced by its affirmative action plans in place, along with above-average minority enrollment? Would you learn more effectively and be more comfortable if all of your fellow students were of the same racial background? If so, you might wish to consider an HBCU (see Chapter 7 for detailed information on HBCUs). As one black graduate of a predominantly and historically white institution commented, "It is not a bad thing to go somewhere where you might be a minority. You learn about different people."[11] Another student commented that attending a college with low minority enrollment figures was not a major concern, as "the high schools and elementary schools I've been to have never been all black... so it doesn't really matter to me whether it's all black or not." Finally, if you are accepted at a top university, in part due to the school's efforts at diversifying its student population, will you feel comfortable at that institution where the actual minority enrollment is below the national or regional averages? Given that "larger colleges are slightly more likely to consider a student's race or ethnicity than smaller colleges,"[12] are you comfortable attending a larger school (with larger class sizes) in order to take advantage of this fact? These are all very hard questions that only prospective students can answer after honestly assessing themselves, their goals, and what they want out of the college experience. More information on evaluating a college or university's true commitment to diversity is provided under Rule Twelve.

RULE FOUR: DO NOT OMIT HISTORICALLY BLACK COLLEGES AND UNIVERSITIES FROM YOUR CONSIDERATION

While HBCUs are discussed in detail in Chapter 7, especially the issue of the application of affirmative action to these predominantly black institutions, it is pertinent to include a very brief reference to these institutions at this point . It is fair to say that HBCUs such as Howard University, Spelman, Morehouse, and Hampton have excellent reputations in terms of high minority enrollment and an aggressively nurturing environment for minority students. One expert, Isaac Black, has commented that

> our experience has generally been that personal attention, hands-on help, and aggressive mentoring are more likely at a historically black college, where extra encouragement and counseling are freely offered particularly if you run into academic difficulty. At too many mainstream schools, students of color are left to sink or swim. Although statistics show that there are more students of color at mainstream schools, the HBCU graduation rate suggests that they often offer more support.[13]

Tom Joyner, in the foreword to the book *8 Steps to Help Black Families Pay for College*, confirmed this notion when he wrote that it was his "belief that Historically Black Colleges and Universities offer African American students the kind of nurturing environment that they are often unable to receive at mainstream institutions."[14] While this point may be debated, few will argue that HBCUs pride themselves on cultivating students on an individual basis, a level of support that is sometimes lacking from mainstream institutions. Thus, students should consider at least one of the top HBCUs in the country, as will be discussed in Chapter 7.

RULE FIVE: A NEW TREND—INVESTIGATE INSTITUTIONS THAT UTILIZE SOCIOECONOMIC STATUS IN THE DECISION-MAKING PROCESS

Unfortunately, recent data and statistical studies have indicated that, to date, students from low socioeconomic levels have not received specialized treatment in the admissions process, or not have been recognized as deserving of attention in light of concerns for diversity on campus. For example, approximately 75 percent of the students enrolled in approximately 150 of the most selective institutions in the country come from the top economic quartile, contrasted with only a minuscule 3 percent of the students enrolled in approximately 150 of the most selective institutions came from the bottom 25 percent economically.[15] However, focus on this factor is changing, and there appears to be a trend toward the consideration of "need-based" or socioeconomic status of the applicant pool. This is confirmed by the results of a new study headed by William Bowen (coauthor of *Shape of the River*, discussed in Chapter 1, as well as former president of Princeton and current president of the Andrew W. Mellon Foundation), who has concluded as follows as to the practices of the nineteen elite institutions:

> Although early decision applicants, legacies, members of underrepresented minority groups, and recruited athletes are anywhere from 19 percentage points (early applicants) to 30 percent (recruited athletes) more likely to be admitted than otherwise similar applicants, candidates from low-income families and those who would be the first in their families to attend college have an admission rate that is virtually identical to that of more-privileged applicants with the same test scores, grades, race, and other characteristics. Those students are not receiving any kind of "admissions advantage;" nor are they being penalized for their disadvantaged backgrounds, as some observers have suggested.[16]

However, this historical disregard is changing, with institutions now refocusing on an applicant's socioeconomic background. As Bowen has commented, "We believe that the time has come for America's wealthiest and most selective institutions to put another 'thumb on the scale,' as a complement to race-sensitive admissions, for students from socioeconomically disadvantaged backgrounds."[17] This shift in focus was promised by several elite universities before the Supreme Court decisions in June 2003. In fact, in an amicus brief (friend-of-the-court brief filed by an interested party) filed by the presidents of many leading elite institutions, these college leaders promised the Supreme Court that they would promote socioeconomically disadvantaged students, commenting that they will give "special attention to applicants from economically and culturally disadvantaged backgrounds...[and] those who would be the first in their families to attend any college."[18]

The reason for this shift is twofold: First, the Supreme Court commanded in *Grutter*, as discussed more fully in Chapter 2, that race-neutral factors should be considered and adopted if practicable. In its explanation of what constitutes a permissible individualized and holistic review of applicants under the justification of diversity, the Court cited socioeconomic factors as factors that ought to be considered along with race, gender, geography, and life experiences. That is, diversity includes recruiting candidates from all walks of life, including lower-income categories. Second, as institutions move away from race-conscious programs (especially in the financial aid, as discussed in the previous chapter), many of these plans are instead advancing a student's need as the primary consideration.

RULE SIX: WHATEVER YOU DO, DON'T LEAVE THE BOX BLANK!

As you begin to fill out the application, one of the first questions one might ask is whether you should leave the question dealing with racial background blank or fill it out. This question on some applications is optional, while some schools do not specify whether answering the question is mandatory or not. For example, the 2004–2005 application for admission to the University of Tampa specifies that "your response to the items in this section is OPTIONAL." This particular section then asks applicants, "How would you describe yourself?" and asks them to first check the appropriate box regarding race background, and then fill in the blank with "your religious affiliation" and "first language (if other than English)." The choices regarding racial background on this application are as follows: American Indian or Alaska Native, Asian, black or African American, Hispanic/Latino, Native Hawaiian or other Pacific Islander, white, nonresident alien, and race/ethnicity unknown.

Students might be reluctant to provide this information for fear of not wanting to make "too much" an issue of race, or may even feel embarrassed at arguably receiving "special treatment" or consideration. Some students want to be accepted based upon their academic qualifications, and not as a result of being a member of an underrepresented minority class. This is illustrated by a question from a student published in the *New York Times*, wherein a minority student opposed to affirmative action asks a columnist dealing with ethics ("The Ethicist") whether it was ethical to reference race in her application when she opposes the use of affirmative action.[19] In answering the question, the *New York Times* Ethicist remarked that if the student was firmly opposed to affirmative action, the student should feel "free to eschew any mention of race in your application and essay." However, the column then went on to advise the student to reconsider her position on the use of race in her application. The columnist wrote persuasively, in part, as follows:

> [R]ace permeates American life for all of us—it has certainly played a significant part in yours—so perhaps you should re-examine your position. One thing

to consider [is] that many universities (most famously the University of Michigan) employ such programs not only to compensate groups that have been disadvantaged—that is, to level the playing field—but also to create a student body that will expose its members to a broad array of experiences, outlooks and ideas. There are, in other worlds, pedagogical rationales akin to those behind the quest for geographic diversity.[20]

As the column accurately points out, one should not feel abashed about referencing race in the application more than about referencing geographical uniqueness or some other unique factor of your background and life experiences that would add value and diversity to the experiences of others.

Furthermore, providing one's race and ethnicity in the application does not amount to special treatment, or an attempt to circumvent or short-step the process. As Cheryl Brown, director of admissions at Binghamton University, State University of New York, has stated, "It isn't so much about favoring a student based upon race, but about creating a certain type of learning environment within which all students will benefit."[21] According to Brown, "Colleges are concerned with putting together a freshman class that is diverse in many ways. Students have many ways to stand out—as athletes, musicians, writers, et cetera."[22] Further, race, along with a bevy of other factors, helps to provide context in evaluating the overall credentials of individual applicants. It is this self-reported information that enables the holistic, individualized review that the Supreme Court has held is required in any admissions program today. So, applicants should not feel abashed at providing this information. Students should also be cognizant of the fact that providing their race or ethnicity will never hurt their chances for admission. It should always be provided so as to give the admissions department the most accurate depiction of yourself as a complete candidate—beyond the mere mathematical data of such things as your GPA and standardized test scores. As Brown stated in a recent article, "We hope students will fill out the question because it gives us more information about the context of the student's credentials. We want to know lots of things about candidates—their motivation, goals, interests, activities, honors, awards, and community service."[23] As another expert has stated, "Don't worry about being accepted into a college 'because you're black'... there are many, many components to a college application that are weighed differently for each student, and your application will be evaluated for its merit and strength just like any other."[24]

Furthermore, leaving this information out could be damaging to your application in two respects. First, the admissions counselors may think that leaving the box blank was accidental, and this might cause a reviewer to think that the applicant does not check his or her work, or has completed the application in a haphazard fashion. Second, and much more important, institutions that employ race as a factor in admissions need you to be as exhaustive as possible in the application. As one college admissions advisor has commented, "Leaving out racial, ethnic, or religious identities can be a big mistake for those students for whom their culture is important. These days, colleges are not just looking at grades and test scores—they are looking at the whole person."[25]

RULE SEVEN: DO NOT SELL YOURSELF SHORT

Despite Rule One, applicants should never take a school's reported median GPA or standardized test scores as a conclusive, definitive barometer on whether they will be accepted. Perhaps one of the most fatal mistakes an applicant can make is to "self-select" oneself out of the process by not applying. There have been numerous instances of how a school's reported median GPA and standardized test scores may not be totally accurate. That is, there have been examples of a school excluding certain categories of individuals (e.g., athletes or legacy applicants) with a lower student average from the overall data that is reported in college guide books, thereby making the averages appear higher than it actually is for the entire admitted class. Not knowing that the median GPA and standardized test scores were lower for the athletes who were admitted, a student athlete might not apply, thinking that a denial would be automatic. That is, the numbers are not definitive, and applicants should not self-select themselves out of contention simply because their standardized test scores or GPA fall below the reported median scores for the entering class. Phrased another way, applicants should not sell themselves short. As Fernando Yarrito, the Director of Admissions at Southwest Texas State University has written, "admission standards aren't designed as barriers, but rather as guidelines to give you a sense of how you compare to others and how competitive you may be."[26]

Rather than focusing exclusively on test scores and GPA, ask yourself whether or not you are generally competitive for the school and, if so, why? Even if your GPA and/or test scores are lower than the average, you might bring other desirable attributes to the table. Under the holistic approach sanctioned by the Supreme Court in 2003, admissions officials are encouraged to consider the applicant's "total package," instead of one or two isolated factors.

RULE EIGHT: SPEND TIME ON COMPLETING THE ESSAYS

As Tables 2 and 3 indicate, students and parents should realize that the application essays, in recent years, have slowly become one of the most significant ways in which colleges and universities now gauge diversity. If one looks at the percentage of colleges and universities that have indicated that the essay is an important factor in the admissions process, one ought to note the strong increase in the use of the essays as an evaluative tool in gauging diversity and other "tip" factors previously referenced in this work. Indeed, it has been said that the essay has become the "uppermost tip factor in the admissions process."[27] In 1993, only 14 percent of colleges and universities indicated that the applicant's essay was of considerable importance to the overall application and chances for admission. Yet, by 2004, that number has steadily risen to 25.2 percent.[28] As was highlighted in

Chapter 3, many universities and colleges, like the University of Michigan and Ohio State University, have spent hundreds of thousands of dollars to increase their admissions staff in order to process and thoroughly read and analyze these essays. Thus, it goes without saying that a student who wishes to gain a competitive advantage through the institution's use of affirmative action and "plus factors" should plan on spending a good amount of time thoughtfully preparing the application essays. Arguably, for many, essays are the most important aspect of the overall application, next to GPAs and standardized test scores.

RULE NINE: EXPAND YOUR MARKETABILITY AS CONTRIBUTING TO UNIVERSITY/CLASSROOM DIVERSITY

If no other rule or point stands out from the *Gratz* and *Grutter* decisions, it is that race is not the only factor important to colleges and universities in promoting diversity. Other factors (which also, by the way, would not even implicate the strict scrutiny standards by the courts) include whether or not you are the first generation in your family to attend college or graduate school, whether you are from a rural or an inner city area, whether you come from a socioeconomically disadvantaged background, whether you have experience working and living in diverse environment, whether you have traveled extensively and/or lived abroad, whether you have demonstrated experience working with underserved or underprivileged populations; and whether you are from a state or city that has been historically underrepresented at the university. Thus, before sitting down and preparing your application, it would be wise to spend a few minutes thinking about these factors in conjunction with your life. As a general rule of thumb, the more unique you are as a person, the more marketable you are to universities and colleges.

RULE TEN: HONESTY IN THE APPLICATION

It goes without saying that you must be honest in the application and in your essays. Admissions counselors generally can spot insincerity or embellishments designed to elicit sympathy in the admissions process. So, do not claim to be a member of a disadvantaged group, or claim some unique life experience, if it is, in fact, not true. Your dishonesty will likely doom the application. In answering the question "What are the worst mistakes you've seen students make on college applications?" one college admissions official responded that "by far the worst mistake is to lie or be dishonest. I could not care how strong a particular student might be, if we catch that student in any form of dishonesty on their application they're going to be immediately denied admission."[29] Furthermore, many universities include a statement at the end of the application, whereby a student swears/certifies as to the accuracy of the information: "I certify that all the information provided in my application is accurate and that I am the author of the attached personal statement. I understand that the university may deny me admission or enrollment if any information is found to be incomplete or inaccurate."[30] This includes not only information inputted by the student, but also substantive additions and/or corrections and editing done by another—usually a parent or friend. As was reported by the *U.S. News & World Report* in 1999, this "benign" form of cheating is often the result of well-intentioned parents. According to one college counselor,

> "I am beginning to think of myself in the role of 'integrity police,'" she says, relating countless stories of college application essays that have been "edited" by Mom or Dad—and often for the worse, as big words replace any shred of youthful personality. "I'm afraid a lot of this cheating comes from home, where the parents' modus operandi is success at any cost."[31]

So, in the words of Shakespeare in his play *Hamlet*, "to thine own self be true." There certainly is nothing wrong with working with your parents on the application. However, parents should ensure that their work and thoughts do not, in the process, entirely supplant the applicant. Students should also not change who they are or what their life experiences have been to reflect what they believe admissions counselors are looking for in an application, or what a book like this might suggest colleges find of interest in applicants. Rather, students should tell their potential schools what sort of person they really are, what they really want to achieve in life, and why the school honestly interests them. It is only through this process of honesty and disclosure that you and the schools will find the right fit and match. This will serve you well in the long run. After all, do you really want to spend four years at an institution that was not the right fit for you to begin with?

RULE ELEVEN: DO *NOT* REQUEST ETHNICITY/RACE BE COVERED IN LETTERS OF RECOMMENDATION

As most readers doubtless are aware, recommendations are one of the key components of any application. In fact the Supreme Court expressly commented on the utility of this part of the application as a way to achieve and ensure diversity, in its *Grutter* decision. Most schools request that recommendations accompany the application, and usually two or three recommendations. So, the essentialness of this component to the applicant naturally raises the question as to whether the teacher or academic adviser writing the letter should include in it references to race or ethnicity. The quick answer is clearly a "no," but for several different reasons. First, the decision to raise and discuss race or ethnicity in your application is ultimately up to you, the applicant. If you want to address your unique life experiences (including membership in a minority class or a certain ethnic group and how that has impacted your life), it is best addressed in the application essays or other personal statements. You should not expect, nor should you request, individuals to write letters of recommendation that discuss this issue. The main reason for this is that you are in the best position to articulate the unique effect such a factor has had on your life visions and goals. The admissions committee or official reviewing your application will be aware that you are from an underrepresented race or ethnicity by virtue of the main application, which normally asks about the race/ethnicity of the applicant. The admissions committee may also learn about this fact via your personal statement or essay. You are simply in the best position to discuss this fact in your application package. The letters of recommendation are best left to cover other attributes of the applicant, such as academic acumen, motivation, intellectual curiosity, leadership, responsibility, athletic prowess, community service, and dedication, among others.

This raises the second reason as to why one's race or ethnicity should not be intentionally addressed in the letter of recommendation. In addition to the fact that you know this information best and can relay it in the most effective manner elsewhere in your application, letters of recommendation that mention race may unintentionally relay the wrong message, that the student needs special treatment in evaluating the application. Phrased another way, the letter might undermine your academic abilities, motivation, or industry by focusing on race. If one is applying at an institution that utilizes an affirmative action plan to recruit and retain minority students, you only need address this at one or two places in your application, but certainly not in the letters of recommendation, which, at a minimum, would be superfluous, and might actually be damaging.

Finally, how do you ensure that your recommender is not including racial or ethnic background statements in your letter of recommendation? There are several ways to avoid this scenario. First, it is a good idea to give the person writing the recommendation a copy of your résumé (if you have one) or at least a one-page summary of factors that you might wish the recommender to address in the letter. At this point, you might also tactfully request that your race or ethnicity not be referenced in the letter. Most recommenders will know not to include such statements, but this would prevent the rare instance when the recommender inadvertently (and presumably from good intentions) would mention this factor. As a college professor, I have written hundreds of letters of recommendation for students as part of their graduate and professional school applications. As a standard practice, it is always recommended that the students provide a résumé and a list of factors that they might ideally wish to see addressed in my letter of recommendation. Over time, it has become apparent that this practice generally correlates into very strong, personal letters, which complement other aspects of the student's application as well as allow the student some control in this part of the application (if the student wants a particular theme or approach to be replete throughout the application).

A second way in which you can "police" letters (to ensure that the information is not inadvertently included in the letter) is to ask for a courtesy copy of the letter or ask that the letter be returned to you for mailing. If a teacher, adviser, or professor is willing to write a letter of recommendation on your behalf, he/she should usually be willing to provide you a courtesy copy for your files. If you notice that the letter includes references to race or ethnicity, you then have the choice of either asking that the letter be revised to omit this information, or, if the recommender will not revise the letter, seeking a letter of recommendation from another individual.

RULE TWELVE: SHOW INTEREST IN THE INSTITUTIONS OF CHOICE

Once your application has been completed and sent in to your schools of choice, you should continue to monitor the applications and show some genuine interest in the institutions. There is some indication that such applicants receive a "boost" in the process. It has been reported that as many as "53 percent of colleges use demonstrated interest in admitting students . . ."[32] This is consistent with the findings of the 2005 NACAC survey on the state of college admissions, wherein it was reported that students' demonstrated interest in the college or university of choice was a factor of considerable importance for 6.9 percent of the institutions polled, a factor of moderate importance for 15.8 percent, and a factor of limited importance for 30.1 percent.[33]

Colleges are increasingly utilizing "demonstrated interest" as a tip factor in admissions. While there is no standard way in which to gauge an applicant's true interest, college admissions departments often subjectively attempt to find out how determined or interested a student truly is based upon a host of factors. This includes such things as arranging for a campus interview, attending a class, statements made on the application and in the personal essay, content in the letters of recommendation indicating demonstrated interest, follow-ups and contact by the student with the admissions department, and whether or not the student applied for early enrollment/decision and submitted an application early in the process.

A few words are in order for each of these ways in which you might express your "demonstrated interest" to the admissions department. First, the initial point/time for an applicant to express his or her interest in a particular university/college is in completing the application, usually the essay section. If possible, applicants should indicate why they wish to attend the institution in question. If done well, this would indicate to the admissions committee not only your strong interest in the institution, but also that you have done your research regarding the institution. Having sat on a faculty admissions appeal committee at the University of Tampa, I can recall multiple instances in which the decision regarding admissions came down to whether the faculty members on the committee thought the applicant truly desired to attend the university. If it was apparent (through the student's essay) that he or she had not researched the university, it showed a definite lack of interest on the part of the student, and often boded very unfavorably for the final disposition of the application.

Second, according to the responses of colleges and universities in several studies and reports, campus visits and personal interviews are the two chief ways in which most schools evaluate whether a student has a genuine interest in the school. Consequently, if you stop by for a campus visit, be sure to let the admissions department know you are on campus (so it may be noted in your file), instead of just anonymously taking the campus tour. As discussed below, it is also a good idea to ask if you can sit in on a class or two, not only to illustrate your interest in the campus, but also to help you make an educated decision between that institution and others from which you might receive acceptances. If you cannot afford a trip to the campus of your dreams, there are other ways to express continued interest, such as writing a short update letter giving your latest information and, of course, an expression of your continued interest in the school. You can also request a telephonic interview with an admissions counselor if you are unable to visit the campus. However, be careful with the use of e-mail. The electronic age is wonderful, and your application may have even been submitted electronically online. But individuals corresponding by e-mail often tend to become much more familiar in the "writing tone," and often the e-mail lacks basic grammatical structure, proper punctuation, and correct spelling. This, of course, would do more damage to your application than it would help, so, as a general rule, you should stay clear of e-mail communications, and try to converse via letters or phone. If you must communicate via e-mail, you should ensure that the message reads like a letter, with proper spelling, punctuation, and grammatical structure.

RULE THIRTEEN: VERIFY THAT THE SCHOOL IS CONCERNED WITH DIVERSITY

Once you have gained acceptance, your work is not complete. The student must now determine, perhaps most important of all, which institution is the best fit. Institutions may claim one thing in their admissions brochures, but in fact practice another. Unfortunately, this sometimes involves claims regarding commitments to diversity on campus; as one college counselor has written, "Some colleges claim to celebrate diversity of ideas, yet most of their classes are biased in one direction, with other ideas presented mainly to be denigrated."[34] However, the student can verify a school's commitment to diversity by taking a variety of steps delineated in this section of the book, including visiting the campus and perusing the college catalogue—with an eye toward not only diversity of classes and departments, but also diversity in the faculty and student college organizations (e.g., the existence of both College Democrats and College Republicans on campus). The student can verify a school's commitment to diversity by asking a lot of questions of the admissions department after being accepted, again using the questions delineated in this section of the book to assist in the process. The next few paragraphs delineate the major steps a student can (and should) take to properly evaluate diversity at his or her college of choice/interest. Following that, Table 3 delineates an exhaustive list of questions and issues that a student should consider when gauging a university's true mettle regarding its commitment to diversity. This list comes from a 2005 article entitled "The Inclusive University: Helping Minority Students Choose a College and Identify Institutions that Value Diversity," published in the *Journal of College Admissions*.

However, before turning to Table 3, a few general words of advice are in order. First, in terms of clubs and diversity, it may be helpful to ascertain whether there are any social clubs (fraternities, sororities, or service organizations) tailored specifically to minority students on campus. There are nine black college fraternities and sororities on the National Pan-Hellenic Council, including Alpha Kappa Alpha Sorority (founded at Howard University in 1908), Delta Sigma Theta Sorority (Howard University, 1913), Alpha Phi Alpha Fraternity (Cornell University, 1906), and Omega Psi Phi Fraternity (Howard University, 1911), just to name a few. Similarly, an applicant should verify whether or not there are places on campus (like an interfaith chapel or cultural center) where students can practice their own religion or meet other students. In terms of classes, college catalogues will list not only the breadth of courses, but also how often such classes are offered.

In terms of faculty, college catalogues often list the entire full-time faculty, along with their academic credentials. Furthermore, many universities allow the public to look up faculty member profiles on the college Web site, so both applicants and students alike may check the qualifications and credentials of professors before enrolling at the university or, if already enrolled, what classes to sign up for the following semester. Colleges with a real concern for diversity will have both faculty and students from different walks of life. Hence, applicants should query the college, or conduct independent research, as to the exact demographic makeup of both the student body and the faculty for the college, as well as on the departmental level. The standard four-year college guides on the market normally provide a plethora of demographic information regarding universities or colleges as a whole. For departmental data, you might have to send a request to the department chair, or review the department's Web page—if one is available. For diversity among faculty members, this would include not only adequate gender and racial representation, but also diverse background of faculty members with various political and religious viewpoints, and also where they received their terminal doctorate degree (Ph.D., M.D., J.D., or others). One would expect to find faculty members who received their terminal doctorate degrees from leading public and private institutions from around the country, and indeed the world. If diversity is important, the college would not want every faculty member to have his or her terminal doctorate degree from Harvard, Georgetown, Stanford, or another institution of similar reputation. Conversely, if every member of the department has his or her degree from the same local college/university, this fact might also raise not only issues of national academic reputation, but also concerns of diversity. One would also expect a healthy amount of diversity among faculty members in the same departments in terms of academic institutions attended, degrees received, research interests, areas of specialty, and publications. Faculty publications, often overlooked by applicants, can serve as a test for whether or not a faculty member has a national reputation as an expert on a subject or is known for his or her research, and also as an indicator of diversity. It also shows that the faculty members at issue are intellectually active and engaged, which often leads to improvements and updates in the classroom as well.

In terms of actual classes offered, it is a good idea for applicants to obtain the class schedule/registration materials for the upcoming year (for upperclassmen), in order to see the breadth of classes actually offered. Additionally, if the applicant can afford to visit the campus, more about the institution can be learned at the campus bookstore (than perhaps anyplace else), by perusing the textbook section for the various disciplines/departments, and the kind of books that are being assigned by professors in given classes. This might also help applicants gauge how much faculty members incorporate concepts from other cultures and different racial/ethnic heritages. Another overlooked source of information is the weekly college newspaper. The college newspaper will give you a decent indication of the amount of academic discourse and debate occurring on campus outside of classes, as well as the level or sophistication of the student body. Reading a week or two of the school's paper will also give you a good idea of an array of other factors that will be important to you as a student, such as student morale, student satisfaction with the school, and special programs and events that are offered on campus. If the paper is filled with a myriad of student editorials complaining about everything from parking availability to the lack of certain classes being offered, this might be an early warning sign for you that the institution is not as responsive as it may claim in its promotional viewbook and other solicitation materials. Many college newspapers are available online. If you cannot locate the paper online, simply call the admissions department and ask them to send you the newspapers of the last week or two. If you visit the campus, the paper for the week should be readily accessible in almost all buildings on the campus you may choose to visit. Be sure to grab a copy of the paper as you make your school visit. As an aside, I regularly scour through the newspapers from other institutions, in order to see what is happening around the state and the country. It is a great way to get to the heartbeat of the institution—to find out what is truly important to the staff, faculty, and students. Finally, if time permits, ask the admissions department to arrange for you to sit in on a class. Usually, admissions departments will be very accommodating regarding this request, and faculty members will often be flattered as well by the request. However, if you pursue this option, you should try to attend classes by at least two different professors (from your discipline, and from a professor you would actually take at the institution if enrolled), to ensure that you are receiving a fair observation of what future classes will be like. A myriad of other considerations are delineated in Table 3.

RULE FOURTEEN: HOPE SPRINGS ETERNAL!

If you have followed all the advice thus far in this book, but have still not been accepted, do not lose hope yet. One of the great aspects of the United States today is that there is a school for virtually everyone in society, ranging from community colleges and associate degree programs to post doctorate graduate

Table 3
Guiding Questions for Examining College and University Campuses and Determining Their Climate toward Diversity

College Major

- Does your institution offer a major in the field of study in which I am interested?
- What is the demographic composition of undergraduate students who are seeking degrees from your department? What is the demographic composition of the faculty within your department?
- What is the departmental commitment to mentoring? Is a faculty member available who is interested and available to mentor me throughout my course of study?
- Are there opportunities to work with faculty members on their research?
- Are there part-time employment opportunities in this department within my field of study?

General Curricular Issues

- What is the typical class size for both general education courses and courses within my major?
- To what extent is small-group learning—fostering communication and cooperation across students—available?
- What are some examples of the uses of technology in courses?
- What type of academic advising is available to help me design my schedule?
- To what extent are the faculty aware, knowledgeable, and sensitive to different cultures?
- To what extent do faculty incorporate diverse perspectives in their courses by including examples, cases, or readings written by authors from different cultures?
- To what extent are service learning opportunities available for course credit?
- To what extent are service learning courses designed to foster multicultural exposure—both in the community and in working with students from diverse backgrounds?

Majors, Graduation Rates, and Job Prospects

- What proportion of students from this department complete their degrees? What is the average time to graduation?
- What proportion of students from this department go on to graduate school?
- What are the job prospects for students who graduate from this institution with a degree in my chosen field of study?
- Can you provide information contrasting majority and minority performance rates on the three questions listed above?
- Give examples of students of color who have achieved success as graduates of this program.

Student Activities

- What types of extracurricular activities are available on your campus?
- What sports, athletic, and recreational activities are available?

(continued)

Table 3 (*continued*)

- Are there gathering places on campus for students of color to meet?
- Are there organized social groups (or sororities and fraternities) for students of color to join?
- Are there cultural centers on campus to celebrate and reinforce students' racial, ethnic, or cultural identities?

Student Services

- Does the university provide access to computers or will I need to purchase one?
- What types of study skills courses are offered at the institution?
- Is tutoring available?
- What are the remedial services you offer students who are having difficulty learning?
- What services do you offer high-achieving students who would like to get better grades?
- What types of services are available for students who want to improve their spoken English or writing skills?

Financial Aid

- What percentage of your student body receives student aid?
- What is the average debt of your students at graduation?
- Describe the availability of merit-based and need-based scholarships.
- To what extent are scholarships available that are earmarked for students from diverse backgrounds? What are the criteria for awarding those scholarships?
- Will my financial aid package cover my tuition, room, board, and books?
- Are your scholarships renewable? What are the criteria that must be met for renewing the scholarships on an annual basis?

Personal Support

- To what extent does the institution sponsor events and activities to help students feel connected to the campus?
- Does the institution or department organize social and professional events?
- Do individuals, on- or off-campus, want to interact with students from diverse backgrounds? Are there community members or host families available to help you orient yourself to the community?

Living Arrangements in the Community

- What types of housing are available on campus?
- Are there special living/learning communities for students of color?
- How are roommates assigned? Can I choose the person I prefer to have as a roommate?
- What food options and special dietary plans are available in residential housing?
- Will I have adequate privacy to study in my residential housing?
- Who do I go to resolve problems with my campus housing or with my roommate?

Transportation

- What types of campus transportation are available? Is there a fee for such services? If so, what is it? Is it covered by my financial aid package?
- What transportation is available between my residential housing area and the academic campus?
- How far is the walk between my particular residential housing unit and the academic campus?

Safety and Security

- How does the campus go about providing a safe environment for all students?
- What measures are taken to protect students from harassment or physical harm?
- How safe and secure is the campus? The area around my residence hall? What data do you have to support the safety of the campus?

Reprinted with permission. Copyright 2005 National Association for College Admission Counseling. Carol Elam and Gilbert Brown, "The Inclusive University: Helping Minority Students Choose a College and Identify Institutions that Value Diversity," NACAC Journal.

programs. In fact, if one considers schools of every ilk, there are over 3,000 four-year colleges in the United States, many of which have "open admissions" (meaning that they accept any student who has completed high school and submitted an application). If you have not been accepted yet, it may mean that you set your sights too high, and did not include "safe" schools in the various schools to which you requested admission. There is still hope—either for this year or next. First, if you were wait-listed, or did not apply at all, there is a way to check if various institutions of interest still have openings. For the first time in May 2005, the NACAC began putting its "Space Availability Survey" on its Web site for public viewing. This is a listing of colleges and universities that still have openings after the normal admissions cycle is complete. Anyone "with access to the internet will be able to tell which schools still have openings, financial aid and/or housing for the incoming class. The survey will help . . . students who still may be looking for a college for the fall."[35] This material may be found on the organization's Web site, at http://www.nacac.com.

RULE FIFTEEN: IF AT FIRST YOU DON'T SUCCEED, TRY . . . TRY AGAIN

Of course, despite all the best efforts, sometimes the rejection letter still arrives in the mail. If you were accepted to a "safe school," but not your dream institution, this often raises the difficult question of whether to attend the "safe school" immediately, or wait a year and reapply. There is evidence to suggest that waiting a year—in what admissions officials call the "gap year strategy"[36]—increases the student's chances of admittance dramatically. This is likely the case for several reasons. First, reapplying the following year shows "demonstrated interest" to the institution at issue (see Rule Twelve). Second, it shows the admissions department representative or committee that you have "grit," tenacity, and perseverance as positive character traits. These same traits may also correlate into success as a student and after graduation. Third, during the off-year or "gap year," the student is doing something to improve deficiencies in his or her academic record, such as studying for and retaking the standardized tests or taking college preparatory courses. In fact, there is a "small but growing number of students who continue to pursue slots at highly selective colleges after striking out the first time" by employing this "gap year" strategy, even when accepted at strong, top-tier institutions.[37] However, a word of caution is in order. If you are contemplating this approach, it is imperative that you spend the year off doing something that is going to improve your demonstrated academic skills, or that might improve your diversifying characteristics (see Rules Two and Nine). Spending your entire gap year at the beach will not likely increase your chances for admission the second time around.

6

Six Steps to Completing the Compelling Application Essay

If you have persevered thus far in the book, you are doubtless aware that one of the most important items in the college application, next to GPA and performance on standardized tests, is the application essay. However, writing this persuasive essay is not simply the reiteration of the usual "sob stories." As one admissions official said to me, "If I have to read one more essay about being poor, I think I will lose my mind." Another admissions official, a former director of admissions for the University of California at Berkeley, has said, "The word on the street is that hardship helps get a person into college. That notion is not true to the extent that many students and parents believe it is...."[1] Unfortunately, given this belief, "students may be tempted to lie about other circumstances as well, including the death of a parent—or both parents or the entire family—the hardships of immigration to this country, or the presence of a debilitating condition or illness in oneself or one's parents."[2] Does this mean that you do not write about your experiences if you have truly lived a "down and out" life to date, or have escaped from living below the poverty line to potentially attending an East Coast Ivy League school? Of course not. It only means that you write about experiences that are true and important to you. Admissions counselors can see through most applicants' attempts at pulling the proverbial wool over the eyes of the admissions department. Untrue or embellished essays usually come across as such, and may ruin an otherwise competitive application.

This chapter is important for several reasons. First, as mentioned above, the application essay is the third most important factor in evaluating the merits of the candidate. As is stated in a 2005–2006 application (from New York University), "The essay offers an opportunity for you to help us become acquainted with you in ways different from grades, test scores, and other objective data ... it allows you to demonstrate your ability to organize your thoughts and express yourself."

This alone might merit a separate chapter for this topic. Second, the essay section of the application allows you to personalize yourself to the college or university to which you are seeking admittance. Admissions officials find out about a student's dreams, aspirations, and life experiences, not through standardized test scores or cumulative GPA, but rather through the student's uniquely crafted essay.

The third reason a separate chapter on essay composition is provided is that many high school students (and some college students) have little or no idea how to plan, construct, and write a compelling, structured, and persuasive essay. I am astonished at occasionally reading essays by college students that lack any semblance of planning and thoughtful wording. Given the confluence of these two aspects of essay writing in the overall importance of the essay to the application, separate coverage of the nuts and bolts of essay writing is merited. Even if you, as an applicant, pride yourself on your writing abilities, reviewing this chapter should be helpful in reminding you of the best way to go about the process. This chapter should also be of assistance to those students who have started college and are writing essays for classes. Hence, do not throw away this book once you have been accepted at the college of your dreams, as at least this chapter will provide you with information that you can continue to use throughout your four years of schooling, and might even be helpful in your applications to graduate or professional schools.

In the weeks before you sit down to complete the essay, it is helpful to keep in mind six steps that lead to a successful and persuasive application essay. These steps will each be explained in detail in this chapter. These are as follows:

1. Generating ideas for the application essay that may (but not necessarily) contain issues relating to diversity.
2. Selecting a topic/theme and organizing the information into an outline for the essay.
3. Preparing the first draft.
4. Revising, and then rewriting the essay into a second draft.
5. Proofreading.
6. Final revisions and preparing the final version of the essay for the application.

After a discussion of the six steps, successful essays written by three very good undergraduate students will be provided as examples.

Most college applications give the applicant a topic to address. Very rarely does a college simply say, "Tell us about yourself." Several examples of application essay questions are referenced in Chapter 4. However, a few more examples are mentioned here, in order to give the reader an idea of the types of questions posed on the applications. For example, in NYU's 2005–2006 application for undergraduate admissions, there is a "personal statements and essays" section. Part 1 of this section consists of a series of questions that must be answered in five or six lines on the application. The questions are as follows:

1. Please explain how you decided which extracurricular activity on your list was the most important to you.
2. Please tell us about something you did last Sunday afternoon (or the Sunday before that, or the Sunday before that...
3. Many students decide to apply to NYU because of our New York City location. Apart from the New York City location, please tell us what other aspects make you feel NYU will be a good match for you.
4. Please tell us what led you to select your anticipated academic program and/or NYU school/college, and what interests you most about your intended discipline.

Part 2 of the essay section asks the applicant to write an essay, in 400–500 words, on one of three proposed topics (provided below), or, if the applicant chooses, on "something about yourself that has not been presented to your satisfaction in this application." The proposed topics are as follows:

1. Tell us about a person, place, or event in your life that has particular meaning for you, and why it is important to you. We'd especially like to hear about someone or something that has affected your life that may not have affected or even been noticed by other people.
2. Select a creative work—a novel, a film, a musical piece, a painting, or other work of art—that has influenced the way you view the world and the way you view yourself. Discuss the impact the work has had on you.
3. New York is a city full of people from other places. Everyone brings with them a story of where they are from. Tell us something about where you're from and what single facet of your hometown experience has shaped you into the person you are today.

As can be seen from the above example, the questions, while giving the applicant some structure in the form of a broad topic, also give much leeway in crafting the response in a way uniquely suitable to that applicant's personality or life experiences. This is your opportunity to let your inner beauty shine. This is your opportunity to show the admissions committee why you are *you,* and that you can contribute to the incoming class in unique ways. So, it almost goes without saying that your topic, themes, words, and ultimately your essay, must all be your own. While it is okay (and in fact recommended) for others to read your essays, offer suggestions and ideas, and proofread for errors, your work must still be your own. Having served on a faculty admissions appeal committee at the University of Tampa (reviewing appeals and requests for reconsideration from denied students), it was often readily apparent to me when an essay or personal statement was written (or substantially written) by a parent or a writing coach.

As a corollary to the basic idea of writing your own essay, you should also have "ownership" of your essay topic/theme. That is, an applicant should not write on a topic that he or she does not "own." Phrased yet another way, applicants should not merely regurgitate what "experts," parents, or friends say ought to go into a successful essay. There are countless books on the market that claim to offer the perfect essays for college applications. This book, while offering you pointers on how best to plan, structure, and compose the essay, will not offer any advice on what specific topics to address, except to encourage applicants to explore their uniqueness and diversity, and to address weaknesses that might be apparent in other parts of the application. If you think you are not unique, you should think again. Every candidate has something unique about himself or herself—it only needs to be identified. It is said that there are no two people, of the billions on the planet, with identical fingerprints or thumbprints. Likewise, there are other factors that make you unique, whether you realize it or not. No other applicant came from the same parents (unless you consider siblings) or grew up in the same household with the same life experiences as you. Part of the process is to identify, and to let the admissions committee know exactly how you are unique (and therefore how you can enhance the learning experiences of others in the entering class). Perhaps, the idea was best captured by the instructions/information section to the 2005 NYU application for admissions, which advised applicants to be "personal" in completing the essays: "The best writing is often very personal. All kinds of experiences—serious, funny, unexplained, fleeting—can influence our lives and help make us who we are."

The essay section of the application not only promotes your uniqueness and diversity but also addresses your weaknesses (like low standardized test scores or GPA) that might be apparent to admissions officials by reviewing other sections of the application. If your application is weak or your GPA and/or standardized test scores are below the applicant averages for the institution at issue, admissions department officials will often look to the essay section for explanations as to why they might discount something that detracts from the overall application. In the legal profession, this is known as "taking the sting out" of information. That is, if adverse information will come out during a trial that might hurt the client, lawyers are taught to take the sting out of the evidence by introducing it to the jury first, with an explanation, rather than waiting for it to be discovered by the jury or exploited by the other side. The idea (at least how it is taught and explained at law school) is that the jury will not think you are hiding information, if you are the one who highlights it. Likewise, if one piece of information stands in the way of an otherwise stellar application, you might wish to take the sting out of that information through the essay. One example of this approach will be analyzed later in this chapter.

This is not to say that applicants should automatically make excuses for poor performance in a particular area or for simple lack of hard work. However, if there are extenuating circumstances that would explain lower-than-average scores (say, the death of a family member), it would be helpful to delineate this in the application. I have met several good students who avoided putting such personal information in the essay for fear of sounding insincere or phony.

My advice to those students is that if the event really had a profound effect on your life, and has defined you as a person, you ought to consider very seriously including it in your application, especially if it might help explain what was happening in your life during a particular period. This is not to elicit sympathy, but rather to offer an insight into your inner being and personality, and again, to provide the admissions committee members information about what was happening in your junior year of high school, for example, when your grade point dipped down for a semester or year.

Indeed, some of the strongest lessons in life are often brought home when losing a loved one, so applicants should not eschew the discussion of such topics. One of the greatest lessons came to me when sitting at the hospital bed of my dying father, Robert C. Beckman. In the last years of his life, especially after retirement, he always sought to improve himself by watching as much History Channel programming as he could each day. During the last few days, he was quickly losing his cognitive and mental facilities due to the ravages of a cruel affliction, Creutzfeldt-Jakob disease (CJD). Yet, as he sat in his hospital bed slipping in and out of consciousness, the television in his room was constantly tuned to the History Channel. At the time, it seemed like a cruel joke that a man who was about to die was watching the History Channel and gaining information that he would immediately forget. For months, it was a bitter memory for me, so much so that watching the History Channel was a painful experience to be avoided. However, in time, I came to draw one of my most important lessons about education from this experience—the pursuit of knowledge should never cease, and one should strive one's entire life to learn, even to the deathbed. Thus, when the semester draws long and nears an end, and like many colleagues, I begin to yearn for a break to the academic year, I recall my father and his pursuit of knowledge. This experience has defined me as a person, and is relevant for anyone to know who attempts to evaluate me as a person. Likewise, students who have gone through similar experiences should not be afraid to discuss their experiences. If it has defined you as a person, or if it reasonably and legitimately explains a hard time in your life, it ought to be considered for the essay section of the application.

So, how does an applicant decide what theme/topic to address, and what information might ultimately be worthy of inclusion in the essay? Step 1 of the process is to simply generate ideas for the essay. There are several ways an applicant might go about generating ideas. First, if time permits, keep a notebook with you, and, when a thought or idea hits you during the day, write it down for later use. If you are thinking about the essays ahead of time, this might be a useful way to generate ideas. Oftentimes, the best ideas come when you are not concentrating intensely on the task at hand. I know of college professors who employ this technique with classes and lesson plans. When they hear something on the radio or see something on television or in the newspaper that might ultimately be useful and relevant to an upcoming class, they jot it down in a notebook for later reference and incorporation into the lesson plans when time permits.

Another way to generate ideas for the application essay is to engage in freewriting or brainstorming. Freewriting is a technique whereby the applicant sits down and writes without stopping (or editing) for a short period of time, usually five to ten minutes. The applicant should write whatever comes to mind, even if it is "I can't think of anything at present!" Eventually, through the process of freewriting, items of merit will make it to the paper, or the computer screen. During this freewriting exercise, the applicant should not worry about spelling, grammar, punctuation, or other formalities, or even whether the comments are of value or not. The idea is to write down as many thoughts as you can, as quickly as possible. Once you have finished, you should read what you have written. If you used a computer, you should print out your writing sample. Finally, underline anything you might find of use in your essay, and strike out those concepts or ideas that you do not think appropriate.

A similar technique, often employed in freshman English classes across the country and corporate boardrooms alike, is brainstorming. Brainstorming is quite similar to freewriting, if done properly, as the person is rapidly listing ideas, concepts, facts, phrases, and other items with little concern for proper punctuation or grammar, and also under a time limit. This will help your ideas come out more quickly. You can brainstorm alone, or with the help of your family. I would recommend family brainstorming, as your family might be able to better recall incidents or examples from your childhood or young adult period. For instance, taking one of the NYU essays asking to describe "a person, place, or event in your life that has particular meaning for you, and why it is important to you," the applicant and his or her family could sit down at the kitchen table and brainstorm regarding old neighbors, teachers, family holidays, trips, and so on. This helps to bring up old memories and details that, while important in forming the applicant's life, may have been internalized and, at least on the conscious level, forgotten. Using the other NYU example of describing "something about where you're from and what single facet of your hometown experience has shaped you into the person you are today," other family members can be quite helpful in coming up with as exhaustive a list as possible. Once done, as with freewriting, you can go back and eliminate those ideas and concepts that are not useful, and highlight those that might be relevant to your essay. Ideally, you can then take those concepts and ideas and put them into whichever topic/theme you have chosen to address.

As this is a book on affirmative action, and the readers presumably have some interest as to how affirmative action will help in college admissions process, a few more points about this concern for diversity and about generating ideas should be noted. Despite the earlier admonishment about writing what is true to you, there is nothing wrong about being mindful of a school's affirmative action program and concerns for diversity. As a separate exercise (via either freewriting or brainstorming), it is helpful to make a list of the factors that make you unique, in terms of life experiences, previous living conditions, physical or financial hurdles, and the like. The whole purpose of generating ideas is to get you to think about your own uniqueness, and how you can best contribute to the university's desire to achieve diversity.

After you have brainstormed and generated ideas, the next step is to organize those ideas into an outline format. At the most basic level, the essay should start with an introduction, followed by the main text or body, and finally, a conclusion. The introduction should identify the topic or theme that the applicant will address in the essay, present a thesis statement, and contain a "hook" or an interesting concept or event that grabs the reader's attention.

In the body of the essay, the applicant should support and explain the thesis statement contained in the introduction. The body of the essay should have four or five paragraphs (depending on the maximum word length), and each paragraph should have a topic sentence, a mini-body proving or establishing the topic sentence, and a conclusion. Each major point that is made to prove or establish the thesis statement should normally be a separate paragraph (as illustrated in the examples). The goal of the body of the essay is to provide ideas, concepts, or events that support the main theme.

Finally, the essay should contain a conclusion, which serves to reemphasize the thesis statement and briefly explain how the thesis statement was proven. The applicant should be careful not to merely restate the thesis statement or main points made in the body of the essay, but rather summarizes them with new wording. It might be helpful to end with a good quotation or a strong concluding statement about your candidacy.

Once a detailed outline, has been constructed, it is time to put "pen to paper," so to speak, and begin to compose your first draft of the essay. If you have a detailed outline and have filled in much of the structure of the essay in the outline, composing the first draft should not be too daunting a process. The first draft should take the outline content and put it into proper narrative format. In doing so, transitional sentences and words will have to be inserted at certain points. Once you have the first draft done, at least one-half of the work is complete. Too many students submit what is, in essence, only a first draft of an essay. As a pre-law advisor at the University of Tampa, I have reviewed the essays of many aspiring law students, some of which were excellent. However, many of these essays were pretty rough in the first-draft stage. The key is to solicit comments and suggestions from family, friends, and teachers, and then write a second draft.

Hence, the fourth step of the essay-crafting process is to revise, and then rewrite the essay into a second draft. It is helpful at this point to circulate a draft family and friends, to solicit critical comments and suggestions that, if employed, would enhance the points of the essay. However, the applicant should be sure to take these ideas and personally rewrite them as his or her own. If the admissions committee believes that an applicant is using vocabulary beyond his or her level of expression, or the essay appears too polished, the committee might discount the essay as being too much the work of someone other than the applicant.

The final steps of the process are to proofread the draft essay (step 5) and to complete the final revisions and prepare the final version of the essay for the application (step 6). When this stage is reached, most of the content is complete, and the essay is merely being "fine-tuned." At this point in the process, the applicant should ensure that all words are spelled correctly, and that grammatical structure is correct. While the spell-check programs on many word processors are excellent, they alone should not be relied upon. Misspelling a word may result in a typo that will not be caught by spell-check programs. For example, if the essay uses the word "poor," and the applicant mistypes a "u" for the second "o," the result is the word "pour," which of course means something entirely different. So, the essay should be carefully proofread to catch any errors that might "slip through the cracks" of a computer program.

Once finalized, the essay should be printed out on nice, clean, white-bond paper, if not applying online. The final printout should not contain any smudges or other superficial errors that might detract from the content of the essay. Contrary to the 2001 Hollywood movie *Legally Blonde*, in which a student obsessed with fashion gets accepted to Harvard Law School, it is not a good idea to complete the essay on pink, perfumed stationery (as in the movie); or letterhead or stationery of other colors or with logos or pictures of animals; or paper types that distract from the content. An admissions official reviewing the application might conclude that the applicant was less than completely serious, or that the applicant lacked the maturity expected of incoming students. While the use of certain pictures and stationery is perfectly suitable for personal correspondence, and usually bears no relation to the maturity level of the writer, the college or graduate school application should be treated as a work product. As such, applicants should keep it simple, and again rely on clean, white-bond paper, free of any superficial errors.

At this point, it might be helpful to read the successful essays by some highly qualified individuals to illustrate the foregoing points. Each of the following essays was part of an actual application for graduate school or law school in 2005, and is reproduced with the student's permission. The first essay, written by a nontraditional University of Tampa Honors Program student, was part of her successful application for graduate school at one of the leading history departments in the state of Florida:

> As a former student of psychology, I was taught that the best predictor of future behavior is past behavior. I believe that this is a valid theory and it is evident in my own academic history. Although I scored poorly on the verbal and quantitative sections of the Graduate Record Exam, I believe that a truer measure of my skills is the excellent score I received on the analytical essay portion of the exam and my past academic history. While I can certainly respect the need for universities to have some kind of quantifiable evidence in order to predict the success rate of potential enrollments, I believe that many students have unfair advantages which result in superior performance on the standardized examinations and thereby acceptance into professional or graduate programs. Admittedly, I am 50 years old and decided to pursue my college

education 15 years after receiving my General Equivalency Diploma. Like my peers, standardized testing was not administered during my elementary and secondary education unlike my current fellow classmates who have been literally drilled to master the "art." There are any number of preparatory courses for the Graduate Record Exams for a fee, but many fine candidates I am certain are unable to afford them and as such are further disadvantaged. This applied to me as I am the widow of a permanent and totally disabled veteran and the mother of a developmentally disabled son struggling to support my household on a widow's pension.

During my academic career, I have been an honor student since my first semester of college and have enjoyed the many challenges I have faced. During my first two years of college, I was active as a student leader in campus clubs and honor societies. The involvement and commitment to campus leadership was one which I enjoyed. I was able to maintain honors status with a GPA of 3.6 while also working 30 hours per week for a time. While attending the University of Tampa, I was unable to become involved with campus activities or work as I had a three hour per day commute. Recently, I was notified that my paper entitled "Perpetrators of the Holocaust" will be published in the University of Tampa honors publication *Respondez!* this spring. I have been rewarded with scholarships; and in my sophomore year, I was invited to sit on the Pasco-Hernando Community College Human Services Advisory Committee as a student consultant, a position I held into my junior year at the University of Tampa. As a student leader, I held positions as a chapter president for an honor society and a club simultaneously with great successes. I also received several awards in the area of campus leadership. My demonstrated abilities for leadership, conducting sound research, analytical reasoning, and my commitment to excellence, I believe, provide me with the qualities expected in a graduate school candidate.

A few comments on the above essay are in order. This candidate seeks to address several main issues/themes. First, the candidate provides explanation as to what she believed was her lower-than-average performance on two different sections of the GRE, while calling attention to portions of the test wherein she scored far above the averages. Then, the applicant introduces several factors that highlight her uniqueness as a candidate, and how she would offer a unique viewpoint as a member of the entering class (namely, being an older, nontraditional student, a widow of a disabled veteran, the chief caretaker of a disabled son, and coming from a background of limited economic resources). The remainder of the essay highlights her many academic achievements, including being an honors program student, maintaining a high GPA, serving in many campus organizations, and publishing an article. The applicant then concludes the essay by commenting that her "demonstrated abilities for leadership, conducting sound research, analytical reasoning, and . . . commitment to excellence" make her a promising graduate school candidate. The essay seamlessly provides information that personalizes her as a candidate, indicates her uniqueness among the sea of other applicants, and strongly illustrates her qualifications and academic credentials for studying at any top-tier graduate program in the country.

The second essay, written by another nontraditional University of Tampa Honors Program student, was part of her successful application to one of the leading law schools in the state of Florida and one of the top fifty law schools in the country. This student completed excellent graduate-level research, and her assistance to me in the writing and researching of this book was quite valuable. Her application essay follows:

> I am the oldest of three children born in 1967 to parents from Puerto Rico who divorced when I was 13 years old. My mother was a single parent who was employed as an insurance agent, a career that provided the family with the necessities of life but not the luxury to finance a college education for her children. I will be the first in my family to complete a bachelor's degree.
>
> Currently, I am married with three children; and for 12 years of the marriage, my husband was a member of the U.S. Navy. It was difficult in the early years for me to pursue a college education as I had to maintain the family while my husband was deployed for six months at a time. Enlisted military life is a series of hardships: deployments, relocations, and near poverty. In addition, my marriage is an interracial one; and we were subjected to discrimination and prejudice, which sparked my interest in studying the law. Determined to progress, when my husband was able to get "shore duty," I immediately went to business school and completed a short, word-processing program. I was hired by the same school, and eventually worked my way up to Director of Admissions as I continued to take classes in legal transcription.
>
> The most significant challenge I had to face in my life was when, in an accident on board his ship, my husband sustained a skull fracture and severe brain injury. He was not expected to survive and his right side was paralyzed. He had numerous cognitive disabilities and eventually learned to walk again. Shortly after his release from the hospital, officers unaware of the severity of his condition expected him to report for duty; and since he was unable to defend himself, I had to become his advocate. It was a struggle to get the military to award him his due benefits and 100% disability rating, but I was able to seek justice for him. Additionally, I took charge in filing for his social security benefits because he was incapable of handling any financial or legal affairs at that time. My husband continued to improve and is currently attending college.
>
> In 2003, I completed my associate degree with honors while I worked full and part-time jobs because the income from social security and my husband's pension were not enough to sustain the family. These experiences have made me stronger, more compassionate, and determined. Although I believe all things are possible if met with perseverance, I know the support and encouragement of my husband and children, now in their teens, has helped me to realize my goals.

I have been active in a number of student organizations and community service projects. A Government and World Affairs major, I chose the field because I wanted to expand my sense of political awareness and study different regimes worldwide, government policies, legal issues, and human rights. My professors have realized my talent for research and writing and have mentored me in two independent study projects this semester, both 4-credit, 400-level courses, which will be used in their upcoming books: affirmative action and higher education, and the other, global population issues in developing countries. Additionally, I have received approval to research K-12 educational policy in Florida, which will culminate into a senior honors thesis next semester. I have a strong interest in constitutional law and was honored by the university when they published my paper, "The Implications and Constitutionality of a Victim's Rights Amendment," in *Respondez!*, the Honor's Program publication.

Civil rights issues are indeed close to my heart. Although I grew up after the civil rights movement of the 1950s and 1960s, I find the issue to be timeless, an issue of significance around the world. While many consider racial inequality when they think of civil rights, it is only one of many. Recently, during a month-long, study-abroad program in Italy, I learned of the expansion of executive power in the country, the allegations concerning the bribery of judges, and the reductions in their freedom of speech, all of which are serious threats to democracy, in my opinion. After witnessing these issues first-hand, I returned to the United States with the realization that political participation is critical to maintaining American freedoms. This awakening came at the perfect time, an election year, and motivated me to volunteer my time to the presidential campaign. Furthermore, as a Hispanic American, I am familiar with the lack of representation in the legal profession. I am eagerly awaiting the challenge. I am certain my convictions, experiences, and talents will be an asset to the law school that accepts me and to the community as a whole.

While both of the foregoing essays were excellently drafted and accomplished the important task of educating admissions representatives on the student's viability as a candidate for admission and their competitiveness for advanced study, the students took two different approaches. The author of the first essay sought to address at the outset of her essay, what she perceived were her lower-than-average scores on some sections of the graduate placement examination—"taking the sting out" of this information. She then led into why her performance was arguably lower than that of other applicants, and why her unique background and life experiences would make her nonetheless an ideal candidate for admission. The second candidate structured her essay as more of a "life story" or biographical sketch. The applicant was able to not only effectively personalize herself to the admissions committee and explain her unique life experiences and background, but also led to a climactic conclusion wherein she established her academic credentials and accomplishments. The second essay also clearly delineated why the student desired to attend law school.

The final example is an excellent illustration of how the essay portion of the application can be utilized to highlight both one's uniqueness and "life story," but also the applicant's creativity in how the essay in composed. This essay, completed by a University of Tampa Honors Program student, displays the creative writing skills of the applicant, while also attempting to explain her personality and qualifications for admissions. This applicant discusses the major influences on her life, from moving to the United States, to finding her father. Indeed, the applicant does not even directly mention law school admissions in her essay until her concluding paragraph. Additionally, the applicant is content to let her GPA, LSAT scores, class rank, etc., speak for itself else where in her application, and rather use the essay section of the application to tell the schools of interest "who she really is" as a person.

> I am so exhausted. It has been a long, but fulfilling night. For the past six hours, I have been engulfed with the law of supply and demand, price discrimination, and the correlation between unemployment and inflation. As I slowly erase the graphs and models depicting the relationship between interest rates and economic trends off the dusty blackboard, my stomach begins growling as it is in dire need for food. Yet at that moment, I never felt better. Explaining the fundamentals of economics to twelve confused students can be challenging, but also very exciting. After all, economics is a social science. I always believed that to understand economics is, in essence, to understand life. Don't we find ourselves buying more price elastic goods, such as trendy clothing, when the price of that good decreases? The theory of economics can be explained through the practical aspects of our day-to-day activities.
>
> As I exit the doors of Plant Hall 400, my second home in the tutoring center at the University of Tampa, my eyes gaze at the beautiful light shining from the sky. The stars that lit up on the Minarets, the historic silver domes found on top of the main university building, were the electrifying pictures that inspired me to attend the University of Tampa. Seeing the reflection of the starlight onto the silver Minarets always reminded me of the many nights I spent attempting to capture the true beauty of the sky. The magnificent aura of nature evoked emotions of strength, motivation, and determination—emotions that economics could never. I can still remember the way it used to make me feel. This feeling takes me back to one of the most memorable nights of my life.
>
> It was a cool, windy night. As the beautiful yellow gleams of light from the sun set on the tranquil dark waters of the Atlantic Ocean, my hands began to shake as I attempted the hardest task ever—to capture the true beauty of the sunset with my brand new Kodak camera. It always seemed that no matter how many pictures I took, I could never truly capture the essence of what was seen through the lens of my eyes. However, my love and my passion for the art of photography inspired in me the motivation and belief that the day would come when my pictures would truly depict the beauty of the skies. As I packed my camera and began to end the night, the skies began releasing a truly captivating

purplish gleaming light that I had never seen before. I quickly got my camera ready to take the picture that would change my album forever. As I looked through the lens of my camera and into the breathtaking picture of the skies, I began to think. I began to think as profoundly as the light's intersection with the sea. I thought of my life, my hardships and my blessings, my happiness and my sorrows, my past and my future, my roots and my legacies. Who am I?

I began to think of my father. I wondered if his face was round like mine. I had always wished that my father could be with me every night when I gazed longingly at the sun setting on such tranquil waters. I closed my eyes hoping that when I opened them I could see him standing before the crystal, sparkling waters. This was when I knew it was time, a time to open the first chapter of the book of my life. It was now time to find my self.

My "mammy" was a Bahamian woman, courageous and strong. As for my father, the one thing I knew of him was that he was an African American. I had always heard that America was the land of dreams, but what I knew was that my father was my dream. It was at that moment, when I saw the purplish light off the skies sparkle onto the dark waters of my island, that I knew it was time to turn my dream into a reality. I had never met my father, and for the next few years of my life I vowed to meet him. It was then that I took a fresh piece of paper out, laid it down gently, and began writing. I had no clue as to how many rough drafts I would have to encounter before I finished the final draft. However, what I did know was that whatever it was, I was determined to stay on course.

Two years later, I finally put my pen and paper down, but only for a moment. I exited the huge jet into the Hartsfield International Airport in Atlanta, Georgia. My hands were wet and shaking. I felt like there were a million caterpillars transforming into fluttering butterflies in my heart all at the same time. My journey had come to an end. As I entered the airport, I was amazed to see thousands and thousands of people, and feelings of fear erupted inside of me. Coming from a country with a population total of 300,000, I was not accustomed to such big crowds. My heart began beating faster and faster. I had never felt so nervous in my life; yet I was also never as excited in my life. Then, a gentleman with light brown eyes like mine, with a round face that looked like mine, and a tall, skinny frame just like mine approached me. My butterflies felt alive and free, a feeling that I can never forget. After meeting the man that I could finally call "Dad", I knew that I had finished the first chapter of my life, but, most importantly, I knew there would be many more chapters as fulfilling and captivating as the first.

Today, four years later, when I gaze at the beautiful sunset, the sunlight shining on the waters, I am forever reminded of the first chapter of my book of life. I had always known that I could never pursue a career as a photographer, because my goal was to pursue a career that would be beneficial to the country I call home. Economic development is the greatest challenge in my developing country. It involves great understanding and little complexities, in my mind. I also knew that I wanted to spend time throughout my journey in the land that my father called home. I was ready to write the next chapter of my life, and that is how I ended up in Plant Hall 400.

My book of life has been filled with many chapters: from finding my father at the age of 16, from the Bahamas to America, from photography to economics. Each step in life that I have encountered has built me into the person I am and has given me a joy that could only be found tucked away in the quiet corners of one's heart. However, my book is not closed yet. Just as I wrap up the finishing touches from photography to economics, I begin a new chapter from the theory of economics to the study of law, from college to law school. I do not know exactly how that chapter will end. What I do know is that it will end with the profound emotion of joy I feel when gazing into my father's eyes; that it will involve my undying commitment to help those in need of finding that joy, and that I will continue to write many more chapters in this book of my life.

The lessons learned from these three examples are many. Despite the divergent approaches of each essay, the reader should note much in common in the essays. First, none of the candidates, while mentioning factors that might make them unique, nontraditional students (age, marital status, socioeconomic status, race, citizenship, etc.), makes these factors the focus of the essay. Rather, each student independently establishes a myriad of reasons why they are qualified for admission. Second, these three examples illustrate how a well-crafted essay will endear and personalize you to the admissions committee. One of the goals of your essay should be to make the readers like you as a person, and want to root and pull for you as an applicant. Each of the foregoing essays are very successful in this regard. Finally, each essay is well organized and contains an introduction, body, and conclusion. Within the body, each essay has put forth several thesis statements, and then proved or illustrated them in the sentences that followed.

The foregoing essays are certainly worthy of emulation and illustrate how a successful application essay looks and feels. However, students must still find their own voice and uniqueness, and craft the voice and the story into a well-worded essay. In concluding this chapter, it might be perhaps helpful to quote the lyrics of a famous song from World War II, by the Andrews Sisters and Bing Crosby, "Ac-cent-tchu-ate the Positive." The song offers advice on how to succeed in life, but could easily be directed toward any aspiring applicant striving to write the best possible application essay. The chorus goes as follows: "You got to accentuate the positive, eliminate the negative, latch on to the affirmative, don't mess with The Mister in between; Spread joy up to the maximum; bring gloom down to the minimum; Have faith, otherwise pandemonium, liable to walk upon the scene." After drafting and reviewing your essay, ask yourself whether you have satisfied the admonition of the Andrews Sisters and Bing Crosby—accentuated the positive and eliminated the negative in your application essay.

7

Consideration of Historically Black Colleges and Universities: Admittedly a "Different World"

Thus far, the focus of this book has been on mainstream colleges and universities. Yet, there exist over 100 institutions in approximately twenty different states, as well as Washington, D.C., whose avowed mission is the education of black Americans. While many Americans became aware of these institutions only with the success of the late-1980s television show *A Different World* called Historically Black Colleges and Universities (HBCUs) have been catering to the educational needs of the black community since the end of the Civil War. Indeed, HBCUs were born out of the rampant racism in the United States at the end of the Civil War and the existence of segregationist Jim Crow laws, which denied black Americans quality education at leading colleges and universities around the country. Immediately after the war, in conjunction with the Freedmen's Bureau and philanthropic church groups in the North, black schools spread throughout the South. Thus, for example, "the town that witnessed John Brown's strike at the institution of slavery in 1859" (one of the sparks of the Civil War) has an HBCU established in 1865, and received a state educational charter by 1867.[1] A few Northern institutions that specialized in the education of blacks prior to the Civil War continued in that role after the war, with renewed vigor. Thus, the oldest HBCU in the United States is Cheyney University in Cheyney, Pennsylvania, initially founded as a school for "colored youth" in 1837. Similarly, Wilberforce University in Ohio and Lincoln University in Pennsylvania were also established before the Civil War.

Today, beyond just a common historical commitment to the African American community, HBCUs come in all sizes and shapes, and include both private and public institutions. In total, there are approximately 105 HBCUs, comprising 40 public four-year institutions, 49 private four-year institutions, 11 public two-year institutions, and 5 private two-year institutions. According to the Higher Education Act of 1965, as amended in 1998, an HBCU is defined as "any historically Black college or university that was established prior to 1964 whose principal mission was, and is, the education of Black Americans..."[2] However, several of the HBCUs no longer have a student body where a majority of the students are black. Generally speaking, since the end of legal segregation in education brought about by the Supreme Court's decision in *Brown v. Board of Education*, many of the HBCUs have struggled to survive, losing some of the best students to mainstream institutions and struggling to fill their classes, while also battling to retain adequate funding. Some schools have even ceased to operate. For example, Storer College, in Harpers Ferry, West Virginia, closed its doors in 1955, a year after *Brown*, when the state of West Virginia indicated that it would not continue to provide separate funding for the all-black school. The U.S. National Park Service now commemorates the school as part of the Harpers Ferry National Historical Park, and many U.S. Park Service rangers receive training at the Mather training center, which was once the center of the Storer College campus.

Despite the long and proud history of HBCUs, the institutions are facing some difficult issues in the twenty-first century also, especially since the Supreme Court's rulings in 2003. With increased acknowledgment of the role and value of diversity on campus, it becomes harder and harder for institutions to justify campuses that are racially segregated—either benign or invidious. That is, at the same time as many universities and colleges around the country are discussing the tangible benefits of diversity in student population, especially the enhancement of overall educational value for students, HBCUs cannot be seen as closing themselves off and voluntarily resegregating, at least not without serious and significant criticisms, and complaints from the Department of Education's Office of Civil Rights. Furthermore, as alluded to briefly above, HBCUs are losing some of the nation's brightest minority students to mainstream institutions as these institutions are now offering better financial aid packages and highly recruiting minority students who meet the academic requirements. Thus, for example, in the 1990s, Florida A&M (an HBCU in Florida) attracted one of the largest classes of National Achievement Scholarship finalists in the country, even surpassing Harvard. However, by 2004, only four National Achievement Scholarship finalists were making their way to Florida A&M, compared to eighty-five to Harvard, sixty-one to Yale, fifty-seven to Stanford, and forty to the flagship public institution in Florida, the University of Florida.[3] In the words of Florida A&M's recruiting director, "Once upon a time, our package was perhaps the best scholarship deal in America. Since then, others have sweetened the kitty."

Many HBCUs recognized the value of diversity in student body long before the Supreme Court's decisions in 2003. This is one of the reasons why white enrollment at a dozen of the HBCUs has recently run between 20 and 50 percent. Generally, white enrollment at HBCUs has grown 65 percent in the last twenty-five years, from 21,000 to 35,000.[4] These changing demographics of the student population at HBCUs can be attributed to multiple factors, including improved perception of the quality of HBCUs and their institutional commitment to diversity beyond the Afrocentric curriculum. There is also a heightened appreciation for the historical nature of these institutions—especially those founded just after the Civil War, like Howard University. HBCUs are also reported as eager to increase the number of nonblack students, as a "black flight" is occurring from HBCUs to mainstream institutions that are seeking to diversify their entering classes. As discrimination on account of race is not permitted under Title VI of the Civil Rights Act, HBCUs have seen an increase in the number of white students who wish to attend. For example, Morgan State, Bowie State, Coppin State, and the University of Maryland Eastern Shore, all HBCUs in Maryland, have agreed with the Department of Education in 2000 (in lieu of legal action) to set no cap or quota for white students. While overall white enrollment at HBCUs was approximately 13 percent as of 2005, the trend of "black flight" and increased white enrollment is pronounced at certain HBCUs.[5] For example, at the historical 110-year-old Bluefield State College in West Virginia, only 12 percent of the students were black in 2005.[6] Similarly, Lincoln University in Missouri now has a student body that is predominantly white. This is ironic given the fact that these institutions were initially set up to accommodate students who were denied attendance at mainstream institutions for racist reasons. One of the most well-known and well-respected HBCUs, Howard University, has a very black demographic composition, where only 1 percent of the students are white (approximately 100 white students out of the total student population of 11,000).[7]

What is also interesting about HBCUs, after *Gratz* and *Grutter*, is that if the academic world so seriously believes that diversity in student population enhances the educational experience of students in the classroom, then HBCUs should also be concerned with bringing in people from other walks of life. As was pointed out in Chapter 2, if an institution claims that racial diversity is valuable on campus, then the institution cannot pick and choose which underrepresented groups ought to be promoted, and which ones ought not. In the HBCU context, this would correlate to the admission of more white applicants, or at least giving nontraditional white students a "tip" or "plus" factor as is given to black students at traditionally white institutions. One concern raised by this increased competition is that as more admissions spots are being given to whites, the chances of black applicants being accepted becomes more competitive with each passing year. While many of the HBCUs have "open admissions," several of the more "elite" of the HBCUs are quite competitive with admissions. For example, in recent years, Spelman College has averaged an acceptance rate of approximately 50 percent per year, meaning that one-half of the applicants are rejected. At a minimum, in light of the increased competition and nonminority enrollment, black applicants should be aware that admission to a competitive HBCU is not automatically granted, and these schools can no longer be viewed as "safe schools," where you can always be assured of admittance.

SHOULD YOU ATTEND AN HBCU?

Perhaps the most difficult question with HBCUs is whether or not you should attend one. Of course, there is no objectively correct (or easy) answer that applies across the board to all applicants. Rather, as the saying goes, beauty is in the eye of the beholder. What might be a right fit for one applicant could be a horrible choice for another. Applicants (and their parents) should candidly consider what the student wishes to take from his or her college experience, and what institution best aligns with those goals/desires. For example, HBCUs are known for providing a nurturing environment for those students who might be in need of personal attention, remedial training or tutoring, or in need of role models of the same racial group. The HBCU approach is very individualized. This might suit some applicants, and would be stifling to others.

Of course, the reputation of HBCUs varies widely, as does the prognosis for their role in the twenty-first century. Few will deny that these are historical institutions that ought to be preserved as part of black and American history. However, the issue of academic rigor at HBCUs has been subject to several critic reviews. For example, Thomas Sowell, conservative critic of HBCUs and programs such as affirmative action, has argued, partly based upon personal experience as a student at Howard, that HBCUs do not compete academically with mainstream institutions. In his 1989 book, *Choosing a College*, Sowell writes about learning bad academic habits at Howard, and not realizing these bad habits until he transferred to Harvard. *Days of Grace*, by Arthur Ashe, while a general supporter of HBCUs, came to the same conclusion as Sowell's book. In this book, his memoir work, Ashe describes becoming disenchanted teaching at an HBCU, and finding numerous academic deficiencies among the written works of the students, and a general lack of discipline, illustrated by showing up late for class. Of course, there are just as many supporters for HBCUs as there are critics. Furthermore, many of the arguments cited by Sowell, Ashe, and others can be rebutted by simply pointing out that the problems are not endemic of only HBCUs, but rather reflect societal problems and attitudes that can be found at most mainstream institutions. For example, Ashe's criticism of students showing up late for class, or turning in assignments late, is not limited to HBCUs. This author, a college professor at a private mainstream (predominately white) university and a law school professor, has yet to have a semester where students do not come into class late, or turn in assignments late. Nonetheless, applicants should at least be aware of this debate when considering HBCUs, even if such criticisms are ultimately disregarded.

What are some of the major positive and negative considerations regarding an HBCU? First, HBCUs have provided yeoman's service to the country, and to African Americans in particular, for the last 140-plus years. These institutions served as the primary seats of learning for a whole class of citizenry, especially during the crucial years of Reconstruction, as blacks made the transition from bondage to freedom. This significant role is illustrated by the fact that "30% of all bachelor's and 15% of all master's degrees awarded to African Americans" were awarded by HBCUs, while at the same time representing only 3 percent of all colleges and universities in the country.[8] The history and heritage of the HBCUs are quite inspiring and certainly are positive considerations in the pursuit of knowledge. Second, as noted above, HBCUs are known for providing an individualized, nurturing environment that allows students to blossom intellectually, spiritually, and culturally. This is illustrated by the fact that a large percentage of black doctoral students received their undergraduate degree from an HBCU. Third, black students are less likely to feel isolated, and can generally assimilate more quickly and completely at an HBCU than would be the case at a mainstream institution, especially one of the larger public universities. However, an admissions recruiter at one HBCU (Florida A&M) stated that black students who have historically attended all-white or near all-white high schools or grade schools might actually have a hard time assimilating at an HBCU. According to this official, "They [black students of all-white high schools] may assimilate fairly easily [at a mostly white college] because it's nothing new to them.... Ironically, the flip side of that is that some... would have more difficulty adjusting to us as a historically black college. They've simply never been around that number of African Americans."[9]

Fourth, financial aid packages at many of the HBCUs have been quite generous to students in need—much more so than at the mainstream colleges. Fifth, there is less possibility of racism or racial hostilities existing on campus. Sixth, there is a greater focus on black culture and history. Seventh, many of the HBCUs employ "open admissions," meaning that applicants with average test scores and high school GPAs have a better chance of admission than is many upper-tier mainstream institutions. It has been argued that HBCUs give students from the margins a chance, in terms of both admission and retention. According to one expert on HBCUs, "Many young people would not survive if they went into majority institutions where the classroom sizes are overwhelming, where they don't see people who look like them who are professors and administrators, because many of them are the first (in their families) to go to college."[10] Finally, for African American applicants, there is an abundance of role models of the same racial group amongst the faculty (higher percentages than at mainstream institutions) and of mentors and previous graduates to emulate. Famous graduates of HBCUs include Oprah Winfrey (Tennessee State), Reverend Jesse Jackson (North Carolina A&T), Reverend Martin Luther King, Jr. (Morehouse), Justice Thurgood Marshall (Lincoln University), Toni Morrison (Howard University), Ed Bradley (Cheyney University), Spike Lee (Morehouse), and Andrew Young (Howard University), just to name a few. HBCUs have also contributed richly to the history and culture of the United States. As one author of a book on HBCUs has stated, "We found that these institutions contributed to the development of jazz, the development of the Harlem Renaissance with black writers coming out of many of these institutions, and that the whole civil rights movement grew out of historically black colleges."[11]

Just as there are many positive factors relating to HBCUs, there are issues/ factors that some have labeled as negative. First, despite the increased enrollment of white students, many HBCUs still lack racial diversity on campus. Second, some of the HBCUs lack the funding or large endowments that mainstream universities enjoy. This sometimes correlates to the lack of equal facilities on campus, and the breadth of academic disciplines and/or studies that are available, and may even impact the caliber of professors. For example, many of the most famous African American scholars are recruited, courted, and employed not by HBCUs, but rather by leading mainstream institutions. Thus, Professor Henry Louis Gates teaches at Harvard, Professor Cornel West at Cornell, Professor Derrick Bell at the University of Pittsburgh, Professor Maya Angelou at Wake Forest, and Toni Morrison at Princeton University, again just to name a few. Finally, some critics argue that HBCUs do not prepare students for the heterogeneous real world. At a college informational interview with prospective applicants, one student stated that he believed he might be happier at an HBCU like Prairie View A&M University. A black graduate of Texas A&M, serving as the college's representative, was trying to convince the student to go to Texas A&M, in part because HBCUs do not reflect the real world. The college representative opined that "the world looks like Texas A&M. It doesn't look like Prairie View."[12] This experience was repeated across the country, in Florida, where a high school student selected the University of Florida, over the nation's leading HBCU, Howard University in Washington, D.C. The student selected UF over Howard because she thought attending UF would help her better succeed in society after graduation, commenting as follows about her decision: "This is what corporate America looks like ... I'm not downing the experience at FAMU and other historically black schools, but this is definitely what corporate America is going to be like."[13] Yet another individual, the admissions director at North Carolina A&T, an HBCU, has agreed with the foregoing sentiments, stating, "Boardrooms are not all black, and classrooms shouldn't be either."[14] This is, of course, a highly debatable and contentious issue—but one that every applicant must consider and reach a conclusion of his or her own, especially if the applicant ultimately attends an HBCU.

8

Congratulations: You've Been Accepted to College, but Now Need to Pay for It: Financial Aid and Student Aid in the Post–*Gratz* and *Grutter* World

OVERVIEW OF CURRENT ISSUES/PROBLEMS

While the number of schools that currently utilize race as a factor in admissions is somewhere in the range of 300–400, the number of institutions that allowed for race-conscious scholarships and financial aid was enormous prior to *Gratz* and *Grutter*. It was cogently argued that concern for diversity in higher education meant little if students were not afforded the means to attend the college or university of their choice. In fact, this was recognized by the U.S. General Accounting Office, when it reported that scholarships and financial aid based on race and ethnicity were "valuable tools for recruiting and retaining" minority students and helped in "overcome[ing] the traditional difficulties ... in enrolling and graduating minority students, such as financial hardships and a perception of cultural isolation."[1] The report also found that the availability of such scholarships "help[ed] build a critical mass of minority enrollment and sen[t] a message that the school sincerely want[ed] to attract [minority and untraditional] students."[2] According to the College Board, based upon data from 1999–2000, approximately "47% of four-year public colleges, 43% of four-year private colleges and one-quarter of community colleges based their non-need awards (at least in part) on students' race or ethnicity."[3]

This consideration of race or ethnicity is important in light of the rapidly increasing cost of attending college. In the 1970s, one could attend a private university for approximately five or six thousand dollars a year. However, in 2002–2003, the College Board reported that the average cost of attending a private college was approximately $18,300 per year. Public schools have increased the costs up to an average of roughly $5,000 a year in tuition. Furthermore, a 2002 report by the National Center for Public Policy, entitled *Losing Ground*, indicated that the amount spent on tuition by low- and middle-income families had increased from 13 percent of the family's income (in 1980) to 25 percent (in 2000–2001).[4] Unfortunately, however, as the price of higher education has skyrocketed, the amount of governmental grant and scholarship funds has dwindled. For example, from 1986 to 1999, "the average federal Pell Grant went from covering 98 percent of the tuition to only 57 percent, while state aid coverage dropped from 75 percent to 64 percent."[5] In 2005, President Bush submitted his budget for the Department of Education that would, according to the original language, eliminate the federal Perkins grants altogether. As a result, students, especially minority students who come in large numbers from low- and middle-class families, have become more dependent on loans and financial aid packages. Hence, the heightened importance and need for financial aid, particularly among minority students.

Yet, despite the skyrocketing costs of education, the reduction of federal grants and scholarships, and the particular need among minority students, the use of race-conscious programs in the financial aid arena has declined tremendously in the aftermath of *Gratz* and *Grutter* (for reasons that will be discussed below). A myriad of newspaper and media reports in 2004 have said that, in part because of the Supreme Court's rulings in 2003, "colleges...nationwide are opening up scholarships previously restricted to Black students. In reporting on this trend, a March 2004 *Chronicle of Higher Education* article, by Peter Schmidt, was entitled 'Not Just for Minority Students Anymore.' Programs aimed at recruiting and retaining minorities have been scrapped or broadened to include White students."[6] This trend of opening up minority student scholarships to a variety of racial and ethnic groups has been found at institutions such as Virginia Tech (which has eliminated the use of race in all areas of admissions, financial aid, and employment), Harvard, Yale, Carnegie Mellon, Indiana University, Washington University in St. Louis, and St. Louis University.[7] These institutions have also opened up the traditionally racially exclusive scholarships to applicants from indigent or low-income families under the idea of socioeconomic or need-based awards being a legitimate factor for consideration and selection. William Gray, former president of the United Negro College Fund, has called this trend "a blatant attempt to narrow the doorway of access for minorities."[8]

Yet, what is surprising about this rapid decline in race-conscious scholarships is that, at least on the surface, the Supreme Court made no express reference to the constitutionality of scholarship programs targeted at minority students in the *Gratz* and *Grutter* decisions. Rightly or wrongly, institutions are applying the standards of *Gratz* and *Grutter* to areas of higher education beyond admissions. As discussed in Chapter 2, the Supreme Court held that the use of race in admissions is permissible to achieve diversity in the classroom, so long as it is only one of a series of different factors utilized. Hence, institutions have been importing these "lessons" of *Gratz* and *Grutter* to the financial aid context, despite some questions as to the correctness of this approach. However, it is no mistake that many schools are eliminating their race-conscious financial aid/scholarship programs in light of threatened litigation by the American Civil Rights Institute (ACRI) and the Center for Equal Opportunity (CEO). These organizations have threatened legal action and sent warning letters to "dozens of colleges and universities... against denying qualified white students access to scholarship and programs offered to minorities."[9] According to Roger Clegg, general counsel for the CEO, they have contacted over 100 different universities about racially exclusive scholarships in the last several months of 2004 and in the beginning of 2005. Indeed, the Center for Equal Opportunity has followed through with the threats, and has filed complaints with the Department of Education's Office for Civil Rights against Virginia Tech, Pepperdine University, and Massachusetts Institute of Technology.[10] In light of this policing, universities and colleges are backing away from race-exclusive scholarships, or finding private funding for such activity. For example, Southern Illinois University funds its summer program for minority engineering students with private money. This trend is illustrated by a comment made by Mary Jo Lively, the general counsel for Carnegie Mellon University, when she said, "When I looked at the Michigan cases and read them carefully, my conclusion, as I think has been the conclusion of practically every scholar around the country and every general counsel with whom I have talked, is that race-exclusive programs—except in certain extreme factual circumstances, are not likely to withstand a legal challenge."[11] Thus, many college administrators, in order to avoid potential problems (even if the question has not been completely resolved by courts), have preemptively dropped racially exclusive scholarships. Finally, for those who have not previously considered race in financial aid/scholarship programs, this trend certainly has not increased the desire to start considering race. For example, Leslie Winner, legal counsel for the University of North Carolina, has commented that "we were already not taking race into account in admissions,"[12] so the expansion into other areas is unlikely.

Despite the avalanche of institutions that seem to be opening up minority programs to students of all races in the aftermath of the *Gratz* and *Grutter* decisions (and because of the threat and possibility of legal action), there are still a handful of institutions that are standing firm against this overwhelming pressure, at least for the time being. For example, the University of Wisconsin system employs the Ben R. Lawton Minority Undergraduate Grant Program, which is designed to ensure that students from certain groups will have sufficient funds to complete their university education. This program, initially authorized in 1985 by a Wisconsin state law, limits eligibility to students who are blacks, Hispanics, or American Indians, or members of immediate family that came to the United States as refugees from Cambodia, Laos, or Vietnam. In 2004, over 2,700 students received annual awards under this program. Despite the Supreme Court's rulings in 2003, and the implications in financial aid and other areas that many administrators feared as a result, administrators within the University of Wisconsin system vowed to continue to offer these racially exclusive funds. As David Glisch-Sanchez, director of academic affairs at the University of

Wisconsin, requested "a strong show of support for programs like the Lawton grants in order to send a clear message to those who would forsake race-conscious efforts."[13] Pepperdine University and the University of Missouri at Columbia have also resisted the trend of opening up minority student scholarships to other races. While the University of Missouri at Columbia announced that it would broaden some of the programs previously offered only to black students to now be available to all "underrepresented minority students," it has continued to not allow white students to qualify for these programs. The Pepperdine University, generally considered to be a conservative university, announced that it refuses to eliminate or alter its race-conscious financial aid packages, saying that "it's our responsibility, given our Christian mission, to be not a white island but to reflect the diversity around us."[14]

It should be noted, however, that the practices of the above institutions and the reluctance to change their programs have prompted scrutiny by the Department of Education's Office for Civil Rights (or in the case of the University of Missouri at Columbia, a threatening complaint). As a result of a complaint filed with the OCR by a retired University of Wisconsin economics professor, the university's Lawton Minority Scholarship program is under scrutiny. The OCR will ultimately decide, after reviewing the program, whether the program violates Title VI of the Civil Rights Act of 1964, or the Fourteenth Amendment. The reader may recall that Title VI outright prohibits racial discrimination (benign or invidious) by any institution, public or private, that receives federal funds. Whether the University of Wisconsin program will be upheld or invalidated, is ultimately an issue that the courts will address in the next several years. The law and practice in this area is clearly in a state of flux. Until additional guidance is provided either by the OCR, or via a federal court case, the information provided in the next three sections remains the only guidance available on the permissibility and availability of financial aid or scholarships that might be based on an affirmative action approach.

It should also be noted that this movement afoot to open up scholarship programs on account of race does not apply to other classifications based on such factors as veteran status, geographical origin of the candidate, physical handicaps, and the like. After having read the first several chapters of this book, the reason should be obvious—the Fourteenth Amendment and Title VI of the Civil Rights Act of 1964 deal with classifications based upon race, and not other types of governmental discrimination.

FLANAGAN V. GEORGETOWN COLLEGE, PODBERESKY V. KIRWAN, AND THE SCARCITY OF CASE LAW ON RACIALLY EXCLUSIVE FINANCIAL AID PROGRAMS

Unlike the question of whether race-conscious affirmative action is permissible for admissions decisions in higher education (for which numerous case-law decisions exist), the question of whether it may be used in the allocation of financial aid and/or scholarships has hardly ever been addressed in federal case law. Indeed, only two cases, the *Flanagan* and the *Podberesky* decisions, have been repeatedly cited as shedding light on the constitutionality of race-conscious financial aid programs. These two pre-1994 Department of Education Guideline cases are lower court rulings and do not apply to all institutions across the country.

The earlier of the two cases, and arguably the less important one, is a federal district court ruling from the District of Columbia, entitled *Flanagan v. Georgetown College*, 417 F. Supp. 377 (D.D.C. 1976). The court in *Flanagan* upheld a challenge to Georgetown University Law Center's affirmative action program, which was designed to increase minority enrollment at the law school by providing roughly 60 percent of the scholarships to minority students, who constituted approximately 11 percent of the population, but comprised only a miniscule percentage of lawyers generally (and Georgetown Law students specifically) at the time. The court held that though the use of affirmative action might in some cases be permissible to ensure that all candidates are equally situated to compete for the available benefits and opportunities, it was impermissible for Georgetown's Law Center to favor one racial group to the disadvantage of another racial group in the distribution of sparse resources like scholarships and financial aid. Thus, the *Flanagan* decision prohibited racially exclusive financial aid programs. However, the reader should also note that the *Flanagan* decision has been criticized in recent years based upon the fact that it predates the *Bakke* decision, and, arguably, might have been decided differently if it came after the Supreme Court's ruling in *Bakke*.

The second case dealing with race and financial aid is *Podberesky v. Kirwan*, 38 F.3d 147 (4th Cir. 1994). Any review of the current state and permissibility of racially exclusive financial aid and scholarship must start with the *Podberesky* decision, as it is the leading federal circuit court decision on the subject. In *Podberesky*, a Hispanic American applicant, Daniel J. Podberesky, claimed that the University of Maryland reversely discriminated against him by denying him a scholarship that was available only to African American applicants. Podberesky claimed that but for his race, he would have received the scholarship. Podberesky based this claim on the fact that he graduated from high school with a 3.56 GPA and a 1340 on the SAT.

The scholarship program at issue, the Banneker Scholarship, had its genesis in 1969, when the then Department of Education's Office of Civil Rights found that Maryland's public higher education system remained unlawfully segregated and in violation of Title VI of the Civil Rights Act of 1964. As a result, the state of Maryland was obligated to submit a desegregation plan. Part of the plan (finally approved in 1985) included race-targeted scholarship programs like the Banneker Scholarship. In litigation, the University of Maryland defended the racially restrictive Banneker program and offered a series of justifications, including the unfavorable reputation of the campus within the African American community, racial tensions and hostility on the campus between blacks and whites, the underrepresentation of African American students on campus, and the low retention and graduation rates of African Americans at the university.

At the federal district court level, Podberesky was not successful in his case. The district court, relying on a leading affirmative action and contracting case called *City of Richmond v. J.A. Croson*, 488 U.S. 469 (1989), which required the strictest of judicial scrutiny when racial discrimination was at issue, concluded that the effects and practices of prior discrimination against African Americans justified the racially exclusive scholarship program. The court ruled that "attempting to remedy the effects of past discrimination was a compelling governmental interest needed to pass the strict scrutiny test" utilized by the court.[15] The district court also found that the scholarship program was narrowly tailored, and offered other sources of scholarships and financial aid for members of other racial groups.

However, on appeal, the United States Court of Appeals for the Fourth Circuit reversed the district court's ruling, and in so doing, held that the Banneker Scholarship program did not meet the strict scrutiny. Specifically, the Fourth Circuit held that it was insufficient to justify the existence of an affirmative action plan based "merely" on past discrimination and wrongs committed against minority groups. In order for the scholarship plan to be proper, the court said that it must be in response to the documented existence of contemporary harm or discrimination and that "mere knowledge of historical fact is not the kind of present effect that can justify a race-exclusive remedy." Furthermore, "while the inequities and indignities visited by past discrimination are undeniable, the use of race as a reparational device risks perpetuating the very race-consciousness such a remedy purports to overcome.... It thus remains our constitutional premise that race is an impermissible arbiter of human fortunes." Phrased another way, the racially exclusive scholarship program only survives constitutional review if the program was designed to remedy the present effects of discrimination. Furthermore, the institution must have "strong evidence" (which it documents) of the institution-specific discrimination (i.e., general societal discrimination is insufficient) and of the lingering effects of this discrimination. The Fourth Circuit held that none of this was established by the University of Maryland with sufficiently strong evidence.

The narrow results of the decision in *Podberesky* was that public-funded scholarships designated for students only of African American race was no longer permissible at the University of Maryland or other public institutions within the state. However, the decision has had greater impact throughout the country in the years following it. First, the decision in *Podberesky* was binding not only on the public institutions of Maryland, but also on the other states that comprised the federal Fourth Circuit, namely, the mid-Atlantic states of Virginia, West Virginia, and Delaware. For example, the University of Delaware publicly announced that it had dropped its racially exclusive scholarships, opening them up to nonminority students as well.[16] Even more telling was a complaint to the OCR, in 1996, claiming that Northern Virginia Community College was violating the *Podberesky* decision. Specifically, the scholarships being offered at the college, unlike the Banneker scholarships at the University of Maryland, were provided by private donors. However, the college administered the funds on behalf of the donors, and selected the recipients for the scholarships. This ultimately led the Department of Education to conclude that the scholarship program was unacceptable under the *Podberesky* decision. The Department held that if Northern Virginia Community College wished to continue the use of such racially exclusive scholarships provided by private donors, the college could not be involved in the process, by either administering the funds or selecting the recipients.[17] As a result of the *Podberesky* decision, administrators around the country wondered about the legality of scholarships at their schools. While the Department of Education tried to quell concerns about racial exclusiveness and improperly administered programs on campuses by sending a letter to colleges and universities in 1996 reaffirming that it is permissible, within the perimeters of the *Podberesky* decision, to consider race in the financial aid context. This attempt to allay fears largely failed. Indeed, as reported by *Black Issues in Higher Education* in 2004, "The decision [in *Podberesky*] [had] a chilling effect on race-conscious scholarship programs around the nation."[18] This chilling effect on scholarship programs has increased since the *Gratz* and *Grutter* decisions in 2003 (as discussed more fully later in this chapter), and has left the status of financial aid in a state of flux and confusion.

BACKGROUND ON THE UNITED STATES DEPARTMENT OF EDUCATION GUIDELINES ON RACE-BASED SCHOLARSHIPS

One cannot entirely blame the court system alone for the confusion as to whether or not financial aid and scholarships may be awarded on the basis of race. Part of the confusion may also be attributed to the flip-flop the U.S. Department of Education made on this issue in the early 1990s. First, on December 4, 1990, a Department official remarked that "Title VI categorically prohibited colleges and universities from awarding scholarships on the basis of race."[19] However, approximately three months after this pronouncement, on March 20, 1991, the then secretary of education, Lamar Alexander, had the policy statement rescinded and stated that the Department of Education would "continue to interpret Title VI as permitting federally funded institutions to provide minority scholarships."[20] On December 10, 1991, the Department of Education published a notice and solicited comments from the public on a draft Public Policy Guidance by the agency relating to whether Title VI allowed for scholarships based on race and national origin. The draft Public Policy Guidance indicated, among other things, that while there had never been a "full policy review and clear set of principles" regarding race-based scholarships, the Department of Education "would continue to interpret Title VI as permitting race-based scholarships in a variety of instances."[21] In January 1994, the Department of Education issued its final version of the policy guidelines. This final 1994 policy remains, to date, the only complete and comprehensive guidance for students and college administrators alike on the permissibility of using race or ethnicity as the chief factor in granting scholarships or financial aid.

1994 TITLE VI FINAL POLICY GUIDELINES AND IMPLICATIONS OF THE GUIDELINES AFTER THE *GRATZ* AND *GRUTTER* DECISIONS

1994 Title VI Final Policy Guidelines

As noted above, while the Department of Education's 1994 guidelines predates the *Gratz* and *Grutter* decisions by a decade, it still remains the only comprehensive guidance by the federal government on the use of race in awarding scholarships or financial aid. It is also worth noting that the 1994 guidelines have never been overturned or invalidated by a subsequent court decision, or even adequately addressed in *any* court decision. Also, it is argued that these guidelines would survive any current Court challenges as they can be defended as employing the same logic and reasoning as is found in *Gratz* and *Grutter*[22] because the Department of Education relied heavily on Justice Powell's diversity rationale, which was approved of by the Supreme Court in *Gratz* and *Grutter*, in putting together the 1994 guidelines. For this reason, it is reported that the Department of Education has no intentions of revising them. It is for these reasons that the 1994 policy guidelines are worthy of discussion, and are reproduced in their entirety as an appendix at the end of this book (see Appendix B).

The 1994 policy guidelines put forth five major principles regarding the use of race or ethnicity as the chief factor that colleges and universities may use in awarding scholarships under Title VI of the Civil Rights Act of 1964. First, the guidelines specify that colleges and universities may always award funds to disadvantaged students, even if this practically means that most of the funds are going to minority students. As the Department of Education specified, "awarding financial aid to disadvantaged students provides a sufficiently strong educational purpose to justify any racially disproportionate effect the use of this criterion may entail."[23] Second, colleges and universities may award financial aid on the grounds of race if justified under another federal statute or law. In so holding, the Department stated that "financial aid programs for minority students that are authorized by a specific federal law cannot be considered to violate another Federal law, i.e., Title VI."[24] Third, the guidelines specify that colleges and universities may use race in the award of financial aid or scholarships if the monetary award is necessary to overcome the present effects of past racial discrimination at the institution. As stated by the Department of Education, "Allowing colleges to implement narrowly tailored remedial affirmative action if there is strong evidentiary support for it—without requiring that it be delayed until a finding is made by OCR, a court or a legislative body—will assist in ensuring that Title VI's mandate against discrimination based on race or national origin is achieved."[25] Fourth, consistent with both Justice Powell's diversity rationale in *Bakke* and the Supreme Court's later rulings in *Gratz* and *Grutter*, colleges and universities may use race and ethnicity, along with other factors, in order to recruit and retain a diverse student population. However, according to the Department in its guidelines (and consistent with later decisions in *Gratz* and *Grutter*), race can be considered only as "one factor, with other factors, in awarding financial aid if necessary to promote diversity" and as "a condition of eligibility in awarding financial aid if it is narrowly tailored to promote diversity."[26] The fifth principle put forth in the guidelines was that private donations and gifts are not limited by application of Title VI. That is, according to the Department's guidelines, Title VI specifies that colleges and universities may not discriminate based upon race. However, Title VI does not apply to private individual donors or groups who are not themselves recipients of federal financial assistance.

An illustration of these rules can be seen in a Department of Education's Office of Civil Rights case dealing with Florida Atlantic University in 1996–1997. In this case, the OCR investigated racially exclusive scholarship programs at Florida Atlantic University, such as the full-tuition Martin Luther King, Jr. Scholarship, employed by the university as a means to increase minority enrollment. However, the OCR contended that this violated the 1994 guidelines. Ultimately, in settling the case, the then president of Florida Atlantic, Anthony Catanese, announced that it would revise its scholarship programs so as not to rely on the applicant's race as a paramount or decisive factor. Rather, the school would open the scholarships to all applicants, and include race as *one* of several factors that might be equally relevant to receiving the scholarship. Florida Atlantic specifically promised to "give equal, if not greater, weight to economic need and scholastic achievement."[27] Thus, "for the first time, a white student attending Florida Atlantic University may be eligible to receive a full-tuition Martin Luther King, Jr. scholarship previously available only to blacks."[28]

However, the Florida Atlantic case did not preclude scholarships that continued to rely on "race-as-a-plus" factor if properly based upon the Department of Education's 1994 guidelines. That is, race-based scholarships or financial aid could still be offered if the award met the 1994 guidance relating to diversifying the student body, correcting the present effects of past discrimination at the school, among other things. In its case investigation (*Florida Atlantic University*, Case Number 04-90-2067), the Department of Education's Office of Civil Rights approved of the "race-as-a-plus" factor under the 1994 guidelines. In the OCR's conclusions, it was specifically persuaded by the following additional factors/evidence relating to the program at Florida Atlantic: (1) the Florida Board of Regents stated that "black student recruitment and retention [were] heavily dependent upon financial assistance programs" and, for black students, financial aid was "among one of the most important criteria... in choosing a college"; (2) statements by several black students indicated that they could not have attended Florida Atlantic without financial assistance; (3) the university program was narrowly tailored in that Florida Atlantic had implemented "numerous non-race exclusive measures," which were generally successful in recruitment of students, but "not...as successful in recruiting black students"; and (4) the "race-plus" approach did not unnecessarily injure nonminority students, in that only 7–8 percent of Florida Atlantic's scholarships utilized race as a significant factor in qualification and selection of recipients.

Implications of the Guidelines after *Gratz* and *Grutter*

As stated above, the Department of Education was greatly influenced by Justice Powell's diversity rationale when it drafted the 1994 guidelines, and so, much of the guidance is consistent with the Court's rulings on the use of affirmative action, as the reader can also see from the 1997 Florida Atlantic case discussed above. Furthermore, Roger Clegg, director of the CEO, has put the issue as follows: "The legal principles are the same. If the various civil rights laws prohibit discrimination in admissions, it has to extend to scholarships, internships, summer programs, and the rest. I think everybody would have to agree to that."[29] As a result, many programs that once had racially exclusive scholarships are now opening them up to a variety of student groups.

However, not all university officials are willing to accept that the *Gratz* and *Grutter* decisions mandate that racially exclusive scholarships must be opened up to nonminority students. For example, Elisie Boddie of the NAACP Legal Defense and Education Fund has pointed out that the *Gratz* and *Grutter* decisions dealt with the use of affirmative action in admissions, and do not speak of any other area of higher education. According to Ms. Boddie, "It's overstating the Court's decision to extend it to other programs."[30] Ms. Boddie further commented that "I'm not saying that institutions should not examine their programs and calibrate them so they are appropriate. But I don't think it's wise for them to so quickly abandon ship. The fact is that these programs are critical, and without them, diversity on campus can very easily unravel."[31] This sentiment is echoed by William H. Gray, III, a former president of the United Negro College Fund, who calls the recent prohibitions on racially exclusive scholarships as "a blatant attempt to narrow the doorway of access for minorities."[32]

However, despite this resistance, if one considers the *Gratz* and *Grutter* decisions, along with the Department of Education's 1994 guidelines, racially exclusive scholarship programs have become almost indefensible by universities and colleges. It is for this reason that the scholarship programs are being broadened to include multiple screening and selection factors, and students should be aware of this fact. While practical advice on admissions and financial aid will be offered in the subsequent chapters of this book, it should be noted that students will now have broader competition for scholarship programs previously restricted to race, and so they should be prepared to focus on other grounds as well (e.g., economic need, unique life experiences, and scholastic achievement).

One more potentially negative trend in race-based scholarships is worth noting. There are many private organizations that currently offer race-based scholarships. For private scholarships funded and administered by private individuals and/or organizations, the above law and Title VI restrictions do not apply, so long as the college or university does not have a role in the administration of the scholarship program. For example, it has been reported that the United Negro College Fund scholarships have been awarded to students attending approximately 900 different institutions.[33] However, there has been some talk among groups critical of affirmative action that perhaps even these types of financial aid or scholarships might not be legal under existing federal law. Specifically, critics point to a statutory provision (42 U.S.C. Section 1981) long on the books, which was first enacted after the Civil War under the Civil Rights Act of 1866. This statutory provision, which applies to both public and private parties, specifies that racial discrimination in the making of private contracts is illegal. This provision was cited by the Supreme Court in both the *Gratz* and *Grutter* decisions. In fact, in *Gratz*, the Court commented that 42 U.S.C. Section 1981 "proscribes discrimination in the making or enforcement of contracts against, or in favor of, any race," and that a "contract for educational services is a 'contract' for purposes of §1981." Critics therefore argue that scholarships conferred by private donors are "contracts" within the meaning of Section 1981, and cannot discriminate on the basis of race.

What this means for future racially exclusive scholarships from private donors is yet to be seen. To date, the focus of anti-affirmative action groups has been to attack practices of colleges and universities that have utilized race in a way that these groups feel goes beyond the limitations placed by the Supreme Court in *Gratz* and *Grutter*. That is to say, to date, most of the resources in combating affirmative action programs have been utilized in ensuring college and university compliance with *Gratz* and *Grutter*. It is for this reason that there has been a rapid decline in racially exclusive scholarships and financial aid around the country. As delineated above, universities are moving away from such scholarships, and opening up the scholarships to candidates from a variety of backgrounds, definitely including candidates from certain underrepresented backgrounds, but also including socioeconomically disadvantaged students or those from underrepresented geographical areas. While scholarships awarded and administered from private donors have not been substantially reduced from pre-2003 levels, and there has not been an attack mounted on these programs by conservative groups under 42 U.S.C. Section 1981, the reader should note that it is possible that these programs might be subject to some restrictions in future years based upon possible challenges and the resulting court cases.

WHERE DOES THIS LEAVE ME? BRIEF CONSIDERATION OF FINANCIAL AID, SCHOLARSHIPS, LOANS, AND DEBT IN THE POST–*GRATZ* AND *GRUTTER* ERA

Given the reduction in funds available based upon race-conscious factors alone, the applicant might be pondering where all of the above information leaves him or her? One part of the successful journey to the college or university of your dreams is to get accepted at the school. However, the second step is equally important, namely, procuring the funds to pay for the costs of attending the school. As was pointed out above, schools are cutting back on race-conscious financial aid packages and programs, and the applicant would do well not to rely too heavily on the availability of these funds in the future. Thus, the remainder of this chapter will briefly highlight other considerations the student/applicant and parents must keep in mind to pay for the school they fought so hard to get into.

The first step to approaching the issue of college costs is to complete the FAFSA (Free Application for Federal Student Aid). This form is often considered the first battle for available money/financial aid, and the award is ultimately a "needs-based" decision, meaning aid is provided based upon the income of the student's parents and assets (unless the student is legally "independent" of the parents, in which case the aid determination is based upon the student's income and assets alone). When the FAFSA is completed, it delineates a whole array of personal financial details and other information, such as the age of the oldest parent, number of household members attending colleges, household size, et cetera. This form should be completed and submitted to the Department of Education as early as possible in the year. For example, the Department of Education's 2004–2005 Student Guide states that students can begin applying as early as January 1, 2004, and they have until June 30 to submit the FAFSA for the upcoming year. So, why should the form be submitted as early as possible? First, the earlier in the year the FAFSA is submitted, the more likely it is that funds will be available and you will receive the Student Aid Report back (delineating the size of your financial aid award from the government) with plenty of time to investigate other avenues of financing if necessary. The Student Guide implies this when it recommends to "apply as early as you can; you don't want to miss out on any source of aid!" Second, colleges have their own internal due dates for financial aid, many of which may be before the FAFSA official due date. If you wait until the last minute to submit the FAFSA, you might miss out on important local financial aid packages.

Delay in submitting the FAFSA is not excusable, as it can now be sent in a matter of minutes over the internet. The form has been made available online by the U.S. Department of Education at its Web site entitled "FAFSA on the Web—U.S. Department of Education Free Application for Federal Student Aid Web Site," at the following link: http://www.fafsa.ed.gov/index.htm. This site not only allows the student/parent to submit the FAFSA online, but also lists deadlines and other information regarding financial aid for the upcoming year. Additionally, the Web page allows students/parents to save their work, and therefore removes the need to complete the entire form in one sitting. The information is protected through the use of a "PIN" and password system that the applicant/student and parents request when visiting the Web site for the first time.

Some states, like Florida for example, use the FAFSA as the state grant application as well. In states such as Florida, the FAFSA not only determines an applicant's eligibility for federal programs such as the Pell Grant, but also state aid programs. In addition to the FAFSA, many colleges require their own set of forms to be completed as well. The most common one is the College Scholarship Service form, or CSS, which is required by close to 800 different colleges and universities. The procedure for the CSS is similar to the FAFSA in that you must obtain a registration form (available at www.collegeboard.com), which must be sent to each college for which you have applied. Of course, a fee of $14.95 is payable to the CSS to forward the data to the colleges in which you are interested. In addition to the CSS, many schools have other specialized forms of their own, or state specific forms, which you should obtain directly from the individual schools. The financial aid department at the school will be able to provide you with information regarding the forms required. Alternatively, a student's guidance office should be able to advise students about how to apply for grant programs within the home state.

After reviewing the submitted forms, the college financial aid department will estimate the student's financial resources and assets, and craft a financial aid package accordingly. This package will be a combination of federal student aid, that all U.S. citizens are entitled to depending on one's financial needs, and college aid. The federal aid comes in the form of grants (which need not be repaid), federal work-study, and federally subsidized loans (e.g., the federal Stafford Loan). College aid comes in the form of grants and tuition reduction. But these aids are often short of the needed amount, and students and parents will have to scramble for a loan to cover the remaining costs. For example, if tuition is $20,000 a year, and the college concludes that you can pay $5,000 a year, it may offer a package worth $15,000, leaving you to deal with the remaining $5,000. Based upon endowments and funding from the state, some colleges are better suited than others at putting together financial aid packages. The goal, of course, is to have a financial aid package that will cover all costs, without having to mortgage the house or charge up the credit cards each semester. If the college of your dreams cannot provide you a financial aid package that covers your needs, and you cannot obtain a scholarship to cover costs, you will be forced to either choose a less expensive college, or one that offers a more generous financial aid package, or turn to unsubsidized private loans or other means of payment (e.g., home equity loan).

The best student loans to obtain are the subsidized federal loans, like the Stafford Loan. This is because the government pays the interest on your loan (unlike unsubsidized loans) until six months after your graduation, and the principal of the loan is not payable until six months after graduation as well. The subsidized Stafford Loan is "need based." If you do not have documented need, then you can apply with a local bank for an unsubsidized Stafford Loan. The main difference is that in this case, the interest is immediately accrued upon disbursement of the loan. Other federal loans include the federal Perkins Loans and the PLUS Loan. Information on these and other loans is readily obtainable through the Department of Education's Student Guide, available at http://studentaid.ed.gov. This Web site is very comprehensive and available free of cost. It will provide an array of resources that should be of help on the issue of federal financial aid. The following Web site, http://www.fedmoney.org, is also a helpful resource.

If all else fails, there is the option of private loans. Actually, a surprising number of students finance their education each year through the use of private loans. The interest rates on these loans are often higher than the federal loans, which are normally capped at 8 percent. Many private loans have adjusted quarterly interest rates, meaning that the rates might be low when you start receiving the aid, but increase to a much higher percentage depending on economic indicators. These loans are based upon one's "good credit," and there is no guarantee or right to receive a private loan if the family credit is bad. Finally, most of these private loans will accept parents as cosigners, in order to qualify a student with no credit history. Your college financial aid office should be able to provide you with a list of private loan options. The following Web sites are also quite helpful to learn about privately funded programs: http://www.fastweb.monster.com; http://www.finaid.org; http://www.collegenet.com; http://www.collegeboard.com; http://www.collegescholarships.com. Additionally, here is a list of private loan programs that will cover a student's tuition and expenses, so long as the credit history is good. Each program has its own application, as well as terms and conditions, which can be obtained by calling the organization that oversees the program. Some leading loan programs are the Education Resource Institute (TERI) Loan (1-800-255-8374), Sallie Mae Signature Loan (1-800-695-3317), Sallie Mae Consolidation Loans (Smart Loans) (1-800-524-9100), The Knight College Resource Group Loans (1-800-225-6783), and Student Support Services "Plato Loan" (1-800-767-5626).

Finally, going to the most expensive private school in the country may not be the soundest financial decision, considering your future plans. For example, if you want to be a high school teacher after graduation, it will not greatly matter (for hiring and income purposes) whether you attended the most expensive Ivy League college in the country, or a solid state university within your state of residency. The difference in tuition between in-state resident tuition at a good state university and a private college can often be tens of thousands of dollars a year. Over the course of four years, this may amount to savings of $50,000 or more in tuition. Public institutions are often overlooked and underrated by many applicants, despite the fact that many of these institutions are ranked by experts as being at the top of the heap in terms of the teaching and scholarship of its faculty, and the overall educational value to the student. Furthermore, if you are interested in a leading public institution in another state, it would be wise to establish residency in that state, in order to receive the in-state tuition. The financial aid department of the school can give you tips on the documentation you will need to provide (e.g., local driver's license, local checking account, lease agreement, etc.) to establish residency in a new state. While it may be a minor nuisance to take such steps as exchanging your old state driver's license for a new one and opening a checking account, or even staying in the state during the summer break, it is definitely worth it over the course of four years in thousands of dollars of saved tuition.

CONCLUDING THOUGHTS ON FINANCIAL AID

Today, with the skyrocketing college costs, it is very hard to make it through college without going into debt. Also, paying back a loan over the course of ten to twenty years is not an attractive option. However, this fact should not dissuade the student from attending college. Once you have a college degree in hand, you will command a higher income level, and can begin to repay the loans in monthly installments. In an era of risky stock market investments and land booms and busts, higher education continues to be one of the most solid investments around, and will certainly pay back dividends for the remainder of the student's life, in terms of enriched life, accrued knowledge, and finer appreciation of one's surroundings, and also in terms of increased income potential and career opportunities.

9

Veterans and Affirmative Action

One does not normally associate affirmative action with veterans. Phrased another way, most people do not think of affirmative action as including within its list of intended beneficiaries veterans of the U.S. armed forces. Perhaps this is because race-conscious affirmative action plans/programs are the ones most often subject to litigation and controversy. Nonetheless, "the Servicemen's Readjustment Act of 1944, usually referred to as the G.I. Bill of Rights [or the Montgomery G.I. Bill], constituted what is possibly the most generous and largest social welfare program in U.S. history" and, arguably, "the most massive affirmative action program in U.S. history."[1] However, the concept of veterans and affirmative action makes more sense if one keeps in mind the basic idea behind affirmative action. On the broadest level, the practice of affirmative action is for institutions to take or provide "positive action to improve the participation of members of certain groups in various aspects of society, such as the workforce and higher education" when those groups have "historically been subject to systematic or institutional discrimination."[2] For veterans, such specialized treatment would be based on rewarding them for their service, or providing a "bump" or "bonus" to their applications because veterans have historically been underrepresented or excluded on college campuses. Thus, today, veteran applicants can expect some benefit both in the admissions process (as a favorable factor in the "diversity analysis" of applicants) and in the financial aid programs, as will be discussed more fully in this chapter.

Yet, sadly, not only do most people not make the association that one's veteran status might be of benefit in the admissions process, but also many veterans who qualify for the educational benefits never utilize them. Officials at the Department of Veterans Affairs estimate that nearly half of the veterans eligible for the Montgomery G.I. Bill benefits fail to utilize them (which lapse, and are no longer useful ten years after the effective date of honorable discharge from the armed forces).[3] This is the equivalent of not cashing in a $36,000 check, or turning down a "no strings attached" scholarship for $36,000, as the benefits currently provide a student approximately $1,034 a month for thirty-six months of full-time schooling. According to the Department of Veterans Affairs, the G.I. Bill pays out sixteen times what was invested by the soldier (i.e., the soldier receives approximately $16 for every $1 originally invested during the service period.[4] What makes the situation almost tragic is that this benefit has already been earned by the service member, "paid for... in advance with cold cash and sweat equity," and utilizing it does not incur any additional obligations on the part of the veteran, and the benefits do not need to be paid back (unlike traditional student loans).

THE MONTGOMERY G.I. BILL

While many people believe that the G.I. Bill is a military benefit for service members (the soldier, the sailor, or the airman) while in service, and that it is administered and handled by the Department of Defense, in reality, both these beliefs are incorrect. The G.I. Bill is actually a "veteran's benefit," and is managed by the Department of Veterans Affairs (VA), and not the Department of Defense. The G.I. Bill started out as a World War II legislation, entitled the Servicemen's Readjustment Act of 1944, and was passed in June 1944 and literally signed into law by President Franklin D. Roosevelt during the famous D-day invasion. The idea was to provide World War II veterans with an array of benefits upon their return from the war. The original provisions of the law dealt with not only education but also the following: readjustment of unemployment benefits (up to a year); guaranteed home, farm, or business loans; life insurance at special low premiums; dental/medical care; advantages/preferences for certain governmental jobs; and pensions and vocational rehabilitation. Many of these programs, like the educational component of the G.I. Bill (discussed below) and the VA-guaranteed home loan, still survive today.

The impact the G.I. Bill had (and still has) on education has been truly revolutionary and has prompted the renowned World War II historian Stephen Ambrose to remark that the "G.I. Bill was the best piece of legislation ever passed by the U.S. Congress and it made modern America."[5] Not only did the legislation ensure that millions of Americans would be able to attend college (a 1988 governmental report indicated that 40 percent of those who attended college under the G.I. Bill would not otherwise have had the opportunity[6]), but it also kept millions of soldiers from flooding the job market immediately after the war. Indeed, almost half (7.8 million soldiers out of 15.4 million) opted for school, rather than immediately returning to the workforce, including "2,230,000 in college, 3,480,000 in other schools, 1,400,000 in on-the-job training and 690,000 in farm training." For this initial group of soldiers, the educational opportunity allowed an economic elevation for themselves and their family that otherwise would not have been possible. For example, "approximately 450,000 became engineers, 240,000 accountants, 238,000 teachers, 67,000 doctors, and 22,000 dentists."[7]

The G.I. Bill still exists today and is thriving, but has been adjusted several times over the years to reflect changes in the economy and time. Today, in order to be eligible for the benefits, the rules require a combination of active duty and modest monthly contributions by the solider during the first year of service. In a nutshell, the G.I. Bill for active duty soldiers extends up to $36,104 worth of benefits, in exchange for at least three years of active duty, along with a reduction in pay of $100 a month for the first year ($1,200 in total contributions). For those soldiers who enlist for only two years of active duty, there is a plan that grants $29,376 worth of benefits, with the same $1,200 in contributions made by the soldier. The monthly payments of $100 a month are actually called "reductions in pay," and not "contributions," because even if one decides not to use the benefit, the payments cannot be refunded. Once the soldier has made the payments, the only way to get the money back is to take advantage of the educational benefits offered by the G.I. Bill by completing the required period of service (as briefly delineated below). In some instances, such as discharge for medical disabilities, hardship, or for the good of the service (e.g., reductions in force), a service member may still receive the educational benefits even if he/she does not complete the required period of service. Readers of this book who wish to have further information on these rules should check with the Veterans Department, or if still in the service, with the respective branch's Educational Service Office. Service members will need to verify that they have served the requisite period before pursuing a voluntary discharge.

Another hitch with the G.I. Bill is that the veteran needs to have decided at the beginning of service obligation if he/she wishes to participate in the G.I. Bill program. That is, upon enlistment, when the new recruit is signing a plethora of paperwork dealing with everything from setting up direct electronic payment and electing (or declining) special service member insurance coverage to arranging for the shipment of household goods, he/she will also need to make a decision (and complete the paperwork) regarding the G.I. Bill. I can recall from my active duty days that this paperwork takes hours to complete, and usually occurs toward the beginning of basic training. Typically, the soldier/sailor/ airman will have a presentation on each of the benefits and forms, so, presumably, the recruit will know what he/she is declining (if the person does elect not to enroll in the particular benefit). If the service member declines enrollment (which must be in writing), the person cannot change the decision at a later point. It is estimated that a small percentage of soldiers certainly do decline the benefits each year. According to one author, "Almost 95 percent of those who enlisted in the armed services in fiscal year 1996 enrolled in the program, and there has been a 75 percent enrollment of all enlistees since the inception of the program."[8] As highlighted at the beginning of this chapter, the bigger problem (than initially signing up for enrollment) is the approximately one-half of all veterans who never actually take advantage of the benefits after paying into the program both in terms of time and reductions in pay.

In addition to those who decline enrollment upon entry into active duty, two other groups of individuals are not eligible to enroll in the G.I. Bill, namely, ROTC Scholarship recipients and U.S. Service Academy graduates. First, if the service member was commissioned into one of the branches of the U.S. armed forces by way of an ROTC Scholarship and received more than $3,400 in any previous academic year, then the service member is declined enrollment. Second, if the service member was commissioned into one of the branches of the U.S. armed forces by way of a service academy (e.g., the U.S. Military Academy at West Point, New York; the U.S. Air Force Academy at Colorado Springs, Colorado; the U.S. Naval Academy at Annapolis, Maryland; or the U.S. Coast Guard Academy at New London, Connecticut), the service member may not enroll in the program. The logic of these exclusions is that the U.S. Government is already providing thousands of dollars for the education of this particular group of service members (via the ROTC Scholarship program or the operation of the service academies), so additional educational benefits are not warranted. It should be noted, however, that if a service member had paid for G.I. Bill benefits prior to entrance into one of the service academies, or into an ROTC program, then the service member retains the earned G.I. Bill benefits for later use. The accrued benefits do not lapse simply because the service member accepts an ROTC Scholarship or an appointment to a service academy.

Once enrolled, the service member can use the educational benefits while on active duty, or within ten years after honorable discharge or retirement from active duty. Service members who wish to use the G.I. Bill while on active duty can obviously do so only if they have first spent a minimum of two years on active duty. Most service members do not use the G.I. Bill benefits while on active duty, but only immediately after leaving the service. In fact, as all branches of the U.S. armed forces now offer 100 percent tuition reimbursement for active duty soldiers under another program called "Teaching Assistance," most service members "save" the G.I. Bill benefits for after discharge from active duty. The rates for payment and other rules regarding the "nuts and bolts" of the G.I. Bill will be discussed in a later section of this chapter. We will also discuss what expenses a service member may offset using the G.I. Bill, and what training or educational expenses do not qualify as legitimate expenses under the bill. However, before that, it is necessary to step back for a moment and discuss the admissions process as it relates to one's veteran status.

VETERAN STATUS IN THE APPLICATION PROCESS

An applicant's status as a veteran might be a diversifying factor that might strengthen the application, depending on the needs of the university/college at issue, and whether or not the institution has decided to include veterans of the armed forces in the list of potential beneficiaries of a given affirmative action program. In political science classes, for example, a veteran may often have unique experiences to share with the class. In one of my Comparative Law classes, a veteran brought great insight into one of the countries being discussed, by virtue of his assignment to that country for a long period of time. Because of this, some colleges might seek to recruit and enroll veterans.

Typically, the most frequently included group of veterans in affirmative action plans as beneficiaries are Vietnam-era veterans. The reason for this lies in the history of affirmative action. When first created and implemented in the modern era, (as described in Chapter 1), the chief purpose of affirmative action was to compensate members of certain groups who had traditionally been subject to institutional discrimination. Sadly, many Vietnam era veterans were discriminated against by some due to their service in Vietnam. As such, institutions decided to give these veterans special consideration in the admissions process, as a remedial compensation measure. While discrimination against Vietnam veterans is now largely a footnote of history, many institutions still retain this restrictive rule regarding giving veterans special consideration in the admissions process only if they served during the Vietnam era. Many colleges ask applicants to identify themselves as Vietnam-era veterans when completing the admissions application.

That is not to say, however, that one's veteran status will not serve as a diversifying factor of interest to admissions committees even if the person served during peacetime, or in another conflict. As stated above, a veteran can bring a unique perspective to classroom debates and discussions in many disciplines, such as history, sociology, and political science, to name a few. Additionally, on some campuses known historically for their liberal leanings (e.g., the University of California at Berkeley), being a veteran might mean being in a nontraditional student group, and some schools (depending on the college) might recruit veterans as a historically underrepresented group on campus. As was pointed out in Chapter 2, if a university or college wishes to employ affirmative action consistent with the Supreme Court's guidelines in *Gratz* and *Grutter*, it should engage in what Professor Killenbeck has characterized as "principled affirmative action," that is, "a diversity policy cannot and should not focus on a single group, either in theory or in practice." As discussed in Chapter 2, this means that not only are African Americans the proper beneficiaries of affirmative action plans, but also are women, the handicapped, socioeconomically disadvantaged, and, as discussed in the subject of this chapter, veterans.

THE MECHANICS OF THE ACTIVE DUTY MONTGOMERY G.I. BILL

If you are still reading this part of the chapter, it is likely that you plan on being eligible in the future for the educational benefits of the Montgomery G.I. Bill. Once you have paid into the system and put in the investment of active duty, the hard work is over. The benefits may be utilized for a wide variety of educational and/or vocational training programs like undergraduate/graduate studies at a college or university, studies leading to a certificate or diploma from a business or vocational school, foreign (overseas) courses of study that lead to a college degree, flight training,[9] apprenticeships or on-the-job training offered by a union or a company, and correspondence courses. In addition to the above courses of study, G.I. Bill benefits may be utilized to take a remedial or prerequisite course needed to enroll in your planned regular course of studies. Benefits may also include a special allowance/allotment for tutoring at a school, if the student is more than a part-time student at the school, if the student has a documented course deficiency (which tutoring is needed for correcting), and if the school has certified the qualifications of the tutor and the number of hours needed. If the student is eligible for tutoring, benefits may be paid out up to $100 a month (for tutoring), with no more than $1,200 in total payments/benefits being expended.

While the above list of studies is pretty broad, the VA does exclude certain programs from the benefits. These include bartending courses, courses on the radio, self-improvement or personality development courses, audited courses, courses that do not lead to a degree, or an educational, professional, or vocational purpose (i.e., courses that are solely recreational and not related to eventual employment), previously completed courses, courses from a school if you have a business interest in the school.[10] In this vein, the reader should note that if he or she is contemplating a course of study outside of a college or university, the VA must ultimately approve the program offered by the institution of interest. For those readers who are planning to use the G.I. Bill benefits at a mainstream college or university, there will be an official at the school who can be contacted for any questions regarding whether a particular program or course of study is approved under the bill. This official can help you complete the related paperwork and will certify your enrollment for VA benefits. This official can be contacted at one of the following departments/offices within the school: Financial Aid, Academic Advising, Registrar's Office, or Admissions. Most institutions will have the VA forms needed for enrollment (VA Form 22-1990, entitled "Application for VA Education Benefits") and will handle the process and send in the application on your behalf. You can also obtain this form by contacting the Veteran's Administration G.I. Bill toll-free number at 1-888-G.I.BILL-1 (1-888-442-4551) or from the Internet site http://www.gibill.va.gov.

PUTTING IT ALL TOGETHER: THE SUM OF ITS WORTH

To paraphrase a 1970s game show, the final 64,000-dollar question is, "What specific dollar amount/rate will a student receive if he/she has paid into the program, and has applied and been approved for study in a course of study covered under the program?" This question relates, after all, to the central point behind the G.I. Bill, namely, to make education and training more affordable to the nation's young men and women who have valiantly and courageously served the country. In order to fully answer this question, the reader must take into account several issues. First, the amount of benefits has changed several times in the past, as the basic law is altered and amended from time to time. For instance, in October 2004, Congress amended the law to provide more expansive coverage to certain service members who were called to active duty (i.e., activated reservists) after September 11, 2001. Therefore, when dealing with the G.I. Bill, the student should always check as to the current status of the benefits and changes to the program when he or she is ready to make use of the benefits. Again, most institutions have a person who is responsible for (and very knowledgeable on) all G.I. Bill–related issues and questions. Further, as discussed before, if your institution does not have such a person, you can always contact the Veterans Administration to find out the latest changes in the law.

The second issue to keep in mind regarding the exact amount of one's entitlement is that the total amount payable will depend on whether or not the service member served on active duty for three years or more, or for less than three years (but more than two). As you might imagine, the benefits are less (by about $7,000) if the three years on active duty is not completed. Finally, the reader would do well to remember that, according to the VA, one's "maximum entitlement" refers not to a total dollar amount, but rather to the number of months of benefits received. Under the active duty Montgomery G.I. Bill, a service member is entitled to thirty-six months of benefits coverage. As such, if one wished to ascertain the exact amount payable, he or she would take the maximum monthly payment for a full-time student (discussed below) and multiply the figure by thirty-six. This yields the total benefit package. For enlistments of three years or more, the total amount is $37,224, and for less than three years, but more than two years, it would be $30,240. For both types, benefits are payable until the total amount is exhausted, or ten years lapses, whichever occurs sooner.

According to the VA, and benefit rates effective October 2005, if the service member served on active duty for three years or more (and, of course, was enrolled in the program), the following monthly benefits are payable. First, for a full-time student (i.e., usually a student taking at least twelve credit hours in a term or semester), $1,034 is payable per month. Second, for a student who is enrolled at three-fourths of the load (i.e., taking approximately nine credit hours in a semester or term), $775 is payable per month. Third, if the student is enrolled as a half-time (part-time) student (i.e., approximately six credit hours during the semester or term), but enrolled for more than one-fourth of a full-time student's credit hour load, then $517 is payable to the student per month. Finally, if the student is enrolled for less than one-fourth (or less) of a full-time load (i.e., enrollment of approximately three credits in a term or semester), the amount payable is $258. The above rates represent the maximum amount payable. Thus, for example, if a student takes only one course at a local community college, and the course is $80 per month, then that student will only receive the $80 per month. However, regardless of how much (or little, depending on perspective) is paid to the veteran each month, payments may continue until the entire allotment is exhausted. Thus, based upon the above rates, a full-time student receiving $1,034 per month would exhaust the benefits in thirty-six months. However, a part-time student receiving benefits of $517 per month would be covered for seventy-two months.

Now, if the service member was on active duty for less than three years (and, of course, was enrolled in the program), the following benefits are payable per month. $840 for a full-time student, $630 for a student enrolled at three-fourths of the load, $420 for a half-time student enrolled for more than one-fourth of a full-time student's credit load, and $210 for one enrolled for less than one-fourth of full-time load. Again, as described above, these rates would be payable to the veteran until the entire entitlement/allotment of $30,240 is exhausted. Thus, while a full-time student would be paid more each month, the benefits would be exhausted twice as quick.

In addition to the above entitlement/allotment scheme, the reader should be aware that several types of education programs are payable at reduced rates/amounts, namely, correspondence courses (tuition reimbursable at only 55 percent of the approved amount for course), flight training (tuition reimbursable at only 60 percent of the approved amount for course), and on-the-job training (tuition reimbursable on a schedule depending on wages received). Finally, the basic rates delineated above for the calendar year—2005–2006 are likely to have fluctuated by the time the reader is perusing this chapter. This is because the monthly allotment/entitlement amounts are increased by the VA in relation or conjunction with increase in Consumer Price Index every October 1, the beginning of the federal government's fiscal year. These rates may also increase at other times at the discretion of Congress (e.g., as rates/benefits changed after 9/11).

OTHER G.I. BILL SPECIAL RULES AND CONSIDERATIONS

The above is a concise rendition of the benefits applicable to service members who elected to participate in the active duty Montgomery G.I. Bill program. However, it is imperative that the reader check with the VA as to the applicability of other possible benefits as well. There are a myriad of other possible programs that may be of assistance to veterans, such as Training and Rehabilitation for Veterans with Service Connected Disabilities (for vocational rehabilitation), Survivors' and Dependents' Educational Assistance, Educational Assistance Test Program, Educational Assistance Pilot Program, and the Post–Vietnam Era Veterans' Educational Assistance Program.

Additionally, there is also a reserve/national guard version of the active duty Montgomery G.I. Bill. The reserve G.I. Bill program is basically the same as the active duty G.I. Bill explained above, except that the payout/entitlement is not nearly as valuable as the active duty version. The total payout for the reserve/national guard program is $10,368. Briefly, to be eligible for this program, one must serve for a period of six years or more on reserves, or in the national guard. While the benefits are notably lower, service members are not required to make payments during the term of their service (as is the case with the active duty program).

Finally, there is a bevy of other rules/restrictions that are too voluminous to discuss in this book. For example, there are eligibility rules for service members who are forced to leave active duty before the eligibility period has been satisfied (for example, in the case of a medical disability or hardship). Additionally, all of the branches of the U.S. armed forces offer Tuition Assistance for classes taken while on active duty (usually, assistance up to $4,500 per year, per service member) with certain rules/restrictions that are individualized to each branch. Furthermore, the national guard and reserves offer another version of Tuition Assistance, with their own unique rules and restrictions. Finally, "add on" programs such as the College Fund may enable the service member to receive additional amounts in tuition reimbursement, and veterans may be eligible for workstudy programs with the VA after discharge from service. As such, it is imperative that the veteran check with the VA as to the full panoply of available benefits at the time of discharge.

10

Affirmative Action in the Coming Years

If you are an applicant reading this book to help gain insight into the college admissions process, the future of affirmative action may not be a relevant topic, or even all that important to you, especially if you have successfully secured a place in the entering class of a college or university after having read this book. However, if the reader is picking up this book for the first time several years from the original publication date, the relevancy of this chapter will become clearer. Additionally, the reader who is academically or intellectually interested in affirmative action as a social policy/program to rectify societal woes (namely, the vestiges of discrimination and racism) may also be interested in a prognosis of the future of such a program in the United States. As such, it is appropriate to conclude the main text of this book with several brief remarks regarding the permanency, or rather lack of permanency, of affirmative action in American society in the coming decades.

In 2003, then Supreme Court Justice Sandra Day O'Connor wrote for the majority of the Supreme Court in the *Grutter* decision, saying, in part, that

> it has been 25 years since Justice Powell first approved the use of race to further an interest in student body diversity in the context of public higher education. Since that time, the number of minority applicants with high grades and test scores has indeed increased. We expect that 25 years from now, the use of racial preferences will no longer be necessary to further the interest approved today.

This twenty-five-year deadline for the use of affirmative action has spurred a variety of comments and predictions from all over the ideological spectrum. Conservatives opposed to affirmative action have argued that this period was meant by the Court to be a strict deadline, meaning colleges and universities should begin phasing out affirmative action programs as the year 2028 draws closer and closer. As was pointed out earlier, this has prompted at least one commentator to wonder that if the Court truly expects affirmative action practices to be discontinued within the next twenty-five years, then the *Grutter* decision is largely a Pyrrhic victory.[1] With each passing year, the clock continues to wind down in terms of this Court-suggested deadline of 2028.

However, supporters of affirmative action are very quick to argue that O'Connor's comments regarding the state of affirmative action in twenty-five years were pure obiter dicta. The term "obiter dictum" is defined by *Black's Law Dictionary* as "words of an opinion entirely unnecessary for the decision of the case ... [and as] such are not binding as precedent."[2] Thus, for supporters of affirmative action, Justice O'Connor's statement is nothing more than her personal opinion and dictum on the subject. Additionally, as Justice O'Connor submitted her resignation from the Court in June 2005, she will not have a say in the enforcement or literal translation or meaning of this clause even in the immediate years to come. In light of these two opposing interpretations of the twenty-five-year timeline prediction by Justice O'Connor, it is no wonder that Justice Scalia lamented in his dissenting opinion that the *Grutter* decision seemed to him "perversely designed to prolong the controversy and the litigation." Critics of affirmative action are already remarking that universities and colleges should begin phasing out affirmative action, while supporters argue that affirmative action should not be phased out, but continued and strengthened. Practically, this means that litigation will continue until the Court again steps in to provide further guidance on the implementation of affirmative action, or a ruling declaring affirmative action to be null and void.

Thus, at present, there is no clear answer as to whether the Court, in twenty-five years, will view this statement by O'Connor as just her personal opinion, or as language central to the Court's decision (and therefore binding as law and precedent). However, one can predict with some confidence several issues. First, there will continue to be a vociferous debate regarding the propriety and efficacy of affirmative action in higher education. Second, one can also predict that with the robust public debate, there will be a variety of practices and preferences of universities and colleges, ranging from the prohibition and discontinuation of affirmative action, to the use of affirmative action not only in admissions, but also in financial aid programs and other areas. Third, as pressure on race-conscious affirmative action plans continues to mount, one can expect universities and colleges to refocus their programs to benefit individuals from disadvantaged socioeconomic classes, instead of allocating benefits based on skin color alone. Fourth, one can also predict with confidence that the lawsuits and litigation will continue until the U.S. Supreme Court reenters the debate—to definitively rule on the subject.

This is merely an academic issue at present, as it is extremely hard to accurately predict what conclusion the Court will come to by 2028 regarding affirmative action. This author can confidently predict only one thing regarding affirmative action in 2028, and that is, the Supreme Court will have to issue another decision as it did in 1979 with *Bakke*, and later, in 2003, with *Gratz* and *Grutter*. It is also very likely that the Court will be composed of nine different members than the Court's composition in 2003. One can only say with confidence that the Court will again issue landmark decisions on affirmative action in the future, and until that time, affirmative action is here to stay—as is the debate and controversy.

Additionally, any decision to further expand or reduce affirmative action must take into account the needs of the growing minority groups in the United States. W.E.B. DuBois once declared that "the problem of the Twentieth Century is the problem of the color line"; it looks like that prediction might as equally apply to the twenty-first century in America. However, it will not be just a white-black issue any longer. Rather, the issue of equality and an egalitarian society will extend to what one author has aptly described as a "mosaic of minorities" of a variety of races and ethnicities.[3] In fact, "today, Hispanics account for 13 percent of the U.S. population and now constitute the largest minority group in the United States."[4] The Hispanic population in the country doubled in the 1990s alone. Thus, by 2050, white Caucasian Americans will constitute a smaller segment of society, than the other minority groups combined. Thus, it is imperative that members of these rapidly expanding minority groups are offered adequate educational opportunities in the here and now. Otherwise, there will be a great divide in wealth and knowledge between the races in the future, and such a divide could spell calamity for the country in terms of global competition and standards of living. How the United States collectively responds to the growing minority groups will also impact the Court's rulings on affirmative action in the coming decades.

Appendix A

Four-Year Degree-Granting Colleges and Universities, The Use of Affirmative Action (or Lack Thereof), and Minority Enrollment Data

The following table is a comprehensive listing of all institutions in the United States authorized to award undergraduate college degrees (Bachelor of Arts, Bachelor of Science, Bachelor of Nursing, etc.) with enrollment of over 500 students. The table delineates the following: first, the use of race in admissions decisions and degree utilized (if at all); second, the use of alumni relations or legacies as factors in admissions and degree utilized (if at all); third, the use of other unique diversity factors (e.g., geographic origin) and degree utilized; and fourth, the total ethnic/minority representation on campus (or lack thereof), as well as the total student population. The data/information delineated below is the same as that provided/reported by the institutions. Thus, for example, if a university utilizes race in the admissions process, but that fact is not indicated in the table, it is because the school did not previously report its use/reliance on race in its public disclosures.

Additionally, there are a plethora of other factors (beyond those reported in the table) that admissions departments obviously view as very important factors (e.g., grades, standardized test scores, personal essays, and class rank, among other things) or important factors (e.g., work experience, interviews, volunteer experience, among others). For a definitive listing of the factors that are most important to a particular college, applicants should check with that particular college, or consult a traditional college reference book such as the Princeton Review's *Complete Book of Colleges* or Peterson's *Guide to Colleges and Universities*. The listing below delineates only those factors typically utilized in the practice/use of affirmative action in admissions. Finally, the symbol "NR" connotes that the information was "not reported" by the institution, meaning that the institution either did not provide information on the topic or likely does not consider or utilize the factor in candidate evaluations and admissions decisions.

College	Use of Race in Admission Decisions and Degree Utilized (if at all)	Use of Alumni Relations or Legacies as Factor and Degree Utilized	Use of Other Factors (e.g., geographic origin or religious affiliation) and Degree Utilized	Reported Ethnic/Minority Representation	Total Student Population
Abilene Christian University (Abilene, TX)	Minority status considered as factor	Alumni relations considered as factor	Religious affiliation and/or commitment is an important factor	African American 7%; Hispanic 7%; Native American 1%; Asian 1%	4,166
Academy of Art College (San Francisco, CA)	NR	NR	NR	African American 4%; Hispanic 8%; Asian 17%	5,324
Adams State College (Alamosa, CO)	NR	NR	Geographic origin/residence considered	African American 5%; Hispanic 28%; Native American 2%; Asian 1%	2,009
Adelphi University (Garden City, NY)	NR	Alumni relations considered as factor	NR	African American 12%; Hispanic 9%; Asian 1%	4,413
Adrian College (Adrian, MI)	NR	NR	NR	African American 6%; Hispanic 1%; Asian 1%	1,010
Agnes Scott College (Atlanta, GA)	Minority status considered as factor	Alumni relations considered as a factor	Geographic origin/residence considered	African American 22%; Hispanic 4%; Asian 6%	857
Alabama A&M University (Normal, AL)	Minority status is an important factor	Alumni relations is a very important factor	Geographic origin/residence is a very important factor	African American 69%; Caucasian 3%	4,744

Alabama State University (Montgomery, AL)	NR	NR	NR	African American 95%; Caucasian 4%	5,125
Albany College of Pharmacy (Albany, NY)	Minority status considered as factor	Alumni relations considered as a factor	NR	African American 2%; Hispanic 1%; Asian 7%	632
Albany State University (Albany, GA)	NR	NR	NR	African American 84%; Caucasian 4%	2,936
Albertson College of Idaho (Caldwell, ID)	NR	Alumni relations considered as a factor	Geographic origin/residence is considered an important factor	Asian 3%; Hispanic 3%; Native American 1%	820
Albertus Magnus College (New Haven, CT)	NR	Alumni relations considered as a factor	NR	African American 21%; Hispanic 8%; Asian 1%	1,788
Albion College (Albion, MI)	Minority status is an important factor	Alumni relations is a very important factor	Geographic origin/residence is considered an important factor	African American 2%; Hispanic 1%; Asian 2%	1,708
Albright College (Reading, PA)	NR	Alumni relations considered as a factor	NR	African American 9%; Hispanic 4%; Asian 2%	2,124
Alcorn State University (Alcorn State, MS)	Minority status considered as factor	NR	NR	African American 91%; Caucasian 7%	2,832

(continued)

College	Use of Race in Admission Decisions and Degree Utilized (if at all)	Use of Alumni Relations or Legacies as Factor and Degree Utilized	Use of Other Factors (e.g., geographic origin or religious affiliation) and Degree Utilized	Reported Ethnic/Minority Representation	Total Student Population
Alderson-Broaddus College (Philippi, WV)	Minority status considered as factor	Alumni relations considered as a factor	Religious affiliation and/or commitment is considered	African American 3%; Hispanic 1%; Asian 1%	671
Alfred University (Alfred, NY)	Minority status considered as factor	NR	NR	African American 5%; Hispanic 4%; Native American 1%; Asian 2%	1,969
Alice Lloyd College (Pippa Passes, KY)	NR	Alumni relations is considered as an important factor	Geographic origin/residence is considered a very important factor	African American 1%; Hispanic 1%	585
Allegheny College (Meadville, PA)	Minority status considered as factor	Alumni relations considered as a factor	Geographic origin/residence considered	African American 1%; Hispanic 1%; Asian 3%	1,929
Alma College (Alma, MI)	NR	Alumni relations considered as a factor	NR	African American 2%; Hispanic 1%; Asian 1%	1,214
Alvernia College (Reading, PA)	Minority status considered as factor	Alumni relations is considered as an important factor	Geographic origin/residence considered; Religious affiliation and/or commitment is considered	African American 12%; Hispanic 3%; Asian 1%	1,866

Alverno College (Milwaukee, WI)	NR	NR	NR	African American 23%; Hispanic 11%; Asian 4%	1,923
American Intercontinental University (Hoffman Estates, IL)	Minority status is an important factor	Alumni relations is considered as a very important factor	NR	African American 27%; Hispanic 2%; Asian 1%	981
American International College (Springfield, MA)	NR	Alumni relations is considered as an important factor	NR	African American 26%; Hispanic 8%; Asian 3%	1,227
American University (Washington, DC)	Minority status considered as factor	Alumni relations considered as a factor	Geographic origin/residence considered	African American 6%; Hispanic 5%; Asian 5%	5,731
American University of Puerto Rico (Bayamon, PR)	NR	NR	NR	Hispanic 100%	4,060
Amherst College (Amherst, MA)	Minority status considered as factor	Alumni relations considered as an important factor	Geographic origin/residence considered	NR	431
Anderson College (Anderson, SC)	NR	Alumni relations considered as a factor	NR	African American 10%; Hispanic 1%	1,441
Anderson University (Anderson, IN)	Minority status considered as factor	Alumni relations considered as a factor	Religious affiliation and/or commitment is an important factor	African American 4%; Hispanic 1%	1,965
Andrews University (Berrien Sprin, MI)	NR	NR	NR	African American 21%; Hispanic 8%; Asian 10%	1,746

(continued)

137

College	Use of Race in Admission Decisions and Degree Utilized (if at all)	Use of Alumni Relations or Legacies as Factor and Degree Utilized	Use of Other Factors (e.g., geographic origin or religious affiliation) and Degree Utilized	Reported Ethnic/Minority Representation	Total Student Population
Angelo State University (San Angelo, TX)	NR	NR	NR	African American 6%; Hispanic 23%; Asian 1%	5,559
Anna Maria College (Paxton, MA)	NR	Alumni relations considered as a factor	NR	African American 3%; Hispanic 3%; Asian 1%	680
Antioch College (Yellow Springs, OH)	Minority status considered as factor	Alumni relations considered as a factor	NR	African American 3%; Hispanic 2%; Native American 1%; Asian 1%	488
Appalachian State University (Boone, NC)	NR	NR	Geographic origin/residence considered	African American 3%; Hispanic 1%; Asian 1%	12,238
Aquinas College (MI) (Grand Rapids, MI)	NR	NR	NR	African American 4%; Hispanic 4%; Asian 1%	1,730
Arcadia University (Glenside, PA)	NR	Alumni relations considered as a factor	NR	African American 9%; Hispanic 2%; Asian 3%	1,924
Arizona State University (Tempe, AZ)	NR	NR	Geographic origin/residence is considered an important factor	African American 4%; Hispanic 12%; Asian 5%	38,117

Arizona State University East (Tempe, AZ)	NR	NR	Geographic origin/residence is considered an important factor	African American 2%; Hispanic 11%; Asian 3%	2,372
Arizona State University West (Phoenix, AZ)	NR	NR	NR	African American 5%; Hispanic 18%; Native American 2%; Asian 4%	4,973
Arkansas State University (Jonesboro, AR)	NR	NR	NR	African American 15%; Hispanic 1%; Asian 1%	9,000
Arkansas Tech University (Russellville, AR)	NR	NR	NR	African American 4%; Hispanic 2%; Native American 2%; Asian 1%	5,967
Armstrong Atlantic State University (Savannah, GA)	NR	NR	NR	African American 22%; Hispanic 3%; Asian 3%	5,281
Art Center College of Design (Pasadena, CA)	Minority status considered as factor	Alumni relations considered as a factor	NR	African American 2%; Hispanic 11%; Asian 35%	1,394
Art Institute of Atlanta (Atlanta, GA)	NR	NR	NR	African American 32%; Hispanic 4%; Asian 3%	2,635
The Art Institute of Boston at Lesley University (Boston, MA)	Minority status considered as factor	Alumni relations considered as a factor	Geographic origin/residence considered	African American 3%; Hispanic 3%; Native American 1%; Asian 4%	511

(continued)

139

College	Use of Race in Admission Decisions and Degree Utilized (if at all)	Use of Alumni Relations or Legacies as Factor and Degree Utilized	Use of Other Factors (e.g., geographic origin or religious affiliation) and Degree Utilized	Reported Ethnic/Minority Representation	Total Student Population
Art Institute of Colorado (Denver, CO)	NR	NR	NR	African American 1%; Hispanic 6%; Native American 1%; Asian 2%	2,320
The Art Institute of Dallas (Dallas, TX)	NR	NR	NR	African American 5%; Hispanic 7%; Asian 3%	1,463
The Art Institute of Pittsburgh (Pittsburgh, PA)	NR	NR	NR	African American 2%	4,864
The Art Institutes International Minnesota (Minneapolis, MN)	NR	NR	NR	African American 2%; Hispanic 1%; Native American 1%; Asian 3%	1,391
Asbury College (Wilmore, KY)	Minority status is a very important factor	Alumni relations considered as a factor	Geographic origin/residence considered; Character, Personal Qualities & Religious Affiliation all important factors	African American 1%; Hispanic 1%; Asian 1%	1,167
Ashland University (Ashland, OH)	NR	Alumni relations considered as a factor	Geographic origin/residence, Character, Personal Qualities & Religious Affiliation all considered	African American 8%; Hispanic 2%	2,789

Assumption College (Worcester, MA)	Minority status considered as factor	Alumni relations considered as a factor	Geographic origin/residence, Character, Personal Qualities & Religious Affiliation all considered	African American 1%; Hispanic 2%; Asian 1%	2,123
Auburn University (Auburn, AL)	Minority status considered as factor	Alumni relations considered as a factor	Geographic origin/residence is considered an important factor	African American 7%; Hispanic 1%; Asian 1%	19,145
Auburn University Montgomery (Montgomery, AL)	NR	Alumni relations considered as a factor	Geographic origin/residence considered	African American 34%; Hispanic 1%; Asian 2%	4,214
Ausburg College (Minneapolis, MN)	NR	Alumni relations considered as a factor	Character and Personal Qualities considered as important factor	African American 5%; Hispanic 2%; Asian 3%	2,720
Augusta State University (Augusta, GA)	NR	NR	NR	African American 28%; Hispanic 3%; Asian 3%	5,408
Augustana College (IL) (Rock Island, IL)	Minority status considered as factor	Alumni relations considered as a factor	Character and Personal Qualities considered as important factor	African American 2%; Hispanic 3%; Asian 2%	2,289
Augustana College (SD) (Sioux Falls, SD)	NR	NR	Character and Personal Qualities considered	African American 1%; Native American 1%; Asian 1%	1,727

(*continued*)

College	Use of Race in Admission Decisions and Degree Utilized (if at all)	Use of Alumni Relations or Legacies as Factor and Degree Utilized	Use of Other Factors (e.g., geographic origin or religious affiliation) and Degree Utilized	Reported Ethnic/Minority Representation	Total Student Population
Aurora University (Aurora, IL)	NR	NR	Character and Personal Qualities considered	African American 14%; Hispanic 13%; Asian 2%	1,699
Austin College (Sherman, TX)	Minority status considered as factor	Alumni relations considered as a factor	Geographic origin/residence, Character, Personal Qualities & Religious Affiliation all considered	African American 4%; Hispanic 8%; Native American 1%; Asian 10%	1,281
Austin Peay State University (Clarksville, TN)	NR	NR	NR	African American 19%; Hispanic 5%; Native American 1%; Asian 2%	7,964
Averett University (Danville, VA)	NR	Alumni relations considered as a factor	Character and Personal Qualities considered	African American 32%; Hispanic 2%; Native American 1%; Asian 1%	2,056
Avila University (Kansas City, MO)	NR	NR	Character and Personal Qualities considered	African American 18%; Hispanic 4%; Native American 1%; Asian 1%	1,096
Azusa Pacific University (Azusa, CA)	Minority status considered as factor	Alumni relations considered as a factor	Geographic origin/residence, Character and Personal Qualities considered as important factors	African American 3%; Hispanic 12%; Asian 5%	4,441

Babson College (Babson Park, MA)	NR	NR	Geographic origin/residence, Character & Personal Qualities considered	African American 3%; Hispanic 5%; Asian 8%	1,697
Baker College of Auburn Hills (Auburn Hills, MI)	NR	NR	NR	African American 20%; Hispanic 4%; Native American 1%; Asian 4%	2,596
Baker College of Jackson (Jackson, MI)	NR	NR	NR	African American 7%; Hispanic 3%	1,392
Baker College of Muskegon (Muskegon, MI)	NR	NR	NR	African American 14%; Hispanic 4%; Native American 1%; Asian 1%	3,442
Baker College of Owosso (Owosso, MI)	NR	NR	NR	African American 2%; Hispanic 2%; Native American 1%	2,361
Baker College of Port Huron (Port Huron, MI)	NR	NR	NR	African American 4%; Hispanic 2%; Native American 1%	1,363
Baker University (Baldwin City, KS)	NR	NR	NR	African American 5%; Hispanic 2%; Native American 1%; Asian 1%	968
Baldwin-Wallace College (Berea, OH)	Minority status considered as factor	Alumni relations considered as a factor	Geographic origin/residence, Character, Personal Qualities & Religious Affiliation all considered	African American 5%; Hispanic 1%; Asian 2%	3,674

(continued)

College	Use of Race in Admission Decisions and Degree Utilized (if at all)	Use of Alumni Relations or Legacies as Factor and Degree Utilized	Use of Other Factors (e.g., geographic origin or religious affiliation) and Degree Utilized	Reported Ethnic/Minority Representation	Total Student Population
Ball State University (Muncie, IN)	NR	Alumni relations considered as a factor	Character and Personal Qualities considered	African American 7%; Hispanic 1%; Asian 1%	17,335
Baptist Bible College and Seminary of Pennsylvania (Clarks Summit, PA)	NR	NR	Character, Personal Qualities & Religious Affiliation very important factors	Hispanic 1%; Asian 1%	709
Baptist College of Florida (Graceville, FL)	NR	Alumni relations considered as important factor	Character, Personal Qualities & Religious Affiliation very important factors	African American 7%; Hispanic 3%; Native American 1%; Asian 1%	572
Barat College of Depaul University (Lake Forest, IL)	NR	Alumni relations considered as a factor	Character and Personal Qualities considered	African American 8%; Hispanic 7%; Asian 3%	708
Barber Scotia College (Concord, NC)	NR	Alumni relations considered as a factor	Geographic origin/ residence, Character and Personal Qualities considered	African American 98%; Caucasian 1%	475

Bard College (Annandale-on-Hudson, NY)	Minority status considered as factor	Alumni relations considered as a factor	Character and Personal Qualities are very important; Geographic origin/residence & Religious Affiliation considered	African American 3%; Hispanic 4%; Asian 5%	1,458
Barnard College (New York, NY)	Minority status considered as factor	Alumni relations considered as a factor	Geographic origin/residence, Character and Personal Qualities considered	African American 5%; Hispanic 7%; Native American 1%; Asian 17%	2,287
Barry University (Miami Shores, FL)	NR	NR	Character and Personal Qualities considered as important factor	NR	5,652
Barton College (Wilson, NC)	NR	NR	Character and Personal Qualities considered	African American 22%; Hispanic 2%; Asian 1%	1,198
Bates College (Lewiston, ME)	Minority status considered as factor	Alumni relations considered as a factor	Character and Personal Qualities considered as very important factors; Geographic origin/residence considered	African American 2%; Hispanic 3%; Asian 4%	1,743
Bay Path College (Longmeadow, MA)	NR	NR	Character and Personal Qualities considered	African American 11%; Hispanic 7%; Asian 1%	1,347

(continued)

145

College	Use of Race in Admission Decisions and Degree Utilized (if at all)	Use of Alumni Relations or Legacies as Factor and Degree Utilized	Use of Other Factors (e.g., geographic origin or religious affiliation) and Degree Utilized	Reported Ethnic/Minority Representation	Total Student Population
Baylor University (Waco, TX)	NR	Alumni relations considered as a factor	Geographic origin/residence, Character, Personal Qualities & Religious Affiliation all considered	African American 7%; Hispanic 8%; Native American 1%; Asian 6%	11,521
Becker College (Worcester, MA)	NR	Alumni relations considered as a factor	Character and Personal Qualities considered	African American 5%; Hispanic 3%; Asian 2%	1,501
Belhaven College (Jackson, MS)	NR	Alumni relations considered as a factor	Character and Personal Qualities considered	African American 28%; Hispanic 1%; Asian 1%	1,428
Bellevue University (Bellevue, NE)	NR	NR	NR	African American 10%; Hispanic 7%; Native American 1%; Asian 1%	3,972
Belmont Abbey College (Belmont, NC)	NR	Alumni relations considered as a factor	Character and Personal Qualities considered as very important factors	African American 12%; Hispanic 5%; Asian 1%	791
Belmont University (Nashville, TN)	Minority status considered as factor	Alumni relations considered as a factor	Religious affiliation and/or commitment is an important factor	African American 4%; Hispanic 2%; Asian 1%	3,269

Beloit College (Beloit, WI)	NR	Alumni relations considered as a factor	Character and Personal Qualities considered	African American 3%; Hispanic 3%; Asian 1%	1,301
Bemidji State University (Bemidji, MN)	NR	NR	NR	Native American 3%	4,168
Benedict College (Columbia, SC)	Minority status considered as factor	Alumni relations considered as a factor	Geographic origin/residence, Character, Personal Qualities & Religious Affiliation all considered	African American 53%	2,128
Benedictine College (Atchison, KS)	Minority status considered as factor	Alumni relations considered as a factor	Character & Personal Qualities considered	African American 4%; Hispanic 8%; Native American 1%; Asian 15%	978
Benedictine University (Lisle, IL)	NR	NR	NR	African American 10%; Hispanic 8%; Asian 13%	2,050
Bennington College (Bennington, VT)	NR	NR	NR	African American 1%; Hispanic 3%; Asian 2%	621
Bentley College (Waltham, MA)	Minority status considered as factor	Alumni relations considered as a factor	Character and Personal Qualities are very important; Geographic origin/residence & Religious Affiliation considered	African American 4%; Hispanic 4%; Asian 1%	4,250

(*continued*)

College	Use of Race in Admission Decisions and Degree Utilized (if at all)	Use of Alumni Relations or Legacies as Factor and Degree Utilized	Use of Other Factors (e.g., geographic origin or religious affiliation) and Degree Utilized	Reported Ethnic/Minority Representation	Total Student Population
Berea College (Berea, KY)	Minority status is considered as a very important factor	NR	Geographic origin/residence are very important; Character and Personal Qualities are important	African American 19%; Hispanic 2%; Native American 1%; Asian 1%	1,514
Berkeley College (West Paterson, NJ)	NR	NR	Character & Personal Qualities considered	African American 17%; Hispanic 33%; Asian 3%	2,125
Berkeley College—New York City Campus (New York, NY)	NR	NR	Character & Personal Qualities considered	African American 30%; Hispanic 31%; Asian 6%	1,652
Berkeley College—Westchester Campus (White Plains, NY)	NR	NR	Character & Personal Qualities considered	African American 25%; Hispanic 23%; Asian 3%	664
Berklee College of Music (Boston, MA)	Minority status considered as factor	Alumni relations considered as a factor	Character and Personal Qualities are important; Geographic origin/residence considered	African American 4%; Hispanic 4%; Asian 3%	3,799

Berry College (Mount Berry, GA)	NR	Alumni relations considered as a factor	Character & Personal Qualities considered	African American 2%; Hispanic 1%; Asian 1%	1,933
Bethany College (KS) (Lindsborg, KS)	NR	NR	NR	African American 8%; Hispanic 4%; Native American 1%; Asian 1%	569
Bethany College (WV) (Bethany, WV)	NR	Alumni relations considered as a factor	NR	African American 2%; Hispanic 1%; Asian 1%	887
Bethel College (IN) (Mishawake, IN)	Minority status considered as factor	Alumni relations considered as a factor	Character and Personal Qualities are very important; Religious affiliation and/or commitment is considered	African American 8%; Hispanic 2%; Native American 1%; Asian 1%	1,624
Bethel College (KS) (North Newton, KS)	NR	Alumni relations considered as a factor	Character & Personal Qualities considered	African American 6%; Hispanic 5%; Native American 1%; Asian 2%	509
Bethel College (MN) (Saint Paul, MN)	Minority status considered as factor	Alumni relations considered as a factor	Character and Personal Qualities are very important	African American 2%; Hispanic 1%; Asian 3%	3,019
Bethel College (TN) (McKenzie, TN)	NR	NR	NR	NR	924
Bethune-Cookman College (Daytona Beach, FL)	NR	Alumni relations considered as a factor	Character and Personal Qualities are very important	African American 90%; Hispanic 1%	2,895

(*continued*)

College	Use of Race in Admission Decisions and Degree Utilized (if at all)	Use of Alumni Relations or Legacies as Factor and Degree Utilized	Use of Other Factors (e.g., geographic origin or religious affiliation) and Degree Utilized	Reported Ethnic/Minority Representation	Total Student Population
Beulah Heights Bible College (Atlanta, GA)	NR	NR	Character and Personal Qualities are very important	African American 24%; Hispanic 1%;	557
Biola University (La Mirada, CA)	Minority status considered as factor	NR	Religious affiliation and/or commitment is a very important factor; Character & Personal Qualities considered	African American 4%; Hispanic 11%; Asian 8%	3,548
Birmingham—Southern College (Birmingham, AL)	NR	NR	Character and Personal Qualities are important; Geographic origin/residence considered	African American 6%; Hispanic 1%; Asian 2%	1,316
Bismarck State College (Bismarck, ND)	NR	NR	NR	Native American 1%	2,594
Black Hills State University (Spearfish, SD)	NR	NR	Character & Personal Qualities considered	African American 1%; Hispanic 2%; Native American 3%; Asian 1%	3,163

Bloomfield College (Bloomfield, NJ)	NR	Alumni relations considered as a factor	Character & Personal Qualities considered	African American 52%; Hispanic 18%; Asian 4%	2,038
Bloomsburg University of Pennsylvania (Bloomsburg, PA)	NR	Alumni relations considered as a factor	Geographic origin/residence, Character & Personal Qualities all considered	African American 5%; Hispanic 2%; Asian 1%	7,325
Bluefield College (Bluefield, VA)	NR	Alumni relations considered as a factor	Character and Personal Qualities are important	African American 17%; Hispanic 1%; Asian 1%	790
Bluefield State College (Bluefield, WV)	NR	NR	NR	African American 11%; Hispanic 1%	3,092
Bluffton College (Bluffton, OH)	NR	NR	NR	African American 2%; Hispanic 1%; Asian 1%	866
Bob Jones University (Greenville, SC)	NR	NR	Character, Personal Qualities & Religious Affiliation are very important factors	NR	3,589
Boise State University (Boise, ID)	NR	NR	NR	African American 1%; Hispanic 5%; Native American 3%; Asian 2%	14,840
Boston Architectural Center (Boston, MA)	NR	NR	NR	African American 2%; Hispanic 4%; Asian 3%	744

(continued)

College	Use of Race in Admission Decisions and Degree Utilized (if at all)	Use of Alumni Relations or Legacies as Factor and Degree Utilized	Use of Other Factors (e.g., geographic origin or religious affiliation) and Degree Utilized	Reported Ethnic/Minority Representation	Total Student Population
Boston College (Chestnut Hill, MA)	Minority status considered as factor	Alumni relations is considered as an important factor	Character, Personal Qualities & Religious Affiliation are important factors	African American 6%; Hispanic 7%; Asian 9%	9,059
Boston University (Boston, MA)	NR	Alumni relations considered as a factor	Character & Personal Qualities considered	African American 2%; Hispanic 5%; Asian 13%	15,953
Bowdoin College (Brunswick, ME)	Minority status is considered as important factor	Alumni relations is considered as an important factor	Character and Personal Qualities are very important; Geographic origin/residence considered	African American 5%; Hispanic 6%; Native American 1%; Asian 11%	1,665
Bowie State University (Bowie, MD)	NR	NR	NR	African American 74%; Hispanic 1%; Asian 1%	3,953
Bowling Green State University (Bowling Green, OH)	Minority status considered as factor	Alumni relations considered as a factor	Character & Personal Qualities considered	African American 6%; Hispanic 3%; Asian 1%	15,628
Bradford College (Haverhill, MA)	Minority status is considered as a very important factor	Alumni relations is considered a very important factor	Geographic origin/residence, Character, Personal Qualities & Religious Affiliation all considered	African American 1%; Hispanic 1%; Native American 1%	577

Bradley University (Peoria, IL)	Minority status considered as a factor	Alumni relations considered as a factor	Character & Personal Qualities considered	African American 6%; Hispanic 2%; Asian 3%	5,111
Brandeis University (Waltham, MA)	Minority status considered as a factor	Alumni relations considered as a factor	Character and Personal Qualities are important	African American 3%; Hispanic 3%; Asian 8%	3,158
Brenau University Women's College (Gainesville, GA)	NR	NR	Character and Personal Qualities are important	African American 9%; Hispanic 2%; Asian 2%	664
Brescia University (Owensboro, KY)	NR	NR	Character and Personal Qualities are important	African American 4%; Hispanic 1%	630
Brevard College (Brevard, NC)	NR	Alumni relations considered as a factor	Character and Personal Qualities are important; Religious Affiliation considered	African American 6%; Hispanic 3%; Asian 1%	571
Brewton-Parker College (Mt. Vernon, GA)	NR	NR	NR	African American 20%; Hispanic 2%	1,124
Briar Cliff University (Sioux City, IA)	NR	Alumni relations considered as a factor	Character & Personal Qualities considered	African American 2%; Hispanic 4%; Asian 1%	1,023
Bridgewater College (Bridgewater, VA)	Minority status considered as factor	Alumni relations considered as a factor	Geographic origin/ residence, Character, Personal Qualities & Religious Affiliation all considered	African American 8%; Hispanic 1%; Asian 1%	1,513

(continued)

College	Use of Race in Admission Decisions and Degree Utilized (if at all)	Use of Alumni Relations or Legacies as Factor and Degree Utilized	Use of Other Factors (e.g., geographic origin or religious affiliation) and Degree Utilized	Reported Ethnic/Minority Representation	Total Student Population
Bridgewater State College (Bridgewater, MA)	Minority status considered as factor	Alumni relations considered as a factor	Character & Personal Qualities considered	African American 4%; Hispanic 2%; Asian 1%	7,420
Brigham Young University (HI) (Laie, HI)	NR	Alumni relations considered as a factor	Geographic origin/residence, Character, Personal Qualities & Religious Affiliation all very important	Hispanic 2%; Native American 1%; Asian 22%	2,341
Brigham Young University (ID) (Rexburg, ID)	NR	NR	NR	Hispanic 3%; Native American 1%; Asian 2%	11,555
Brigham Young University (Provo, UT)	Minority status is considered as important factor	NR	Character, Personal Qualities & Religious Affiliation all very important	Hispanic 3%; Native American 1%; Asian 3%	30,847
Broome Community College (Binghamton, NY)	NR	NR	NR	African American 1%; Hispanic 1%; Asian 1%	4,519
Brown University (Providence, RI)	Minority status considered as factor	Alumni relations considered as a factor	Geographic origin/residence considered	African American 6%; Hispanic 6%; Native American 1%; Asian 13%	5,806

Bryant College (Smithfield, RI)	Minority status considered as factor	Alumni relations is considered as an important factor	Character and Personal Qualities are very important; Geographic origin/ residence considered	African American 3%; Hispanic 3%; Asian 3%	3,030
Bryn Mawr College (Bryn Mawr, PA)	NR	NR	NR	African American 5%; Hispanic 3%; Asian 11%	1,313
Bucknell University (Lewisburg, PA)	Minority status is considered as important factor	Alumni relations considered as a factor	Character and Personal Qualities are very important; Geographic origin/ residence & Religious Affiliation considered	African American 3%; Hispanic 1%; Asian 3%	3,419
Buena Vista University (Strom Lake, IA)	NR	Alumni relations considered as a factor	Character & Personal Qualities considered	African American 2%; Hispanic 2%; Asian 2%	1,242
Butler University (Indianpolis, IN)	Minority status considered as factor	Alumni relations considered as a factor	Character & Personal Qualities considered	African American 4%; Hispanic 2%; Asian 2%	3,706
Cabrini College (Radnor, PA)	NR	NR	Character and Personal Qualities are important; Geographic origin/ residence considered	African American 7%; Hispanic 2%; Asian 2%	1,610

(*continued*)

College	Use of Race in Admission Decisions and Degree Utilized (if at all)	Use of Alumni Relations or Legacies as Factor and Degree Utilized	Use of Other Factors (e.g., geographic origin or religious affiliation) and Degree Utilized	Reported Ethnic/Minority Representation	Total Student Population
Caldwell College (Caldwell, NJ)	NR	Alumni relations considered as a factor	Character & Personal Qualities considered	African American 18%; Hispanic 10%; Asian 2%	1,687
California Baptist University (Riverside, CA)	NR	NR	Character and Personal Qualities are important	African American 7%; Hispanic 16%; Native American 1%; Asian 3%	2,222
California College of the Arts (San Francisco, CA)	NR	NR	Character & Personal Qualities considered	African American 2%; Hispanic 7%; Native American 1%; Asian 12%	1,284
California Institute of the Arts (Valencia, CA)	NR	NR	Character & Personal Qualities considered	African American 7%; Hispanic 11%; Native American 1%; Asian 11%	812
California Institute of Technology (Pasadena, CA)	Minority status considered as factor	NR	Character and Personal Qualities are very important	African American 1%; Hispanic 7%; Native American 1%; Asian 31%	896
California Lutheran University (Thousand Oaks, CA)	Minority status considered as factor	Alumni relations considered as a factor	Character and Personal Qualities are important; Geographic origin/ residence considered	African American 2%; Hispanic 14%; Native American 1%; Asian 5%	1,888

California Maritime Academy of California State University (Vallejo, CA)	NR	NR	Character & Personal Qualities and Geographic origin/residence considered	African American 4%; Hispanic 7%; Native American 1%; Asian 11%	606
California Polytechnic State University—San Luis Obispo (San Luis Obispo, CA)	NR	NR	NR	African American 1%; Hispanic 10%; Native American 1%; Asian 12%	16,565
California State Polytechnic University—Pomona (Pomona, CA)	NR	NR	NR	African American 4%; Hispanic 25%; Asian 33%	16,484
California State University Bakersfield (Bakersfield, CA)	NR	NR	NR	African American 7%; Hispanic 27%; Native American 2%; Asian 7%	4,309
California State University—Chico (Chico, CA)	NR	NR	Geographic origin/residence considered	African American 2%; Hispanic 11%; Native American 1%; Asian 5%	14,279
California State University—Dominguez Hills (Carson, CA)	NR	NR	NR	African American 29%; Hispanic 33%; Native American 1%; Asian 9%	8,041
California State University—Fresno (Fresno, CA)	NR	NR	NR	African American 5%; Hispanic 29%; Native American 1%; Asian 13%	16,650

(*continued*)

College	Use of Race in Admission Decisions and Degree Utilized (if at all)	Use of Alumni Relations or Legacies as Factor and Degree Utilized	Use of Other Factors (e.g., geographic origin or religious affiliation) and Degree Utilized	Reported Ethnic/Minority Representation	Total Student Population
California State University—Fullerton (Fullerton, CA)	NR	NR	Geographic origin/residence considered	African American 3%; Hispanic 24%; Native American 1%; Asian 24%	25,261
California State University—Hayward (Hayward, CA)	NR	NR	Geographic origin/residence considered	African American 11%; Hispanic 12%; Native American 1%; Asian 28%	9,385
California State University—Long Beach (Long Beach, CA)	NR	NR	NR	African American 6%; Hispanic 24%; Native American 1%; Asian 22%	27,180
California State University—Los Angeles (Los Angeles, CA)	NR	NR	Geographic origin/residence considered	African American 8%; Hispanic 49%; Asian 20%	13,898
California State University—Northridge (Northridge, CA)	NR	NR	NR	African American 9%; Hispanic 24%; Native American 1%; Asian 15%	20,955

California State University—Sacramento (Sacramento, CA)	NR	NR	Geographic origin/residence considered	African American 6%; Hispanic 14%; Native American 1%; Asian 19%	22,555
California State University—San Bernardino (San Bernardino, CA)	NR	NR	Geographic origin/residence an important factor	African American 12%; Hispanic 33%; Native American 1%; Asian 8%	12,109
California State University—San Marcos (San Marcos, CA)	NR	NR	NR	African American 2%; Hispanic 16%; Native American 1%; Asian 9%	6,344
California State University—Stanislaus (Turlock, CA)	NR	NR	Geographic origin/residence an important factor; Character & Personal Qualities considered	African American 3%; Hispanic 27%; Native American 1%; Asian 9%	6,154
California University of Pennsylvania (California, PA)	Minority status considered as factor	Alumni relations considered as a factor	NR	African American 5%	5,339
Calumet College of Saint Joseph (Whiting, IN)	NR	NR	Character & Personal Qualities considered	African American 28%; Hispanic 17%; Asian 1%	1,004
Calvin College (Grand Rapids, MI)	NR	NR	Religious affiliation and/or commitment is a very important factor; Character & Personal Qualities considered	African American 1%; Hispanic 1%; Asian 3%	4,028

(continued)

College	Use of Race in Admission Decisions and Degree Utilized (if at all)	Use of Alumni Relations or Legacies as Factor and Degree Utilized	Use of Other Factors (e.g., geographic origin or religious affiliation) and Degree Utilized	Reported Ethnic/Minority Representation	Total Student Population
Cameron University (Lawton, OK)	NR	NR	Geographic origin/residence an important factor; Character & Personal Qualities considered	African American 19%; Hispanic 9%; Native American 7%; Asian 3%	5,482
Campbell University (Buies Creek, NC)	NR	Alumni relations considered as a factor	Character and Personal Qualities are important	African American 10%; Hispanic 2%; Native American 1%	2,672
Campbellsville University (Campbellsville, KY)	NR	Alumni relations considered as a factor	Character and Personal Qualities are important; Religious affiliation and/or commitment considered	African American 6%; Hispanic 1%	1,373
Canisius College (Buffalo, NY)	NR	Alumni relations is considered as important factor	Character and Personal Qualities are important	African American 6%; Hispanic 2%; Native American 1%; Asian 2%	3,339
Capital University (Columbus, OH)	Minority status is considered as important factor	Alumni relations is considered as important factor	Character & Personal Qualities and Geographic origin/residence considered as important factors	African American 13%; Hispanic 1%; Asian 2%	2,706

Capitol College (Laurel, MD)	NR	Alumni relations considered as a factor	Character & Personal Qualities considered	African American 36%; Hispanic 2%; Asian 7%	452
Cardinal Stritch College (Milwaukee, WI)	Minority status considered as factor	NR	Character and Personal Qualities are important	African American 16%; Hispanic 3%; Asian 2%	3,069
Carleton College (Northfield, MN)	Minority status is considered as important factor	Alumni relations considered as a factor	Character and Personal Qualities are important; Geographic origin/residence considered	African American 6%; Hispanic 4%; Native American 1%; Asian 9%	1,932
Carlos Albizu University (Miami, FL)	NR	NR	NR	African American 17%	563
Carlow College (Pittsburgh, PA)	Minority status considered as factor	Alumni relations considered as a factor	Character and Personal Qualities are important	African American 17%	1,103
Carnegie Mellon University (Pittsburgh, PA)	Minority status considered as factor	Alumni relations is considered as important factor	Character and Personal Qualities are important	African American 5%; Hispanic 5%; Native American 1%; Asian 23%	5,389
Carroll College (MT) (Helena, MT)	NR	Alumni relations considered as a factor	Character and Personal Qualities are important; Geographic origin/residence considered	Hispanic 2%; Native American 1%; Asian 1%	1,321
Carroll College (WI) (Waukesha, WI)	NR	Alumni relations considered as a factor	Character & Personal Qualities considered	African American 4%; Hispanic 3%; Asian 2%	2,310

(continued)

161

College	Use of Race in Admission Decisions and Degree Utilized (if at all)	Use of Alumni Relations or Legacies as Factor and Degree Utilized	Use of Other Factors (e.g., geographic origin or religious affiliation) and Degree Utilized	Reported Ethnic/Minority Representation	Total Student Population
Carson-Newman College (Jefferson City, TN)	NR	Alumni relations considered as a factor	Character & Personal Qualities considered; Religious affiliation and/or commitment considered	African American 8%	1,970
Carthage College (Kenosha, WI)	Minority status considered as factor	Alumni relations considered as a factor	Character and Personal Qualities are very important; Geographic origin/residence considered	African American 6%; Hispanic 4%; Asian 1%	2,213
Case Western Reserve University (Cleveland, OH)	Minority status considered as factor	Alumni relations considered as a factor	Character & Personal Qualities considered	African American 5%; Hispanic 2%; Asian 15%	3,424
Castleton State College (Castleton, VT)	NR	Alumni relations considered as a factor	Character and Personal Qualities are very important	Hispanic 1%; Native American 1%; Asian 1%	1,740
Catawba College (Salisbury, NC)	Minority status considered as factor	Alumni relations considered as a factor	Character and Personal Qualities are important	African American 15%; Hispanic 2%; Native American 1%; Asian 1%	1,365

The Catholic University of America (Washington, DC)	Minority status considered as factor	Alumni relations considered as a factor	Character and Personal Qualities are very important	African American 7%; Hispanic 5%; Asian 3%	2,871
Cazenovia College (Cazenovia, NY)	NR	Alumni relations considered as a factor	Character and Personal Qualities are very important	African American 4%; Hispanic 3%; Native American 1%; Asian 1%	891
Cedar Crest College (Allentown, PA)	NR	Alumni relations considered as a factor	Character and Personal Qualities are important	African American 5%; Hispanic 5%; Asian 2%	1,523
Cedarville University (Cedarville, OH)	Minority status is considered as important factor	Alumni relations considered as a factor	Character, Personal Qualities & Religious Affiliation are very important factors	African American 2%; Hispanic 1%; Asian 1%	3,006
Centenary College of New Jersey (Hackettstown, NJ)	NR	Alumni relations is considered as important factor	Character and Personal Qualities are important	African American 3%; Hispanic 4%; Asian 5%	1,549
Centenary College of Louisiana (Shreveport, LA)	Minority status considered as factor	Alumni relations considered as a factor	Character and Personal Qualities are important; Geographic origin/residence and religious affiliation considered	African American 8%; Hispanic 2%; Native American 1%; Asian 3%	891

(*continued*)

College	Use of Race in Admission Decisions and Degree Utilized (if at all)	Use of Alumni Relations or Legacies as Factor and Degree Utilized	Use of Other Factors (e.g., geographic origin or religious affiliation) and Degree Utilized	Reported Ethnic/Minority Representation	Total Student Population
Central College (Pella, IA)	NR	NR	Character & Personal Qualities considered	African American 1%; Hispanic 2%; Asian 1%	1,530
Central Connecticut State University (New Britain, CT)	Minority status considered as factor	NR	Geographic origin/ residence considered	African American 8%; Hispanic 6%; Native American 1%; Asian 3%	9,016
Central Methodist College (Fayette, MO)	Minority status is considered as important factor	Alumni relations is considered as important factor	Geographic origin/ residence, Character, Personal Qualities & Religious Affiliation all important	African American 7%; Hispanic 1%	829
Central Michigan University (Mount Pleasant, MI)	Minority status considered as factor	Alumni relations considered as a factor	Character & Personal Qualities considered	African American 6%; Hispanic 2%; Native American 1%; Asian 1%	19,616
Central Missouri State University (Warrensburg, MO)	NR	Alumni relations considered as a factor	Character & Personal Qualities considered	African American 6%; Hispanic 2%; Native American 1%; Asian 1%	8,143
Central Pennsylvania College (Summerdale, PA)	NR	NR	Character & Personal Qualities considered	African American 14%; Hispanic 3%; Native American 1%; Asian 2%	859

Central State University (Wilberforce, OH)	NR	NR	Geographic origin/residence, Character and Personal Qualities all important factors	African American 88%	1,394
Central Washington University (Ellensburg, WA)	NR	NR	Geographic origin/residence, Character and Personal Qualities all considered	African American 2%; Hispanic 2%; Native American 2%; Asian 5%	8,745
Centre College (Danville, KY)	NR	Alumni relations considered as a factor	Character & Personal Qualities considered	African American 2%; Hispanic 1%; Asian 3%	1,060
Chadron State College (Chadron, NE)	NR	Alumni relations considered as a factor	Character & Personal Qualities considered	African American 2%; Hispanic 3%; Native American 3%; Asian 1%	2,066
Chaminade University of Honolulu (Honolulu, HI)	NR	NR	Character & Personal Qualities considered	African American 4%; Hispanic 6%; Native American 1%; Asian 64%	1,066
Champlain College (Burlington, VT)	NR	Alumni relations considered as a factor	Geographic origin/residence, Character and Personal Qualities all considered	African American 1%; Hispanic 1%; Native American 1%; Asian 2%	2,295
Chapman University (Orange, CA)	Minority status considered as factor	Alumni relations considered as a factor	Character and Personal Qualities are very important	African American 2%; Hispanic 10%; Native American 1%; Asian 8%	3,708

(*continued*)

College	Use of Race in Admission Decisions and Degree Utilized (if at all)	Use of Alumni Relations or Legacies as Factor and Degree Utilized	Use of Other Factors (e.g., geographic origin or religious affiliation) and Degree Utilized	Reported Ethnic/Minority Representation	Total Student Population
Charleston Southern University (Charleston, SC)	NR	NR	Character, Personal Qualities & Religious Affiliation are considered	African American 27%; Hispanic 1%; Native American 1%; Asian 2%	2,473
Charter Oak State College (New Britain, CT)	NR	NR	NR	African American 9%; Hispanic 4%; Native American 1%; Asian 2%	1,495
Chestnut Hill College (Philadelphia, PA)	NR	Alumni relations considered as a factor	Character and Personal Qualities are important	African American 41%; Hispanic 6%; Asian 2%	887
Cheyney University of Pennsylvania (Cheyney, PA)	Minority status considered as factor	NR	NR	African American 98%	1087
Chicago State University (Chicago, IL)	NR	NR	NR	African American 87%; Hispanic 6%; Asian 1%	4,818
Chowan College (Murfreesboro, NC)	NR	Alumni relations considered as a factor	Character & Personal Qualities considered	African American 27%; Hispanic 2%; Native American 1%; Asian 1%	753

Christian Brothers University (Memphis, TN)	NR	Alumni relations considered as a factor	Character and Personal Qualities are important	African American 25%; Hispanic 2%; Asian 5%	1,550
Christian Heritage College (El Cajon, CA)	NR	NR	Religious affiliation and/or commitment is a very important factor; Character & Personal Qualities considered	African American 7%; Hispanic 14%; Native American 1%; Asian 3%	503
Christopher Newport University (Newport News, VA)	NR	NR	Character & Personal Qualities considered	African American 10%; Hispanic 2%; Asian 3%	4,608
Cincinnati Bible College and Seminary (Cincinnati, OH)	NR	NR	Religious affiliation and/or commitment and Character & Personal Qualities considered important	NR	625
The Citadel, The Military College of SC (Charleston, SC)	Minority status is considered as important factor	Alumni relations considered as a factor	Character and Personal Qualities are important; Geographic origin/residence considered	African American 8%; Hispanic 4%; Asian 3%	2,120
City University of New York—Baruch College (New York, NY)	NR	Alumni relations considered as a factor	Character & Personal Qualities considered	African American 14%; Hispanic 18%; Asian 27%	12,493

(continued)

College	Use of Race in Admission Decisions and Degree Utilized (if at all)	Use of Alumni Relations or Legacies as Factor and Degree Utilized	Use of Other Factors (e.g., geographic origin or religious affiliation) and Degree Utilized	Reported Ethnic/Minority Representation	Total Student Population
City University of New York—Borough of Manhattan Community College (New York, NY)	NR	NR	NR	African American 37%; Hispanic 30%; Asian 10%	16,732
City University of New York—Brooklyn College (Brooklyn, NY)	NR	NR	NR	African American 29%; Hispanic 11%; Asian 10%	10,789
City University of New York—City College (New York, NY)	NR	NR	NR	African American 29%; Hispanic 32%; Asian 16%	8,816
City University of New York—College of Staten Island (Staten Island, NY)	NR	NR	NR	African American 11%; Hispanic 12%; Asian 8%	10,778
City University of New York—Hostos Community College (Bronx, NY)	NR	NR	NR	African American 26%; Hispanic 59%; Asian 3%	3,577

City University of New York—Hunter College (New York, NY)	NR	NR	African American 16%; Hispanic 21%; Asian 17%	14,109
City University of New York—John Jay College of Criminal Justice (New York, NY)	NR	NR	African American 25%; Hispanic 36%; Asian 6%	12,224
City University of New York—Kingsborough Community College (Brooklyn, NY)	NR	NR	African American 34%; Hispanic 14%; Asian 9%	10,455
City University of New York—Laguardia Community College (Long Island, NY)	NR	NR	African American 16%; Hispanic 34%; Asian 11%	11,182
City University of New York—Lehman College (Bronx, NY)	NR	NR	African American 34%; Hispanic 47%; Asian 4%	7,597
City University of New York—Medgar Evers College (Brooklyn, NY)	NR	Geographic origin/residence considered	African American 87%; Hispanic 5%; Asian 1%	4,742

(continued)

169

College	Use of Race in Admission Decisions and Degree Utilized (if at all)	Use of Alumni Relations or Legacies as Factor and Degree Utilized	Use of Other Factors (e.g., geographic origin or religious affiliation) and Degree Utilized	Reported Ethnic/Minority Representation	Total Student Population
City University of New York—New York City College of Technology (Brooklyn, NY)	NR	NR	NR	African American 46%; Hispanic 26%; Asian 12%	11,420
City University of New York—Queens College (Flushing, NY)	NR	NR	NR	African American 10%; Hispanic 17%; Asian 19%	11,859
City University of New York—Queensborough Community College (Bayside, NY)	NR	NR	NR	African American 27%; Hispanic 23%; Asian 20%	9,898
City University of New York—York College (Jamaica, NY)	NR	NR	NR	African American 44%; Hispanic 14%; Asian 8%	5,311
Claflin University (Orangeburg, SC)	NR	Alumni relations is considered as important factor	Character and Personal Qualities are very important; Geographic origin/residence considered	African American 93%	1,772

Claremont McKenna College (Claremont, CA)	NR	Alumni relations considered as a factor	Character and Personal Qualities are very important; Geographic origin/residence considered	African American 4%; Hispanic 10%; Native American 1%; Asian 16%	1,050
Clarion University of Pennsylvania (Clarion, PA)	Minority status considered as factor	NR	Character & Personal Qualities considered	African American 5%; Hispanic 1%; Asian 1%	5,855
Clark Atlanta University (Atlanta, GA)	NR	Alumni relations is considered as important factor	NR	African American 94%	3,920
Clark University (Worcester, MA)	Minority status considered as factor	Alumni relations considered as a factor	Character and Personal Qualities are very important; Geographic origin/residence considered	African American 3%; Hispanic 3%; Asian 4%	2,075
Clarke College (Dubuque, IA)	Minority status considered as factor	NR	NR	African American 2%; Hispanic 2%	939
Clarkson University (Potsdam, NY)	NR	NR	NR	African American 5%; Hispanic 2%; Asian 1%	2,717
Clayton College & State University (Morrow, GA)	NR	NR	NR	African American 48%; Hispanic 3%; Native American 1%; Asian 4%	5,661
Clearwater Christian College (Clearwater, FL)	Minority status considered as factor	Alumni relations considered as a factor	Character and Personal Qualities are very important; Geographic origin/residence considered	African American 1%; Hispanic 4%; Asian 1%	641

(continued)

171

College	Use of Race in Admission Decisions and Degree Utilized (if at all)	Use of Alumni Relations or Legacies as Factor and Degree Utilized	Use of Other Factors (e.g., geographic origin or religious affiliation) and Degree Utilized	Reported Ethnic/Minority Representation	Total Student Population
Cleary University (Howell, MI)	NR	NR	NR	African American 11%; Hispanic 2%; Native American 1%; Asian 2%	812
Clemson University (Clemson, SC)	NR	Alumni relations considered as a factor	Geographic origin/ residence important	African American 7%; Hispanic 1%; Asian 2%	13,808
Cleveland Institute of Art (Cleveland, OH)	NR	NR	NR	African American 5%; Hispanic 3%; Asian 4%	597
Cleveland State University (Cleveland, OH)	NR	NR	NR	African American 20%; Hispanic 3%; Asian 2%	10,176
Coastal Carolina University (Conway, SC)	NR	NR	Geographic origin/ residence, Character and Personal Qualities all considered	African American 11%; Hispanic 2%; Asian 1%	5,743
Coe College (Cedar Rapids, IA)	Minority status considered as factor	Alumni relations considered as a factor	Character & Personal Qualities considered	African American 2%; Asian 1%	1,212

Coker College (Hartsville, SC)	NR	Alumni relations considered as a factor	Character & Personal Qualities considered	African American 26%; Hispanic 2%	482
Colby College (Waterville, ME)	Minority status is considered as important factor	Alumni relations considered as a factor	Character and Personal Qualities are very important; Geographic origin/residence considered	African American 1%; Hispanic 3%; Native American 1%; Asian 5%	1,820
Colby-Sawyer College (New London, NH)	NR	Alumni relations considered as a factor	Character and Personal Qualities are very important; Geographic origin/residence considered	Asian 1%	954
Colgate University (Hamilton, NY)	Minority status considered as factor	Alumni relations considered as a factor	Character and Personal Qualities are important; Geographic origin/residence considered	African American 4%; Hispanic 4%; Native American 1%; Asian 6%	2,800
College for Creative Studies (Detroit, MI)	NR	NR	Character & Personal Qualities considered	African American 7%; Hispanic 3%; Asian 5%	1,204
College Misericordia (Dallas, PA)	Minority status considered as factor	NR	Character and Personal Qualities are very important	African American 2%; Hispanic 1%; Asian 1%	1,934
College of Aeronautics (Flushing, NY)	NR	Alumni relations considered as a factor	NR	NR	1,316

(continued)

College	Use of Race in Admission Decisions and Degree Utilized (if at all)	Use of Alumni Relations or Legacies as Factor and Degree Utilized	Use of Other Factors (e.g., geographic origin or religious affiliation) and Degree Utilized	Reported Ethnic/Minority Representation	Total Student Population
College of Charleston (Charleston, SC)	Minority status considered as factor	NR	Geographic origin/residence, Character and Personal Qualities all considered important	African American 8%; Hispanic 1%; Asian 1%	9,479
College of the Holy Cross (Worcester, MA)	Minority status considered as factor	Alumni relations is considered as important factor	Character and Personal Qualities are important; Geographic origin/residence considered	African American 3%; Hispanic 5%; Asian 5%	2,718
College of Mount Saint Joseph (Cincinnati, OH)	NR	NR	NR	African American 8%; Asian 1%	2,113
College of Mount Saint Vincent (Riverdale, NY)	NR	Alumni relations considered as a factor	Character and Personal Qualities are very important	African American 12%; Hispanic 30%; Asian 11%	1,360
The College of New Jersey (Ewing, NJ)	Minority status considered as factor	Alumni relations considered as a factor	Character and Personal Qualities are important; Geographic origin/residence considered	African American 6%; Hispanic 7%; Asian 5%	5,840

The College of New Rochelle (New Rochelle, NY)	NR	Alumni relations considered as a factor	Character & Personal Qualities considered	African American 26%; Hispanic 10%; Asian 4%	926
College of Notre Dame of Maryland (Baltimore, MD)	NR	Alumni relations considered as a factor	Character & Personal Qualities considered	African American 26%; Hispanic 3%; Asian 3%	1,686
College of the Ozarks (Point Lookout, MD)	NR	Alumni relations considered as a factor	Character and Personal Qualities are very important; Geographic origin/residence considered	African American 1%; Hispanic 1%; Native American 1%; Asian 1%	1,346
College of Saint Benedict/Saint John's University (Collegeville, MN)	Minority status is considered as important factor	Alumni relations is considered as important factor	Geographic origin/residence, Character and Personal Qualities all considered important	African American 1%; Hispanic 1%; Asian 2%	3,828
College of St. Catherine (Saint Paul, MN)	Minority status considered as factor	NR	Character & Personal Qualities considered	African American 7%; Hispanic 2%; Native American 1%; Asian 5%	3,593
College of Saint Elizabeth (Morristown, NJ)	NR	Alumni relations considered as a factor	Character and Personal Qualities are important; Geographic origin/residence considered	African American 16%; Hispanic 14%; Asian 5%	1,186
College of Saint Mary (Omaha, NE)	NR	Alumni relations considered as a factor	Character & Personal Qualities considered	African American 6%; Hispanic 5%; Native American 1%; Asian 1%	950

(continued)

College	Use of Race in Admission Decisions and Degree Utilized (if at all)	Use of Alumni Relations or Legacies as Factor and Degree Utilized	Use of Other Factors (e.g., geographic origin or religious affiliation) and Degree Utilized	Reported Ethnic/Minority Representation	Total Student Population
The College of Saint Rose (Albany, NY)	Minority status considered as factor	Alumni relations considered as a factor	Geographic origin/residence, Character and Personal Qualities all considered important	African American 2%; Hispanic 2%; Asian 1%	2,780
The College of Saint Scholastica (Duluth, MN)	NR	Alumni relations is considered as important factor	Character and Personal Qualities are important	African American 1%; Hispanic 1%; Native American 1%; Asian 1%	1,841
College of Santa Fe (Santa Fe, NM)	Minority status considered as factor	Alumni relations considered as a factor	Character and Personal Qualities are very important; Geographic origin/residence considered	African American 2%; Hispanic 25%; Native American 3%; Asian 2%	1,279
College of the Siskiyous (Weed, CA)	NR	NR	NR	African American 5%; Hispanic 8%; Native American 5%; Asian 4%	1,153
College of the Southwest (Hobbs, MN)	NR	NR	NR	African American 3%; Hispanic 31%; Native American 4%; Asian 1%	562

College of William and Mary (Williamsburg, VA)	Minority status considered as factor	Alumni relations considered as a factor	Geographic origin/residence, Character and Personal Qualities all considered	African American 6%; Hispanic 3%; Asian 7%	5,686
The College of Wooster (Wooster, OH)	Minority status considered as factor	Alumni relations considered as a factor	Geographic origin/residence, Character and Personal Qualities all considered important	African American 5%; Hispanic 1%; Asian 1%	1,776
Colorado Christian University (Lakewood, CO)	Minority status is considered as important factor	Alumni relations considered as a factor	Religious affiliation and/or commitment and Character & Personal Qualities considered very important; Geographic origin/residence considered	African American 4%; Hispanic 6%; Native American 1%; Asian 1%	1,422
Colorado College (Colorado Springs, CO)	Minority status considered as factor	Alumni relations considered as a factor	Geographic origin/residence, Character and Personal Qualities all considered	African American 2%; Hispanic 7%; Native American 2%; Asian 4%	1,929
Colorado Mountain College—Alpine Campus (Steamboat Springs, CO)	NR	NR	NR	African American 1%; Hispanic 3%; Native American 1%; Asian 1%	1,293

(continued)

College	Use of Race in Admission Decisions and Degree Utilized (if at all)	Use of Alumni Relations or Legacies as Factor and Degree Utilized	Use of Other Factors (e.g., geographic origin or religious affiliation) and Degree Utilized	Reported Ethnic/Minority Representation	Total Student Population
Colorado Mountain College—Spring Valley (Glenwood Springs, CO)	NR	NR	NR	Hispanic 4%; Native American 1%; Asian 1%	827
Colorado School of Mines (Golden, CO)	NR	NR	NR	African American 1%; Hispanic 7%; Native American 1%; Asian 5%	2,667
Colorado State University (Fort Collins, CO)	Minority status considered as factor	Alumni relations considered as a factor	Geographic origin/residence, Character and Personal Qualities all considered	African American 2%; Hispanic 6%; Native American 1%; Asian 3%	20,678
Colorado Technical University (Colorado Springs, CO)	NR	Alumni relations considered as a factor	Character and Personal Qualities considered	African American 8%; Hispanic 6%; Asian 4%	1,261
Columbia College (SC) (Columbia, SC)	NR	Alumni relations considered as a factor	Character and Personal Qualities considered important	African American 45%; Hispanic 2%; Asian 1%	1,130
Columbia College Chicago (Chicago, IL)	NR	NR	NR	African American 16%; Hispanic 10%; Native American 1%; Asian 3%	9,602

Columbia College of Missouri (Columbia, MO)	NR	NR	African American 6%; Hispanic 2%; Native American 1%; Asian 2%	921
Columbia International University (Columbia, SC)	NR	Religious affiliation and/or commitment and Character & Personal Qualities considered very important	African American 1%; Hispanic 1%	568
Columbia Union College (Takoma Park, MD)	NR	Religious affiliation and/or commitment and Character & Personal Qualities considered important	African American 48%; Hispanic 9%; Asian 8%	1,162
Columbia University—Columbia College (New York, NY)	Minority status considered as factor	Alumni relations considered as a factor	Character & Personal Qualities considered very important; Geographic origin/residence considered	African American 9%; Hispanic 8%; Asian 12%	4,115
Columbia University, School of Engineering and Applied Science (New York, NY)	Minority status considered as factor	Alumni relations considered as a factor	Character & Personal Qualities considered very important; Geographic origin/residence considered	African American 3%; Hispanic 5%; Asian 33%	1,387
Columbus College of Art & Design (Columbus, OH)	NR	NR	Character and Personal Qualities considered important	African American 6%; Hispanic 2%; Asian 4%	1,359

(continued)

College	Use of Race in Admission Decisions and Degree Utilized (if at all)	Use of Alumni Relations or Legacies as Factor and Degree Utilized	Use of Other Factors (e.g., geographic origin or religious affiliation) and Degree Utilized	Reported Ethnic/Minority Representation	Total Student Population
Columbus State University (Columbus, GA)	NR	NR	Geographic origin/residence considered	African American 30%; Hispanic 3%; Asian 2%	5,994
Concord College—Athens (Athens, WV)	Minority status considered as factor	Alumni relations considered as a factor	Geographic origin/residence, Character and Personal Qualities all considered	African American 3%; Asian 1%	3,023
Concordia College (Moorhead, MN)	Minority status considered as factor	Alumni relations considered as a factor	Character and Personal Qualities considered	African American 1%; Hispanic 1%; Asian 2%	2,793
Concordia College (Bronxville, NY)	NR	Alumni relations considered as a factor	Religious affiliation and/or commitment and Character & Personal Qualities considered important	African American 10%; Hispanic 10%; Asian 2%	540
Concordia College—Austin (Austin, TX)	NR	NR	NR	African American 9%; Hispanic 14%; Native American 1%; Asian 2%	966

Concordia College—Irvine (Irvine, CA)	Minority status considered as factor	Alumni relations considered as a factor	Religious affiliation and/or commitment and Character & Personal Qualities considered important	African American 3%; Hispanic 12%; Native American 1%; Asian 5%	1,265
Concordia College—Nebraska (Seward, NE)	NR	NR	NR	African American 1%; Hispanic 1%; Asian 1%	1,116
Concordia College—Oregon (Portland, OR)	NR	NR	Character and Personal Qualities considered	African American 5%; Hispanic 3%; Native American 1%; Asian 5%	844
Concordia College—River Forest (River Forest, IL)	NR	NR	NR	African American 6%; Hispanic 5%; Asian 2%	1,072
Concordia University—Wisconsin (Cequon, WI)	NR	Alumni relations considered as a factor	Religious affiliation and/or commitment and Character & Personal Qualities considered important	African American 11%; Hispanic 2%; Native American 1%; Asian 1%	3,962
Connecticut College (New London, CT)	Minority status is considered a very important factor	Alumni relations is considered as important factor	Character and Personal Qualities are important; Geographic origin/residence considered	African American 4%; Hispanic 4%; Asian 4%	1,796
Converse College (Spartanburg, SC)	NR	Alumni relations considered as a factor	Character and Personal Qualities considered	African American 10%; Hispanic 1%	756

(continued)

College	Use of Race in Admission Decisions and Degree Utilized (if at all)	Use of Alumni Relations or Legacies as Factor and Degree Utilized	Use of Other Factors (e.g., geographic origin or religious affiliation) and Degree Utilized	Reported Ethnic/Minority Representation	Total Student Population
Cooper Union (New York, NY)	NR	NR	Character and Personal Qualities considered	African American 5%; Hispanic 8%; Asian 25%	845
Coppin State College (Baltimore, MD)	Minority status considered as factor	Alumni relations considered as a factor	Geographic origin/residence, Character and Personal Qualities all considered	African American 95%	3,185
Cornell College (Mount Vernon, IA)	NR	Alumni relations considered as a factor	Character and Personal Qualities considered	African American 3%; Hispanic 3%; Asian 1%	1,143
Cornell University (Ithaca, NY)	Minority status considered as factor	Alumni relations considered as a factor	Geographic origin/residence, Character and Personal Qualities all considered	African American 5%; Hispanic 5%; Asian 16%	13,577
Cornerstone University (Grand Rapids, MI)	Minority status considered as factor	NR	Character & Personal Qualities considered very important	African American 19%; Hispanic 2%; Asian 1%	2,042

Cornish College of the Arts (Seattle, WA)	NR	NR	NR	African American 2%; Hispanic 4%; Native American 1%; Asian 5%	649
Covenant College (Lookout Mountain, GA)	Minority status considered as factor	NR	Religious affiliation and/or commitment and Character & Personal Qualities considered important	African American 6%; Hispanic 2%; Asian 1%	1,215
Creighton University (Omaha, NE)	Minority status considered as factor	NR	Character and Personal Qualities considered	African American 3%; Hispanic 3%; Native American 1%; Asian 8%	3,358
Crichton College (Memphis, TN)	NR	NR	NR	African American 51%	969
Crown College (St. Bonifacius, MN)	NR	NR	Religious affiliation and/or commitment and Character & Personal Qualities considered important	African American 2%; Hispanic 2%; Asian 7%	936
The Culinary Institute of America (Hyde Park, NY)	NR	Alumni relations is considered as important factor	Character and Personal Qualities are important	African American 2%; Hispanic 4%; Asian 3%	2,294
Culver-Stockton College (Canton, MO)	NR	Alumni relations is considered as important factor	Character and Personal Qualities are important	African American 7%; Hispanic 3%	855
Cumberland College (Williamsburg, KY)	NR	NR	NR	African American 7%; Hispanic 2%	1,422

(continued)

183

College	Use of Race in Admission Decisions and Degree Utilized (if at all)	Use of Alumni Relations or Legacies as Factor and Degree Utilized	Use of Other Factors (e.g., geographic origin or religious affiliation) and Degree Utilized	Reported Ethnic/Minority Representation	Total Student Population
Cumberland University (Lebaonon, TN)	NR	Alumni relations considered as a factor	NR	African American 14%; Hispanic 1%; Asian 2%	921
Curry College (Milton, MA)	NR	Alumni relations considered as a factor	Character and Personal Qualities considered	African American 4%; Hispanic 2%; Asian 1%	1,709
Daemen College (Amherst, NY)	NR	Alumni relations considered as a factor	Character and Personal Qualities considered	African American 16%; Hispanic 2%; Native American 1%; Asian 1%	1,409
Dakota State University (Madison, SD)	NR	NR	NR	African American 1%; Hispanic 1%; Native American 1%; Asian 1%	1,430
Dakota Wesleyan University (Mitchell, SD)	NR	NR	NR	African American 4%; Hispanic 2%; Native American 2%; Asian 1%	654
Dallas Baptist University (Dallas, TX)	NR	NR	Religious affiliation and/or commitment and Character & Personal Qualities considered important	African American 19%; Hispanic 9%; Native American 1%; Asian 2%	3,541

Dana College (Blair, NE)	NR	NR	NR	African American 5%; Hispanic 4%; Asian 1%	637
Daniel Webster College (Nashua, NH)	NR	NR	Character and Personal Qualities considered	African American 2%; Hispanic 2%; Asian 1%	988
Dartmouth College (Hanover, NH)	Minority status considered as factor	Alumni relations considered as a factor	Character & Personal Qualities considered very important; Geographic origin/residence considered	African American 7%; Hispanic 6%; Native American 4%; Asian 13%	3,996
Davenport University (Dearborn, MI)	NR	NR	NR	African American 37%; Hispanic 1%; Asian 1%	5,335
Davidson College (Davidson, NC)	Minority status considered as factor	NR	Character & Personal Qualities considered very important	African American 6%; Hispanic 4%; Asian 2%	1,702
Davis & Elkins College (Elkins, WV)	Minority status considered as factor	Alumni relations considered as a factor	Geographic origin/residence, Character and Personal Qualities, and Religious Affiliation/Commitment all considered	African American 2%; Hispanic 1%; Asian 4%	625
Defiance College (Defiance, OH)	NR	Alumni relations considered as a factor	Character and Personal Qualities considered	African American 4%; Hispanic 3%	918

(continued)

185

College	Use of Race in Admission Decisions and Degree Utilized (if at all)	Use of Alumni Relations or Legacies as Factor and Degree Utilized	Use of Other Factors (e.g., geographic origin or religious affiliation) and Degree Utilized	Reported Ethnic/Minority Representation	Total Student Population
Delaware State University (Dover, DE)	NR	Alumni relations considered as a factor	Character & Personal Qualities considered important; Geographic origin/residence considered	African American 79%; Hispanic 2%; Asian 1%	3,149
Delaware Valley College (Doylestown, PA)	NR	Alumni relations considered as a factor	NR	African American 4%; Hispanic 1%; Asian 1%	1,744
Delta State University (Cleveland, MS)	NR	NR	NR	African American 33%; Hispanic 1%; Asian 1%	3,156
Denison University (Granville, OH)	Minority status considered as factor	Alumni relations considered as a factor	Geographic origin/residence, Character and Personal Qualities, and Religious Affiliation/Commitment all considered	African American 5%; Hispanic 3%; Asian 3%	2,198
Depaul Univiersity (Chicago, IL)	Minority status considered as factor	Alumni relations considered as a factor	Character & Personal Qualities considered very important; Geographic origin/	African American 9%; Hispanic 11%; Asian 8%	14,239

Depauw University (Greencastle, IN)	Minority status considered as factor	Alumni relations considered as a factor	residence, and Religious Affiliation and/or Commitment considered Geographic origin/ residence, Character and Personal Qualities all considered	African American 5%; Hispanic 3%; Asian 2%	2,350
Desales University (Center Valley, PA)	Minority status considered as factor	NR	Character & Personal Qualities considered important; Geographic origin/ residence considered	African American 1%; Hispanic 1%; Asian 1%	2,167
Dickinson College (Carlisle, PA)	Minority status is considered a very important factor	Alumni relations is considered as important factor	Geographic origin/ residence, Character and Personal Qualities all considered	African American 4%; Hispanic 3%; Asian 4%	2,280
Dickinson State University (Dickinson, ND)	NR	NR	NR	African American 2%; Hispanic 1%; Native American 1%	2,479
Dillard University (New Orleans, LA)	NR	Alumni relations considered as a factor	NR	African American 99%	2,155
Doane College (Crete, NE)	Minority status considered as factor	Alumni relations is considered as important factor	Character & Personal Qualities considered important	African American 3%; Hispanic 2%; Asian 1%	1,618

(continued)

College	Use of Race in Admission Decisions and Degree Utilized (if at all)	Use of Alumni Relations or Legacies as Factor and Degree Utilized	Use of Other Factors (e.g., geographic origin or religious affiliation) and Degree Utilized	Reported Ethnic/Minority Representation	Total Student Population
Dominican College of Blauvelt (Orangeburg, NY)	NR	NR	NR	African American 16%; Hispanic 14%; Asian 6%	1,297
Dominican University (IL) (River Forest, IL)	NR	Alumni relations considered as a factor	Character & Personal Qualities considered important; Geographic origin/residence considered	African American 7%; Hispanic 16%; Asian 2%	1,209
Dominican University of California (San Rafael, CA)	Minority status is considered as important factor	Alumni relations considered as a factor	Character & Personal Qualities considered very important; Geographic origin/residence considered	African American 8%; Hispanic 15%; Native American 1%; Asian 17%	1,226
Dowling College (Oakdale, NY)	NR	Alumni relations considered as a factor	Character and Personal Qualities considered	African American 10%; Hispanic 10%; Asian 2%	3,357
Drake University (Des Moines, IA)	NR	NR	Character and Personal Qualities considered	African American 3%; Hispanic 1%; Asian 3%	3,118
Drew University (Madison, NJ)	Minority status considered as factor	Alumni relations considered as a factor	Character & Personal Qualities considered	African American 4%; Hispanic 6%; Asian 6%	1,578

Drexel University (Philadelphia, PA)	NR	Alumni relations is considered as important factor	Character & Personal Qualities considered important	African American 10%; Hispanic 3%; Asian 12%	11,544
Drury University (Springfield, MO)	Minority status considered as factor	Alumni relations considered as a factor	Character & Personal Qualities considered important; Geographic origin/residence considered	African American 1%; Hispanic 4%; Native American 2%; Asian 1%	1,588
Duke University (Durham, NC)	Minority status considered as factor	Alumni relations considered as a factor	Character & Personal Qualities considered important; Geographic origin/residence considered	African American 10%; Hispanic 7%; Asian 12%	6,066
Duquesne University (Pittsburgh, PA)	NR	Alumni relations considered as a factor	Character & Personal Qualities considered important	African American 4%; Hispanic 1%; Asian 1%	5,549
D'Vouville College (Buffalo, NY)	NR	Alumni relations considered as a factor	Character & Personal Qualities considered	African American 23%; Hispanic 5%; Native American 1%; Asian 3%	1,136
Earlham College (Richmond, IN)	Minority status is considered a very important factor	Alumni relations considered as a factor	Character & Personal Qualities considered very important; Geographic origin/residence and Religious Affiliation considered	African American 7%; Hispanic 3%; Asian 2%	1,149

(continued)

College	Use of Race in Admission Decisions and Degree Utilized (if at all)	Use of Alumni Relations or Legacies as Factor and Degree Utilized	Use of Other Factors (e.g., geographic origin or religious affiliation) and Degree Utilized	Reported Ethnic/Minority Representation	Total Student Population
East Carolina University (Greenville, NC)	NR	Alumni relations considered as a factor	Geographic origin/residence, Character and Personal Qualities all considered	African American 15%; Hispanic 2%; Native American 1%; Asian 2%	17,406
East Central University (Ada, OK)	NR	NR	NR	African American 5%; Hispanic 3%; Native American 19%; Asian 1%	3,870
East Stroudsburg University of Pennsylvania (East Stroudsburg, PA)	NR	Alumni relations considered as a factor	Geographic origin/residence, Character and Personal Qualities all considered	African American 4%; Hispanic 4%; Asian 1%	5,282
East Tennessee State University (Johnson City, TN)	Minority status considered as factor	NR	Character & Personal Qualities considered important	African American 4%; Hispanic 1%; Asian 1%	9,355
East Texas Baptist University (Marshall, TX)	NR	NR	Character & Personal Qualities considered	African American 13%; Hispanic 4%; Native American 1%	1,271

Eastern Connecticut State University (Willimantic, CT)	NR	NR	Geographic origin/residence, Character and Personal Qualities all considered	African American 7%; Hispanic 4%; Native American 1%; Asian 1%	4,513
Eastern Illinois University (Charleston, IL)	NR	NR	NR	African American 7%; Hispanic 2%; Asian 1%	9,714
Eastern Kentucky University (Richmond, KY)	NR	NR	NR	African American 4%; Hispanic 1%; Asian 1%	12,944
Eastern Mennonite University (Harrisonburg, VA)	NR	NR	Religious affiliation and/or commitment and Character & Personal Qualities considered important	African American 6%; Hispanic 2%; Asian 2%	1,008
Eastern Michigan University (Ypsilanti, MI)	NR	NR	Character & Personal Qualities considered important	African American 17%; Hispanic 2%; Native American 1%; Asian 2%	18,485
Eastern Nazarene College (Quincy, MA)	NR	NR	Religious affiliation and/or commitment and Character & Personal Qualities considered	NR	525
Eastern New Mexico University (Portales, NM)	NR	NR	NR	African American 7%; Hispanic 29%; Native American 3%; Asian 1%	3,010

(*continued*)

College	Use of Race in Admission Decisions and Degree Utilized (if at all)	Use of Alumni Relations or Legacies as Factor and Degree Utilized	Use of Other Factors (e.g., geographic origin or religious affiliation) and Degree Utilized	Reported Ethnic/Minority Representation	Total Student Population
Eastern Oregon University (LaGrande, OR)	Minority status considered as factor	NR	Geographic origin/residence considered	African American 2%; Hispanic 3%; Native American 2%; Asian 3%	2,876
Eastern University (St. Davids, PA)	NR	Alumni relations considered as a factor	Character & Personal Qualities considered important; Religious affiliation and/or commitment considered	African American 12%; Hispanic 5%; Asian 1%	2,054
Eastern Washington University (Cheney, WA)	NR	NR	Character & Personal Qualities considered	African American 3%; Hispanic 6%; Native American 2%; Asian 4%	9,390
Eastman School of Music, University of Rochester (Rochester, NY)	Minority status considered as factor	Alumni relations considered as a factor	Character & Personal Qualities considered	African American 3%; Hispanic 2%; Asian 6%	495
East-West University (Chicago, IL)	NR	NR	Geographic origin/residence is very important; Character & Personal Qualities considered	African American 71%; Hispanic 11%; Asian 1%	1,113

Eckerd College (St. Petersburg, FL)	NR	NR	Character & Personal Qualities considered very important	African American 3%; Hispanic 4%; Asian 2%	1,662
Edgewood College (Madison, WI)	Minority status considered as factor	Alumni relations considered as a factor	Character & Personal Qualities considered	African American 2%; Hispanic 2%; Asian 2%	1,806
Edinboro University of Pennsylvania (Edinboro, PA)	Minority status is considered as important factor	Alumni relations considered as a factor	Geographic origin/residence is important; Character & Personal Qualities considered	African American 7%; Hispanic 1%; Asian 1%	6,587
Elizabeth City State University (Elizabeth City, NC)	Minority status is considered as important factor	Alumni relations considered as a factor	Geographic origin/residence, and Character & Personal Qualities considered very important	African American 77%; Hispanic 1%	2,015
Elizabethtown College (Elizabethtown, PA)	Minority status is considered as important factor	Alumni relations considered as a factor	Geographic origin/residence, Character and Personal Qualities, and Religious Affiliation/Commitment all considered	African American 1%; Hispanic 1%; Asian 2%	2,096
Elmhurst College (Elmhurst, IL)	NR	Alumni relations considered as a factor	Character & Personal Qualities considered	African American 6%; Hispanic 6%; Asian 3%	2,339

(*continued*)

College	Use of Race in Admission Decisions and Degree Utilized (if at all)	Use of Alumni Relations or Legacies as Factor and Degree Utilized	Use of Other Factors (e.g., geographic origin or religious affiliation) and Degree Utilized	Reported Ethnic/Minority Representation	Total Student Population
Elmira College (Elmira, NY)	Minority status considered as factor	Alumni relations considered as a factor	Character & Personal Qualities considered very important; Geographic origin/residence considered	African American 1%; Hispanic 1%	1,448
Elms College (Chicopee, MA)	NR	Alumni relations is considered as important factor	Character & Personal Qualities considered important	African American 3%; Hispanic 2%; Asian 1%	685
Elon University (Elon, NC)	Minority status considered as factor	Alumni relations is considered as important factor	Geographic origin/residence, Character and Personal Qualities, considered	African American 7%; Hispanic 1%; Asian 1%	4,622
Embry-Riddle Aeronautical University (AZ) (Prescott, AZ)	NR	Alumni relations considered as a factor	Character & Personal Qualities considered	African American 2%; Hispanic 7%; Native American 1%; Asian 6%	1,631
Embry-Riddle Aeronautical University (FL) (Daytona Beach, FL)	NR	Alumni relations considered as a factor	Character & Personal Qualities considered	African American 5%; Hispanic 7%; Asian 4%	4,389

Emerson College (Boston, MA)	Minority status considered as factor	Alumni relations considered as a factor	Character & Personal Qualities considered important	African American 2%; Hispanic 5%; Asian 4%	3,076
Emmanuel College (GA) (Franklin Springs, GA)	NR	NR	NR	African American 16%; Hispanic 1%; Asian 1%	754
Emmanuel College (MA) (Boston, MA)	NR	Alumni relations considered as a factor	NR	African American 9%; Hispanic 4%; Asian 4%	1,628
Emory and Henry College (Emory, VA)	Minority status considered as factor	Alumni relations considered as a factor	Geographic origin/residence, Character and Personal Qualities, and Religious Affiliation/Commitment all considered	African American 4%; Hispanic 1%; Asian 1%	886
Emory University (Atlanta, GA)	Minority status considered as factor	Alumni relations considered as a factor	Geographic origin/residence, Character and Personal Qualities considered	African American 9%; Hispanic 3%; Asian 16%	6,260
Emporia State University (Emporia, KS)	NR	NR	NR	African American 4%; Hispanic 4%; Native American 1%; Asian 1%	4,209
Endicott College (Beverly, MA)	Minority status considered as factor	Alumni relations is considered as important factor	Geographic origin/residence, Character and Personal Qualities, considered important	African American 1%; Hispanic 2%; Asian 1%	1,973

(*continued*)

College	Use of Race in Admission Decisions and Degree Utilized (if at all)	Use of Alumni Relations or Legacies as Factor and Degree Utilized	Use of Other Factors (e.g., geographic origin or religious affiliation) and Degree Utilized	Reported Ethnic/Minority Representation	Total Student Population
Erie Community College—City Campus (Buffalo, NY)	NR	NR	NR	African American 39%; Hispanic 9%; Native American 2%; Asian 2%	1,982
Erie Community College—North Campus (Williamsville, NY)	NR	NR	NR	African American 10%; Hispanic 2%; Asian 2%	4,301
Erie Community College—South Campus (Orchard Park, NY)	NR	NR	NR	African American 2%; Hispanic 1%; Native American 1%; Asian 1%	2,660
Erskine College (Due West, SC)	NR	Alumni relations is considered as very important	Character & Personal Qualities considered	African American 7%; Hispanic 1%;	607
Eugene Lang College/New School University (New York, NY)	Minority status considered as factor	Alumni relations considered as a factor	Character & Personal Qualities considered important; Geographic origin/residence considered	African American 5%; Hispanic 5%; Asian 4%	733

Eureka College (Eureka, IL)	NR	Alumni relations considered as a factor	Character & Personal Qualities considered very important	African American 9%; Hispanic 1%; Asian 1%	516
Evangel University (Springfield, MO)	NR	NR	Religious affiliation and/or commitment and Character & Personal Qualities considered important	African American 2%	1,616
The Evergreen State College (Olympia, WA)	Minority status considered as factor	NR	Geographic origin/residence considered important	African American 5%; Hispanic 5%; Native American 4%; Asian 5%	3,907
Excelsior College (Albany, NY)	NR	NR	NR	African American 15%; Hispanic 7%; Native American 1%; Asian 9%	26,022
Fairfield University (Fairfield, CT)	Minority status considered as factor	Alumni relations considered as a factor	Geographic origin/residence, Character and Personal Qualities considered	African American 2%; Hispanic 5%; Asian 3%	3,552
Fairleigh Dickinson University, College at Florham (Madison, NJ)	NR	Alumni relations considered as a factor	Character & Personal Qualities considered important	African American 7%; Hispanic 7%; Asian 3%	2,518
Fairleigh Dickinson University, Metropolitan Campus (Teaneck, NJ)	NR	Alumni relations considered as a factor	Character & Personal Qualities considered important	African American 21%; Hispanic 17%; Asian 5%	3,114

(continued)

College	Use of Race in Admission Decisions and Degree Utilized (if at all)	Use of Alumni Relations or Legacies as Factor and Degree Utilized	Use of Other Factors (e.g., geographic origin or religious affiliation) and Degree Utilized	Reported Ethnic/Minority Representation	Total Student Population
Fairmont State College (Fairmont, WV)	NR	NR	NR	African American 2%	6,496
Farmingdale State University (Farmingdale, NY)	NR	Alumni relations considered as a factor	Character & Personal Qualities considered	African American 15%; Hispanic 9%; Asian 4%	3,909
Fashion Institute of Technology (New York, NY)	NR	NR	NR	African American 7%; Hispanic 9%; Asian 10%	6,537
Faulkner University (Montgomery, AL)	NR	Alumni relations is considered as important factor	Religious affiliation and/or commitment and Character & Personal Qualities considered important	African American 44%; Hispanic 1%; Asian 1%	2,225
Fayetteville State University (Fayetteville, NC)	NR	NR	Character & Personal Qualities considered important	African American 80%; Hispanic 4%; Native American 1%; Asian 1%	3,660
Felician College (Lodi, NJ)	Minority status considered as factor	Alumni relations considered as a factor	Character & Personal Qualities considered	African American 14%; Hispanic 16%; Asian 5%	1,416

Ferris State University (Big Rapids, MI)	Minority status considered as factor	Alumni relations considered as a factor	Character & Personal Qualities considered	African American 6%; Hispanic 1%; Native American 1%; Asian 1%	10,300
Ferrum College (Ferrum, VA)	NR	NR	Character & Personal Qualities considered important	African American 18%; Hispanic 1%; Asian 1%	951
Fisk University (Nashville, TN)	NR	Alumni relations is considered as important factor	Character & Personal Qualities considered very important	African American 98%	812
Fitchburg State College (Fitchburg, MA)	NR	Alumni relations considered as a factor	NR	African American 3%; Hispanic 3%; Asian 2%	3,157
Five Towns College (Dix Hills, NY)	NR	NR	Character & Personal Qualities considered very important	African American 20%; Hispanic 14%; Asian 2%	1,026
Flagler College (St. Augustine, FL)	NR	Alumni relations is considered as important factor	Geographic origin/residence, Character and Personal Qualities considered	African American 2%; Hispanic 4%; Asian 6%	2,106
Florida A&M University (Tallahassee, FL)	Minority status considered as factor	Alumni relations considered as a factor	Geographic origin/residence, Character and Personal Qualities considered	African American 97%	10,592
Florida Atlantic University (Boca Raton, FL)	Minority status considered as factor	Alumni relations considered as a factor	NR	African American 18%; Hispanic 15%; Asian 5%	19,081

(continued)

College	Use of Race in Admission Decisions and Degree Utilized (if at all)	Use of Alumni Relations or Legacies as Factor and Degree Utilized	Use of Other Factors (e.g., geographic origin or religious affiliation) and Degree Utilized	Reported Ethnic/Minority Representation	Total Student Population
Florida College (Temple Terrace, FL)	NR	NR	NR	African American 2%; Hispanic 2%	503
Florida Gulf Coast University (Fort Myers, FL)	Minority status considered as factor	NR	Character & Personal Qualities considered	African American 5%; Hispanic 9%; Asian 2%	4,776
Florida Institute of Technology (Melbourne, FL)	NR	NR	Character & Personal Qualities considered	African American 4%; Hispanic 7%; Asian 3%	2,298
Florida International University (Miami, FL)	NR	NR	Geographic origin/residence, Character and Personal Qualities considered very important	African American 14%; Hispanic 56%; Asian 4%	25,729
Florida Southern College (Lakeland, FL)	NR	Alumni relations considered as a factor	Character & Personal Qualities considered important	African American 6%; Hispanic 5%; Asian 1%	1,894
Florida State University (Tallahassee, FL)	NR	Alumni relations considered as a factor	Geographic origin/residence, Character and Personal Qualities considered important	African American 12%; Hispanic 10%; Asian 3%	29,820

Fontbonne University (St. Louis, MO)	NR	Alumni relations considered as a factor	Character & Personal Qualities considered important	African American 33%; Hispanic 1%; Asian 1%	1,888
Fordham University (New York, NY)	Minority status considered as factor	Alumni relations considered as a factor	Character & Personal Qualities considered important; Geographic origin/residence considered	African American 6%; Hispanic 11%; Asian 6%	7,244
Fort Hays State University (Hays, KS)	NR	NR	NR	African American 1%; Hispanic 2%; Asian 1%	5,710
Fort Lewis College (Durango, CO)	NR	NR	NR	African American 1%; Hispanic 4%; Native American 14%; Asian 1%	4,056
Fort Valley State University (Fort Valley, GA)	Minority status is considered as important factor	Alumni relations considered as a factor	Geographic origin/residence, Character and Personal Qualities considered	African American 95%; Hispanic 1%; Native American 1%	2,088
Framingham State College (Framingham, MA)	NR	Alumni relations considered as a factor	Geographic origin/residence, Character and Personal Qualities considered	African American 3%; Hispanic 3%; Asian 3%	3,476
Francis Marion University (Florence, SC)	NR	NR	NR	African American 40%; Hispanic 1%; Native American 1%; Asian 1%	3,068

(continued)

College	Use of Race in Admission Decisions and Degree Utilized (if at all)	Use of Alumni Relations or Legacies as Factor and Degree Utilized	Use of Other Factors (e.g., geographic origin or religious affiliation) and Degree Utilized	Reported Ethnic/Minority Representation	Total Student Population
The Franciscan University (Clinton, IA)	NR	NR	Character and Personal Qualities considered very important	Hispanic 4%; Asian 2%	1,832
Franklin & Marshall College (Lancaster, PA)	Minority status is considered as important factor	Alumni relations considered as a factor	Character & Personal Qualities considered important; Geographic origin/residence considered	African American 2%; Hispanic 3%; Asian 4%	1,931
Franklin College (Franklin, IN)	Minority status is considered as important factor	Alumni relations considered as a factor	Character & Personal Qualities considered important; Geographic origin/residence considered	African American 4%; Hispanic 2%; Asian 1%	994
Franklin Pierce College (Rindge, NH)	NR	NR	Character and Personal Qualities considered very important	African American 4%; Hispanic 2%; Asian 1%	1,586
Franklin University (Columbus, OH)	NR	NR	NR	African American 19%; Hispanic 2%; Asian 3%	5,682

Freed-Hardeman University (Henderson, TN)	NR	Alumni relations considered as a factor	Character & Personal Qualities and Religious Affiliation considered	African American 4%	1,367
Fresno Pacific University (Fresno, CA)	NR	NR	NR	African American 4%; Hispanic 22%; Native American 1%; Asian 2%	1,304
Frostburg State University (Frostburg, MD)	NR	Alumni relations considered as a factor	Character & Personal Qualities considered	African American 13%; Hispanic 2%; Asian 2%	4,453
Furman University (Greenville, SC)	Minority status considered as factor	Alumni relations considered as a factor	Character & Personal Qualities considered important	African American 6%; Hispanic 1%; Asian 2%	2,807
Gallaudet University (Washington, DC)	NR	NR	Character & Personal Qualities considered important	African American 10%; Hispanic 7%; Native American 1%; Asian 4%	1,178
Gannon University (Erie, PA)	NR	Alumni relations is considered as important factor	Character & Personal Qualities considered important	African American 5%; Hispanic 1%; Asian 1%	2,309
Gardner-Webb University (Boiling Springs, NC)	NR	NR	NR	African American 16%; Hispanic 1%; Native American 1%; Asian 1%	2,551
Geneva College (Beaver Falls, PA)	NR	Alumni relations considered as a factor	Character & Personal Qualities considered	African American 9%; Hispanic 1%; Asian 1%	1,589
George Fox University (Newberg, OR)	NR	NR	Character & Personal Qualities considered	African American 1%; Hispanic 3%; Native American 2%; Asian 4%	1,713

(*continued*)

College	Use of Race in Admission Decisions and Degree Utilized (if at all)	Use of Alumni Relations or Legacies as Factor and Degree Utilized	Use of Other Factors (e.g., geographic origin or religious affiliation) and Degree Utilized	Reported Ethnic/Minority Representation	Total Student Population
George Mason University (Fairfax, VA)	Minority status considered as factor	Alumni relations considered as a factor	Character & Personal Qualities considered important; Geographic origin/residence considered	African American 8%; Hispanic 8%; Asian 17%	16,579
The George Washington University (Washington, DC)	Minority status considered as factor	Alumni relations considered as a factor	Geographic origin/residence, Character and Personal Qualities considered	African American 5%; Hispanic 5%; Asian 9%	9,953
Georgetown College (Georgetown, KY)	Minority status considered as factor	Alumni relations considered as a factor	Character & Personal Qualities considered important; Geographic origin/residence and Religious Affiliation considered	African American 4%; Hispanic 1%	1,277
Georgetown University (Washington, DC)	Minority status considered as factor	Alumni relations considered as a factor	Character & Personal Qualities considered very important; Geographic origin/residence considered	African American 7%; Hispanic 6%; Asian 10%	6,282

Georgia College & State University (Milledgeville, GA)	NR	NR	NR	African American 9%; Hispanic 1%; Asian 1%	4,632
Georgia Institute of Technology (Atlanta, GA)	NR	NR	Character & Personal Qualities considered important; Geographic origin/residence considered	African American 7%; Hispanic 3%; Asian 15%	11,354
Georgia Southern University (Statesboro, GA)	NR	NR	NR	African American 23%; Hispanic 1%; Asian 1%	13,526
Georgia Southwestern State University (Americus, GA)	NR	NR	NR	African American 31%; Hispanic 1%	2,053
Georgia State University (Atlanta Georgia)	NR	Alumni relations considered as a factor	Geographic origin/residence, Character and Personal Qualities considered	African American 32%; Hispanic 3%; Asian 10%	19,239
Georgian Court College (Lakewood, NJ)	NR	Alumni relations considered as a factor	Character & Personal Qualities considered	African American 5%; Hispanic 6%; Asian 2%	1,805
Gettysburg College (Gettysburg, PA)	Minority status considered as factor	Alumni relations considered as a factor	Character & Personal Qualities considered important; Geographic origin/residence considered	African American 4%; Hispanic 1%; Asian 2%	2,453

(continued)

College	Use of Race in Admission Decisions and Degree Utilized (if at all)	Use of Alumni Relations or Legacies as Factor and Degree Utilized	Use of Other Factors (e.g., geographic origin or religious affiliation) and Degree Utilized	Reported Ethnic/Minority Representation	Total Student Population
Glenville State College (Glenville, WV)	NR	NR	NR	African American 6%; Hispanic 1%; Asian 1%	1,374
Globe Institute of Technology (New York, NY)	Minority status is considered a very important factor	Alumni relations considered as a very important factor	Character & Personal Qualities considered very important	African American 21%; Hispanic 19%; Asian 26%	2,100
Golden Gate University (San Francisco, CA)	Minority status considered as factor	NR	NR	African American 7%; Hispanic 10%; Asian 17%	614
Gonzaga University (Spokane, WA)	Minority status considered as factor	Alumni relations considered as a factor	Character & Personal Qualities considered important	African American 1%; Hispanic 3%; Native American 1%; Asian 6%	4,007
Gordon College (Wenham, MA)	Minority status considered as factor	Alumni relations considered as a factor	Religious affiliation and/or commitment and Character & Personal Qualities considered important	African American 1%; Hispanic 2%; Asian 2%	1,621
Goshen College (Goshen, IN)	NR	Alumni relations is considered as important factor	Character & Personal Qualities considered important	African American 3%; Hispanic 4%; Asian 1%	882

Goucher College (Baltimore, MD)	NR	Alumni relations considered as a factor	Character & Personal Qualities considered	African American 5%; Hispanic 3%; Asian 3%	1,345
Governors State University (University Park, IL)	NR	NR	NR	African American 32%; Hispanic 6%; Asian 2%	2,623
Grace College and Seminary (Winona Lake, IN)	NR	Alumni relations considered as a factor	Religious affiliation and/or commitment and Character & Personal Qualities considered important	African American 2%; Hispanic 2%; Native American 1%	1,054
Graceland University (Lamoni, IA)	Minority status considered as factor	NR	Character & Personal Qualities considered important	African American 3%; Hispanic 2%; Native American 1%; Asian 2%	1,878
Grambling State University (Grambling, LA)	NR	Alumni relations considered as a factor	NR	African American 96%	4,171
Grand Canyon University (Phoenix, AZ)	NR	NR	Character & Personal Qualities considered	African American 3%; Hispanic 7%; Native American 1%; Asian 2%	1,609
Grand Valley State University (Allendale, MI)	Minority status considered as factor	Alumni relations considered as a factor	Geographic origin/residence, Character and Personal Qualities considered	African American 5%; Hispanic 3%; Native American 1%; Asian 2%	18,160
Grand View College (Des Moines, IA)	NR	Alumni relations considered as a factor	Character & Personal Qualities considered very important	African American 3%; Hispanic 1%; Asian 2%	1,697

(*continued*)

College	Use of Race in Admission Decisions and Degree Utilized (if at all)	Use of Alumni Relations or Legacies as Factor and Degree Utilized	Use of Other Factors (e.g., geographic origin or religious affiliation) and Degree Utilized	Reported Ethnic/Minority Representation	Total Student Population
Green Mountain College (Poultney, VT)	Minority status considered as factor	NR	Character & Personal Qualities considered very important	African American 1%; Hispanic 3%; Native American 1%; Asian 1%	591
Greensboro College (Greensboro, NC)	NR	Alumni relations considered as a factor	Character & Personal Qualities considered important; Religious affiliation and/or commitment considered	African American 15%; Hispanic 1%; Asian 2%	1,178
Greenville College (Greenville, IL)	NR	Alumni relations considered as a factor	Religious affiliation and/or commitment and Character & Personal Qualities considered important	African American 7%; Hispanic 2%; Native American 1%; Asian 1%	1,135
Grinnell College (Grinnell, IA)	Minority status is considered as important factor	Alumni relations considered as a factor	Geographic origin/ residence, Character and Personal Qualities considered	African American 4%; Hispanic 4%; Native American 1%; Asian 5%	1,518
Grove City College (Grove City, PA)	Minority status considered as factor	Alumni relations considered as a factor	Religious affiliation and/or commitment and Character &	Asian 2%	2,318

Guilford College (Greensboro, NC)	Minority status considered as factor	Alumni relations considered as a factor	Personal Qualities considered very important; Geographic origin/residence considered	African American 19%; Hispanic 2%; Native American 1%; Asian 2%	2,101
Gustavus Adolphus College (Saint Peter, MN)	Minority status considered as factor	Alumni relations considered as a factor	Geographic origin/residence, Character and Personal Qualities, and Religious Affiliation/Commitment all considered	African American 1%; Hispanic 1%; Asian 4%	2,506
Gwynedd-Mercy College (Gwynedd Valley, PA)	NR	Alumni relations considered as a factor	Character & Personal Qualities considered	African American 13%; Hispanic 2%; Asian 3%	1,939
Hamilton College (Clinton, NY)	Minority status is considered as important factor	Alumni relations considered as a factor	Character & Personal Qualities considered important; Geographic origin/residence considered	African American 4%; Hispanic 4%; Native American 1%; Asian 5%	1,762
Hamline University (Saint Paul, MN)	Minority status considered as factor	Alumni relations considered as a factor	Character & Personal Qualities considered	African American 4%; Hispanic 2%; Native American 1%; Asian 6%	1,895

(continued)

College	Use of Race in Admission Decisions and Degree Utilized (if at all)	Use of Alumni Relations or Legacies as Factor and Degree Utilized	Use of Other Factors (e.g., geographic origin or religious affiliation) and Degree Utilized	Reported Ethnic/Minority Representation	Total Student Population
Hampden-Sydney College (Hampden-Sydney, VA)	Minority status considered as factor	Alumni relations considered as a factor	Character & Personal Qualities considered very important	African American 2%; Hispanic 1%; Asian 1%	1,082
Hampshire College (Amherst, MA)	Minority status considered as factor	Alumni relations considered as a factor	Character & Personal Qualities considered important	African American 3%; Hispanic 5%; Asian 4%	1,344
Hampton University (Hampton, VA)	NR	Alumni relations considered as a factor	Character & Personal Qualities considered very important	African American 95%	5,200
Hannibal-Lagrange College (Hannibal, MO)	NR	NR	NR	African American 2%; Hispanic 1%	815
Hanover College (Hanover, IN)	NR	Alumni relations considered as a factor	Character & Personal Qualities considered important; Geographic origin/residence considered	African American 2%; Hispanic 2%; Asian 3%	989
Harding University (Searcy, AR)	NR	Alumni relations considered as a factor	Character & Personal Qualities considered very important; Geographic origin/residence considered	African American 4%; Hispanic 1%; Native American 1%; Asian 1%	4,023

Institution	Admissions Factor 1	Admissions Factor 2	Admissions Factor 3	Enrollment
Hardin-Simmons University (Abilene, TX)	NR	Alumni relations considered as a factor	Character & Personal Qualities considered important	African American 5%; Hispanic 9%; Native American 1%; Asian 1%	1,937
Hartwick College (Oneonta, NY)	Minority status considered as factor	Alumni relations considered as a factor	Geographic origin/residence, Character and Personal Qualities considered	African American 5%; Hispanic 4%; Native American 1%; Asian 1%	1,455
Harvard College (Cambridge, MA)	Minority status considered as factor	Alumni relations considered as a factor	Character & Personal Qualities considered very important; Geographic origin/residence considered	African American 8%; Hispanic 8%; Native American 1%; Asian 18%	6,649
Harvey Mudd College (Claremont, CA)	Minority status considered as factor	Alumni relations is considered as important factor	Character & Personal Qualities considered very important; Geographic origin/residence considered	African American 1%; Hispanic 6%; Asian 18%	720
Hastings College (Hastings, NE)	Minority status considered as factor	Alumni relations considered as a factor	Character & Personal Qualities considered important	African American 3%; Hispanic 2%; Asian 1%	1,091
Haverford College (Haverford, PA)	Minority status considered as factor	Alumni relations considered as a factor	Character & Personal Qualities considered very important; Geographic origin/residence considered	African American 6%; Hispanic 6%; Native American 1%; Asian 13%	1,172
Hawaii Pacific University (Honolulu, HI)	NR	NR	Character & Personal Qualities considered	African American 7%; Hispanic 6%; Native American 1%; Asian 29%	5,985

(*continued*)

College	Use of Race in Admission Decisions and Degree Utilized (if at all)	Use of Alumni Relations or Legacies as Factor and Degree Utilized	Use of Other Factors (e.g., geographic origin or religious affiliation) and Degree Utilized	Reported Ethnic/Minority Representation	Total Student Population
Heidelberg College (Tiffin, OH)	NR	Alumni relations is considered as important factor	Character & Personal Qualities considered very important; Geographic origin/residence and Religious Affiliation considered	African American 4%; Hispanic 1%	1,111
Henderson State University (Arkadelphia, AR)	NR	NR	Character & Personal Qualities considered	African American 15%; Hispanic 1%; Native American 1%	2,709
Hendrix College (Conway, AR)	Minority status considered as factor	NR	Character & Personal Qualities considered important	African American 4%; Hispanic 3%; Native American 2%; Asian 3%	1,036
Heritage College (Toppenish, WA)	NR	NR	NR	African American 1%; Hispanic 58%; Native American 13%	751
Herkimer County Community College (Herkimer, NY)	NR	NR	NR	African American 3%; Hispanic 2%; Native American 1%; Asian 1%	2,195
High Point University (High Point, NC)	NR	NR	Character & Personal Qualities considered important	African American 22%; Hispanic 2%; Asian 1%	2,605

Hilbert College (Hamburg, NY)	NR	NR	Character & Personal Qualities considered	African American 4%; Hispanic 2%; Native American 1%; Asian 1%	1,052
Hillsdale College (Hillsdale, MI)	NR	Alumni relations considered as a factor	Character & Personal Qualities considered very important	NR	1,115
Hiram College (Hiram, OH)	Minority status considered as factor	Alumni relations considered as a factor	Character & Personal Qualities considered important	African American 11%; Hispanic 1%; Asian 1%	1,087
Hobart and William Smith Colleges (Geneva, NY)	Minority status considered as factor	Alumni relations considered as a factor	Character & Personal Qualities considered important; Geographic origin/residence considered	African American 4%; Hispanic 4%; Asian 2%	1,825
Hofstra University (Hempstead, NY)	Minority status considered as factor	Alumni relations considered as a factor	Character & Personal Qualities considered important; Geographic origin/residence considered	African American 10%; Hispanic 8%; Asian 4%	8,869
Hollins University (Roanoke, VA)	Minority status considered as factor	Alumni relations considered as a factor	Character & Personal Qualities considered	African American 9%; Hispanic 2%; Native American 1%; Asian 2%	805
Holy Family University (Philadelphia, PA)	NR	Alumni relations is considered as important factor	Character & Personal Qualities considered important	African American 3%; Hispanic 2%; Asian 3%	1,600
Holy Names College (Oakland, CA)	NR	Alumni relations considered as a factor	Character & Personal Qualities considered	African American 32%; Hispanic 16%; Native American 1%; Asian 6%	592

(continued)

College	Use of Race in Admission Decisions and Degree Utilized (if at all)	Use of Alumni Relations or Legacies as Factor and Degree Utilized	Use of Other Factors (e.g., geographic origin or religious affiliation) and Degree Utilized	Reported Ethnic/Minority Representation	Total Student Population
Hood College (Frederick, MD)	Minority status considered as factor	Alumni relations considered as a factor	Character & Personal Qualities considered	African American 13%; Hispanic 2%; Asian 2%	808
Hope College (Holland, MI)	NR	Alumni relations considered as a factor	Character & Personal Qualities considered	African American 1%; Hispanic 2%; Asian 2%	3,496
Hope International University (Fullerton, CA)	NR	NR	Religious affiliation and/or commitment and Character & Personal Qualities considered	African American 8%; Hispanic 19%; Native American 1%; Asian 4%	978
Houghton College (Houghton, NY)	Minority status considered as factor	Alumni relations considered as a factor	Religious affiliation and/or commitment and Character & Personal Qualities considered very important	African American 2%; Hispanic 1%; Asian 2%	1,428
Houston Baptist University (Houston, TX)	NR	Alumni relations considered as a factor	Geographic origin/ residence, Character and Personal Qualities, and	African American 19%; Hispanic 14%; Native American 1%; Asian 13%	1,761

Institution				
Howard Payne University (Brownwood, TX)	NR	NR	Character & Personal Qualities considered	African American 8%; Hispanic 12%; Native American 1%; Asian 1%	1,303
Howard University (Washington, DC)	NR	Alumni relations considered as a factor	Character & Personal Qualities considered important	African American 84%	7,063
Humboldt State University (Arcata, CA)	Minority status considered as factor	NR	Character & Personal Qualities considered important	African American 2%; Hispanic 6%; Native American 2%; Asian 2%	6,450
Humphreys College (Stockton, CA)	NR	NR	NR	African American 9%; Hispanic 21%; Native American 2%; Asian 8%	692
Huntingdon College (Montgomery, AL)	Minority status considered as factor	Alumni relations considered as a factor	Character & Personal Qualities considered	African American 8%; Native American 1%; Asian 1%	602
Huntington College (Huntington, IN)	Minority status considered as factor	Alumni relations considered as a factor	Religious affiliation and/or commitment and Character & Personal Qualities considered important	African American 1%; Hispanic 1%; Asian 1%	878
Huron University (Huron, SD)	Minority status considered as factor	Alumni relations considered as a factor	Character & Personal Qualities considered important; Geographic origin/residence considered	African American 11%; Hispanic 6%; Native American 3%; Asian 1%	540

(continued)

College	Use of Race in Admission Decisions and Degree Utilized (if at all)	Use of Alumni Relations or Legacies as Factor and Degree Utilized	Use of Other Factors (e.g., geographic origin or religious affiliation) and Degree Utilized	Reported Ethnic/Minority Representation	Total Student Population
Husson College (Bangor, ME)	NR	Alumni relations considered as a factor	Character & Personal Qualities considered important	African American 2%; Hispanic 1%; Asian 1%	1,442
Huston-Tillotson College (Austin, TX)	NR	NR	Character & Personal Qualities considered	African American 78%; Hispanic 10%; Asian 1%	583
Idaho State University (Pocatello, ID)	NR	Alumni relations considered as a factor	Character & Personal Qualities considered	Hispanic 3%; Native American 1%; Asian 1%	11,040
Illinois College (Jacksonville, IL)	Minority status considered as factor	NR	Character & Personal Qualities considered important; Geographic origin/residence considered	Hispanic 3%; Hispanic 1%; Native American 1%	891
The Illinois Institute of Art—Schaumburg (Schaumburg, IL)	Minority status considered as factor	Alumni relations is considered as important factor	NR	African American 3%; Hispanic 6%; Asian 8%	699
Illinois Institute of Technology (Chicago, IL)	NR	NR	Character & Personal Qualities considered	African American 6%; Hispanic 7%; Asian 14%	1,961
Illinois State University (Normal, IL)	NR	NR	Character & Personal Qualities considered	African American 6%; Hispanic 3%; Asian 2%	17,806

Illinois Wesleyan University (Bloomington, IL)	Minority status considered as factor	Alumni relations considered as a factor	Character & Personal Qualities considered important; Geographic origin/residence considered	African American 3%; Hispanic 3%; Asian 2%	2,111
Immaculata University (Immaculata, PA)	NR	Alumni relations considered as a factor	NR	African American 6%; Hispanic 1%; Asian 1%	2,850
Indiana Institute of Technology (Fort Wayne, IN)	Minority status is considered as important factor	Alumni relations is considered as very important	Character & Personal Qualities considered	African American 17%; Hispanic 2%; Native American 1%; Asian 1%	2,985
Indiana State University (Terre Haute, IN)	NR	NR	Character & Personal Qualities considered	African American 12%; Hispanic 1%; Asian 1%	9,085
Indiana University—Bloomington (Bloomington, IN)	Minority status considered as factor	Alumni relations considered as a factor	Character & Personal Qualities considered important; Geographic origin/residence considered	African American 4%; Hispanic 2%; Asian 3%	29,062
Indiana University East (Richmond, IN)	NR	NR	Geographic origin/residence considered	African American 5%; Hispanic 1%; Asian 1%	2,176
Indiana University Kokomo (Kokomo, IN)	NR	NR	NR	African American 3%; Hispanic 1%; Asian 1%	2,505
Indiana University Northwest (Gary, IN)	NR	NR	NR	African American 21%; Hispanic 12%; Asian 1%	4,190

(continued)

College	Use of Race in Admission Decisions and Degree Utilized (if at all)	Use of Alumni Relations or Legacies as Factor and Degree Utilized	Use of Other Factors (e.g., geographic origin or religious affiliation) and Degree Utilized	Reported Ethnic/Minority Representation	Total Student Population
Indiana University of Pennsylvania (Indiana, PA)	NR	Alumni relations considered as a factor	Character & Personal Qualities considered	African American 6%; Hispanic 1%; Asian 1%	11,861
Indiana University—Purdue University Fort Wayne (Fort Wayne, IN)	NR	NR	Geographic origin/residence considered	African American 5%; Hispanic 2%; Asian 2%	10,587
Indiana University—Purdue University Indianapolis (Indianapolis, IN)	NR	NR	Character & Personal Qualities considered	African American 11%; Hispanic 2%; Asian 2%	20,844
Indiana University South Bend (South Bend, IN)	NR	NR	Geographic origin/residence considered	African American 7%; Hispanic 3%; Native American 1%; Asian 1%	5,967
Indiana University Southeast (New Albany, IN)	NR	NR	Geographic origin/residence considered	African American 3%; Hispanic 1%; Asian 1%	5,219
Indiana Wesleyan University (Marion, IN)	NR	NR	NR	African American 11%; Hispanic 1%; Asian 1%	6,554

Institution				
International College (Naples, FL)	NR	NR	African American 13%; Hispanic 14%; Native American 1%; Asian 1%	1,327
Iona College (New Rochelle, NY)	NR	Alumni relations considered as a factor	Character & Personal Qualities considered important; Geographic origin/residence considered	African American 7%; Hispanic 11%; Asian 1%	3,413
Iowa State University (Ames, IA)	NR	NR	Character & Personal Qualities considered important; Geographic origin/residence considered	African American 3%; Hispanic 2%; Asian 3%	20,993
Iowa Wesleyan College (Mt. Pleasant, IA)	NR	NR	Geographic origin/residence considered important; Religious Affiliation considered	African American 5%; Hispanic 2%; Asian 1%	785
Ithaca College (Ithaca, NY)	NR	Alumni relations considered as a factor	Character & Personal Qualities considered important	African American 2%; Hispanic 3%; Asian 3%	6,159
Jackson State University (Jackson, MS)	NR	NR	Geographic origin/residence considered	African American 98%	5,471
Jacksonville State University (Jacksonville, AL)	NR	NR	NR	African American 22%; Hispanic 1%; Native American 1%; Asian 1%	7,096

(*continued*)

College	Use of Race in Admission Decisions and Degree Utilized (if at all)	Use of Alumni Relations or Legacies as Factor and Degree Utilized	Use of Other Factors (e.g., geographic origin or religious affiliation) and Degree Utilized	Reported Ethnic/Minority Representation	Total Student Population
Jacksonville University (Jacksonville, FL)	NR	Alumni relations considered as a factor	Character & Personal Qualities considered	African American 15%; Hispanic 5%; Native American 1%; Asian 3%	2,194
James Madison University (Harrisonburg, VA)	Minority status considered as factor	Alumni relations considered as a factor	Character & Personal Qualities considered important; Geographic origin/residence considered	African American 3%; Hispanic 2%; Asian 5%	14,677
Jamestown College (Jamestown, ND)	NR	Alumni relations considered as a factor	Character & Personal Qualities considered	African American 2%; Hispanic 2%; Native American 1%; Asian 1%	1,152
Jarvis Christian College (Hawkins, TX)	NR	NR	NR	African American 98%; Hispanic 1%	538
John Brown University (Siloam Springs, AR)	NR	Alumni relations considered as a factor	Religious affiliation and/or commitment and Character & Personal Qualities considered	African American 3%; Hispanic 2%; Native American 2%; Asian 2%	1,674

John Carroll University (University Heights, OH)	Minority status considered as factor	Alumni relations considered as a factor	Character & Personal Qualities considered important; Geographic origin/residence considered	African American 4%; Hispanic 2%; Asian 3%	3,442
Johns Hopkins University (Baltimore, MD)	Minority status considered as factor	Alumni relations considered as a factor	Character & Personal Qualities considered very important; Geographic origin/residence considered	African American 5%; Hispanic 5%; Asian 22%	4,201
Johnson & Wales University—Charleston (Charleston, SC)	NR	NR	NR	African American 8%; Hispanic 1%; Native American 1%; Asian 1%	1,497
Johnson & Wales University—Denver (Denver, CO)	NR	Alumni relations considered as a factor	NR	African American 6%; Hispanic 12%; Native American 1%; Asian 4%	1,512
Johnson & Wales University—Norfolk (Norfolk, VA)	NR	NR	NR	African American 33%; Hispanic 5%; Native American 1%; Asian 2%	709
Johnson & Wales University—North Miami (Miami, FL)	NR	Alumni relations considered as a factor	NR	African American 32%; Hispanic 21%; Asian 2%	2,388
Johnson & Wales University—Providence (Providence, RI)	NR	Alumni relations considered as a factor	NR	African American 11%; Hispanic 6%; Asian 3%	9,145

(continued)

College	Use of Race in Admission Decisions and Degree Utilized (if at all)	Use of Alumni Relations or Legacies as Factor and Degree Utilized	Use of Other Factors (e.g., geographic origin or religious affiliation) and Degree Utilized	Reported Ethnic/Minority Representation	Total Student Population
Johnson Bible College (Knoxville, TN)	NR	Alumni relations considered as a factor	Religious affiliation and/or commitment and Character & Personal Qualities considered important	African American 2%; Hispanic 1%; Asian 1%	744
Johnson C. Smith University (Charlotte, NC)	NR	NR	NR	African American 99%	1,415
Johnson State College (Johnson, VT)	NR	NR	Character & Personal Qualities considered important	African American 1%; Hispanic 2%;	1,441
Judson College (Elgin, IL)	NR	NR	Character & Personal Qualities considered important	African American 4%; Hispanic 5%; Asian 1%	1,132
The Juilliard School (New York, NY)	NR	NR	Character & Personal Qualities considered important	African American 13%; Hispanic 5%; Asian 12%	504
Juniata College (Huntington, PA)	Minority status considered as factor	Alumni relations considered as a factor	Character & Personal Qualities considered very important	African American 1%; Hispanic 1%; Asian 1%	1,378

Kalamazoo College (Kalamazoo, MI)	Minority status considered as factor	Alumni relations considered as a factor	Character & Personal Qualities considered important; Geographic origin/residence considered	African American 3%; Hispanic 1%; Asian 5%	1,242
Kansas City Art Institute (Kansas City, MO)	NR	NR	Character & Personal Qualities considered very important	African American 3%; Hispanic 7%; Native American 2%; Asian 4%	579
Kansas State University (Manhattan, KS)	NR	NR	NR	African American 3%; Hispanic 2%; Asian 1%	18,893
Kansas Wesleyan University (Salina, KS)	NR	NR	NR	African American 8%; Hispanic 4%; Native American 1%; Asian 1%	640
Kean University (Union, NJ)	Minority status considered as factor	Alumni relations considered as a factor	Character & Personal Qualities considered	African American 20%; Hispanic 20%; Asian 6%	9,710
Keene State College (Keene, NH)	NR	Alumni relations considered as a factor	NR	Hispanic 1%; Asian 1%	4,779
Kendall College (Chicago, IL)	NR	NR	Character & Personal Qualities considered	African American 14%; Hispanic 6%; Native American 1%; Asian 5%	628
Kendall College of Art and Design of Ferris State University (Grand Rapids, MI)	NR	NR	Character & Personal Qualities considered	African American 2%; Hispanic 1%; Native American 1%; Asian 2%	932

(*continued*)

College	Use of Race in Admission Decisions and Degree Utilized (if at all)	Use of Alumni Relations or Legacies as Factor and Degree Utilized	Use of Other Factors (e.g., geographic origin or religious affiliation) and Degree Utilized	Reported Ethnic/Minority Representation	Total Student Population
Kennesaw State University (Kennesaw, GA)	NR	NR	NR	African American 10%; Hispanic 3%; Asian 3%	15,917
Kent State University—Kent Campus (Kent, Ohio)	NR	NR	NR	African American 8%; Hispanic 1%; Asian 1%	19,061
Kentucky Christian College (Grayson, KY)	NR	NR	Religious affiliation and/or commitment and Character & Personal Qualities considered important	African American 1%	569
Kentucky State University (Frankfort, KY)	NR	Alumni relations considered as a factor	Geographic origin/ residence considered	African American 67%; Hispanic 1%; Asian 1%	1,942
Kentucky Wesleyan College (Owensboro, KY)	Minority status considered as factor	Alumni relations considered as a factor	Character & Personal Qualities considered important	African American 8%; Hispanic 2%; Asian 1%	657
Kenyon College (Bambier, OH)	Minority status considered as factor	Alumni relations considered as a factor	Character & Personal Qualities considered important;	African American 3%; Hispanic 2%; Asian 3%	1,605

Kettering University (Flint, MI)	NR	NR	Geographic origin/residence considered	African American 6%; Hispanic 2%; Asian 5%	2,511
Keuka College (Keuka Park, NY)	NR	Alumni relations considered as a factor	Character & Personal Qualities considered important	African American 3%; Hispanic 1%; Native American 1%	1,154
King College (Bristol, TN)	NR	NR	Character & Personal Qualities considered	African American 1%; Hispanic 1%; Asian 1%	670
King's College (Wilkes-Barre, PA)	NR	NR	Religious affiliation and/or commitment and Character & Personal Qualities considered important; Geographic Origin/Residence considered	African American 2%; Hispanic 1%	1,999
Knox College (Galesburg, IL)	Minority status considered as factor	Alumni relations considered as a factor	Character & Personal Qualities considered	African American 5%; Hispanic 4%; Asian 5%	1,167
Kutztown University of Pennsylvania (Kutztown, PA)	Minority status considered as factor	NR	Geographic origin/residence, Character and Personal Qualities considered	African American 6%; Hispanic 3%; Asian 1%	8,141

(*continued*)

College	Use of Race in Admission Decisions and Degree Utilized (if at all)	Use of Alumni Relations or Legacies as Factor and Degree Utilized	Use of Other Factors (e.g., geographic origin or religious affiliation) and Degree Utilized	Reported Ethnic/Minority Representation	Total Student Population
La Sierra University (Riverside, CA)	NR	NR	Religious affiliation and/or commitment and Character & Personal Qualities considered important; Geographic Origin/Residence considered	African American 6%; Hispanic 18%; Native American 1%; Asian 26%	1,148
Laboratory Institute of Merchandising (New York, NY)	NR	Alumni relations considered as a factor	Character & Personal Qualities considered	African American 10%; Hispanic 15%; Asian 6%	608
Lafayette College (Easton, PA)	Minority status considered as important factor	Alumni relations considered as important factor	Character & Personal Qualities considered important; Geographic origin/residence considered	African American 5%; Hispanic 3%; Asian 2%	2,251
LaGrange College (LaGrange, GA)	NR	Alumni relations considered as a factor	Character & Personal Qualities considered	African American 13%; Hispanic 1%; Asian 1%	881

Lake Erie College (Painesville, OH)	Minority status considered as factor	Alumni relations considered as a factor	Geographic origin/residence, Character and Personal Qualities, and Religious Affiliation/Commitment all considered	African American 6%; Hispanic 1%	760
Lake Forest College (Lake Forest, IL)	NR	Alumni relations considered as a factor	Character & Personal Qualities considered important; Geographic origin/residence considered	African American 4%; Hispanic 5%; Asian 4%	1,361
Lake Region State College (Devils Lake, ND)	NR	NR	NR	African American 2%; Hispanic 2%; Native American 7%; Asian 1%	656
Lake Superior State University (Sault Saint Marie, MI)	NR	NR	Geographic origin/residence considered	African American 1%; Hispanic 1%; Native American 8%; Asian 1%	3,022
Lakeland College (Sheboygan, WI)	Minority status considered as important factor	Alumni relations considered as important factor	NR	African American 5%; Hispanic 1%; Native American 1%; Asian 2%	2,920
Lamar University (Beaumont, TX)	NR	NR	NR	African American 22%; Hispanic 5%; Native American 1%; Asian 3%	9,057

(continued)

College	Use of Race in Admission Decisions and Degree Utilized (if at all)	Use of Alumni Relations or Legacies as Factor and Degree Utilized	Use of Other Factors (e.g., geographic origin or religious affiliation) and Degree Utilized	Reported Ethnic/Minority Representation	Total Student Population
Lambuth University (Jackson, TN)	NR	NR	NR	African American 17%; Hispanic 2%; Asian 1%	785
Lancaster Bible College (Lancaster, PA)	NR	NR	Religious affiliation and/or commitment and Character & Personal Qualities considered important	African American 3%; Hispanic 1%; Native American 1%	641
Lander University (Greenwood, SC)	NR	Alumni relations considered as a factor	Character & Personal Qualities considered	African American 22%; Hispanic 1%; Asian 1%	2,655
Lane College (Jackson, TN)	NR	Alumni relations considered as a factor	Character & Personal Qualities considered very important	African American 68%	952
La Roche College (Pittsburgh, PA)	NR	NR	Character & Personal Qualities considered very important	African American 4%; Hispanic 1%; Native American 1%; Asian 1%	1,355
LaSalle University (Philadelphia, PA)	NR	Alumni relations considered as a factor	Character & Personal Qualities considered	African American 11%; Hispanic 6%; Asian 2%	4,044

Lasell College (Newton, MA)	NR	Alumni relations considered as a factor	Character & Personal Qualities considered	African American 10%; Hispanic 6%; Asian 5%	1,081
Lawrence Technological University (Southfield, MI)	NR	NR	NR	African American 13%; Hispanic 2%; Asian 3%	2,566
Lawrence University (Appleton, WI)	Minority status considered as important factor	Alumni relations considered as important factor	Character & Personal Qualities considered	African American 2%; Hispanic 3%; Asian 3%	1,344
Le Moyne College (Syracuse, NY)	Minority status considered as factor	Alumni relations considered as a factor	Geographic origin/residence, and Character and Personal Qualities are considered	African American 5%; Hispanic 3%; Native American 1%; Asian 3%	2,437
Lebanon Valley College (Annville, PA)	Minority status considered as factor	Alumni relations considered as a factor	Character & Personal Qualities considered important; Geographic origin/residence considered	African American 2%; Hispanic 1%; Asian 2%	1,668
Lee University (Cleveland, TN)	Minority status considered as factor	Alumni relations considered as a factor	Character & Personal Qualities considered important; Religious Affiliation considered	African American 5%; Hispanic 3%; Asian 1%	3,479

(continued)

College	Use of Race in Admission Decisions and Degree Utilized (if at all)	Use of Alumni Relations or Legacies as Factor and Degree Utilized	Use of Other Factors (e.g., geographic origin or religious affiliation) and Degree Utilized	Reported Ethnic/Minority Representation	Total Student Population
Lees-McRae College (Banner Elk, NC)	NR	Alumni relations considered as a factor	Character & Personal Qualities considered	African American 6%; Hispanic 1%; Asian 1%	792
Lehigh University (Bethlehem, PA)	Minority status considered as factor	Alumni relations considered as a factor	Character & Personal Qualities considered very important	African American 3%; Hispanic 2%; Asian 6%	4,553
LeMoyne-Owen College (Memphis, TN)	NR	NR	NR	African American 98%	720
Lenoir-Rhyne College (Hickory, NC)	NR	NR	Character & Personal Qualities considered	African American 7%; Hispanic 1%; Asian 1%	1,358
Lesley College (Cambridge, MA)	Minority status considered as factor	Alumni relations considered as a factor	Character & Personal Qualities considered important; Geographic origin/residence considered	African American 6%; Hispanic 4%; Native American 1%; Asian 5%	1,028
Letourneau University (Longview, TX)	NR	Alumni relations considered as a factor	Religious affiliation and/or commitment and Character & Personal Qualities considered important	African American 17%; Hispanic 9%; Asian 1%	2,658

Lewis & Clark College (Portland, OR)	Minority status considered very important	Alumni relations considered very important	Character & Personal Qualities considered important; Geographic origin/residence considered	African American 1%; Hispanic 4%; Native American 1%; Asian 5%	1,845
Lewis University (Romeoville, IL)	Minority status considered as factor	Alumni relations considered as a factor	Character & Personal Qualities considered	African American 14%; Hispanic 7%; Asian 3%	3,366
Lewis-Clarke State College (Lewiston, ID)	NR	NR	NR	Hispanic 4%; Native American 5%; Asian 1%	2,908
Liberty University (Lynchburg, VA)	NR	NR	Character & Personal Qualities considered	African American 13%; Hispanic 3%; Native American 1%; Asian 2%	10,505
Life Bible College (San Dimas, CA)	NR	NR	Religious affiliation and/or commitment and Character & Personal Qualities considered important	African American 6%; Hispanic 1%; Native American 1%	481
Life University (Marietta, GA)	NR	NR	Character & Personal Qualities considered	African American 7%	823
Limestone College (Gaffey, SC)	NR	NR	NR	African American 19%; Hispanic 1%; Native American 1%; Asian 1%	625
Lincoln Memorial University (Harrogate, TN)	Minority status considered as factor	Alumni relations considered important	Character & Personal Qualities considered important	African American 4%	1,048

(*continued*)

College	Use of Race in Admission Decisions and Degree Utilized (if at all)	Use of Alumni Relations or Legacies as Factor and Degree Utilized	Use of Other Factors (e.g., geographic origin or religious affiliation) and Degree Utilized	Reported Ethnic/Minority Representation	Total Student Population
Lincoln University (MO) (Jefferson City, MO)	NR	NR	NR	African American 42%; Hispanic 1%; Asian 1%	2,644
Lincoln University (PA) (Lincoln University, PA)	NR	Alumni relations considered as a factor	Geographic origin/residence, and Character and Personal Qualities are considered	African American 91%	1,520
Lindenwood University (St. Charles, MO)	NR	Alumni relations considered as a factor	Character & Personal Qualities considered very important; Geographic origin/residence considered	African American 11%; Hispanic 2%	4,900
Lindsey Wilson College (Columbia, KY)	NR	NR	NR	African American 7%; Hispanic 1%; Asian 1%	1,451
Linfield College (McMinnville, OR)	Minority status considered as factor	Alumni relations considered as a factor	Geographic origin/residence, and Character and Personal Qualities are considered	African American 1%; Hispanic 2%; Native American 1%; Asian 7%	1,608

Lipscomb University (Nashville, TN)	NR	Alumni relations considered as a factor	Character & Personal Qualities considered important; Religious Affiliation considered	African American 4%; Asian 1%	2,315
Livingstone College/Hood Theological Seminary (Salisbury, NC)	NR	NR	NR	African American 93%; Hispanic 1%	1,016
Lock Haven University of Pennsylvania (Lock Haven, PA)	NR	NR	Character & Personal Qualities considered very important	African American 3%; Hispanic 1%; Asian 1%	4,240
Loma Linda University (Loma Linda, CA)	NR	Alumni relations considered as a factor	Religious affiliation and/or commitment and Character & Personal Qualities considered important	African American 6%; Hispanic 17%; Native American 1%; Asian 19%	789
Long Island University—Brooklyn (Brooklyn, NY)	NR	NR	NR	African American 42%; Hispanic 13%; Asian 14%	4,406
Long Island University—C.W. Post (Brookville, NY)	NR	Alumni relations considered as a factor	Character & Personal Qualities considered	African American 7%; Hispanic 7%; Native American 1%; Asian 2%	5,748

(continued)

College	Use of Race in Admission Decisions and Degree Utilized (if at all)	Use of Alumni Relations or Legacies as Factor and Degree Utilized	Use of Other Factors (e.g., geographic origin or religious affiliation) and Degree Utilized	Reported Ethnic/Minority Representation	Total Student Population
Longwood University (Farmville, VA)	Minority status considered as factor	Alumni relations considered as a factor	Geographic origin/residence, and Character and Personal Qualities are considered	African American 6%; Hispanic 2%; Asian 2%	3,694
Loras College (Dubuque, IA)	Minority status considered as factor	NR	Character & Personal Qualities considered	African American 1%; Hispanic 1%; Asian 1%	1,615
Louisiana College (Pineville, LA)	Minority status considered as factor	Alumni relations considered as a factor	Geographic origin/residence, Character and Personal Qualities, and Religious Affiliation/Commitment all considered	African American 7%; Hispanic 2%; Asian 1%	1,014
Louisiana State University—Baton Rouge (Baton Rouge, LA)	NR	NR	Character & Personal Qualities considered	African American 9%; Hispanic 2%; Native American 3%	25,849
Louisiana State University—Shreveport (Shreveport, LA)	NR	NR	NR	African American 22%; Hispanic 2%; Native American 1%; Asian 2%	3,594

Louisiana Tech University (Ruston, LA)	Minority status considered as factor	Alumni relations considered as a factor	NR	African American 15%; Hispanic 2%; Native American 1%; Asian 1%	8,666
Lourdes College (Sylvania, OH)	NR	NR	Character & Personal Qualities considered	African American 15%; Hispanic 2%; Native American 1%; Asian 1%	1,295
Loyola College in Maryland (Baltimore, MD)	Minority status considered as factor	Alumni relations considered as a factor	Character & Personal Qualities considered	African American 5%; Hispanic 2%; Asian 2%	3,414
Loyola Marymount University (Los Angeles, CA)	NR	Alumni relations considered as a factor	Geographic origin/residence, and Character and Personal Qualities are considered	African American 7%; Hispanic 19%; Native American 1%; Asian 11%	5,465
Loyola University Chicago (Chicago, IL)	Minority status considered as factor	Alumni relations considered as a factor	Character & Personal Qualities considered important; Geographic origin/residence considered	African American 8%; Hispanic 11%; Asian 11%	7,320
Loyola University New Orleans (New Orleans, LA)	NR	Alumni relations considered as a factor	Character & Personal Qualities considered	African American 8%; Hispanic 10%; Asian 4%	3,649
Lubbock Christian University (Lubbock, TX)	Minority status considered as factor	Alumni relations considered as a factor	Character & Personal Qualities considered important; Religious Affiliation considered	African American 6%; Hispanic 14%; Native American 1%; Asian 1%	1,728

(*continued*)

College	Use of Race in Admission Decisions and Degree Utilized (if at all)	Use of Alumni Relations or Legacies as Factor and Degree Utilized	Use of Other Factors (e.g., geographic origin or religious affiliation) and Degree Utilized	Reported Ethnic/Minority Representation	Total Student Population
Luther College (Decorah, IA)	Minority status is considered as important factor	Alumni relations considered as a factor	Character & Personal Qualities considered important; Geographic origin/residence and Religious Affiliation considered	African American 1%; Hispanic 1%; Asian 1%	2,508
Lycoming College (Williamsport, PA)	NR	Alumni relations considered as a factor	Character & Personal Qualities considered important	African American 2%; Hispanic 1%; Asian 1%	1,486
Lynchburg College (Lynchburg, VA)	NR	NR	NR	African American 7%; Hispanic 3%; Asian 1%	1,741
Lyndon State College (Lyndonville, VT)	NR	Alumni relations considered as a factor	Character & Personal Qualities considered important	Hispanic 1%	1,280
Lynn University (Boca Raton, FL)	NR	Alumni relations considered as a factor	Character & Personal Qualities considered	African American 5%; Hispanic 5%	1,903
Lyon College (Batesville, AR)	NR	NR	Character & Personal Qualities considered	African American 4%; Hispanic 2%; Native American 2%; Asian 1%	508

Macalester College (St. Paul, MN)	Minority status considered as factor	Alumni relations considered as a factor	Character & Personal Qualities considered important	African American 3%; Hispanic 3; Native American 1%; Asian 6%	1,867
Macmurray College (Jacksonville, IL)	NR	NR	Character & Personal Qualities considered important	African American 13%; Hispanic 3%	667
Madonna University (Livonia, MI)	NR	Alumni relations considered as a factor	Character & Personal Qualities considered important; Religious Affiliation considered	African American 3%; Hispanic 1%	2,910
Maine Maritime Academy (Castine, ME)	NR	Alumni relations considered as a factor	Character & Personal Qualities considered important	Hispanic 1%	747
Malone College (Canton, OH)	Minority status considered as factor	Alumni relations considered as a factor	Religious affiliation and/or commitment and Character & Personal Qualities considered important	African American 6%; Hispanic 1%; Asian 1%	1,866
Manchester College (Manchester, NH)	NR	Alumni relations considered as a factor	Religious affiliation and/or commitment and Character & Personal Qualities considered	African American 4%; Hispanic 2%; Native American 2%; Asian 1%	1,113
Manhattan College (Riverdale, NY)	NR	Alumni relations considered as a factor	Character & Personal Qualities considered	African American 3%; Hispanic 2%; Native American 1%; Asian 1%	2,905

(*continued*)

College	Use of Race in Admission Decisions and Degree Utilized (if at all)	Use of Alumni Relations or Legacies as Factor and Degree Utilized	Use of Other Factors (e.g., geographic origin or religious affiliation) and Degree Utilized	Reported Ethnic/Minority Representation	Total Student Population
Manhattanville College (Purchase, NY)	NR	Alumni relations considered as a factor	Geographic origin/residence, and Character and Personal Qualities are considered	African American 5%; Hispanic 11%; Asian 4%	1,606
Mansfield University of Pennsylvania (Mansfield, PA)	Minority status considered as factor	Alumni relations considered as a factor	Character & Personal Qualities considered	African American 6%; Hispanic 1%; Native American 1%; Asian 1%	2,971
Marian College (IN) (Indianapolis, IN)	NR	Alumni relations considered as a factor	Geographic origin/residence, and Character and Personal Qualities are considered	African American 18%; Hispanic 2%; Native American 1%; Asian 1%	1,412
Marian College of Fond du Lac (Fond du Lac, WI)	NR	Alumni relations considered as a factor	Character & Personal Qualities considered	African American 5%; Hispanic 2%; Native American 1%; Asian 1%	1,815
Marietta College (Marietta, OH)	Minority status considered as factor	Alumni relations considered as a factor	Character & Personal Qualities considered important	African American 3%; Hispanic 1%; Asian 1%	1,343

Marist College (Poughkeepsie, NY)	Minority status is considered as important factor	Alumni relations considered as a factor	Geographic origin/residence, and Character and Personal Qualities are considered important	African American 4%; Hispanic 6%; Asian 2%	4,686
Marquette University (Milwaukee, WI)	Minority status considered as factor	Alumni relations considered as a factor	Geographic origin/residence, Character and Personal Qualities, and Religious Affiliation/Commitment all considered	African American 5%; Hispanic 4%; Asian 4%	7,709
Mars Hill College (Mars Hill, NC)	NR	Alumni relations considered as a factor	Religious affiliation and/or commitment and Character & Personal Qualities considered	African American 8%; Hispanic 1%; Asian 1%	1,177
Marshall University (Huntington, WV)	NR	NR	NR	African American 5%; Hispanic 1%; Asian 1%	9,411
Martin Luther College (New Ulm, MN)	NR	NR	Religious affiliation and/or commitment and Character & Personal Qualities considered important	African American 1%; Hispanic 1%; Asian 1%	804
Mary Baldwin College (Staunton, VA)	NR	Alumni relations considered as a factor	Character & Personal Qualities considered	African American 17%; Hispanic 3%; Asian 2%	1,296

(continued)

College	Use of Race in Admission Decisions and Degree Utilized (if at all)	Use of Alumni Relations or Legacies as Factor and Degree Utilized	Use of Other Factors (e.g., geographic origin or religious affiliation) and Degree Utilized	Reported Ethnic/Minority Representation	Total Student Population
Mary Washington College (Fredericksburg, VA)	Minority status considered as factor	Alumni relations considered as a factor	Geographic origin/residence, and Character and Personal Qualities are considered	African American 4%; Hispanic 3%; Asian 5%	4,039
Marygrove College (Detroit, MI)	NR	NR	Character & Personal Qualities considered very important	African American 70%; Hispanic 2%	662
Maryland Institute College of Art (Baltimore, MD)	Minority status considered as factor	Alumni relations considered as a factor	Character & Personal Qualities considered	African American 3%; Hispanic 4%; Asian 6%	1,399
Marylhurst University (Marylhurst, OR)	NR	NR	NR	NR	672
Marymount College of Fordham University (Tarrytown, NY)	NR	Alumni relations considered as a factor	Character & Personal Qualities considered important	African American 17%; Hispanic 14%; Asian 5%	1,021
Marymount Manhattan College (New York, NY)	NR	Alumni relations considered as a factor	Geographic origin/residence, and Character and Personal Qualities are considered	African American 22%; Hispanic 16%; Asian 4%	2,244

Marymount University (Arlington, VA)	NR	Alumni relations considered as a factor	Character & Personal Qualities considered	African American 16%; Hispanic 10%; Asian 8%	2,160
Maryville College (Maryville, TN)	NR	NR	Character & Personal Qualities considered important	African American 6%; Hispanic 1%; Asian 1%	1,016
Maryville University of Saint Louis (St. Louis, MO)	Minority status considered as factor	NR	Character & Personal Qualities considered	African American 6%; Hispanic 1%; Asian 1%	2,537
Marywood University (Scranton, PA)	NR	NR	Character & Personal Qualities considered very important	African American 2%; Hispanic 2%; Asian 1%	1,741
Massachusetts College of Art (Boston, MA)	Minority status considered as factor	NR	Character & Personal Qualities considered	African American 3%; Hispanic 4%; Asian 5%	1,386
Massachusetts College of Liberal Arts (North Adams, MA)	NR	NR	Character & Personal Qualities considered very important	African American 5%; Hispanic 2%; Native American 1%; Asian 1%	1,246
Massachusetts College of Pharmacy & Health Science (Boston, MA)	NR	NR	NR	African American 5%; Hispanic 2%; Asian 28%	1,594
Massachusetts Institute of Technology (Cambridge, MA)	Minority status considered as factor	Alumni relations considered as a factor	Character & Personal Qualities considered important; Geographic origin/residence considered	African American 6%; Hispanic 12%; Native American 2%; Asian 28%	4,132

(*continued*)

College	Use of Race in Admission Decisions and Degree Utilized (if at all)	Use of Alumni Relations or Legacies as Factor and Degree Utilized	Use of Other Factors (e.g., geographic origin or religious affiliation) and Degree Utilized	Reported Ethnic/Minority Representation	Total Student Population
Massachusetts Maritime Academy (Buzzards Bay, MA)	NR	Alumni relations considered as a factor	Character & Personal Qualities considered important	NR	923
Master's College and Seminary (Santa Clarita, CA)	NR	Alumni relations considered as a factor	Religious affiliation and/or commitment and Character & Personal Qualities considered important	African American 2%; Hispanic 6%; Native American 1%; Asian 4%	1,124
Mayville State University (Mayville, ND)	NR	NR	Character & Personal Qualities considered	African American 4%; Hispanic 1%; Asian 4%	897
McDaniel College (Westminster, MD)	Minority status is considered as important factor	NR	NR	African American 8%; Hispanic 2%; Native American 1%; Asian 2%	1,581
McKendree College (Lebanon, IL)	NR	Alumni relations considered as a factor	Character & Personal Qualities considered	African American 10%; Hispanic 1%; Asian 1%	2,035
McMurry University (Abilene, TX)	NR	Alumni relations considered as a factor	Religious affiliation and/or commitment and Character & Personal Qualities	African American 8%; Hispanic 12%; Native American 1%; Asian 1%	1,408

McNeese State University (Lake Charles, LA)	NR	NR	African American 17%; Hispanic 1%; Native American 1%; Asian 1%	7,045
Medaille College (Buffalo, NY)	NR	Alumni relations considered as a factor	African American 16%; Hispanic 3%; Native American 1%; Asian 1%	1,650
Medical College of Georgia (Augusta, GA)	NR	NR	African American 15%; Hispanic 1%; Asian 2%	712
Menlo College (Atherton, CA)	NR	Alumni relations considered as a factor	African American 8%; Hispanic 14%; Native American 1%; Asian 13%	749
Mercer University—Macon (Macon, GA)	NR	Character & Personal Qualities considered very important	African American 29%; Hispanic 2%; Asian 3%	4,561
Mercy College (Dobbs Ferry, NY)	Minority status considered as factor	Character & Personal Qualities considered	African American 27%; Hispanic 30%; Asian 3%	2,312
Mercyhurst College (Erie, PA)	Minority status considered as factor	Geographic origin/residence, Character and Personal Qualities, and Religious Affiliation/Commitment all considered	African American 3%; Hispanic 1%	3,537

(continued)

College	Use of Race in Admission Decisions and Degree Utilized (if at all)	Use of Alumni Relations or Legacies as Factor and Degree Utilized	Use of Other Factors (e.g., geographic origin or religious affiliation) and Degree Utilized	Reported Ethnic/Minority Representation	Total Student Population
Meredith College (Raleigh, NC)	NR	Alumni relations considered as a factor	Character & Personal Qualities considered important	African American 9%; Hispanic 2%; Asian 2%	1,807
Merrimack College (North Andover, MA)	NR	Alumni relations considered as a factor	Character & Personal Qualities considered important; Geographic origin/residence considered	African American 1%; Hispanic 2%; Asian 1%	2,232
Mesa State College (Grand Junction, CO)	NR	NR	Geographic origin/residence, and Character and Personal Qualities considered	African American 1%; Hispanic 7%; Native American 1%; Asian 1%	4,832
Messiah College (Grantham, PA)	Minority status considered as factor	Alumni relations considered as a factor	Religious affiliation and/or commitment and Character & Personal Qualities considered important	African American 3%; Hispanic 2%; Asian 2%	2,887
Methodist College (Fayetteville, NC)	NR	Alumni relations considered as a factor	NR	African American 22%; Hispanic 5%; Native American 1%; Asian 2%	1,941

244

Metropolitan College of New York (New York, NY)	NR	NR	Character & Personal Qualities considered	Hispanic 18%; Native American 1%; Asian 1%	1,093
Metropolitan State College of Denver (Denver, CO)	NR	NR	Character & Personal Qualities considered important	African American 6%; Hispanic 12%; Native American 1%; Asian 4%	18,013
Miami University (Oxford, OH)	Minority status considered as factor	Alumni relations considered as a factor	Geographic origin/residence, Character and Personal Qualities, and Religious Affiliation/Commitment all considered	African American 3%; Hispanic 2%; Native American 1%; Asian 3%	15,011
Michigan State University (East Lansing, MI)	Minority status considered as factor	Alumni relations considered as a factor	Geographic origin/residence considered	African American 8%; Hispanic 3%; Native American 1%; Asian 5%	35,107
Michigan Technological University (Houghton, MI)	NR	Alumni relations considered as a factor	Character & Personal Qualities considered	African American 2%; Hispanic 1%; Native American 1%; Asian 1%	5,622
MidAmerica Nazarene University (Olathe, KS)	NR	NR	Character & Personal Qualities considered	African American 6%; Hispanic 2%; Native American 1%; Asian 1%	1,411
Middle Tennessee State University (Murfreesboro, TN)	NR	NR	NR	African American 12%; Hispanic 2%; Asian 3%	17,130

(continued)

College	Use of Race in Admission Decisions and Degree Utilized (if at all)	Use of Alumni Relations or Legacies as Factor and Degree Utilized	Use of Other Factors (e.g, geographic origin or religious affiliation) and Degree Utilized	Reported Ethnic/Minority Representation	Total Student Population
Middlebury College (Middlebury, VT)	Minority status is considered as important factor	Alumni relations considered as a factor	Character & Personal Qualities considered important; Geographic origin/residence considered	African American 3%; Hispanic 5%; Asian 7%	2,357
Midland Lutheran College (Fremont, NE)	NR	NR	NR	African American 4%; Hispanic 1%	1,033
Midway College (Midway, KY)	NR	Alumni relations considered as a factor	Character & Personal Qualities considered	African American 5%	1,249
Midwestern State University (Wichita Falls, TX)	NR	NR	Geographic origin/residence considered	African American 10%; Hispanic 9%; Native American 1%; Asian 3%	5,601
Miles College (Fairfield, AL)	NR	Alumni relations considered as a factor	NR	African American 98%	1,660
Miles Community College (Miles City, MT)	NR	NR	NR	Hispanic 2%; Native American 4%; Asian 1%	458

Millersville University of Pennsylvania (Millersville, PA)	Minority status is considered as important factor	Alumni relations considered as a factor	Character & Personal Qualities considered important; Geographic origin/ residence considered	African American 5%; Hispanic 3%; Asian 2%	7,998
Milligan College (Milligan College, TN)	Minority status considered as factor	Alumni relations considered as a factor	Religious affiliation and/or commitment and Character & Personal Qualities considered important	African American 2%; Hispanic 1%; Asian 1%	751
Millikin University (Decatur, IL)	Minority status considered as factor	Alumni relations considered as a factor	Character & Personal Qualities considered	African American 9%; Hispanic 2%; Asian 1%	2,630
Mills College (Oakland, CA)	Minority status considered as factor	Alumni relations considered as a factor	Character & Personal Qualities considered important	African American 9%; Hispanic 9%; Native American 1%; Asian 9%	762
Millsaps College (Jackson, MS)	NR	NR	Character & Personal Qualities considered very important	African American 10%; Hispanic 1%; Native American 1%; Asian 4%	1,109
Milwaukee Institute of Art and Design (Milwaukee, WI)	NR	NR	Character & Personal Qualities considered very important	African American 3%; Hispanic 7%; Native American 1%; Asian 3%	629
Milwaukee School of Engineering (Milwaukee, WI)	NR	NR	NR	African American 2%; Hispanic 2%; Native American 1%; Asian 3%	2,089

(continued)

College	Use of Race in Admission Decisions and Degree Utilized (if at all)	Use of Alumni Relations or Legacies as Factor and Degree Utilized	Use of Other Factors (e.g, geographic origin or religious affiliation) and Degree Utilized	Reported Ethnic/Minority Representation	Total Student Population
Minneapolis College of Art and Design (Minneapolis, MN)	NR	NR	Character & Personal Qualities considered important	African American 3%; Hispanic 3%; Native American 1%; Asian 4%	627
Minnesota State University—Mankato (Mankato, MN)	NR	NR	NR	African American 2%; Hispanic 1%; Asian 2%	12,131
Minnesota State University—Moorhead (Moorhead, MN)	NR	NR	NR	African American 1%; Hispanic 1%; Native American 1%; Asian 1%	7,045
Minot State University—Bottineau Campus (Bottineau, ND)	NR	NR	NR	African American 1%; Hispanic 8%; Asian 1%	450
Minot State University—Minot (Minot, ND)	NR	NR	NR	African American 3%; Hispanic 2%; Native American 4%; Asian 1%	3,425
Mississippi College (Clinton, MS)	NR	Alumni relations considered as a factor	Character & Personal Qualities considered important	African American 15%; Hispanic 1%; Asian 1%	2,356

Mississippi State University (Mississippi State, MS)	NR	NR	NR	African American 19%; Hispanic 1%; Asian 1%	12,839
Mississippi University for Women (Columbus, MS)	NR	Alumni relations considered as a factor	Character & Personal Qualities considered	African American 28%; Hispanic 1%	3,180
Mississippi Valley State University (Itta Bena, MS)	NR	NR	Geographic origin/ residence considered	African American 57%	4,838
Missouri Baptist College (St. Louis, MO)	NR	Alumni relations considered as a factor	Religious affiliation and/or commitment and Character & Personal Qualities considered important	African American 5%; Hispanic 2%	1,151
Missouri Southern State University (Joplin, MO)	NR	NR	NR	African American 3%; Hispanic 2%; Native American 3%; Asian 1%	4,673
Missouri Valley College (Marshall, MO)	NR	Alumni relations considered as a factor	Character & Personal Qualities considered very important	African American 13%; Hispanic 4%; Native American 1%; Asian 4%	1,425
Missouri Western State College (Saint Joseph, MO)	NR	NR	NR	African American 11%; Hispanic 2%; Native American 1%; Asian 1%	4,652

(continued)

College	Use of Race in Admission Decisions and Degree Utilized (if at all)	Use of Alumni Relations or Legacies as Factor and Degree Utilized	Use of Other Factors (e.g., geographic origin or religious affiliation) and Degree Utilized	Reported Ethnic/Minority Representation	Total Student Population
Mitchell College (New London, CT)	NR	Alumni relations considered as a factor	Character & Personal Qualities considered important	African American 10%; Hispanic 3%; Native American 4%	508
Mohawk Valley Community College (Utica, NY)	NR	NR	NR	African American 6%; Hispanic 3%; Native American 1%; Asian 2%	4,410
Molloy College (Rockville Centre, NY)	NR	Alumni relations considered as a factor	Character & Personal Qualities considered	African American 19%; Hispanic 8%; Asian 4%	2,247
Monmouth College (Monmouth, IL)	NR	NR	Character & Personal Qualities considered	African American 3%; Hispanic 3%; Asian 1%	1,246
Monmouth University (West Long Beach, NJ)	NR	Alumni relations considered as a factor	Character & Personal Qualities considered	African American 5%; Hispanic 4%; Asian 2%	1,246
Monroe College (Bronx, NY)	Minority status considered as factor	Alumni relations considered as a factor	Geographic origin/residence, Character and Personal Qualities, and Religious Affiliation/Commitment all considered	African American 45%; Hispanic 42%; Asian 1%	5,689

Montana State University College of Technology—Great Falls (Great Falls, MT)	NR	NR	African American 2%; Hispanic 2%; Native American 3%; Asian 1%	1,241
Montana State University—Billings (Billings, MT)	NR	Character & Personal Qualities considered	African American 1%; Hispanic 3%; Native American 6%; Asian 1%	4,166
Montana State University—Bozeman (Bozeman, MT)	NR	NR	Hispanic 1%; Native American 2%; Asian 1%	10,639
Montana State University—Northern (Havre, MT)	NR	Geographic origin/residence considered	African American 1%; Hispanic 1%; Native American 10%; Asian 1%	1,367
Montana Tech of the University of Montana (Butte, MT)	NR	NR	Hispanic 1%; Native American 1%	1,913
Montclair State University (Upper Montclair, NJ)	NR	Character & Personal Qualities considered	African American 11%; Hispanic 16%; Asian 5%	11,195
Montreat College (Montreat, NC)	NR	Alumni relations considered as a factor	African American 18%; Hispanic 1%; Native American 7%; Asian 1%	943

(*continued*)

College	Use of Race in Admission Decisions and Degree Utilized (if at all)	Use of Alumni Relations or Legacies as Factor and Degree Utilized	Use of Other Factors (e.g., geographic origin or religious affiliation) and Degree Utilized	Reported Ethnic/Minority Representation	Total Student Population
Moravian College (Bethlehem, PA)	NR	Alumni relations considered as a factor	Character & Personal Qualities considered very important; Geographic origin/residence considered	African American 2%; Hispanic 3%; Asian 2%	1,828
Morehead State University (Morehead, KY)	Minority status is considered as a very important factor	Alumni relations considered as a very important factor	Character & Personal Qualities considered important; Geographic origin/residence considered very important	African American 3%; Hispanic 1%	7,270
Morehouse College (Atlanta, GA)	Minority status considered as factor	Alumni relations considered as a factor	Geographic origin/residence, and Character & Personal Qualities considered	African American 89%	2,891
Morgan State University (Baltimore, MD)	NR	NR	NR	African American 91%	6,005
Morningside College (Sioux City, IA)	NR	NR	NR	African American 3%; Hispanic 4%; Asian 1%	983

252

Morris Brown College (Atlanta, GA)	NR	Alumni relations considered as important factor	Geographic origin/residence, Character and Personal Qualities, and Religious Affiliation/Commitment all considered	African American 96%	2,501
Morris College (Sumter, SC)	NR	NR	NR	African American 100%	897
Mount Aloysius College (Cresson, PA)	NR	Alumni relations considered as a factor	Character & Personal Qualities considered	African American 1%; Hispanic 1%	1,382
Mount Holyoke College (South Hadley, MA)	Minority status considered as factor	Alumni relations considered as a factor	Character & Personal Qualities considered important; Geographic origin/residence considered	African American 4%; Hispanic 5%; Native American 1%; Asian 11%	2,095
Mount Ida College (Newton, MA)	NR	Alumni relations considered as a factor	Character & Personal Qualities considered important	African American 12%; Hispanic 6%; Asian 3%	1,297
Mount Marty College (Yankton, SD)	NR	Alumni relations considered as a factor	Character & Personal Qualities considered	African American 2%; Hispanic 1%; Asian 1%	889
Mount Mary College (Milwaukee, WI)	NR	Alumni relations considered as a factor	Character & Personal Qualities considered	African American 16%; Hispanic 5%; Native American 1%; Asian 3%	1,193

(continued)

College	Use of Race in Admission Decisions and Degree Utilized (if at all)	Use of Alumni Relations or Legacies as Factor and Degree Utilized	Use of Other Factors (e.g., geographic origin or religious affiliation) and Degree Utilized	Reported Ethnic/Minority Representation	Total Student Population
Mount Mercy College (Cedar Rapids, IA)	NR	NR	Character & Personal Qualities considered	African American 2%; Hispanic 1%; Asian 1%	1,434
Mount Olive College (Mount Olive, NC)	NR	Alumni relations considered as a factor	Character & Personal Qualities considered	NR	2,289
Mount Saint Mary College (Newburgh, NY)	NR	Alumni relations considered as a factor	Character & Personal Qualities considered	African American 12%; Hispanic 8%; Asian 2%	1,973
Mount St. Mary's College (Los Angeles, CA)	NR	Alumni relations considered as a factor	Character & Personal Qualities considered; Geographic origin/residence considered	African American 10%; Hispanic 35%; Asian 13%	1,719
Mount Saint Mary's University (MD) (Emmitsburg, MD)	NR	Alumni relations considered as a factor	Character & Personal Qualities considered	African American 6%; Hispanic 3%; Asian 2%	1,612
Mount Senario Colege (Ladysmith, WI)	NR	NR	NR	African American 14%; Hispanic 3%; Native American 2%; Asian 2%	672
Mount Union College (Alliance, OH)	Minority status considered as factor	Alumni relations considered as a factor	Character & Personal Qualities considered	African American 4%; Hispanic 1%	2,131

Mount Vernon Nazarene University (Mount Vernon, OH)	NR	NR	African American 3%; Hispanic 1%; Asian 1%	2,001
Mountain State University (Beckley, WV)	Minority status is considered as a very important factor	Alumni relations considered as a very important factor	Geographic origin/residence, Character and Personal Qualities, and Religious Affiliation/Commitment all considered	3,467
Muhlenberg College (Allentown, PA)	Minority status considered as factor	Alumni relations considered as a factor	Geographic origin/residence, Character and Personal Qualities, and Religious Affiliation/Commitment all considered important	African American 10%; Hispanic 2%; Native American 1%; Asian 1%
Multnomah Bible College and Biblical Seminary (Portland, OR)	NR	Alumni relations considered as a factor	Character & Personal Qualities considered very important; Geographic origin/residence considered	African American 2%; Hispanic 4%; Asian 2%	2,378
Murray State University (Murray, KY)	Minority status considered as factor	Alumni relations considered as important factor	Religious affiliation and/or commitment and Character & Personal Qualities considered important	African American 1%; Hispanic 3%; Asian 4%	527
			Geographic origin/residence, and Character and Personal Qualities considered	African American 6%; Hispanic 1%; Asian 1%	7,814

(continued)

College	Use of Race in Admission Decisions and Degree Utilized (if at all)	Use of Alumni Relations or Legacies as Factor and Degree Utilized	Use of Other Factors (e.g., geographic origin or religious affiliation) and Degree Utilized	Reported Ethnic/Minority Representation	Total Student Population
Muskingum College (New Concord, OH)	Minority status considered as factor	Alumni relations considered as a factor	Geographic origin/residence, and Character and Personal Qualities considered	African American 4%	1,615
Naropa College at Naropa University (Boulder, CO)	Minority status considered as factor	Alumni relations considered as a factor	Character & Personal Qualities considered important	African American 2%; Hispanic 6%; Asian 2%	457
National University (La Jolla, CA)	NR	NR	NR	African American 13%; Hispanic 18%; Native American 1%; Asian 9%	4,776
National-Louis University (Evanston, IL)	NR	NR	NR	African American 26%; Hispanic 8%; Asian 3%	3,545
Nazareth College of Rochester (Rochester, NY)	Minority status considered as factor	Alumni relations considered as a factor	Geographic origin/residence, and Character and Personal Qualities considered	African American 4%; Hispanic 2%; Asian 2%	1,905

Nebraska Wesleyan University (Lincoln, NE)	Minority status is considered as important factor	Alumni relations considered as a factor	Character & Personal Qualities considered important; Geographic origin/residence considered	African American 1%; Hispanic 2%; Asian 1%	1,759
Neumann College (Aston, PA)	Minority status considered as factor	Alumni relations considered as important factor	Religious affiliation and/or commitment and Character & Personal Qualities considered	African American 13%; Hispanic 1%; Asian 1%	2,197
New College of Florida (Sarasota, FL)	NR	Alumni relations considered as a factor	Character & Personal Qualities considered important; Geographic origin/residence considered	African American 2%; Hispanic 9%; Asian 3%	692
New England College (Henniker, NH)	NR	Alumni relations considered as a factor	Character & Personal Qualities considered important	African American 2%; Hispanic 2%; Asian 1%	919
New Jersey City University (Jersey City, NJ)	NR	Alumni relations considered as a factor	Character & Personal Qualities considered	African American 20%; Hispanic 34%; Asian 9%	5,835
New Jersey Institute of Technology (Newark, NJ)	Minority status considered as factor	Alumni relations considered as a factor	Geographic origin/residence, Character and Personal Qualities, and Religious Affiliation/Commitment all considered	African American 10%; Hispanic 12%; Asian 20%	5,366

(continued)

College	Use of Race in Admission Decisions and Degree Utilized (if at all)	Use of Alumni Relations or Legacies as Factor and Degree Utilized	Use of Other Factors (e.g., geographic origin or religious affiliation) and Degree Utilized	Reported Ethnic/Minority Representation	Total Student Population
New Mexico Highlands University (Las Vegas, NM)	NR	NR	NR	African American 5%; Hispanic 57%; Native American 9%; Asian 1%	1,931
New Mexico Institute of Mining & Technology (Socorro, NM)	NR	NR	NR	African American 1%; Hispanic 19%; Native American 3%; Asian 1%	1,148
New Mexico State University (Las Cruces, NM)	NR	NR	NR	African American 3%; Hispanic 45%; Native American 3%; Asian 1%	12,145
New York Institute of Technology (Old Westbury, NY)	NR	NR	Character & Personal Qualities considered	African American 11%; Hispanic 10%; Asian 10%	5,141
New York University (New York, NY)	Minority status considered as factor	Alumni relations considered as a factor	Character & Personal Qualities considered important	African American 4%; Hispanic 5%; Asian 10%	19,826
Newberry College (Newberry, SC)	Minority status considered as factor	Alumni relations considered as a factor	Geographic origin/residence, Character and Personal Qualities, and	African American 27%; Hispanic 1%; Asian 1%	764

Institution		Religious Affiliation/ Commitment all considered		
Newman University (Wichita, KS)	NR	NR	African American 5%; Hispanic 7%; Native American 2%; Asian 3%	1,843
Niagara County Community College (Sanborn, NY)	NR	NR	African American 5%; Hispanic 1%; Native American 2%; Asian 1%	3,707
Niagara University (Niagara Falls, NY)	NR	Alumni relations considered as a factor	Character & Personal Qualities considered	African American 5%; Hispanic 2%; Native American 1%; Asian 1%	2,825
Nicholls State University (Thibodaux, LA)	NR	NR	Geographic origin/ residence considered	African American 17%; Hispanic 1%; Native American 2%; Asian 1%	6,784
Nichols College (Dudley, MA)	NR	NR	Character & Personal Qualities considered	African American 7%; Hispanic 4%; Asian 2%	1,432
Norfolk State University (Norfolk, VA)	NR	Alumni relations considered as a factor	Geographic origin/ residence considered	African American 92%; Hispanic 1%; Asian 1%	5,810
North Carolina A&T State University (Greensboro, NC)	NR	Alumni relations considered as a factor	Geographic origin/ residence considered	African American 92%; Hispanic 1%	7,245

(continued)

College	Use of Race in Admission Decisions and Degree Utilized (if at all)	Use of Alumni Relations or Legacies as Factor and Degree Utilized	Use of Other Factors (e.g., geographic origin or religious affiliation) and Degree Utilized	Reported Ethnic/Minority Representation	Total Student Population
North Carolina Central University (Durham, NC)	Minority status considered as factor	Alumni relations considered as a factor	Geographic origin/residence considered	African American 89%; Hispanic 1%; Asian 1%	4,471
North Carolina School of the Arts (Winston-Salem, NC)	Minority status considered as factor	NR	Character & Personal Qualities considered	African American 10%; Hispanic 2%; Asian 3%	721
North Carolina State University (Raleigh, NC)	Minority status considered as factor	Alumni relations considered as a factor	Geographic origin/residence, and Character and Personal Qualities considered	African American 10%; Hispanic 2%; Native American 1%; Asian 5%	20,302
North Carolina Wesleyan College (Rocky Mount, NC)	NR	Alumni relations considered as important factor	Character & Personal Qualities considered important	African American 40%; Hispanic 1%; Native American 1%; Asian 1%	1,695
North Central College (Naperville, IL)	NR	Alumni relations considered as a factor	Character & Personal Qualities considered important	African American 3%; Hispanic 5%; Asian 3%	1,937
North Central University (Minneapolis, MN)	NR	NR	Religious affiliation and/or commitment and Character & Personal Qualities considered important	African American 4%; Hispanic 2%; Asian 2%	1,241

North Dakota State University (Fargo, ND)	NR	NR	NR	African American 1%; Native American 1%; Asian 1%	10,545
North Georgia College and State University (Dahlonega, GA)	NR	Alumni relations considered as a factor	NR	African American 3%; Hispanic 2%; Asian 1%	3,972
North Greenville College (Tigerville, SC)	NR	NR	NR	African American 10%	1,570
North Park University (Chicago, IL)	Minority status is considered as important factor	Alumni relations considered as a factor	Character & Personal Qualities considered important	African American 12%; Hispanic 9%; Asian 8%	1,665
Northeastern Illinois University (Chicago, IL)	NR	NR	NR	African American 12%; Hispanic 29%; Asian 11%	9,076
Northeastern State University (Tahlequah, OK)	NR	NR	NR	African American 5%; Hispanic 1%; Native American 29%; Asian 1%	7,777
Northeastern University (Boston, MA)	Minority status considered as factor	Alumni relations considered as a factor	Character & Personal Qualities considered important; Geographic origin/residence considered	African American 6%; Hispanic 5%; Asian 7%	14,618
Northern Arizona University (Flagstaff, AZ)	NR	NR	NR	African American 2%; Hispanic 11%; Native American 7%; Asian 2%	13,135

(*continued*)

College	Use of Race in Admission Decisions and Degree Utilized (if at all)	Use of Alumni Relations or Legacies as Factor and Degree Utilized	Use of Other Factors (e.g., geographic origin or religious affiliation) and Degree Utilized	Reported Ethnic/Minority Representation	Total Student Population
Northern Illinois University (Dekalb, IL)	Minority status considered as factor	NR	NR	African American 12%; Hispanic 6%; Asian 6%	18,025
Northern Kentucky University (Highland Heights, KY)	NR	NR	NR	African American 5%; Hispanic 1%; Asian 1%	11,656
Northern Michigan University (Marquette, MI)	NR	NR	Character & Personal Qualities considered	African American 2%; Hispanic 1%; Native American 2%; Asian 1%	8,312
Northern State University (Aberdeen, SD)	NR	NR	NR	African American 1%; Hispanic 1%; Native American 3%; Asian 2%	1,870
Northland College (Ashland, WI)	Minority status considered as factor	Alumni relations considered as a factor	Geographic origin/residence, and Character and Personal Qualities considered	African American 1%; Hispanic 1%; Native American 2%; Asian 1%	752
Northwest College (Kirkland, WA)	NR	NR	Character & Personal Qualities considered	African American 3%; Hispanic 3%; Native American 1%; Asian 4%	1,054

Northwest Missouri State University (Maryville, MO)	NR	Character & Personal Qualities considered	African American 3%; Hispanic 1%; Asian 1%	5,568
Northwest Nazarene University (Nampa, ID)	NR	Alumni relations considered as a factor	Character & Personal Qualities considered important; Religious Affiliation considered	African American 1%; Hispanic 1%; Asian 1%	1,162
Northwestern College (IA) (Orange City, IA)	NR	NR	Character & Personal Qualities considered important; Religious Affiliation considered	Hispanic 1%; Asian 1%	1,246
Northwestern College (MN) (Saint Paul, MN)	NR	NR	Religious affiliation and/or commitment and Character & Personal Qualities considered important	African American 4%; Hispanic 1%; Asian 2%	2,199
Northwestern Oklahoma State University (Alva, OK)	NR	NR	NR	African American 5%; Hispanic 1%; Native American 3%	1,648
Northwestern State University (Natchitoches, LA)	Minority status considered as factor	Alumni relations considered as a factor	Geographic origin/residence considered	African American 32%; Hispanic 2%; Native American 2%; Asian 1%	9,241
Northwestern University (Evanston, IL)	Minority status considered as factor	Alumni relations considered as a factor	Character & Personal Qualities considered important	African American 5%; Hispanic 5%; Asian 17%	7,988

(continued)

College	Use of Race in Admission Decisions and Degree Utilized (if at all)	Use of Alumni Relations or Legacies as Factor and Degree Utilized	Use of Other Factors (e.g., geographic origin or religious affiliation) and Degree Utilized	Reported Ethnic/Minority Representation	Total Student Population
Northwood University (Midland, MI)	NR	Alumni relations considered as a factor	Character & Personal Qualities considered	African American 13%; Hispanic 2%; Asian 1%	1,811
Northwood University—Florida (West Palm Beach, FL)	NR	Alumni relations considered as a factor	Character & Personal Qualities considered	African American 10%; Hispanic 10%; Asian 2%	728
Northwood University—Texas (Cedar Hill, TX)	NR	Alumni relations considered as a factor	Character & Personal Qualities considered	African American 21%; Hispanic 26%; Asian 3%	638
Norwich University (Northfield, VT)	NR	Alumni relations considered as a factor	Character & Personal Qualities considered	African American 3%; Hispanic 4%; Asian 2%	2,099
Notre Dame De Namur University (Belmont, CA)	NR	NR	NR	African American 7%; Hispanic 20%; Native American 1%; Asian 14%	913
Nova Southeastern University (Ft. Lauderdale, FL)	NR	Alumni relations considered as a factor	Character & Personal Qualities considered	African American 28%; Hispanic 25%; Asian 4%	5,088

Institution				
Nyack College (Nyack, NY)	NR	NR	Religious affiliation and/or commitment and Character & Personal Qualities considered important	African American 30%; Hispanic 22%; Asian 6%	1,964
Oakland City University (Oakland City, IN)	NR	NR	Character & Personal Qualities considered	African American 15%; Hispanic 2%; Native American 1%; Asian 1%	1,258
Oakland University (Rochester, MI)	NR	Alumni relations considered as a factor	Character & Personal Qualities considered	African American 9%; Hispanic 2%; Asian 3%	12,608
Oberlin College (Oberlin, OH)	Minority status considered as factor	Alumni relations considered as a very important factor	Character & Personal Qualities considered important; Geographic origin/residence considered	African American 6%; Hispanic 5%; Native American 1%; Asian 8%	2,807
Occidental College (Los Angeles, CA)	Minority status considered as factor	Alumni relations considered as a factor	Character & Personal Qualities considered important; Geographic origin/residence considered	African American 7%; Hispanic 15%; Native American 1%; Asian 11%	1,848
Oglethorpe University (Atlanta, GA)	NR	Alumni relations considered as a factor	Character & Personal Qualities considered	African American 20%; Hispanic 3%; Asian 3%	900
Ohio Dominican University (Columbus, OH)	NR	NR	Character & Personal Qualities considered	African American 24%; Hispanic 1%; Asian 14%	2,170

(continued)

College	Use of Race in Admission Decisions and Degree Utilized (if at all)	Use of Alumni Relations or Legacies as Factor and Degree Utilized	Use of Other Factors (e.g., geographic origin or religious affiliation) and Degree Utilized	Reported Ethnic/Minority Representation	Total Student Population
Ohio Northern University (Ada, OH)	NR	NR	Character & Personal Qualities considered	African American 1%; Hispanic 1%; Asian 1%	2,065
Ohio State University—Columbus (Columbus, OH)	Minority status is considered as important factor	NR	Geographic origin/residence, and Character and Personal Qualities considered	African American 8%; Hispanic 2%; Asian 5%	36,097
Ohio State University—Lima (Lima, OH)	NR	NR	NR	African American 3%; Hispanic 1%; Asian 1%	1,198
Ohio State University—Mansfield (Mansfield, OH)	NR	NR	NR	African American 5%; Hispanic 1%; Asian 1%	1,498
Ohio State University—Marion (Marion, OH)	NR	NR	NR	African American 2%; Hispanic 2%; Asian 2%	1,403
Ohio State University—Newark (Newark, OH)	NR	NR	NR	African American 4%; Hispanic 1%; Asian 2%	1,951

Ohio University—Athens (Athens, OH)	Minority status considered as factor	Alumni relations considered as a factor	Character & Personal Qualities considered	African American 3%; Hispanic 1%; Asian 1%	16,802
Ohio University—Southern (Ironton, OH)	NR	NR	NR	African American 2%	2,510
Ohio University—Zanesville (Zanesville, OH)	NR	NR	NR	African American 2%; Hispanic 1%	1,824
Ohio Valley College (Vienna, WV)	NR	Alumni relations considered as important factor	Religious affiliation and/or commitment and Character & Personal Qualities considered	African American 4%; Hispanic 1%; Asian 1%	492
Ohio Wesleyan University (Delaware, OH)	Minority status is considered as important factor	Alumni relations considered as important factor	Character & Personal Qualities considered very important; Geographic origin/residence considered	African American 4%; Hispanic 1%; Asian 2%	1,917
Oklahoma Baptist University (Shawnee, OK)	NR	Alumni relations considered as a factor	Character & Personal Qualities considered important; Geographic origin/residence and Religious Affiliation considered	African American 2%; Hispanic 2%; Native American 5%; Asian 1%	1,480

(*continued*)

College	Use of Race in Admission Decisions and Degree Utilized (if at all)	Use of Alumni Relations or Legacies as Factor and Degree Utilized	Use of Other Factors (e.g., geographic origin or religious affiliation) and Degree Utilized	Reported Ethnic/Minority Representation	Total Student Population
Oklahoma Christian University (Oklahoma City, OK)	NR	NR	NR	African American 7%; Hispanic 3%; Native American 2%; Asian 1%	1,748
Oklahoma City University (Oklahoma City, OK)	Minority status is considered as important factor	Alumni relations considered as a factor	Character & Personal Qualities considered important; Religious Affiliation considered	African American 7%; Hispanic 4%; Native American 3%; Asian 2%	1,869
Oklahoma Panhandle State University (Goodwell, OK)	NR	NR	NR	African American 4%; Hispanic 10%; Native American 2%	1,226
Oklahoma State University (Stillwater, OK)	NR	NR	Character & Personal Qualities considered	African American 4%; Hispanic 2%; Native American 9%; Asian 2%	18,636
Oklahoma Wesleyan University (Bartlesville, OK)	Minority status is considered as important factor	Alumni relations considered as important factor	Religious affiliation and/or commitment and Character & Personal Qualities considered important; Geographic origin/residence considered	African American 3%; Hispanic 3%; Native American 8%; Asian 1%	539

Old Dominion University (Norfolk, Va)	NR	Alumni relations considered as a factor	Character & Personal Qualities considered	African American 23%; Hispanic 3%; Native American 1%; Asian 6%	13,679
Olivet College (Olivet, MI)	Minority status is considered as important factor	Alumni relations considered very important	Character & Personal Qualities considered very important; Geographic origin/residence and Religious Affiliation considered	African American 16%; Hispanic 2%; Native American 1%; Asian 1%	912
Olivet Nazarene University (Bourbonnais, IL)	NR	Alumni relations considered as a factor	Religious affiliation and/or commitment and Character & Personal Qualities considered important	African American 5%; Hispanic 2%; Asian 1%	2,251
Oral Roberts University (Tulsa, OK)	NR	NR	NR	African American 18%; Hispanic 5%; Native American 2%; Asian 2%	3,670
Oregon Health Sciences University (Portland, OR)	NR	NR	NR	African American 1%; Hispanic 2%; Native American 2%; Asian 6%	609
Oregon Institute of Technology (Klamath Falls, OR 97601)	NR	NR	Character & Personal Qualities considered	African American 1%; Hispanic 4%; Native American 2%; Asian 5%	2,663
Oregon State University (Corvallis, OR)	NR	NR	Character & Personal Qualities considered	African American 1%; Hispanic 3%; Native American 1%; Asian 8%	15,137

(continued)

College	Use of Race in Admission Decisions and Degree Utilized (if at all)	Use of Alumni Relations or Legacies as Factor and Degree Utilized	Use of Other Factors (e.g., geographic origin or religious affiliation) and Degree Utilized	Reported Ethnic/Minority Representation	Total Student Population
Otis College of Art & Design (Los Angeles, CA)	NR	Alumni relations considered as a factor	Character & Personal Qualities considered	African American 2%; Hispanic 12%; Native American 1%; Asian 30%	1,016
Ottawa University (Ottawa, KS)	NR	Alumni relations considered as a factor	Religious affiliation and/or commitment and Character & Personal Qualities considered important	African American 11%; Hispanic 2%; Native American 2%; Asian 1%	490
Otterbein College (Westerville, OH)	Minority status considered as factor	Alumni relations considered as a factor	Character & Personal Qualities considered	African American 7%; Hispanic 1%; Asian 1%	2,759
Ouachita Baptist University (Arkadelphia, AR)	NR	NR	Religious affiliation and/or commitment and Character & Personal Qualities considered	African American 3%; Hispanic 1%	1,536
Our Lady of Holy Cross College (New Orleans, LA)	Minority status considered as factor	NR	NR	African American 13%; Hispanic 5%; Native American 1%; Asian 3%	1,199

Our Lady of the Lake University (San Antonio, TX)	NR	NR	African American 7%; Hispanic 67%; Asian 1%	2,195
Oxford College of Emory University (Oxford, GA)	NR	Alumni relations considered as a factor	NR	569
Ozark Christian College (Joplin, MO)	NR	NR	Religious affiliation and/or commitment and Character & Personal Qualities considered important	772
Pace University—New York City (New York, NY)	NR	Alumni relations considered as a factor	Character & Personal Qualities considered	8,044
Pace University—Pleasantville/Briarcliff (Pleasantville, NY)	NR	Alumni relations considered as a factor	Character & Personal Qualities considered	2,760
Pacific Lutheran University (Tacoma, WA)	NR	NR	Character & Personal Qualities considered very important	3,281
Pacific University (Forest Grove, OR)	Minority status considered as factor	Alumni relations considered as a factor	Character & Personal Qualities considered	1,212

(continued)

College	Use of Race in Admission Decisions and Degree Utilized (if at all)	Use of Alumni Relations or Legacies as Factor and Degree Utilized	Use of Other Factors (e.g., geographic origin or religious affiliation) and Degree Utilized	Reported Ethnic/Minority Representation	Total Student Population
Paine College (Augusta, GA)	NR	NR	NR	African American 97%	863
Palm Beach Atlantic University (West Palm Beach, FL)	Minority status considered as factor	Alumni relations considered as a factor	Geographic origin/residence, Character & Personal Qualities, and Religious Affiliation/Commitment all considered	African American 15%; Hispanic 8%; Asian 1%	2,355
Park University (Parkville, MO)	NR	NR	NR	African American 21%; Hispanic 16%; Native American 1%; Asian 3%	11,990
Parsons School of Design, New School University (New York, NY)	NR	NR	NR	African American 3%; Hispanic 6%; Asian 18%	2,474
Pennsylvania State University—Abington (Abington, PA)	NR	Alumni relations considered as a factor	Character & Personal Qualities considered	African American 10%; Hispanic 4%; Asian 11%	2,723
Pennsylvania State University—Altoona (Altoona, PA)	NR	Alumni relations considered as a factor	Character & Personal Qualities considered	African American 5%; Hispanic 2%; Asian 2%	3,663

Pennsylvania State University—Beaver (Monaca, PA)	NR	Alumni relations considered as a factor	Character & Personal Qualities considered	African American 3%; Hispanic 1%; Asian 2%	676
Pennsylvania State University—Berks (Reading, PA)	NR	Alumni relations considered as a factor	Character & Personal Qualities considered	African American 6%; Hispanic 3%; Asian 5%	2,239
Pennsylvania State University—Delaware County (Media, PA)	NR	Alumni relations considered as a factor	Character & Personal Qualities considered	African American 12%; Hispanic 1%; Asian 9%	1,485
Pennsylvania State University—DuBois (DuBois, PA)	NR	Alumni relations considered as a factor	Character & Personal Qualities considered	African American 1%; Asian 1%	791
Pennsylvania State University—Erie, The Behrend College (Erie, PA)	NR	Alumni relations considered as a factor	Character & Personal Qualities considered	African American 3%; Hispanic 1%; Asian 2%	3,446
Pennsylvania State University—Fayette (Uniontown, PA)	NR	Alumni relations considered as a factor	Character & Personal Qualities considered	African American 4%	879
Pennsylvania State University—Harrisburg (Middletown, PA)	NR	Alumni relations considered as a factor	Character & Personal Qualities considered	African American 5%; Hispanic 1%; Asian 6%	1,536
Pennsylvania State University—Hazleton (Hazleton, PA)	NR	Alumni relations considered as a factor	Character & Personal Qualities considered	African American 4%; Hispanic 3%; Asian 4%	1,181

(*continued*)

College	Use of Race in Admission Decisions and Degree Utilized (if at all)	Use of Alumni Relations or Legacies as Factor and Degree Utilized	Use of Other Factors (e.g., geographic origin or religious affiliation) and Degree Utilized	Reported Ethnic/Minority Representation	Total Student Population
Pennsylvania State University—Lehigh Valley (Fogelsville, PA)	NR	Alumni relations considered as a factor	Character & Personal Qualities considered	African American 2%; Hispanic 4%; Asian 8%	609
Pennsylvania State University—McKeesport (McKeesport, PA)	NR	Alumni relations considered as a factor	Character & Personal Qualities considered	African American 13%; Hispanic 2%; Asian 3%	827
Pennsylvania State University—Mont Alto (Mont Alto, PA)	NR	Alumni relations considered as a factor	Character & Personal Qualities considered	African American 8%; Hispanic 3%; Asian 4%	939
Pennsylvania State University—New Kensignton (Upper Barrell, PA)	NR	Alumni relations considered as a factor	Character & Personal Qualities considered	African American 2%; Asian 2%	852
Pennsylvania State University—Schuylkill (Schuylkill Haven, PA)	NR	Alumni relations considered as a factor	Character & Personal Qualities considered	African American 12%; Hispanic 3%; Asian 4%	869

Pennsylvania State University—Shenango (Sharon, PA)	NR	Alumni relations considered as a factor	Character & Personal Qualities considered	African American 4%; Hispanic 1%; Asian 1%	679
Pennsylvania State University—University Park (University Park, PA)	NR	Alumni relations considered as a factor	Character & Personal Qualities considered	African American 4%; Hispanic 3%; Asian 6%	34,056
Pennsylvania State University—Wilkes-Barre (Lehman, PA)	NR	Alumni relations considered as a factor	Character & Personal Qualities considered	African American 2%; Hispanic 1%; Asian 2%	644
Pennsylvania State University—Worthington Scranton (Dunmore, PA)	NR	Alumni relations considered as a factor	Character & Personal Qualities considered	African American 1%; Hispanic 1%; Asian 1%	1,166
Pennsylvania State University—York (York, PA)	NR	Alumni relations considered as a factor	Character & Personal Qualities considered	African American 4%; Hispanic 3%; Asian 5%	1,244
Pepperdine University (Malibu, CA)	Minority status considered as factor	Alumni relations considered as a factor	Religious affiliation and/or commitment and Character & Personal Qualities considered important	African American 7%; Hispanic 11%; Native American 1%; Asian 10%	3,115
Peru State University (Peru, NE)	NR	NR	NR	African American 3%; Hispanic 2%; Native American 1%; Asian 1%	1,482

(continued)

College	Use of Race in Admission Decisions and Degree Utilized (if at all)	Use of Alumni Relations or Legacies as Factor and Degree Utilized	Use of Other Factors (e.g., geographic origin or religious affiliation) and Degree Utilized	Reported Ethnic/Minority Representation	Total Student Population
Pfeiffer University (Misenheimer, NC)	NR	Alumni relations considered as a factor	Religious affiliation and/or commitment and Character & Personal Qualities considered important	African American 16%; Hispanic 1%; Asian 1%	1,188
Philadelphia Biblical University (Langhorne, PA)	NR	Alumni relations considered as a factor	Religious affiliation and/or commitment and Character & Personal Qualities considered important	African American 10%; Hispanic 2%; Asian 2%	1,018
Philadelphia University (Philadelphia, PA)	NR	NR	NR	African American 9%; Hispanic 3%; Asian 4%	2,676
Philander Smith College (Little Rock, AR)	NR	NR	NR	African American 79%	918
Piedmont College (Demorest, GA)	NR	Alumni relations considered as a factor	Character & Personal Qualities considered	African American 5%; Hispanic 2%; Asian 1%	1,010
Pikeville College (Pikeville, KY)	NR	NR	NR	African American 6%; Hispanic 1%	799

Pine Manor College (Chestnut Hill, MA)	NR	Alumni relations considered as a factor	Character & Personal Qualities considered	African American 32%; Hispanic 21%; Asian 4%	477
Pittsburgh State University (Pittsburg, KS)	NR	NR	NR	African American 2%; Hispanic 1%; Native American 2%	5,422
Pitzer College (Claremont, CA)	Minority status considered as factor	Alumni relations considered as a factor	Character & Personal Qualities considered important; Geographic origin/residence considered	African American 5%; Hispanic 13%; Native American 1%; Asian 10%	942
Plymouth State University (Plymouth, NH)	Minority status considered as factor	Alumni relations considered as a factor	Character & Personal Qualities considered important	African American 1%; Hispanic 1%; Asian 1%	4,019
Point Loma Nazarene University (San Diego, CA)	NR	Alumni relations considered as a factor	Religious affiliation and/or commitment and Character & Personal Qualities considered important	African American 2%; Hispanic 8%; Native American 1%; Asian 4%	2,390
Point Park University (Pittsburgh, PA)	NR	NR	Character & Personal Qualities considered	African American 17%; Hispanic 1%; Asian 1%	2,797
Polytechnic University (Brooklyn, NY)	NR	NR	NR	African American 11%; Hispanic 9%; Asian 35%	1,543
Pomona College (Claremont, CA)	Minority status considered as factor	Alumni relations considered as a factor	Character & Personal Qualities considered important; Geographic origin/residence considered	African American 6%; Hispanic 9%; Asian 13%	1,540

(continued)

College	Use of Race in Admission Decisions and Degree Utilized (if at all)	Use of Alumni Relations or Legacies as Factor and Degree Utilized	Use of Other Factors (e.g., geographic origin or religious affiliation) and Degree Utilized	Reported Ethnic/Minority Representation	Total Student Population
Portland State University (Portland, OR)	NR	NR	NR	African American 3%; Hispanic 4%; Native American 1%; Asian 10%	14,791
Prairie View A&M University (Prairie View, TX)	NR	NR	NR	African American 92%; Hispanic 3%; Asian 1%	6,324
Pratt Institute (Brooklyn, NY)	Minority status considered as factor	Alumni relations considered as a factor	Character & Personal Qualities considered	African American 7%; Hispanic 8%; Asian 13%	2,994
Presbyterian College (Clinton, SC)	NR	Alumni relations considered as a factor	Character & Personal Qualities considered very important; Geographic origin/residence considered	African American 5%; Hispanic 1%; Asian 1%	1,165
Prescott College (Prescott, AZ)	NR	NR	Character & Personal Qualities considered	African American 2%; Hispanic 4%; Native American 2%; Asian 2%	771
Princeton University (Princeton, NJ)	Minority status considered as factor	Alumni relations considered as important factor	Character & Personal Qualities considered very important; Geographic origin/residence considered	African American 8%; Hispanic 7%; Native American 1%; Asian 13%	4,678

Principia College (Elsah, IL)	Minority status considered as factor	Alumni relations considered as a factor	Religious affiliation and/or commitment and Character & Personal Qualities considered important	Hispanic 1%; Asian 1%	531
Providence College (Providence, RI)	Minority status considered as factor	Alumni relations considered as a factor	Geographic origin/residence, Character & Personal Qualities, and Religious Affiliation/Commitment all considered	African American 2%; Hispanic 2%; Asian 2%	4,125
Purdue University—Calumet (Hammond, IN)	NR	NR	NR	African American 12%; Hispanic 14%; Asian 1%	8,350
Purdue University—North Central (Westville, IN)	NR	NR	Character & Personal Qualities considered	African American 3%; Hispanic 3%; Native American 1%; Asian 1%	3,434
Purdue University—West Lafayette (West Lafayette, IN)	NR	Alumni relations considered as a factor	Geographic origin/residence considered	African American 3%; Hispanic 2%; Asian 5%	30,391
Queens University of Charlotte (Charlotte, NC)	NR	NR	Character & Personal Qualities considered very important	African American 18%; Hispanic 3%; Native American 1%; Asian 1%	1,487
Quincy University (Quincy, IL)	NR	NR	Character & Personal Qualities considered	African American 6%; Hispanic 3%; Asian 1%	1,010

(*continued*)

College	Use of Race in Admission Decisions and Degree Utilized (if at all)	Use of Alumni Relations or Legacies as Factor and Degree Utilized	Use of Other Factors (e.g., geographic origin or religious affiliation) and Degree Utilized	Reported Ethnic/Minority Representation	Total Student Population
Quinnipiac University (Hamden, CT)	Minority status considered as factor	Alumni relations considered as a factor	NR	African American 2%; Hispanic 4%; Asian 2%	5,329
Radford University (Radford, VT)	Minority status considered as factor	Alumni relations considered as a factor	Geographic origin/residence, and Character and Personal Qualities considered	African American 6%; Hispanic 2%; Asian 2%	8,329
Ramapo College of New Jersey (Mahwah, NJ)	NR	Alumni relations considered as a factor	Character & Personal Qualities considered important	African American 7%; Hispanic 8%; Asian 4%	4,767
Randolph-Macon College (Ashland, VA)	Minority status considered as factor	Alumni relations considered as a factor	Character & Personal Qualities considered	African American 6%; Hispanic 1%; Asian 1%	1,102
Randolph-Macon Woman's College (Lynchburg, VA)	Minority status considered as factor	Alumni relations considered as a factor	Character & Personal Qualities considered very important	African American 9%; Hispanic 4%; Asian 3%	705
Reed College (Portland, OR)	Minority status considered as factor	Alumni relations considered as a factor	Character & Personal Qualities considered	African American 2%; Hispanic 5%; Native American 1%; Asian 6%	1,273

Reedley College (Reedley, CA)	NR	NR	African American 3%; Hispanic 41%; Native American 2%; Asian 4%	7,334
Regis College (Weston, MA)	NR	Alumni relations considered as a factor	Character & Personal Qualities considered very important	African American 11%; Hispanic 9%; Asian 5%	897
Regis University (Denver, CO)	NR	NR	Character & Personal Qualities considered	African American 5%; Hispanic 8%; Native American 1%; Asian 3%	5,430
Reinhardt College (Waleska, GA)	NR	NR	Character & Personal Qualities considered	African American 8%; Hispanic 2%; Asian 1%	1,054
Rensselaer Polytechnic Institute (Troy, NY)	Minority status considered as factor	Alumni relations considered as a factor	Character & Personal Qualities considered important; Geographic origin/residence considered	African American 4%; Hispanic 5%; Asian 12%	4,888
Rhode Island College (Providence, RI)	NR	Alumni relations considered as a factor	NR	African American 4%; Hispanic 5%; Asian 2%	6,531
Rhode Island School of Design (Providence, RI)	Minority status considered as factor	Alumni relations considered as a factor	Character & Personal Qualities considered important	African American 2%; Hispanic 5%; Asian 14%	1,882
Rhodes College (Memphis, TN)	Minority status considered as important factor	Alumni relations considered as important factor	Character & Personal Qualities considered important	African American 4%; Hispanic 1%; Asian 3%	1,528

(continued)

College	Use of Race in Admission Decisions and Degree Utilized (if at all)	Use of Alumni Relations or Legacies as Factor and Degree Utilized	Use of Other Factors (e.g., geographic origin or religious affiliation) and Degree Utilized	Reported Ethnic/Minority Representation	Total Student Population
Rice University (Houston, TX)	Minority status considered as factor	Alumni relations considered as a factor	Character & Personal Qualities considered very important; Geographic origin/residence considered	African American 7%; Hispanic 11%; Native American 1%; Asian 15%	2,933
Richard Stockton College of New Jersey (Pomona, NJ)	NR	Alumni relations considered as a factor	Character & Personal Qualities considered	African American 7%; Hispanic 6%; Asian 4%	6,251
Rider University (Lawrenceville, NJ)	NR	NR	Character & Personal Qualities considered	African American 8%; Hispanic 5%; Asian 3%	4,038
Ringling School of Art & Design (Sarasota, FL)	Minority status considered as factor	Alumni relations considered as a factor	Character & Personal Qualities considered important; Geographic origin/residence considered	African American 2%; Hispanic 9%; Native American 1%; Asian 4%	1,008
Ripon College (Ripon, WI)	NR	Alumni relations considered as a factor	Character & Personal Qualities considered important	African American 2%; Hispanic 3%; Native American 1%; Asian 3%	885
Rivier College (Nashua, NH)	NR	NR	NR	African American 2%; Hispanic 2%; Asian 2%	1,447

Roanoke College (Salem, VA)	Minority status considered as factor	Alumni relations considered as a factor	Character & Personal Qualities considered very important	African American 4%; Hispanic 2%; Native American 1%; Asian 2%	1,781
Robert Morris College (IL) (Chicago, IL)	NR	NR	Character & Personal Qualities considered	African American 42%; Hispanic 23%; Asian 3%	4,878
Robert Morris University (Moon Township, PA)	NR	NR	Character & Personal Qualities considered important; Geographic origin/residence considered	African American 8%; Hispanic 1%; Asian 1%	3,788
Roberts Wesleyan College (Rochester, NY)	Minority status considered as factor	Alumni relations considered as a factor	Geographic origin/residence, Character & Personal Qualities, and Religious Affiliation/Commitment all considered	African American 6%; Hispanic 3%; Asian 1%	1,376
Rochester College (Rochester Hills, MI)	NR	NR	NR	African American 11%; Hispanic 1%; Native American 1%; Asian 1%	927
Rochester Institute of Technology (Rochester, NY)	Minority status considered as factor	Alumni relations considered as a factor	Geographic origin/residence, and Character and Personal Qualities considered	African American 5%; Hispanic 3%; Asian 7%	11,750

(continued)

College	Use of Race in Admission Decisions and Degree Utilized (if at all)	Use of Alumni Relations or Legacies as Factor and Degree Utilized	Use of Other Factors (e.g., geographic origin or religious affiliation) and Degree Utilized	Reported Ethnic/Minority Representation	Total Student Population
Rockford College (Rockford, IL)	NR	Alumni relations considered as a factor	Character & Personal Qualities considered	African American 5%; Hispanic 3%; Asian 1%	954
Rockhurst University (Kansas City, MO)	NR	Alumni relations considered as a factor	Character & Personal Qualities considered important	African American 9%; Hispanic 5%; Native American 1%; Asian 2%	1,279
Rocky Mountain College (Billings, MT)	NR	Alumni relations considered as a factor	Character & Personal Qualities considered important	African American 1%; Hispanic 3%; Native American 9%; Asian 1%	920
Roger Williams University (Bristol, RI)	NR	NR	Character & Personal Qualities considered important	African American 1%; Hispanic 2%; Asian 2%	4,188
Rollins College (Winter Park, FL)	Minority status considered as factor	Alumni relations considered as a factor	Geographic origin/residence, Character & Personal Qualities, and Religious Affiliation/Commitment all considered	African American 5%; Hispanic 8%; Native American 1%; Asian 4%	1,759
Roosevelt University (Chicago, IL)	NR	Alumni relations considered as a factor	Character & Personal Qualities considered important	African American 25%; Hispanic 11%; Asian 5%	3,863

Rose-Hulman Institute of Technology (Terre Haute, IN)	Minority status is considered as important factor	Alumni relations considered as a factor	Character & Personal Qualities considered important	African American 3%; Hispanic 2%; Asian 3%	1,730
Rosemont College (Rosemont, PA)	NR	Alumni relations considered as a factor	Character & Personal Qualities considered	African American 28%; Hispanic 6%; Asian 8%	583
Rowan University (Glassboro, NJ)	Minority status considered as factor	Alumni relations considered as a factor	Character & Personal Qualities considered	African American 9%; Hispanic 6%; Asian 3%	7,970
Russell Sage College (Troy, NY)	NR	Alumni relations considered as a factor	Character & Personal Qualities considered	African American 4%; Hispanic 3%; Asian 2%	824
Rust College (Holly Springs, MS)	NR	NR	Character & Personal Qualities considered	African American 90%	988
Rutgers University (Camden, NJ)	Minority status considered as factor	NR	Geographic origin/residence considered	African American 15%; Hispanic 6%; Asian 9%	3,959
Rutgers University (Piscataway, NJ)	Minority status considered as factor	NR	Geographic origin/residence considered	African American 9%; Hispanic 8%; Asian 22%	26,366
Rutgers University (Newark, NJ)	Minority status considered as factor	NR	Geographic origin/residence considered	African American 20%; Hispanic 18%; Asian 22%	6,075
Sacred Heart University (Fairfield, CT)	NR	NR	NR	African American 6%; Hispanic 6%; Asian 1%	3,088

(continued)

College	Use of Race in Admission Decisions and Degree Utilized (if at all)	Use of Alumni Relations or Legacies as Factor and Degree Utilized	Use of Other Factors (e.g., geographic origin or religious affiliation) and Degree Utilized	Reported Ethnic/Minority Representation	Total Student Population
Saginaw Valley State University (University Center, MI)	NR	NR	NR	African American 6%; Hispanic 1%; Asian 2%	7,587
Saint Ambrose University (Davenport, IA)	NR	Alumni relations considered as a factor	Character & Personal Qualities considered	African American 2%; Hispanic 3%; Asian 1%	2,394
Saint Andrews Presbyterian College (Laurinburg, NC)	NR	NR	NR	African American 12%; Hispanic 2%; Native American 1%; Asian 1%	707
Saint Anselm College	Minority status considered as factor	Alumni relations considered as a factor	Character & Personal Qualities considered important; Geographic origin/residence considered	African American 1%; Hispanic 1%; Asian 1%	1,960
Saint Augustine's College (Raleigh, NC)	Minority status considered as factor	Alumni relations considered as a factor	Geographic origin/residence, Character and Personal Qualities, and Religious Affiliation/Commitment all considered	African American 60%	1,493

St. Bonaventure University (Bonaventure, NY)	NR	Alumni relations considered as a factor	Character & Personal Qualities considered important	African American 1%; Hispanic 1%	2,170
Saint Cloud State University (Saint Cloud, MN)	Minority status considered as factor	NR	NR	African American 2%; Hispanic 1%; Native American 1%; Asian 2%	13,210
St. Edward's University (Austin, TX)	Minority status considered as factor	NR	Geographic origin/residence, Character & Personal Qualities, and Religious Affiliation/Commitment all considered	African American 5%; Hispanic 30%; Native American 1%; Asian 2%	3,690
Saint Francis College (Brooklyn Heights, NY)	NR	Alumni relations considered as a factor	Character & Personal Qualities considered important	African American 20%; Hispanic 14%; Asian 2%	2,294
Saint Francis University (Loretto, PA)	NR	Alumni relations considered as a factor	Character & Personal Qualities considered important; Geographic origin/residence considered	African American 6%; Hispanic 1%	1,300
Saint John Fisher College (Rochester, NY)	Minority status is considered as important factor	Alumni relations considered very important	Character & Personal Qualities considered important; Geographic origin/residence considered	African American 4%; Hispanic 3%; Asian 2%	2,588

(continued)

287

College	Use of Race in Admission Decisions and Degree Utilized (if at all)	Use of Alumni Relations or Legacies as Factor and Degree Utilized	Use of Other Factors (e.g., geographic origin or religious affiliation) and Degree Utilized	Reported Ethnic/Minority Representation	Total Student Population
St. John's College (MD) (Annapolis, MD)	Minority status considered as factor	Alumni relations considered as important factor	Character & Personal Qualities considered important	African American 1%; Hispanic 3%; Native American 1%; Asian 2%	473
St. John's College (NM) (Sante Fe, NM)	NR	NR	Character & Personal Qualities considered very important	African American 1%; Hispanic 7%; Native American 1%; Asian 2%	450
St. John's University (Jamaica, NY)	NR	NR	Character & Personal Qualities considered	African American 16%; Hispanic 15%; Asian 15%	12,505
Saint Joseph College (West Hartford, CT)	NR	Alumni relations considered as a factor	Character & Personal Qualities considered	African American 14%; Hispanic 8%; Asian 2%	1,093
Saint Joseph's College (IN) (Rensselaer, IN)	NR	Alumni relations considered as a factor	Character & Personal Qualities considered	African American 5%; Hispanic 4%	980
Saint Joseph's College (ME) (Standish, ME)	NR	NR	Character & Personal Qualities considered	African American 12%; Hispanic 1%; Asian 1%	960
St. Joseph's College—Brooklyn (Brooklyn, NY)	NR	Alumni relations considered as a factor	Character & Personal Qualities considered	African American 39%; Hispanic 8%; Asian 4%	1,194

St. Joseph's College—Patchogue (Patchogue, NY)	NR	NR	NR	African American 3%; Hispanic 4%; Asian 1%	3,094
Saint Joseph's University (Philadelphia, PA)	NR	Alumni relations considered as a factor	Character & Personal Qualities considered	African American 7%; Hispanic 2%; Asian 2%	4,823
St. Lawrence University (Canton, NY)	Minority status is considered as important factor	Alumni relations considered as a factor	Character & Personal Qualities considered very important; Geographic origin/residence considered	African American 2%; Hispanic 3%; Asian 1%	2,102
Saint Leo University (Saint Leo, FL)	Minority status considered as factor	Alumni relations considered as important factor	Character & Personal Qualities considered very important	African American 8%; Hispanic 7%; Native American 1%; Asian 1%	1,076
Saint Louis University (Saint Louis, MO)	NR	Alumni relations considered as a factor	Character & Personal Qualities considered	African American 8%; Hispanic 2%; Asian 5%	6,928
Saint Martin's College (Lacey, WA)	NR	Alumni relations considered as a factor	Character & Personal Qualities considered important	African American 9%; Hispanic 6%; Native American 2%; Asian 9%	1,173
Saint Mary's College (Notre Dame, IN)	Minority status considered as factor	Alumni relations considered as a factor	NR	African American 1%; Hispanic 5%; Native American 1%; Asian 2%	1,388

(continued)

College	Use of Race in Admission Decisions and Degree Utilized (if at all)	Use of Alumni Relations or Legacies as Factor and Degree Utilized	Use of Other Factors (e.g., geographic origin or religious affiliation) and Degree Utilized	Reported Ethnic/Minority Representation	Total Student Population
Saint Mary's College of California (Moraga, CA)	Minority status considered as factor	Alumni relations considered as a factor	Geographic origin/residence, Character & Personal Qualities, and Religious Affiliation/Commitment all considered	African American 5%; Hispanic 14%; Native American 1%; Asian 7%	3,330
St. Mary's College of Maryland (St. Mary's City, MD)	Minority status considered as factor	Alumni relations considered as a factor	Geographic origin/residence, and Character & Personal Qualities considered	African American 7%; Hispanic 3%; Asian 4%	1,833
Saint Mary-of-the-Woods College (Saint Mary-of-the-Woods, IN)	NR	NR	Character & Personal Qualities considered	African American 4%; Hispanic 2%	1,354
St. Mary's University (San Antonio, TX)	NR	Alumni relations considered as a factor	Religious affiliation and/or commitment and Character & Personal Qualities considered important	African American 3%; Hispanic 68%; Asian 3%	2,531

Saint Mary's University of Minnesota (Winona, MN)	Minority status considered as factor	Alumni relations considered as a factor	Character & Personal Qualities considered important	African American 4%; Hispanic 3%; Native American 1%; Asian 2%	1,591
Saint Michael's College (Colchester, VT)	Minority status considered as factor	Alumni relations considered as a factor	Character & Personal Qualities considered important; Geographic origin/residence considered	African American 1%; Hispanic 1%; Asian 1%	1,930
St. Norbert College (De Pere, WI)	NR	Alumni relations considered as a factor	Character & Personal Qualities considered	African American 1%; Hispanic 1%; Native American 1%; Asian 1%	1,972
Saint Olaf College (Northfield, MN)	Minority status considered as factor	Alumni relations considered as a factor	Geographic origin/residence, Character & Personal Qualities, and Religious Affiliation/Commitment all considered	African American 1%; Hispanic 2%; Asian 4%	2,920
Saint Paul's College (Lawrenceville, VA)	NR	NR	Character & Personal Qualities considered important	African American 98%	677
Saint Peter's College (Jersey City, NJ)	NR	NR	Character & Personal Qualities considered	NR	2,282
Saint Thomas Aquinas College (Sparkill, NY)	Minority status considered as factor	Alumni relations considered as a factor	Character & Personal Qualities considered important	African American 5%; Hispanic 16%; Asian 4%	1,451

(continued)

College	Use of Race in Admission Decisions and Degree Utilized (if at all)	Use of Alumni Relations or Legacies as Factor and Degree Utilized	Use of Other Factors (e.g., geographic origin or religious affiliation) and Degree Utilized	Reported Ethnic/Minority Representation	Total Student Population
St. Thomas University (Miami, FL)	NR	Alumni relations considered as a factor	Character & Personal Qualities considered	African American 28%; Hispanic 45%; Asian 1%	1,169
Saint Vincent College (Latrobe, PA)	NR	Alumni relations considered as a factor	Character & Personal Qualities considered	African American 2%; Hispanic 1%; Asian 1%	1,280
Saint Xavier University (Chicago, IL)	Minority status considered as factor	Alumni relations considered as a factor	Geographic origin/ residence, Character & Personal Qualities, and Religious Affiliation/ Commitment all considered	African American 18%; Hispanic 11%; Asian 2%	3,009
Salem College (Winston-Salem, NC)	Minority status considered as factor	Alumni relations considered as a factor	Character & Personal Qualities considered important	African American 19%; Hispanic 2%; Asian 1%	858
Salem International University (Salem, WV)	NR	Alumni relations considered as a factor	Character & Personal Qualities considered	African American 8%; Hispanic 2%; Native American 1%; Asian 1%	450
Salem State College (Salem, MA)	NR	Alumni relations considered as a factor	Character & Personal Qualities considered	African American 4%; Hispanic 4%; Native American 1%; Asian 2%	5,751

Salisbury University (Salisbury, MD)	Minority status considered as factor	Alumni relations considered as important factor	Geographic origin/residence considered important; Character & Personal Qualities considered	African American 8%; Hispanic 2%; Asian 3%	6,022
Salve Regina University (Newport, RI)	Minority status is considered as important factor	Alumni relations considered as a factor	Character & Personal Qualities considered important	African American 1%; Hispanic 2%; Asian 2%	2,039
Sam Houston State University (Huntsville, TX)	NR	NR	NR	African American 15%; Hispanic 11%; Native American 1%; Asian 1%	12,270
Samford University (Birmingham, AL)	Minority status considered as factor	Alumni relations considered as important factor	Religious affiliation and/or commitment and Character & Personal Qualities considered very important	African American 6%; Hispanic 1%; Asian 1%	2,855
San Diego State University (San Diego, CA)	NR	NR	Geographic origin/residence considered	African American 4%; Hispanic 21%; Native American 1%; Asian 15%	27,345
San Francisco State University (San Francisco, CA)	NR	Alumni relations considered as a factor	Geographic origin/residence considered	African American 6%; Hispanic 13%; Native American 1%; Asian 31%	22,291
San Jose State University (San Jose, CA)	NR	NR	NR	African American 4%; Hispanic 13%; Asian 34%	21,663

(continued)

College	Use of Race in Admission Decisions and Degree Utilized (if at all)	Use of Alumni Relations or Legacies as Factor and Degree Utilized	Use of Other Factors (e.g., geographic origin or religious affiliation) and Degree Utilized	Reported Ethnic/Minority Representation	Total Student Population
Santa Clara University (Santa Clara, CA)	Minority status considered as factor	Alumni relations considered as a factor	Character & Personal Qualities considered important; Geographic origin/residence considered	African American 3%; Hispanic 13%; Native American 1%; Asian 19%	4,391
Sarah Lawrence College (Bronxville, NY)	Minority status considered as factor	Alumni relations considered as a factor	Character & Personal Qualities considered important; Geographic origin/residence considered	African American 5%; Hispanic 3%; Native American 1%; Asian 4%	1,185
Savannah College of Art & Design (Savannah, GA)	NR	Alumni relations considered as a factor	Character & Personal Qualities considered important	African American 5%; Hispanic 3%; Asian 2%	5,698
Savannah State University (Savannah, GA)	NR	NR	NR	African American 96%	2,635
School the Art Institute of Chicago (Chicago, IL)	NR	NR	Character & Personal Qualities considered important	African American 3%; Hispanic 7%; Native American 1%; Asian 10%	1,992

School of the Museum of Fine Arts (Boston, MA)	NR	Alumni relations considered as a factor	Geographic origin/residence, and Character & Personal Qualities considered	African American 3%; Hispanic 5%; Native American 1%; Asian 3%	664
School of Visual Arts (New York, NY)	Minority status considered as factor	Alumni relations considered as a factor	Character & Personal Qualities considered important	African American 4%; Hispanic 9%; Asian 12%	2,887
Schreiner University (Kerrville, TX)	NR	NR	Character & Personal Qualities considered	African American 2%; Hispanic 16%; Native American 1%; Asian 1%	730
Scripps College (Claremont, CA)	Minority status is considered as a very important factor	Alumni relations considered as a very important factor	Character & Personal Qualities considered important; Geographic origin/residence considered	African American 3%; Hispanic 6%; Asian 13%	815
Seattle Pacific University (Seattle, WA)	Minority status considered as factor	Alumni relations considered as a factor	Religious affiliation and/or commitment and Character & Personal Qualities considered important; Geographic origin/residence considered	African American 3%; Hispanic 3%; Native American 1%; Asian 8%	2,288
Seattle University (Seattle, WA)	Minority status considered as factor	Alumni relations considered as a factor	Character & Personal Qualities considered important; Geographic origin/residence considered	African American 5%; Hispanic 7%; Native American 1%; Asian 21%	3,739

(*continued*)

College	Use of Race in Admission Decisions and Degree Utilized (if at all)	Use of Alumni Relations or Legacies as Factor and Degree Utilized	Use of Other Factors (e.g., geographic origin or religious affiliation) and Degree Utilized	Reported Ethnic/Minority Representation	Total Student Population
Seton Hall University (South Orange, NJ)	NR	NR	Character & Personal Qualities considered	African American 11%; Hispanic 9%; Asian 8%	5,009
Seton Hill University (Greensburg, PA)	NR	Alumni relations considered as a factor	Character & Personal Qualities considered important	African American 6%; Hispanic 1%; Asian 1%	1,347
Sewanee—The University of the South (Sewanee, TN)	Minority status considered as factor	Alumni relations considered as a factor	Character & Personal Qualities considered important; Geographic origin/residence considered	African American 4%; Hispanic 2%; Asian 2%	1,359
Shaw University (Raleigh, NC)	NR	Alumni relations considered as a factor	Character & Personal Qualities considered important; Geographic origin/residence considered	African American 84%	2,424
Shawnee State University (Portsmouth, OH)	Minority status considered as factor	Alumni relations considered as a factor	Geographic origin/residence, Character & Personal Qualities, and Religious Affiliation/Commitment all considered	African American 3%; Hispanic 1%; Native American 1%	3,368

Shenandoah University (Winchester, VA)	NR	Alumni relations considered as a factor	Character & Personal Qualities considered important	African American 4%; Hispanic 1%; Asian 1%	1,511
Shepherd University (Shepherdstown, WV)	NR	Alumni relations considered as a factor	Geographic origin/ residence, and Character & Personal Qualities considered	African American 5%; Hispanic 2%; Asian 1%	3,918
Shippensburg University of Pennsylvania (Shippensburg, PA)	NR	NR	Character & Personal Qualities considered important	African American 4%; Hispanic 1%; Asian 1%	6,496
Shorter College (Rome, GA)	NR	Alumni relations considered as a factor	Character & Personal Qualities considered	African American 6%; Hispanic 1%; Asian 1%	877
Siena College (Loudonville, NY)	Minority status considered as factor	Alumni relations considered as a factor	Geographic origin/ residence, and Character & Personal Qualities considered	African American 2%; Hispanic 3%; Asian 3%	3,213
Siena Heights University (Adrian, MI)	NR	NR	NR	African American 10%; Hispanic 2%	1,886
Sierra College (Rocklin, CA)	NR	NR	NR	African American 1%; Hispanic 7%; Native American 2%; Asian 4%	20,173

(continued)

College	Use of Race in Admission Decisions and Degree Utilized (if at all)	Use of Alumni Relations or Legacies as Factor and Degree Utilized	Use of Other Factors (e.g., geographic origin or religious affiliation) and Degree Utilized	Reported Ethnic/Minority Representation	Total Student Population
Silver Lake College (Manitowac, WI)	NR	Alumni relations considered as a factor	Character & Personal Qualities considered important	African American 1%; Hispanic 2%; Native American 5%; Asian 2%	489
Simmons College (Boston, MA)	NR	Alumni relations considered as a factor	Character & Personal Qualities considered important	African American 6%; Hispanic 3%; Asian 6%	1,294
Simpson College (Indianola, IA)	NR	Alumni relations considered as a factor	Character & Personal Qualities considered important	African American 1%; Hispanic 1%; Asian 1%	1,758
Simpson College and Graduate School (Redding, CA)	NR	NR	Religious affiliation and/or commitment and Character & Personal Qualities considered important	African American 1%; Hispanic 4%; Native American 1%; Asian 6%	953
Skidmore College (Saratoga Springs, NY)	Minority status considered as factor	Alumni relations considered as a factor	Geographic origin/ residence considered	African American 3%; Hispanic 3%; Asian 5%	2,609
Slippery Rock University of Pennsylvania (Slippery Rock, PA)	Minority status considered as factor	Alumni relations considered as a factor	Character & Personal Qualities considered	African American 4%; Hispanic 1%; Asian 1%	6,889

Smith College (Northampton, MA)	Minority status considered as factor	NR	Character & Personal Qualities considered very important	African American 6%; Hispanic 6%; Native American 1%; Asian 10%	2,682
Sonoma State University (Rohnert Park, CA)	Minority status considered as factor	NR	Geographic origin/ residence considered	African American 2%; Hispanic 11%; Native American 1%; Asian 5%	6,677
South Carolina State University (Orangesburg, SC)	NR	NR	NR	African American 98%	3,345
South College (Savannah, GA)	NR	NR	NR	African American 34%; Hispanic 2%; Native American 1%; Asian 2%	450
South Dakota School of Mines & Technology (Rapid City, SD)	NR	NR	Character & Personal Qualities considered	African American 1%; Hispanic 1%; Native American 3%; Asian 1%	1,921
South Dakota State University (Brookings, SD)	NR	NR	NR	African American 1%; Native American 1%; Asian 1%	8,447
Southampton College of Long Island University (Southampton, NY)	NR	NR	Character & Personal Qualities considered	African American 5%; Hispanic 5%; Native American 1%; Asian 1%	1,147
Southeast Missouri State University (Cape Girardeau, MO)	NR	NR	NR	African American 8%; Hispanic 1%; Native American 1%; Asian 1%	7,899

(*continued*)

College	Use of Race in Admission Decisions and Degree Utilized (if at all)	Use of Alumni Relations or Legacies as Factor and Degree Utilized	Use of Other Factors (e.g., geographic origin or religious affiliation) and Degree Utilized	Reported Ethnic/Minority Representation	Total Student Population
Southeastern College of the Assemblies of God (Lakeland, FL)	NR	NR	NR	African American 4%; Hispanic 8%; Native American 1%; Asian 1%	1,078
Southeastern Louisiana University (Hammond, LA)	NR	NR	NR	African American 16%; Hispanic 1%; Asian 1%	13,599
Southeastern Oklahoma State University (Durant, OK)	NR	NR	Geographic origin/residence, and Character & Personal Qualities considered	African American 4%; Hispanic 2%; Native American 23%	3,597
Southeastern University (Washington, DC)	NR	Alumni relations considered as a factor	Character & Personal Qualities considered	African American 78%; Hispanic 9%; Asian 3%	490
Southern Adventist University (Collegedale, TN)	Minority status considered as factor	Alumni relations considered as a factor	Religious affiliation and/or commitment and Character & Personal Qualities considered important	African American 7%; Hispanic 10%; Native American 1%; Asian 4%	2,199

Institution	Admissions Factor	Additional Factor	Enrollment	Demographics
Southern Arkansas University (Magnolia, AR)	NR	NR	2,609	African American 27%; Hispanic 1%; Native American 1%; Asian 1%
Southern Connecticut State University (New Haven, CT)	Minority status considered as factor	NR	7,624	African American 11%; Hispanic 5%; Asian 2%
Southern Illinois University—Carbondale (Carbondale, IL)	NR	NR	16,786	African American 15%; Hispanic 3%; Asian 2%
Southern Illinois University—Edwardsville (Edwardsville, IL)	NR	NR	10,709	African American 11%; Hispanic 2%; Asian 2%
Southern Maine Community College (Portland, ME)	Minority status considered as factor	Geographic origin/residence considered important; Character & Personal Qualities considered	2,728	African American 2%; Hispanic 1%; Native American 1%; Asian 1%
Southern Methodist University (Dallas, TX)	NR	Alumni relations considered as a factor	Character & Personal Qualities considered important	6,090	African American 5%; Hispanic 9%; Native American 1%; Asian 6%
Southern Nazarene University (Bethany, OK)	NR	NR	1,780	African American 8%; Hispanic 4%; Native American 3%; Asian 2%

(*continued*)

College	Use of Race in Admission Decisions and Degree Utilized (if at all)	Use of Alumni Relations or Legacies as Factor and Degree Utilized	Use of Other Factors (e.g., geographic origin or religious affiliation) and Degree Utilized	Reported Ethnic/Minority Representation	Total Student Population
Southern New Hampshire University (Manchester, NH)	NR	Alumni relations considered as a factor	Character & Personal Qualities considered	African American 1%; Hispanic 2%; Asian 1%	3,255
Southern Oregon University (Ashland, OR)	NR	NR	Character & Personal Qualities considered	African American 2%; Hispanic 4%; Native American 2%; Asian 4%	4,429
Southern Polytechnic State University (Marietta, GA)	NR	NR	NR	African American 22%; Hispanic 3%; Asian 6%	3,111
Southern University and A&M College (Baton Rouge, LA)	NR	NR	NR	African American 98%	7,868
Southern University at Shreveport (Shreveport, LA)	NR	NR	Geographic origin/residence considered	African American 91%	1,342
Southern Utah University (Cedar City, UT)	NR	NR	NR	African American 1%; Hispanic 2%; Native American 1%; Asian 2%	4,802

Southern Vermont College (Bennington, VT)	NR	NR	Character & Personal Qualities considered	NR	464
Southern Wesleyan University (Central, SC)	NR	NR	Religious affiliation and/or commitment and Character & Personal Qualities considered important	African American 34%; Hispanic 2%; Asian 1%	2,028
Southwest Baptist University (Bolivar, MO)	NR	NR	Character & Personal Qualities considered	African American 2%; Hispanic 1%; Native American 1%; Asian 1%	2,387
Southwest Missouri State University (Springfield, MO)	Minority status considered as factor	Alumni relations considered as a factor	Character & Personal Qualities considered	African American 3%; Hispanic 1%; Native American 1%; Asian 1%	14,565
Southwestern Christian University (Bethany, OK)	NR	NR	Religious affiliation and/or commitment and Character & Personal Qualities considered important	African American 1%; Native American 1%	637
Southwestern College (Winfield, KS)	NR	Alumni relations considered as a factor	Character & Personal Qualities considered	African American 9%; Hispanic 4%; Native American 2%; Asian 1%	1,122
Southwestern Oklahoma State University (Weatherford, OK)	NR	NR	NR	African American 4%; Hispanic 3%; Native American 6%; Asian 1%	3,967

(continued)

College	Use of Race in Admission Decisions and Degree Utilized (if at all)	Use of Alumni Relations or Legacies as Factor and Degree Utilized	Use of Other Factors (e.g., geographic origin or religious affiliation) and Degree Utilized	Reported Ethnic/Minority Representation	Total Student Population
Southwestern University (Georgetown, TX)	Minority status considered as factor	Alumni relations considered as a factor	Character & Personal Qualities considered important; Geographic origin/residence considered	African American 4%; Hispanic 13%; Native American 1%; Asian 4%	1,276
Spalding University (Louisville, KY)	NR	NR	Character & Personal Qualities considered	African American 13%; Hispanic 1%; Asian 1%	1,128
Spelman College (Atlanta, GA)	NR	Alumni relations considered as a factor	Character & Personal Qualities considered	African American 95%	2,063
Spring Arbor University (Spring Arbor, MI)	Minority status considered as factor	Alumni relations considered as a factor	Religious affiliation and/or commitment and Character & Personal Qualities considered very important	African American 2%; Hispanic 1%; Asian 1%	2,390
Spring Hill College (Mobile, AL)	NR	Alumni relations considered as a factor	Character & Personal Qualities considered	African American 14%; Hispanic 6%; Native American 1%; Asian 1%	1,174

Springfield College (Springfield, MA)	Minority status considered as factor	Alumni relations considered as a factor	Geographic origin/residence, Character & Personal Qualities, and Religious Affiliation/Commitment all considered	African American 3%; Hispanic 3%; Asian 1%	2,238
Stanford University (Stanford, CA)	Minority status considered as factor	Alumni relations considered as a factor	Character & Personal Qualities considered very important; Geographic origin/residence considered	African American 11%; Hispanic 12%; Native American 2%; Asian 24%	6,500
State University of New York at Albany (Albany, NY)	Minority status considered as factor	NR	Character & Personal Qualities considered very important; Geographic origin/residence considered	African American 8%; Hispanic 7%; Asian 6%	11,309
State University of New York at Binghamton (Binghamton, NY)	Minority status considered as factor	Alumni relations considered as a factor	Geographic origin/residence, and Character & Personal Qualities considered	African American 5%; Hispanic 6%; Asian 17%	10,898
State University of New York at Buffalo (Buffalo, NY)	Minority status considered as factor	NR	Geographic origin/residence, and Character & Personal Qualities considered	African American 7%; Hispanic 4%; Asian 9%	17,509

(continued)

College	Use of Race in Admission Decisions and Degree Utilized (if at all)	Use of Alumni Relations or Legacies as Factor and Degree Utilized	Use of Other Factors (e.g., geographic origin or religious affiliation) and Degree Utilized	Reported Ethnic/Minority Representation	Total Student Population
State University of New York College at Brockport (Brockport, NY)	NR	NR	Character & Personal Qualities considered	African American 5%; Hispanic 3%; Asian 1%	6,854
State University of New York College at Buffalo (Buffalo, NY)	NR	NR	Character & Personal Qualities considered	African American 11%; Hispanic 4%; Native American 1%; Asian 2%	8,751
State University of New York College at Cortland (Cortland, NY)	Minority status considered as factor	Alumni relations considered as a factor	Geographic origin/ residence considered	African American 3%; Hispanic 3%; Asian 1%	5,607
State University of New York College at Fredonia (Fredonia, NY)	Minority status considered as factor	Alumni relations considered as a factor	Character & Personal Qualities considered	African American 1%; Hispanic 2%; Native American 1%; Asian 1%	4,824
State University of New York College at Geneseo (Geneseo, NY)	Minority status considered as factor	NR	Character & Personal Qualities considered	African American 2%; Hispanic 3%; Asian 5%	5,375

State University of New York College at New Paltz (New Paltz, NY)	NR	NR	NR	Hispanic 9%; Asian 4%	6,169
State University of New York College at Old Westbury (Old Westbury, NY)	NR	NR	Character & Personal Qualities considered	African American 26%; Hispanic 16%; Asian 8%	3,169
State University of New York College at Oneonta (Oneonta, NY)	Minority status considered as factor	Alumni relations considered as a factor	Character & Personal Qualities considered	African American 3%; Hispanic 4%; Asian 2%	5,512
State University of New York College at Oswego (Oswego, NY)	Minority status considered as factor	Alumni relations considered as a factor	Character & Personal Qualities considered	African American 4%; Hispanic 4%; Asian 2%	6,945
State University of New York College at Plattsburgh (Plattsburgh, NY)	Minority status considered as factor	Alumni relations considered as a factor	Character & Personal Qualities considered	African American 5%; Hispanic 3%; Asian 2%	5,328
State University of New York College at Potsdam (Potsdam, NY)	NR	Alumni relations considered as a factor	Character & Personal Qualities considered	African American 2%; Hispanic 2%; Native American 2%; Asian 1%	3,435
State University of New York College at Purchase (Purchase, NY)	NR	NR	NR	African American 8%; Hispanic 10%; Asian 4%	3,344

(*continued*)

College	Use of Race in Admission Decisions and Degree Utilized (if at all)	Use of Alumni Relations or Legacies as Factor and Degree Utilized	Use of Other Factors (e.g., geographic origin or religious affiliation) and Degree Utilized	Reported Ethnic/Minority Representation	Total Student Population
State University of New York College of A&T at Cobleskill (Cobleskill, NY)	NR	Alumni relations considered as a factor	Geographic origin/residence considered	African American 7%; Hispanic 4%; Asian 1%	2,510
State University of New York College of Environmental Science and Forestry (Syracuse, NY)	NR	Alumni relations considered as a factor	Character & Personal Qualities considered important	African American 3%; Hispanic 2%; Asian 1%	1,156
State University of New York College of Technology at Alfred (Alfred, NY)	NR	Alumni relations considered as a factor	Character & Personal Qualities considered	Hispanic 3%; Asian 1%	3,471
State University of New York College of Technology at Canton (Canton, NY)	NR	NR	Character & Personal Qualities considered	Hispanic 3%; Native American 2%	2,119
State University of New York College of Technology at Delphi (Delhi, NY)	NR	Alumni relations considered as a factor	Character & Personal Qualities considered important; Geographic origin/residence considered	African American 11%; Hispanic 7%; Asian 2%	1,791

State University of New York Empire State College (Saratoga, NY)	NR	Character & Personal Qualities considered very important	African American 12%; Hispanic 7%; Asian 1%	8,495
State University of New York Institute of Technology at Utica/Rome (Utica, NY)	NR	NR	Hispanic 3%; Asian 3%	1,747
State University of New York Maritime College (Throggs Neck, NY)	NR	NR	Hispanic 7%; Asian 4%	713
State University of West Georgia (Carrollton, GA)	NR	NR	African American 23%; Hispanic 1%; Asian 1%	8,279
Stephen F. Austin State University (Nacogdoches, TX)	NR	Geographic origin/residence considered	African American 16%; Hispanic 7%; Native American 1%; Asian 1%	9,747
Stephens College (Columbia, MO)	NR	Character & Personal Qualities considered very important	African American 8%; Hispanic 4%; Native American 1%; Asian 1%	564
Stetson University (Deland, FL)	Minority status considered as factor	Alumni relations considered as a factor	Character & Personal Qualities considered important; Geographic origin/residence considered	African American 4%; Hispanic 6%; Asian 2%	2,181

(continued)

College	Use of Race in Admission Decisions and Degree Utilized (if at all)	Use of Alumni Relations or Legacies as Factor and Degree Utilized	Use of Other Factors (e.g., geographic origin or religious affiliation) and Degree Utilized	Reported Ethnic/Minority Representation	Total Student Population
Stevens Institute of Technology (Hoboken, NJ)	NR	Alumni relations considered as a factor	Character & Personal Qualities considered	African American 4%; Hispanic 9%; Asian 16%	1,726
Stonehill College (Easton, MA)	Minority status considered as factor	Alumni relations considered as a factor	Character & Personal Qualities considered important; Geographic origin/residence considered	African American 3%; Hispanic 3%; Asian 3%	2,401
Strayer University (Washington, DC)	NR	Alumni relations considered as a factor	Character & Personal Qualities considered	African American 40%; Hispanic 4%; Asian 5%	12,703
Suffolk University (Boston, MA)	NR	Alumni relations considered as a factor	Character & Personal Qualities considered important; Geographic origin/residence considered	African American 3%; Hispanic 5%; Asian 7%	4,244
Sul Ross State University (Alpine, TX)	NR	NR	NR	African American 4%; Hispanic 48%; Native American 1%; Asian 1%	1,402

Sullivan County Community College (Loch Sheldrake, NY)	NR	NR	NR	African American 20%; Hispanic 12%; Asian 3%	1,552
Susquehanna University (Selinsgrove, PA)	Minority status is considered as important factor	Alumni relations considered as a factor	Geographic origin/residence, Character & Personal Qualities, and Religious Affiliation/Commitment all considered	Hispanic 2%; Asian 2%	1,972
Swarthmore College (Swarthmore, PA)	Minority status considered as factor	Alumni relations considered as a factor	Character & Personal Qualities considered very important; Geographic origin/residence considered	Hispanic 9%; Native American 1%; Asian 16%	1,459
Sweet Briar College (Sweet Briar, VA)	Minority status considered as factor	Alumni relations considered as a factor	Character & Personal Qualities considered	Hispanic 2%; Native American 2%; Asian 1%	524
Syracuse University (Syracuse, NY)	Minority status considered as factor	NR	Character & Personal Qualities considered	Hispanic 4%; Asian 6%	10,750
Tabor College (Hillsboro, KS)	NR	NR	Religious affiliation and/or commitment and Character & Personal Qualities considered important	Hispanic 2%; Native American 1%; Asian 9%	544

(*continued*)

College	Use of Race in Admission Decisions and Degree Utilized (if at all)	Use of Alumni Relations or Legacies as Factor and Degree Utilized	Use of Other Factors (e.g., geographic origin or religious affiliation) and Degree Utilized	Reported Ethnic/Minority Representation	Total Student Population
Talladega College (Talladega, AL)	NR	NR	Character & Personal Qualities considered important	Hispanic 1%	468
Tarleton State University (Stephenville, TX)	NR	NR	NR	Hispanic 7%; Native American 1%; Asian 1%	7,451
Taylor University—Fort Wayne Campus (Fort Wayne, IL)	NR	NR	Religious affiliation and/or commitment and Character & Personal Qualities considered important	Hispanic 2%; Asian 1%	521
Taylor University—Upland (Upland, NY)	Minority status considered as factor	Alumni relations considered as a factor	Religious affiliation and/or commitment and Character & Personal Qualities considered important	African American 2%; Hispanic 1%; Asian 2%	1,851
Teikyo Post University (Waterbury, CT)	NR	Alumni relations considered as a factor	Character & Personal Qualities considered important	African American 18%; Hispanic 11%; Asian 2%	1,198

Temple University (Philadelphia, PA)	NR	Alumni relations considered as a factor	Character & Personal Qualities considered	African American 6%; Hispanic 6%; Asian 18%	22,780
Tennessee State University (Nashville, TN)	NR	Alumni relations considered as a factor	Geographic origin/residence considered important; Character & Personal Qualities considered	African American 82%; Asian 1%	7,000
Tennessee Technological University (Cookeville, TN)	NR	Alumni relations considered as a factor	Character & Personal Qualities considered	African American 4%; Asian 1%	7,143
Tennessee Wesleyan College (Athens, TN)	NR	NR	NR	African American 3%; Hispanic 2%	779
Texas A&M University (College Station, TX)	NR	Alumni relations considered as a factor	Geographic origin/residence considered important; Character & Personal Qualities considered	African American 2%; Hispanic 10%; Native American 1%; Asian 3%	35,605
Texas A&M University—Commerce (Commerce, TX)	NR	NR	NR	African American 17%; Hispanic 5%; Native American 1%; Asian 1%	4,815
Texas A&M University—Corpus Christi (Corpus Christi, TX)	NR	NR	Character & Personal Qualities considered	African American 2%; Hispanic 37%; Asian 2%	6,017

(continued)

College	Use of Race in Admission Decisions and Degree Utilized (if at all)	Use of Alumni Relations or Legacies as Factor and Degree Utilized	Use of Other Factors (e.g., geographic origin or religious affiliation) and Degree Utilized	Reported Ethnic/Minority Representation	Total Student Population
Texas A&M University—Galveston (Galveston, TX)	NR	Alumni relations considered as a factor	Character & Personal Qualities considered	African American 3%; Hispanic 9%; Native American 1%; Asian 1%	1,577
Texas A&M University—Kingsville (Kingsville, TX)	NR	NR	NR	African American 5%; Hispanic 66%; Asian 1%	4,373
Texas A&M University—Texarkana (Texarkana, TX)	NR	NR	NR	African American 12%; Hispanic 3%; Asian 1%	969
Texas Christian University (Fort Worth, TX)	Minority status is considered as important factor	Alumni relations considered as a factor	Character & Personal Qualities considered very important; Geographic origin/residence and Religious Affiliation considered	African American 5%; Hispanic 6%; Native American 1%; Asian 2%	7,024
Texas College (Tyler, TX)	NR	NR	NR	African American 95%; Hispanic 2%	1,035

Texas Lutheran University (Seguin, TX)	NR	NR	Character & Personal Qualities considered	African American 7%; Hispanic 17%; Asian 1%	1,358
Texas Southern University (Houston, TX)	NR	NR	NR	African American 90%; Hispanic 3%; Asian 2%	9,585
Texas State University—San Marcos (San Marcos, TX)	NR	NR	NR	African American 5%; Hispanic 19%; Native American 1%; Asian 2%	22,402
Texas Tech University (Lubbock, TX)	NR	Alumni relations considered as important factor	Character & Personal Qualities considered important	African American 3%; Hispanic 11%; Native American 1%; Asian 2%	23,329
Texas Wesleyan University (Fort Worth, TX)	NR	Alumni relations considered as a factor	Character & Personal Qualities considered very important	African American 20%; Hispanic 18%; Native American 1%; Asian 2%	1,407
Texas Woman's University (Denton, TX)	NR	NR	NR	African American 22%; Hispanic 13%; Native American 1%; Asian 10%	5,790
Thiel College (Greenville, PA)	NR	Alumni relations considered as a factor	Character & Personal Qualities considered important	African American 6%; Hispanic 1%; Asian 1%	1,217
Thomas College (Waterville, ME)	NR	Alumni relations considered as a factor	Character & Personal Qualities considered	African American 18%; Hispanic 1%	693

(*continued*)

College	Use of Race in Admission Decisions and Degree Utilized (if at all)	Use of Alumni Relations or Legacies as Factor and Degree Utilized	Use of Other Factors (e.g., geographic origin or religious affiliation) and Degree Utilized	Reported Ethnic/Minority Representation	Total Student Population
Thomas Edison State College (Trenton, NJ)	NR	NR	NR	African American 10%; Hispanic 4%; Native American 1%; Asian 2%	9,012
Thomas Jefferson University (Philadelphia, PA)	NR	NR	NR	African American 11%; Hispanic 2%; Asian 6%	656
Thomas More College (Crestview Hill, KY)	NR	NR	Character & Personal Qualities considered	African American 5%; Asian 1%	1,371
Thomas University (Thomasville, GA)	NR	NR	NR	African American 38%; Hispanic 2%; Asian 1%	530
Tiffin University (Tiffin, OH)	NR	Alumni relations considered as a factor	NR	African American 17%; Hispanic 2%	1,145
Toccoa Falls College (Toccoa Falls, GA)	NR	NR	Religious affiliation and/or commitment and Character & Personal Qualities considered important	African American 3%; Hispanic 2%; Asian 5	814
Tougaloo College (Tougaloo, MS)	NR	Alumni relations considered as a factor	Character & Personal Qualities considered important	NR	967

Touro College (Brooklyn, NY)	Minority status considered as factor	Alumni relations considered as a factor	NR	African American 12; Hispanic 9; Asian 4	8,741
Towson University (Towson, MD)	NR	NR	NR	African American 10%; Hispanic 2%; Asian 3%	13,627
Transylvania University (Lexington, KY)	NR	Alumni relations considered as a factor	Geographic origin/residence, and Character & Personal Qualities considered	African American 2%; Hispanic 1%; Asian 2%	1,109
Trevecca Nazarene University (Nashville, TX)	NR	NR	Character & Personal Qualities considered very important	African American 7%; Hispanic 2%; Asian 1%	1,133
Trinity Christian College (Palos Heights, IL)	Minority status is considered as important factor	Alumni relations considered as a factor	Religious affiliation and/or commitment and Character & Personal Qualities considered important; Geographic origin/residence considered	African American 7%; Hispanic 4%; Asian 2%	1,080
Trinity College (Hartford, CT)	Minority status is considered as important factor	Alumni relations considered as a factor	Character & Personal Qualities considered important; Geographic origin/residence considered	African American 5%; Hispanic 5%; Asian 6%	2,145

(continued)

College	Use of Race in Admission Decisions and Degree Utilized (if at all)	Use of Alumni Relations or Legacies as Factor and Degree Utilized	Use of Other Factors (e.g., geographic origin or religious affiliation) and Degree Utilized	Reported Ethnic/Minority Representation	Total Student Population
Trinity College (DC) (Washington, DC)	NR	Alumni relations considered as a factor	Character & Personal Qualities considered very important; Geographic origin/residence considered	African American 68%; Hispanic 8%; Asian 2%	1,001
Trinity College of Vermont (Burlington, VT)	NR	Alumni relations considered as a factor	Character & Personal Qualities considered	African American 3%; Hispanic 1%; Native American 1%; Asian 1%	569
Trinity International University (Deerfield, IL)	NR	NR	Religious affiliation and/or commitment and Character & Personal Qualities considered important	African American 11%; Hispanic 2%; Asian 2%	1,291
Trinity University (San Antonio, TX)	NR	Alumni relations considered as a factor	Character & Personal Qualities considered very important; Geographic origin/residence considered	African American 2%; Hispanic 11%; Asian 6%	2,406
Trinity Western University (Blaine, WA)	NR	NR	Religious affiliation and/or commitment and Character &	NR	1,968

Tri-State University (Angola, IN)	NR	Alumni relations considered as a factor	Personal Qualities considered important Character & Personal Qualities considered	African American 3%; Hispanic 1%; Asian 1%	1,172
Troy State University at Troy (Troy, AL)	NR	NR	Character & Personal Qualities considered	African American 28%; Hispanic 1%; Native American 1%; Asian 1%	5,198
Troy State University—Dothan (Dothan, AL)	NR	NR	Geographic origin/residence considered important; Character & Personal Qualities considered	African American 22%; Hispanic 2%; Native American 1%; Asian 1%	1,470
Troy State University—Montgomery (Montgomery, AL)	NR	NR	NR	African American 52%; Hispanic 1%; Asian 1%	2,893
Truman State University (Kirksville, MO)	Minority status considered as factor	Alumni relations considered as a factor	Geographic origin/residence, and Character & Personal Qualities considered	African American 4%; Hispanic 2%; Asian 2%	5,482
Tufts University (Medford, MA)	Minority status is considered as important factor	Alumni relations considered as a factor	Character & Personal Qualities considered important; Geographic origin/residence considered	African American 7%; Hispanic 8%; Asian 13%	4,888

(continued)

College	Use of Race in Admission Decisions and Degree Utilized (if at all)	Use of Alumni Relations or Legacies as Factor and Degree Utilized	Use of Other Factors (e.g., geographic origin or religious affiliation) and Degree Utilized	Reported Ethnic/Minority Representation	Total Student Population
Tulane University (New Orleans, LA)	NR	Alumni relations considered as a factor	Character & Personal Qualities considered important	African American 8%; Hispanic 3%; Asian 3%	7,952
Tusculum College (Greenville, TN)	NR	NR	Character & Personal Qualities considered	African American 13%; Hispanic 1%; Asian 1%	2,053
Tuskegee University (Tuskegee, AL)	NR	Alumni relations considered as a factor	Geographic origin/residence, and Character & Personal Qualities considered	African American 78%	2,580
UM College of Technology (Missoula, MO)	NR	NR	NR	African American 1%; Hispanic 1%; Native American 3%; Asian 1%	10,357
Union College (KY) (Barbourville, KY)	NR	Alumni relations considered as a factor	Character & Personal Qualities considered	African American 8%; Hispanic 2%; Native American 1%; Asian 1%	588
Union College (NE) (Lincoln, NE)	NR	Alumni relations considered as a factor	Religious affiliation and/or commitment and Character & Personal Qualities	African American 2%; Hispanic 6%; Native American 1%; Asian 2%	883

Union College (NY) (Schenectady, NY)	Minority status considered as factor	Alumni relations considered as a factor	considered important; Geographic origin/residence considered	2,144
			African American 3%; Hispanic 4%; Asian 6%	
Union Institute & University (Cincinnati, OH)	NR	NR	Character & Personal Qualities considered important; Geographic origin/residence considered	1,288
			African American 26%; Hispanic 8%; Asian 1%	
Union University (Jackson, TN)	NR	Alumni relations considered as a factor	Character & Personal Qualities considered	2,045
			African American 8%; Hispanic 1%; Asian 1%	
United States Air Force Academy (Colorado Springs, CO)	Minority status considered as factor	Alumni relations considered as a factor	Religious affiliation and/or commitment and Character & Personal Qualities considered important	4,157
			African American 5%; Hispanic 6%; Native American 1%; Asian 5%	
United States Coast Guard Academy (New London, CT)	Minority status considered as factor	Alumni relations considered as a factor	Character & Personal Qualities considered very important	994
			African American 3%; Hispanic 5%; Native American 1%; Asian 4%	
Unites States Merchant Marine Academy (Kings Point, NY)	Minority status considered as factor	NR	Character & Personal Qualities considered very important	1,007
			Character & Personal Qualities considered important; Geographic origin/residence considered	
			NR	

(continued)

College	Use of Race in Admission Decisions and Degree Utilized (if at all)	Use of Alumni Relations or Legacies as Factor and Degree Utilized	Use of Other Factors (e.g., geographic origin or religious affiliation) and Degree Utilized	Reported Ethnic/Minority Representation	Total Student Population
United States Military Academy (West Point, NY)	Minority status considered as factor	NR	Character & Personal Qualities considered important; Geographic origin/residence considered	African American 7%; Hispanic 6%; Native American 1%; Asian 7%	4,175
United States Naval Academy (Annapolis, MD)	Minority status considered as factor	Alumni relations considered as a factor	Character & Personal Qualities considered important; Geographic origin/residence considered	African American 7%; Hispanic 9%; Native American 2%; Asian 5%	4,349
Unity College (Unity, ME)	NR	Alumni relations considered as a factor	Character & Personal Qualities considered	African American 1%	512
University of Advancing Technology (Tempe, AZ)	NR	NR	NR	African American 4%; Hispanic 14%; Native American 2%; Asian 3%	931
University of Akron (Akron, OH)	NR	NR	NR	African American 15%; Hispanic 1%; Asian 2%	16,887

University of Alabama—Birmingham (Birmingham, AL)	NR	NR	African American 33%; Hispanic 1%; Asian 3%	10,854
University of Alabama—Huntsville (Huntsville, AL)	NR	NR	African American 15%; Hispanic 2%; Native American 1%; Asian 4%	5,125
University of Alabama—Tuscaloosa (Tuscaloosa, AL)	NR	Alumni relations considered as a factor	Character & Personal Qualities considered	African American 13%; Hispanic 1%; Native American 1%; Asian 1%	16,202
University of Alaska—Anchorage (Anchorage, AK)	NR	NR	African American 4%; Hispanic 4%; Native American 10%; Asian 5%	9,341
University of Alaska—Fairbanks (Fairbanks, AL)	NR	NR	African American 3%; Hispanic 3%; Native American 17%; Asian 3%	4,793
University of Alaska—Southeast (Juneau, AK)	NR	NR	African American 3%; Hispanic 3%; Native American 17%; Asian 3%	894
University of Arizona (Tucson, AZ)	Minority status considered as factor	NR	Geographic origin/residence, and Character & Personal Qualities considered	African American 3%; Hispanic 15%; Native American 2%; Asian 6%	27,853

(continued)

College	Use of Race in Admission Decisions and Degree Utilized (if at all)	Use of Alumni Relations or Legacies as Factor and Degree Utilized	Use of Other Factors (e.g., geographic origin or religious affiliation) and Degree Utilized	Reported Ethnic/Minority Representation	Total Student Population
University of Arkansas—Fayetteville (Fayetteville, AR)	NR	NR	Geographic origin/residence, and Character & Personal Qualities considered	African American 5%; Hispanic 2%; Native American 2%; Asian 3%	13,124
University of Arkansas—Little Rock (Little Rock, AR)	NR	NR	NR	NR	NR
University of Arkansas—Monticello (Monticello, AR)	NR	NR	NR	NR	NR
University of Arkansas—Pine Bluff (Pine Bluff, AR)	NR	NR	NR	African American 96%	2,971
University of Baltimore (Baltimore, MD)	NR	NR	NR	African American 34%; Hispanic 2%; Native American 1%; Asian 3%	2,012

University of Bridgeport (Bridgeport, CT)	NR	Alumni relations considered as a factor	Character & Personal Qualities considered	African American 25%; Hispanic 11%; Asian 5%	1,100
University of California—Berkeley (Berkeley, CA)	NR	NR	Geographic origin/residence, and Character & Personal Qualities considered	African American 4%; Hispanic 11%; Native American 1%; Asian 41%	22,880
University of California—Davis (Davis, CA)	NR	NR	Geographic origin/residence, and Character & Personal Qualities considered	African American 3%; Hispanic 10%; Native American 1%; Asian 38%	23,360
University of California—Irvine (Irvine, CA)	NR	NR	Character & Personal Qualities considered	African American 2%; Hispanic 19%; Asian 49%	19,862
University of California—Los Angeles (Los Angeles, CA)	NR	NR	Geographic origin/residence, and Character & Personal Qualities considered	African American 3%; Hispanic 15%; Asian 37%	24,946
University of California—Riverside (Riverside, CA)	NR	NR	Geographic origin/residence considered	African American 7%; Hispanic 24%; Asian 42%	15,089

(continued)

College	Use of Race in Admission Decisions and Degree Utilized (if at all)	Use of Alumni Relations or Legacies as Factor and Degree Utilized	Use of Other Factors (e.g., geographic origin or religious affiliation) and Degree Utilized	Reported Ethnic/Minority Representation	Total Student Population
University of California—San Diego (San Diego, CA)	NR	NR	Geographic origin/residence, and Character & Personal Qualities considered	African American 1%; Hispanic 10%; Asian 38%	20,339
University of California—Santa Barbara (Santa Barbara, CA)	NR	NR	Character & Personal Qualities considered	African American 3%; Hispanic 17%; Native American 1%; Asian 16%	18,114
University of California—Santa Cruz (Santa Cruz, CA)	NR	NR	Geographic origin/residence, and Character & Personal Qualities considered	African American 3%; Hispanic 14%; Native American 1%; Asian 18%	13,647
University of Central Arkansas (Conway, AR)	NR	NR	Character & Personal Qualities considered important	African American 17%; Hispanic 1%; Native American 1%; Asian 1%	9,031
University of Central Florida (Orlando, FL)	NR	Alumni relations considered as a factor	Geographic origin/residence, and Character & Personal Qualities considered	African American 8%; Hispanic 12%; Native American 1%; Asian 5%	34,940

University of Central Oklahoma (Edmond, OK)	NR	NR	NR	African American 9%; Hispanic 3%; Native American 6%; Asian 3%	13,668
University of Charleston (Charleston, WV)	NR	Alumni relations considered as a factor	Character & Personal Qualities considered	African American 3%; Hispanic 1%; Native American 1%; Asian 1%	995
University of Chicago (Chicago, IL)	Minority status considered as factor	Alumni relations considered as a factor	Character & Personal Qualities considered	African American 4%; Hispanic 8%; Asian 15%	4,325
University of Cincinnati (Cincinnati, OH)	NR	NR	NR	African American 13%; Hispanic 1%; Asian 3%	18,993
University of Colorado Health Sciences Center (Denver, CO)	NR	NR	NR	African American 4%; Hispanic 7%; Native American 1%; Asian 8%	450
University of Colorado—Boulder (Boulder, CO)	Minority status considered as factor	Alumni relations considered as a factor	Geographic origin/ residence considered important; Character & Personal Qualities considered	African American 2%; Hispanic 6%; Native American 1%; Asian 6%	25,607
University of Colorado—Colorado Springs (Colorado Springs, CO)	Minority status considered as factor	Alumni relations considered as a factor	Geographic origin/ residence, and Character & Personal Qualities considered	African American 4%; Hispanic 9%; Native American 1%; Asian 5%	5,886

(continued)

College	Use of Race in Admission Decisions and Degree Utilized (if at all)	Use of Alumni Relations or Legacies as Factor and Degree Utilized	Use of Other Factors (e.g., geographic origin or religious affiliation) and Degree Utilized	Reported Ethnic/Minority Representation	Total Student Population
University of Colorado—Denver (Denver, CO)	NR	Alumni relations considered as a factor	Character & Personal Qualities considered	African American 4%; Hispanic 10%; Native American 1%; Asian 10%	6,980
University of Connecticut (Storrs, CT)	Minority status considered as factor	Alumni relations considered as a factor	Character & Personal Qualities considered important; Geographic origin/residence considered	African American 5%; Hispanic 4%; Asian 7%	15,260
University of Dallas (Irving, TX)	NR	Alumni relations considered as a factor	Character & Personal Qualities considered very important	African American 1%; Hispanic 16%; Asian 6%	1,087
University of Dayton (Dayton, OH)	Minority status considered as factor	Alumni relations considered as a factor	Character & Personal Qualities considered	African American 4%; Hispanic 2%; Asian 1%	7,008
University of Delaware (Newark, DE)	Minority status considered as factor	Alumni relations considered as a factor	Geographic origin/residence, and Character & Personal Qualities considered	African American 6%; Hispanic 4%; Asian 3%	16,023

University of Denver (Denver, CO)	NR	NR	Character & Personal Qualities considered very important	African American 3%; Hispanic 7%; Native American 1%; Asian 5%	4,643
University of Detroit Mercy (Detroit, MI)	NR	Alumni relations considered as a factor	NR	African American 32%; Hispanic 2%; Native American 1%; Asian 2%	2,986
University of the District of Columbia (Washington, DC)	NR	NR	NR	African American 75%; Hispanic 5%; Asian 2%	1,935
University of Dubuque (Dubuque, IA)	NR	Alumni relations considered as a factor	Character & Personal Qualities considered	African American 10%; Hispanic 4%; Native American 3%; Asian 1%	1,101
University of Evansville (Evansville, IN)	NR	Alumni relations considered as a factor	Character & Personal Qualities considered	African American 2%; Hispanic 1%; Asian 1%	2,477
University of Findlay (Findlay, OH)	NR	Alumni relations considered as a factor	Religious affiliation and/or commitment and Character & Personal Qualities considered important	African American 4%; Hispanic 2%; Asian 4%	3,381
University of Florida (Gainesville, FL)	NR	NR	NR	African American 9%; Hispanic 12%; Native American 1%; Asian 7%	33,094
University of Georgia (Athens, GA)	NR	NR	NR	African American 5%; Hispanic 2%; Asian 4%	24,975

(*continued*)

College	Use of Race in Admission Decisions and Degree Utilized (if at all)	Use of Alumni Relations or Legacies as Factor and Degree Utilized	Use of Other Factors (e.g., geographic origin or religious affiliation) and Degree Utilized	Reported Ethnic/Minority Representation	Total Student Population
University of Great Falls (Great Falls, MT)	Minority status considered as factor	NR	Religious affiliation and/or commitment and Character & Personal Qualities considered important	African American 2%; Hispanic 3%; Native American 7%; Asian 1%	654
University of Hartford (Hartford, CT)	NR	NR	Character & Personal Qualities considered	African American 10%; Hispanic 4%; Asian 2%	5,254
University of Hawaii—HILO (Hilo, HI)	NR	NR	NR	African American 1%; Hispanic 2%; Native American 1%; Asian 47%	2,790
University of Hawaii—Manoa (Honolulu, HI)	NR	NR	Geographic origin/residence, and Character & Personal Qualities considered	African American 1%; Hispanic 2%; Asian 56%	13,070
University of Hawaii—West Oahu (Pearl City, HI)	NR	NR	NR	NR	792

Institution			
University of Houston—Clear Lake (Houston, TX)	NR	NR	African American 8%; Hispanic 17%; Asian 6%	3,779
University of Houston—Downtown (Houston, TX)	NR	NR	African American 26%; Hispanic 36%; Asian 10%	11,261
University of Houston—Houston (Houston, TX)	NR	Alumni relations considered as a factor	Geographic origin/residence considered	African American 15%; Hispanic 21%; Asian 21%	26,366
University of Houston—Victoria Campus (Victoria, TX)	NR	NR	NR	African American 9%; Hispanic 22%; Asian 4%	1,052
University of Idaho (Moscow, ID)	NR	NR	NR	African American 1%; Hispanic 4%; Native American 1%; Asian 2%	9,047
University of Illinois—Chicago (Chicago, IL)	Minority status considered as factor	NR	Character & Personal Qualities considered	African American 9%; Hispanic 17%; Asian 24%	15,828
University of Illinois—Springfield (Springfield, IL)	NR	NR	NR	African American 8%; Hispanic 2%; Asian 2%	2,328
University of Illinois—Urbana-Champaign (Urbana, IL)	Minority status considered as factor	Alumni relations considered as a factor	Character & Personal Qualities considered important; Geographic origin/residence considered	African American 7%; Hispanic 6%; Asian 13%	27,744

(continued)

College	Use of Race in Admission Decisions and Degree Utilized (if at all)	Use of Alumni Relations or Legacies as Factor and Degree Utilized	Use of Other Factors (e.g., geographic origin or religious affiliation) and Degree Utilized	Reported Ethnic/Minority Representation	Total Student Population
University of Indianapolis (Indianapolis, IN)	NR	NR	NR	African American 10%; Hispanic 2%; Asian 1%	3,100
University of Iowa (Iowa City, IA)	Minority status considered as factor	Alumni relations considered as a factor	Geographic origin/residence considered	African American 2%; Hispanic 2%; Asian 3%	19,401
University of Kansas (Lawrence, KS)	Minority status considered as factor	Alumni relations considered as a factor	Character & Personal Qualities considered	African American 3%; Hispanic 3%; Native American 1%; Asian 4%	20,766
University of Kentucky (Lexington, KY)	Minority status considered as factor	NR	Geographic origin/residence, and Character & Personal Qualities considered	African American 6%; Hispanic 1%; Asian 2%	18,102
University of La Verne (La Verne, CA)	NR	Alumni relations considered as a factor	Character & Personal Qualities considered	African American 9%; Hispanic 38%; Native American 1%; Asian 5%	1,636
University of Louisiana—Lafayette (Lafayette, LA)	NR	NR	NR	African American 19%; Hispanic 2%; Asian 1%	14,564

University of Louisiana—Monroe (Monroe, LA)	NR	NR	NR	8,542
University of Louisville (Louisville, KY)	Minority status considered as factor	NR	Geographic origin/residence, and Character & Personal Qualities considered	African American 13%; Hispanic 1%; Asian 3%	13,818
University of Maine (Orono, ME)	NR	Alumni relations considered as a factor	Character & Personal Qualities considered	African American 1%; Hispanic 1%; Native American 2%; Asian 1%	8,397
University of Maine—Augusta (Augusta, ME)	NR	NR	Character & Personal Qualities considered	African American 1%; Hispanic 1%; Asian 3%	4,482
University of Maine—Farmington (Farmington, ME)	Minority status considered as factor	Alumni relations considered as a factor	Character & Personal Qualities considered important; Geographic origin/residence considered	Hispanic 1%; Native American 1%; Asian 1%	2,237
University of Maine—Fort Kent (Fort Kent, ME)	NR	NR	Character & Personal Qualities considered	NR	926
University of Maine—Machias (Machias, ME)	NR	NR	Character & Personal Qualities considered	African American 1%; Hispanic 2%; Native American 4%	625

(*continued*)

College	Use of Race in Admission Decisions and Degree Utilized (if at all)	Use of Alumni Relations or Legacies as Factor and Degree Utilized	Use of Other Factors (e.g., geographic origin or religious affiliation) and Degree Utilized	Reported Ethnic/Minority Representation	Total Student Population
University of Maine—Presque Isle (Presque Isle, ME)	Minority status considered as factor	Alumni relations considered as a factor	Geographic origin/residence, and Character & Personal Qualities considered	African American 1%; Hispanic 1%; Native American 4%; Asian 1%	1,321
University of Mary (Bismarck, ND)	NR	NR	NR	Native American 1%	1,722
University of Mary Hardin-Baylor (Belton, TX)	Minority status considered as factor	Alumni relations considered as a factor	Geographic origin/residence, Character & Personal Qualities, and Religious Affiliation/Commitment all considered	African American 10%; Hispanic 11%; Asian 1%	2,576
University of Maryland—Baltimore County (Baltimore, MD)	NR	NR	Character & Personal Qualities considered	African American 14%; Hispanic 3%; Asian 19%	9,651
University of Maryland—College Park (College Park, MD)	Minority status considered as factor	Alumni relations considered as a factor	Geographic origin/residence, and Character & Personal Qualities considered	African American 12%; Hispanic 6%; Asian 14%	24,590

University of Maryland—Eastern Shore (Princess Anne, MD)	NR	Alumni relations considered as a factor	Character & Personal Qualities considered very important	African American 80% Hispanic 1%; Asian 1%	2,704
University of Maryland—University College (Adelphi, MD)	NR	NR	NR	NR	17,527
University of Massachusetts—Amherst (Amherst, MA)	Minority status considered as factor	Alumni relations considered as a factor	Geographic origin/residence, and Character & Personal Qualities considered	African American 4%; Hispanic 3%; Asian 7%	18,064
University of Massachusetts—Boston (Boston, MA)	NR	NR	Character & Personal Qualities considered	African American 11% Hispanic 5%; Asian 8%	8,666
University of Massachusetts—Dartmouth (Dartmouth, MA)	NR	Alumni relations considered as a factor	Character & Personal Qualities considered	African American 6%; Hispanic 2%; Asian 3%	6,860
University of Massachusetts—Lowell (Lowell, MA)	NR	NR	Character & Personal Qualities considered	African American 4%; Hispanic 5%; Asian 8%	6,343
The University of Memphis (Memphis, TN)	NR	NR	NR	NR	11,722

(*continued*)

College	Use of Race in Admission Decisions and Degree Utilized (if at all)	Use of Alumni Relations or Legacies as Factor and Degree Utilized	Use of Other Factors (e.g., geographic origin or religious affiliation) and Degree Utilized	Reported Ethnic/Minority Representation	Total Student Population
University of Miami (Coral Gables, FL)	Minority status considered as factor	Alumni relations considered as a factor	Geographic origin/residence, and Character & Personal Qualities considered	African American 9%; Hispanic 24%; Asian 6%	9,741
University of Michigan—Ann Arbor (Ann Arbor, MI)	Minority status considered as factor	Alumni relations considered as a factor	Geographic origin/residence, and Character & Personal Qualities considered important	African American 8%; Hispanic 5%; Native American 1%; Asian 12%	24,677
University of Michigan—Dearborn (Dearborn, MI)	NR	NR	NR	African American 7%; Hispanic 2%; Asian 6%	5,895
University of Michigan—Flint (Flint, MI)	NR	Alumni relations considered as a factor	Geographic origin/residence considered	African American 10%; Hispanic 2%; Native American 1%; Asian 1%	5,357
University of Minnesota—Crookston (Crookston, MN)	NR	NR	NR	African American 2%; Hispanic 2%; Native American 1%; Asian 1%	1,152

336

University of Minnesota—Duluth (Duluth, MN)	Minority status considered as factor	NR	NR	9,014
University of Minnesota—Morris (Morris, MN)	Minority status considered as factor	Alumni relations considered as a factor	Character & Personal Qualities considered important	1,685
University of Minnesota—Twin Cities (Minneapolis, MN)	Minority status considered as factor	NR	Geographic origin/residence, and Character & Personal Qualities considered	African American 4%; Hispanic 2%; Native American 1%; Asian 8%	28,103
University of Mississippi (University, MS)	NR	Alumni relations considered as a factor	Geographic origin/residence considered	African American 13%; Hispanic 1%; Asian 1%	11,765
University of Missouri—Columbia (Columbia, MO)	Minority status considered as factor	NR	NR	African American 6%; Hispanic 2%; Native American 1%; Asian 3%	20,541
University of Missouri—Kansas City (Kansas City, MO)	NR	NR	Character & Personal Qualities considered	African American 14%; Hispanic 4%; Native American 1%; Asian 5%	6,512
University of Missouri—Rolla (Rolla, MO)	NR	NR	Character & Personal Qualities considered	African American 4%; Hispanic 2%; Asian 3%	4,019
University of Missouri—Saint Louis (Saint Louis, MO)	NR	NR	NR	African American 15%; Hispanic 1%; Asian 3%	8,904

(continued)

Note: Row 1 shows "African American 2%; Hispanic 1%; Asian 3%" for University of Minnesota—Morris.

College	Use of Race in Admission Decisions and Degree Utilized (if at all)	Use of Alumni Relations or Legacies as Factor and Degree Utilized	Use of Other Factors (e.g., geographic origin or religious affiliation) and Degree Utilized	Reported Ethnic/Minority Representation	Total Student Population
University of Mobile (Mobile, AL)	NR	NR	NR	African American 21%; Hispanic 1%; Native American 2%	1,675
University of Montana—Missoula (Missoula, MT)	NR	NR	NR	Hispanic 1%; Native American 4%; Asian 1%	10,943
University of Montana—Western (Dillon, MT)	Minority status considered as factor	Alumni relations considered as a factor	Geographic origin/residence considered	African American 1%; Hispanic 3%; Native American 3%; Asian 2%	1,046
University of Montevallo (Montevallo, AL)	NR	Alumni relations considered as a factor	Character & Personal Qualities considered	NR	1,696
University of Nebraska—Kearney (Kearney, NE)	NR	NR	Religious affiliation and/or commitment considered	African American 1%; Hispanic 2%; Asian 1%	5,886
University of Nebraska—Lincoln (Lincoln, NE)	Minority status considered as factor	Alumni relations considered as a factor	Geographic origin/residence considered	African American 2%; Hispanic 2%; Native American 1%; Asian 2%	17,137
University of Nebraska Medical Center (Omaha, NE)	NR	NR	NR	African American 2%; Hispanic 2%; Native American 1%; Asian 1%	771

University of Nebraska—Omaha (Omaha, NE)	NR	Character & Personal Qualities considered	African American 5%; Hispanic 3%; Native American 1%; Asian 3%	10,732
University of Nevada—Las Vegas (Las Vegas, NV)	NR	NR	African American 8%; Hispanic 10%; Native American 1%; Asian 14%	19,525
University of Nevada—Reno (Reno, NV)	NR	NR	African American 2%; Hispanic 7%; Native American 1%; Asian 7%	11,605
University of New England (Biddeford, NE)	Alumni relations considered as a factor	Geographic origin/residence, and Character & Personal Qualities considered	NR	1,660
University of New Hampshire—Durham (Durham, NH)	Alumni relations considered as a factor	Geographic origin/residence, and Character & Personal Qualities considered	Minority status considered as factor; African American 1%; Hispanic 1%; Asian 2%	10,942
University of New Hampshire—Manchester (Manchester, NH)	Alumni relations considered as a factor	Geographic origin/residence, and Character & Personal Qualities considered	Minority status considered as factor; African American 2%; Hispanic 1%; Asian 1%	704
University of New Haven (West Haven, CT)	Alumni relations considered as a factor	Character & Personal Qualities considered	NR; African American 9%; Hispanic 4%; Asian 1%	2,627

(continued)

College	Use of Race in Admission Decisions and Degree Utilized (if at all)	Use of Alumni Relations or Legacies as Factor and Degree Utilized	Use of Other Factors (e.g., geographic origin or religious affiliation) and Degree Utilized	Reported Ethnic/Minority Representation	Total Student Population
University of New Mexico (Albuquerque, NM)	NR	NR	NR	African American 3%; Hispanic 33%; Native American 7%; Asian 3%	16,603
University of New Orleans (New Orleans, LA)	NR	Alumni relations considered as a factor	Geographic origin/residence considered	African American 25%; Hispanic 7%; Asian 6%	13,225
University of North Alabama (Florence, AL)	NR	NR	Character & Personal Qualities considered	African American 10%; Hispanic 1%; Native American 2%; Asian 1%	4,798
University of North Carolina—Asheville (Asheville, NC)	Minority status considered as factor	Alumni relations considered as a factor	Geographic origin/residence, and Character & Personal Qualities considered	African American 3%; Hispanic 2%; Asian 1%	3,232
University of North Carolina—Chapel Hill (Chapel Hill, NC)	Minority status considered as factor	Alumni relations considered as a factor	Geographic origin/residence, and Character & Personal Qualities considered very important	African American 11%; Hispanic 2%; Native American 1%; Asian 6%	15,711

University of North Carolina—Charlotte (Charlotte, NC)	NR	NR	Geographic origin/residence, and Character & Personal Qualities considered	African American 15%; Hispanic 3%; Asian 5%	15,472
University of North Carolina—Greensboro (Greensboro, NC)	NR	NR	NR	African American 19%; Hispanic 2%; Asian 3%	11,241
University of North Carolina—Pembroke (Pembroke, NC)	NR	Alumni relations considered as a factor	Character & Personal Qualities considered	African American 22%; Hispanic 2%; Native American 20%; Asian 2%	4,309
University of North Carolina—Wilmington (Wilmington, DC)	Minority status considered as factor	Alumni relations considered as a factor	Geographic origin/residence, and Character & Personal Qualities considered	African American 4%; Hispanic 2%; Native American 1%; Asian 2%	10,030
University of North Dakota (Grand Forks, ND)	NR	NR	NR	African American 1%; Hispanic 1%; Native American 3%; Asian 1%	10,710
University of North Florida (Jacksonville, FL)	NR	NR	NR	African American 10%; Hispanic 6%; Native American 1%; Asian 5%	12,237
University of North Texas (Denton, TX)	NR	NR	Character & Personal Qualities considered	African American 12%; Hispanic 10%; Native American 1%; Asian 4%	24,274

(*continued*)

College	Use of Race in Admission Decisions and Degree Utilized (if at all)	Use of Alumni Relations or Legacies as Factor and Degree Utilized	Use of Other Factors (e.g., geographic origin or religious affiliation) and Degree Utilized	Reported Ethnic/Minority Representation	Total Student Population
University of Northern Colorado (Greenley, CO)	Minority status considered as factor	NR	Geographic origin/residence, and Character & Personal Qualities considered	African American 2%; Hispanic 8%; Native American 1%; Asian 3%	9,921
University of Northern Iowa (Cedar Falls, IA)	Minority status considered as factor	NR	Geographic origin/residence considered	African American 3%; Hispanic 2%; Asian 1%	11,032
University of Notre Dame (Notre Dame, IN)	Minority status considered as factor	Alumni relations considered as a factor	Character & Personal Qualities considered very important; Religious Commitment and/or Affiliation considered	African American 4%; Hispanic 8%; Native American 1%; Asian 5%	8,322
University of Oklahoma (Norman, OK)	NR	NR	Geographic origin/residence considered	African American 5%; Hispanic 4%; Native American 8%; Asian 5%	20,843
University of Oregon (Eugene, OR)	Minority status considered as factor	NR	Geographic origin/residence considered	African American 2%; Hispanic 3%; Native American 1%; Asian 6%	16,024

University of Pennsylvania (Philadelphia, PA)	Minority status considered as factor	Alumni relations considered as a factor	Character & Personal Qualities considered very important; Geographic origin/ residence considered	African American 6%; Hispanic 6%; Asian 18%	9,719
University of Pittsburgh—Bradford (Bradford, PA)	NR	Alumni relations considered as a factor	Character & Personal Qualities considered	African American 3%; Hispanic 1%; Asian 1%	1,239
University of Pittsburgh—Greensburg (Greensburg, PA)	NR	Alumni relations considered as a factor	Character & Personal Qualities considered	African American 2%; Hispanic 1%; Asian 1%	1,878
University of Pittsburgh—Johnstown (Johnstown, PA)	Minority status considered as factor	NR	Character & Personal Qualities considered	African American 1%; Asian 1%	2,946
University of Pittsburgh—Pittsburgh (Pittsburgh, PA)	Minority status considered as factor	NR	Geographic origin/ residence, and Character & Personal Qualities considered	African American 9%; Hispanic 1%; Asian 4%	16,677
University of Portland (Portland, OR)	Minority status considered as factor	Alumni relations considered as a factor	Geographic origin/ residence, Character & Personal Qualities, and Religious Affiliation/ Commitment all considered	African American 2%; Hispanic 4%; Native American 1%; Asian 9%	2,768

(continued)

College	Use of Race in Admission Decisions and Degree Utilized (if at all)	Use of Alumni Relations or Legacies as Factor and Degree Utilized	Use of Other Factors (e.g., geographic origin or religious affiliation) and Degree Utilized	Reported Ethnic/Minority Representation	Total Student Population
University of Puget Sound (Tacoma, WA)	Minority status considered important factor	Alumni relations considered important factor	Character & Personal Qualities considered	African American 2%; Hispanic 3%; Native American 1%; Asian 8%	2,595
University of Redlands (Redlands, CA)	Minority status considered as factor	Alumni relations considered as a factor	Character & Personal Qualities considered very important; Geographic origin/residence considered	African American 2%; Hispanic 12%; Native American 1%; Asian 6%	2,345
University of Rhode Island (Kingston, RI)	Minority status considered as factor	Alumni relations considered as a factor	Geographic origin/residence, and Character & Personal Qualities considered	African American 4%; Hispanic 4%; Asian 3%	10,957
University of Richmond (Richmond, VA)	Minority status considered as factor	Alumni relations considered as a factor	Character & Personal Qualities considered important; Geographic origin/residence considered	African American 5%; Hispanic 2%; Asian 4%	2,909
University of Rio Grande (Rio Grande, OH)	NR	NR	NR	African American 3%	1,453

University of Rochester (Rochester, NY)	Minority status considered important factor	Alumni relations considered as a factor	Character & Personal Qualities considered very important	African American 4%; Hispanic 4%; Asian 11%	4,449
University of St. Francis (IL) (Joliet, IL)	NR	NR	NR	African American 8%; Hispanic 7%; Asian 3%	1,213
The University of Saint Francis (IN) (Fort Wayne, IN)	NR	NR	NR	African American 7%; Hispanic 2%; Native American 1%; Asian 1%	1,413
University of Saint Mary (KS)	NR	Alumni relations considered as a factor	Character & Personal Qualities considered	African American 13%; Hispanic 7%; Asian 2%	450
University of Saint Thomas (MN)	Minority status considered as factor	Alumni relations considered as a factor	Geographic origin/residence, and Character & Personal Qualities considered	African American 2%; Hispanic 2%; Native American 1%; Asian 5%	5,292
University of St. Thomas (TX) (Houston, TX)	NR	NR	Character & Personal Qualities considered	African American 5%; Hispanic 29%; Native American 1%; Asian 12%	1,781
University of San Diego (San Diego, CA)	Minority status considered as factor	Alumni relations considered as a factor	Religious affiliation and/or commitment and Character & Personal Qualities considered important	African American 2%; Hispanic 15%; Native American 1%; Asian 7%	4,904
University of San Francisco (San Francisco, CA)	Minority status considered as factor	Alumni relations considered as a factor	Character & Personal Qualities considered	African American 5%; Hispanic 13%; Asian 26%	4,274

(continued)

College	Use of Race in Admission Decisions and Degree Utilized (if at all)	Use of Alumni Relations or Legacies as Factor and Degree Utilized	Use of Other Factors (e.g., geographic origin or religious affiliation) and Degree Utilized	Reported Ethnic/Minority Representation	Total Student Population
University of Science and Arts of Oklahoma (Chickasha, OK)	NR	NR	Character & Personal Qualities considered	African American 7%; Hispanic 2%; Native American 14%; Asian 1%	1,207
University of the Sciences in Philadelphia (Philadelphia, PA)				African American 6%; Hispanic 2%; Asian 32%	1,953
The University of Scranton (Scranton, PA)	Minority status considered as factor	Alumni relations considered as a factor	Character & Personal Qualities considered	African American 1%; Hispanic 4%; Asian 2%	3,982
University of Sioux Falls (Sioux Falls, SD)	NR	NR	NR	African American 2%; Hispanic 1%; Native American 1%	1,186
University of South Alabama (Mobile, AL)	NR	NR	NR	African American 18%; Hispanic 2%; Native American 1%; Asian 2%	10,350
University of South Carolina—Aiken (Aiken, SC)	NR	NR	NR	African American 25%; Hispanic 2%; Asian 1%	3,015

University of South Carolina—Columbia (Columbia, SC)	NR	NR	African American 15%; Hispanic 2%; Asian 3%	17,016
University of South Carolina—Spartansburg (Spartansburg, SC)	NR	NR	African American 26%; Hispanic 1%; Asian 3%	4,237
The University of South Dakota (Vermillon, SD)	Minority status considered as factor	NR	African American 1%; Hispanic 1%; Native American 2%; Asian 1%	5,315
University of South Florida (Tampa, FL)	Minority status considered as factor	NR	Character & Personal Qualities considered	32,458
University of Southern California (Los Angeles, CA)	Minority status considered as factor	Alumni relations considered as a factor	Character & Personal Qualities considered	16,271
University of Southern Colorado (Pueblo, CO)	Minority status considered as factor	NR	Character & Personal Qualities considered	4,457
University of Southern Indiana (Evansville, IN)	NR	Alumni relations considered as a factor	Character & Personal Qualities considered	8,925
University of Southern Maine (Gorham, ME)	Minority status considered as factor	Alumni relations considered as a factor	Geographic origin/residence, and Character & Personal Qualities considered	6,842

African American 13%; Hispanic 11%; Asian 6%

African American 7%; Hispanic 13%; Native American 1%; Asian 21%

African American 5%; Hispanic 27%; Native American 2%; Asian 2%

African American 5%; Hispanic 1%; Asian 1%

African American 1%; Hispanic 1%; Native American 1%; Asian 1%

(continued)

College	Use of Race in Admission Decisions and Degree Utilized (if at all)	Use of Alumni Relations or Legacies as Factor and Degree Utilized	Use of Other Factors (e.g., geographic origin or religious affiliation) and Degree Utilized	Reported Ethnic/Minority Representation	Total Student Population
University of Southern Mississippi (Hattiesburg, MS)	NR	Alumni relations considered as a factor	NR	African American 28%; Hispanic 1%; Asian 1%	12,520
University of Tampa (Tampa, FL)	NR	Alumni relations considered as a factor	Character & Personal Qualities considered	African American 6%; Hispanic 9%; Native American 1%; Asian 2%	4,329
University of Tennessee—Chattanooga (Chattanooga, TN)	Minority status considered as factor	NR	NR	African American 22%; Hispanic 1%; Asian 2%	7,181
University of Tennessee—Knoxville (Knoxville, TN)	Minority status considered as factor	Alumni relations considered as a factor	Geographic origin/residence, and Character & Personal Qualities considered	African American 7%; Hispanic 1%; Asian 3%	19,580
University of Tennessee—Martin (Martin, TN)	NR	NR	NR	African American 16%; Hispanic 1%; Asian 1%	4,932

University of Texas—Arlington (Arlington, TX)	NR	Alumni relations considered as a factor	Geographic origin/residence, and Character & Personal Qualities considered	African American 14%; Hispanic 13%; Native American 1%; Asian 11%	18,176
University of Texas—Austin (Austin, TX)	Minority status considered as factor	NR	Geographic origin/residence, and Character & Personal Qualities considered	African American 4%; Hispanic 15%; Asian 17%	36,473
University of Texas—Brownsville (Brownsville, TX)	NR	NR	NR	Hispanic 94%	9,753
University of Texas—Dallas (Richardson, TX)	NR	NR	Geographic origin/residence, and Character & Personal Qualities considered	African American 7%; Hispanic 10%; Native American 1%; Asian 19%	8,904
University of Texas—El Paso (El Paso, TX)	NR	Alumni relations considered as a factor	Geographic origin/residence, and Character & Personal Qualities considered	African American 2%; Hispanic 74%; Asian 1%	14,957
University of Texas Medical Branch (Galveston, TX)	NR	NR	NR	African American 10%; Hispanic 15%; Native American 1%; Asian 9%	511

(*continued*)

College	Use of Race in Admission Decisions and Degree Utilized (if at all)	Use of Alumni Relations or Legacies as Factor and Degree Utilized	Use of Other Factors (e.g., geographic origin or religious affiliation) and Degree Utilized	Reported Ethnic/Minority Representation	Total Student Population
University of Texas—Pan American (Edinburg, TX)	NR	NR	NR	Hispanic 88%; Asian 1%	12,915
University of Texas—Permian Basin (Odessa, TX)	NR	NR	NR	African American 4%; Hispanic 1%; Native American 1%; Asian 1%	1,984
University of Texas—San Antonio (San Antonio, TX)	NR	NR	NR	African American 5%; Hispanic 47%; Asian 3%	15,484
University of Texas—Tyler (Tyler, TX)	NR	NR	Character & Personal Qualities considered	African American 10%; Hispanic 5%; Native American 1%; Asian 2%	4,063
University of the Arts (Philadelphia, PA)	Minority status considered as factor	Alumni relations considered as a factor	Character & Personal Qualities considered important	African American 9%; Hispanic 4%; Asian 3%	1,939
University of the Incarnate Word (San Antonio, TX)	Minority status considered as factor	Alumni relations considered as a factor	Geographic origin/ residence, and Character & Personal Qualities considered	African American 7%; Hispanic 54%; Native American 1%; Asian 2%	3,943

University of the Ozarks (Clarksville, AK)	NR	Alumni relations considered as a factor	Geographic origin/residence, and Character & Personal Qualities considered	African American 2%; Hispanic 3%; Native American 3%; Asian 2%	612
University of the Pacific (Stockton, CA)	Minority status considered as factor	Alumni relations considered as a factor	Geographic origin/residence, and Character & Personal Qualities considered	African American 3%; Hispanic 10%; Native American 1%; Asian 29%	3,446
University of Toledo (Toledo, OH)	NR	NR	Geographic origin/residence considered	African American 12%; Hispanic 2%; Asian 2%	15,640
University of Tulsa (Tulsa, OK)	Minority status considered as factor	Alumni relations considered as a factor	Character & Personal Qualities considered	African American 7%; Hispanic 3%; Native American 5%; Asian 2%	2,699
University of Utah (Salt Lake City, UT)	Minority status considered as factor	NR	NR	African American 1%; Hispanic 4%; Native American 1%; Asian 5%	21,626
University of Vermont (Burlington, VT)	Minority status considered as factor	Alumni relations considered as a factor	Geographic origin/residence, and Character & Personal Qualities considered important	African American 1%; Hispanic 2%; Asian 2	8,143
University of Virginia (Charlottesville, VA)	Minority status considered as factor	Alumni relations considered as very important factor	Geographic origin/residence, and Character & Personal Qualities considered important	African American 9%; Hispanic 3%; Asian 11%	13,231

(continued)

College	Use of Race in Admission Decisions and Degree Utilized (if at all)	Use of Alumni Relations or Legacies as Factor and Degree Utilized	Use of Other Factors (e.g, geographic origin or religious affiliation) and Degree Utilized	Reported Ethnic/Minority Representation	Total Student Population
University of Virginia's College at Wise (Wise, VA)	Minority status considered as factor	NR	Character & Personal Qualities considered	African American 5%; Hispanic 1%; Asian 1%	1,505
University of Washington (Seattle, WA)	NR	Alumni relations considered as a factor	Geographic origin/residence, and Character & Personal Qualities considered	African American 3%; Hispanic 3%; Native American 1%; Asian 24%	26,042
University of West Alabama (Livingston, AL)	NR	NR	NR	African American 40%	1,586
University of West Florida (Pensacola, FL)	Minority status considered as factor	Alumni relations considered as a factor	Geographic origin/residence, and Character & Personal Qualities considered	African American 10%; Hispanic 5%; Native American 1%; Asian 4%	7,586
University of Wisconsin—Eau Claire (Eau Claire, WI)	Minority status considered as factor	Alumni relations considered as a factor	NR	Hispanic 1%; Native American 1%; Asian 3%	9,871

University of Wisconsin—Green Bay (Green Bay, WI)	Minority status considered as factor	NR	Character & Personal Qualities considered	African American 1%; Hispanic 1%; Native American 1%; Asian 3%	5,228
University of Wisconsin—Lacrosse (LoCrosse, WI)	Minority status considered important factor	NR	Geographic origin/residence, and Character & Personal Qualities considered	African American 1%; Hispanic 1%; Native American 1%; Asian 3%	7,614
University of Wisconsin—Madison (Madison, WI)	Minority status considered as factor	Alumni relations considered as a factor	Geographic origin/residence, and Character & Personal Qualities considered	African American 2%; Hispanic 3%; Native American 1%; Asian 5%	28,217
University of Wisconsin—Milwaukee (Milwaukee, WI)	NR	NR	Geographic origin/residence considered	African American 7%; Hispanic 4%; Native American 1%; Asian 5%	19,785
University of Wisconsin—Oskkosh (Oshkosh, WI)	Minority status considered as factor	NR	NR	African American 1%; Hispanic 1%; Native American 1%; Asian 2%	9,510
University of Wisconsin—Parkside (Kenosha, WI)	Minority status considered as factor	Alumni relations considered as a factor	Character & Personal Qualities considered	African American 10%; Hispanic 6%; Native American 1%; Asian 3%	4,615
University of Wisconsin—Platteville (Platteviile, WI)	NR	NR	Geographic origin/residence considered important	African American 1%; Hispanic 1%; Asian 1%	5,500

(continued)

College	Use of Race in Admission Decisions and Degree Utilized (if at all)	Use of Alumni Relations or Legacies as Factor and Degree Utilized	Use of Other Factors (e.g., geographic origin or religious affiliation) and Degree Utilized	Reported Ethnic/Minority Representation	Total Student Population
University of Wisconsin—River Falls (River Falls, WI)	NR	NR	NR	African American 1%; Hispanic 1%; Asian 3%	5,257
University of Wisconsin—Stevens Point (Stevens Point, WI)	Minority status considered as factor	NR	Character & Personal Qualities considered	African American 1%; Hispanic 1%; Native American 1%; Asian 2%	8,536
University of Wisconsin—Stout (Menomonie, WI)	Minority status considered as factor	Alumni relations considered as a factor	Character & Personal Qualities considered	African American 1%; Hispanic 1%; Asian 2%	6,887
University of Wisconsin—Superior (Superior, WI)	Minority status considered as factor	NR	NR	African American 1%; Native American 2%; Asian 1%	2,463
University of Wisconsin—Whitewater (Whitewater, WI)	Minority status considered as factor	Alumni relations considered as a factor	Character & Personal Qualities considered	African American 4%; Hispanic 2%; Asian 2%	9,174
University of Wyoming (Laramie, WY)	NR	NR	Geographic origin/ residence, and Character & Personal Qualities considered	African American 1%; Hispanic 4%; Native American 1%; Asian 1%	8,927

Upper Iowa University (Fayette, IA)	NR	Alumni relations considered as a factor	Character & Personal Qualities considered important	African American 12%; Hispanic 5%; Asian 4%	697
Urbana University (Urbana, OH)	Minority status considered as factor	Alumni relations considered as a factor	Character & Personal Qualities considered	NR	1,221
Ursinus College (Collegeville, PA)	Minority status considered as factor	NR	Character & Personal Qualities considered	African American 7%; Hispanic 3%; Asian 4%	1,481
Ursuline College (Pepper Pike, OH)	Minority status considered as factor	Alumni relations considered as a factor	Character & Personal Qualities considered	African American 25%; Hispanic 2%; Asian 1%	1,106
Utah State University (Logan, UT)	NR	NR	NR	African American 1%; Hispanic 2%; Asian 1%	13,402
Utica College—Offering the Syracuse University Degree (Utica, NY)	NR	Alumni relations considered as a factor	Character & Personal Qualities considered	African American 8%; Hispanic 4%; Native American 1%; Asian 2%	2,171
Valdosta State University (Valdosta, GA)	NR	NR	NR	African American 21%; Hispanic 2%; Asian 1%	8,962
Valley City State University (Valley City, ND)	NR	NR	NR	African American 2%; Hispanic 2%; Native American 2%	1,033
Valparaiso University (Valparaiso, IN)	Minority status considered as factor	Alumni relations considered as a factor	Religious affiliation and/or commitment and Character & Personal Qualities considered important	African American 4%; Hispanic 3%; Asian 2%	3,041

(continued)

College	Use of Race in Admission Decisions and Degree Utilized (if at all)	Use of Alumni Relations or Legacies as Factor and Degree Utilized	Use of Other Factors (e.g., geographic origin or religious affiliation) and Degree Utilized	Reported Ethnic/Minority Representation	Total Student Population
Vanderbilt University (Nashville, TN)	Minority status considered as factor	Alumni relations considered as a factor	Character & Personal Qualities considered very important	African American 7%; Hispanic 4%; Asian 6%	6,231
Vanguard University of Southern California (Costa Mesa, CA)	NR	NR	Religious affiliation and/or commitment and Character & Personal Qualities considered important	African American 3%; Hispanic 15%; Native American 1%; Asian 4%	1,760
Vassar College (Poughkeepsie, NY)	Minority status considered as factor	Alumni relations considered as a factor	Geographic origin/residence, and Character & Personal Qualities considered	African American 5%; Hispanic 5%; Asian 9%	2,428
Villa Julie College (Stevenson, MD)	NR	Alumni relations considered as a factor	Character & Personal Qualities considered	African American 13%; Hispanic 1%; Asian 3%	2,607
Villa Maria College of Buffalo (Buffalo, NY)	NR	Alumni relations considered as a factor	Character & Personal Qualities considered	African American 31%; Hispanic 1%; Native American 1%; Asian 1%	489

Villanova University (Villanova, PA)	Minority status considered as factor	Alumni relations considered as a factor	Geographic origin/residence, and Character & Personal Qualities considered	African American 3%; Hispanic 5%; Asian 6%	6,892
Virginia Commonwealth University (Richmond, VA)	NR	NR	NR	African American 13%; Hispanic 2%; Asian 6%	27,811
Virginia Intermont College (Bristol, VA)	NR	Alumni relations considered as a factor	Character & Personal Qualities considered	African American 7%; Hispanic 2%; Native American 1%; Asian 1%	1,114
Virginia Military Institute (Lexington, VA)	Minority status considered important factor	Alumni relations considered as a factor	Character & Personal Qualities considered very important; Geographic origin/residence considered	African American 5%; Hispanic 3%; Asian 3%	1,362
Virginia State University (Petersburg, VA)	NR	Alumni relations considered as a factor	Geographic origin/residence, and Character & Personal Qualities considered	African American 92%; Hispanic 1%	4,111
Virginia Tech (Blacksburg, VA)	Minority status considered as factor	Alumni relations considered as a factor	Geographic origin/residence considered	African American 6%; Hispanic 2%; Asian 7%	21,332
Virginia Wesleyan College (Norfolk, VA)	NR	Alumni relations considered as a factor	Character & Personal Qualities considered	African American 14%; Hispanic 3%; Native American 1%; Asian 2%	1,353

(*continued*)

College	Use of Race in Admission Decisions and Degree Utilized (if at all)	Use of Alumni Relations or Legacies as Factor and Degree Utilized	Use of Other Factors (e.g., geographic origin or religious affiliation) and Degree Utilized	Reported Ethnic/Minority Representation	Total Student Population
Viterbo University (La Crosse, WI)	NR	Alumni relations considered as a factor	Character & Personal Qualities considered	African American 1%; Hispanic 1%; Asian 2%	1,830
Voorhees College (Denmark, SC)	NR	Alumni relations considered as important factor	Character & Personal Qualities considered important	African American 98%	738
Wabash College (Crawfordsville, IN)	Minority status considered as factor	Alumni relations considered as a factor	Character & Personal Qualities considered important; Geographic origin/residence considered	African American 7%; Hispanic 4%; Asian 3%	845
Wagner College (Staten Island, NY)	NR	NR	Character & Personal Qualities considered	African American 5%; Hispanic 5%; Asian 3%	1,929
Wake Forest University (Winston-Salem, NY)	Minority status considered important factor	Alumni relations considered as important factor	Religious affiliation and/or commitment and Character & Personal Qualities considered important; Geographic origin/residence	African American 6%; Hispanic 2%; Asian 4%	4,104

	Minority status considered as factor	Alumni relations considered as a factor	Religious affiliation and/or commitment and Character & Personal Qualities considered	Hispanic 1%	573
Waldorf College (St. Forest City, IA)					
Walla Walla College (College Place, WA)	NR	NR	Character & Personal Qualities considered very important	African American 3%; Hispanic 6%; Asian 5%	1,649
Walsh College of Accountancy and Business Administration (Troy, MI)	NR	NR	NR	African American 4%; Hispanic 1%; Asian 5%	1,098
Walsh University (North Canton, OH)	NR	NR	Character & Personal Qualities considered important	African American 6%; Hispanic 1%; Asian 1%	1,694
Warner Pacific College (Portland, OR)	NR	NR	NR	African American 3%; Hispanic 3%; Native American 1%; Asian 2%	569
Warner Southern College (Lake Wales, FL)	NR	Alumni relations considered as a factor	Character & Personal Qualities considered	African American 16%; Hispanic 7%; Native American 1%	912
Warren Wilson College (Asheville, NC)	NR	Alumni relations considered as a factor	Character & Personal Qualities considered very important	African American 2%; Hispanic 1%; Native American 1%; Asian 1%	781

(*continued*)

College	Use of Race in Admission Decisions and Degree Utilized (if at all)	Use of Alumni Relations or Legacies as Factor and Degree Utilized	Use of Other Factors (e.g., geographic origin or religious affiliation) and Degree Utilized	Reported Ethnic/Minority Representation	Total Student Population
Wartburg College (Waverly, PA)	Minority status considered as factor	NR	Character & Personal Qualities considered important	African American 3%; Hispanic 1%; Asian 2%	1,772
Washburn University (Topeka, KS)	NR	Alumni relations considered as a factor	Character & Personal Qualities considered	African American 6%; Hispanic 4%; Native American 1%; Asian 2%	5,098
Washington College (Chestertown, MD)	Minority status considered as factor	Alumni relations considered as a factor	Character & Personal Qualities considered important; Geographic origin/residence considered	African American 2%; Hispanic 1%; Asian 1%	1,335
Washington and Lee University (Lexington, VA)	Minority status considered as factor	Alumni relations considered as a factor	Character & Personal Qualities considered very important; Geographic origin/residence considered	African American 4%; Hispanic 1%; Asian 3%	1,754
Washington & Jefferson College (Washington, PA)	NR	Alumni relations considered as a factor	Character & Personal Qualities considered important; Geographic origin/residence considered	African American 2%; Hispanic 1%; Asian 1%	1,334

Washington State University (Pullman, WA)	NR	NR	NR	African American 3%; Hispanic 4%; Native American 1%; Asian 6%	18,825
Washington University in St. Louis (St. Louis, MO)	Minority status considered as factor	Alumni relations considered as a factor	Character & Personal Qualities considered	African American 9%; Hispanic 3%; Asian 9%	6,355
Wayland Baptist University (Plainview, TX)	NR	NR	NR	African American 4%; Hispanic 22%; Native American 1%; Asian 1%	946
Wayne State College (Wayne, NE)	NR	NR	NR	African American 3%; Hispanic 3%; Asian 1%	2,750
Wayne State University (Detroit, MI)	NR	NR	NR	African American 32%; Hispanic 3%; Asian 5%	19,113
Waynesburg College (Waynesburg, PA)	NR	NR	Character & Personal Qualities considered	African American 4%	1,478
Webber International University (Babson Park, FL)	NR	Alumni relations considered as important factor	NR	African American 22%; Hispanic 6%	585
Weber State University (Ogden, UT)	NR	NR	Character & Personal Qualities considered	African American 1%; Hispanic 4%; Native American 1%; Asian 1%	18,046
Webster University (Saint Louis, MO)	Minority status considered important factor	NR	Character & Personal Qualities considered important; Geographic origin/residence considered	African American 13%; Hispanic 2%; Asian 1%	3,465

(*continued*)

College	Use of Race in Admission Decisions and Degree Utilized (if at all)	Use of Alumni Relations or Legacies as Factor and Degree Utilized	Use of Other Factors (e.g., geographic origin or religious affiliation) and Degree Utilized	Reported Ethnic/Minority Representation	Total Student Population
Wellesley College (Wellesley, MA)	Minority status considered as factor	Alumni relations considered as a factor	Character & Personal Qualities considered important; Geographic origin/residence considered	African American 6%; Hispanic 6%; Asian 28%	2,229
Wentworth Institute of Technology (Boston, MA)	NR	NR	NR	African American 3%; Hispanic 4%; Asian 6%	3,248
Wesley College (Dover, DE)	Minority status considered as factor	Alumni relations considered very important factor	NR	African American 25%; Hispanic 3%; Asian 2%	1,820
Wesleyan College (Macon, GA)	NR	Alumni relations considered as a factor	Character & Personal Qualities considered important	African American 31%; Hispanic 2%; Asian 2%	547
Wesleyan University (Middletown, CT)	Minority status considered important factor	Alumni relations considered as important factor	Character & Personal Qualities considered important; Geographic origin/residence considered	African American 7%; Hispanic 7%; Asian 9%	2,755

West Chester University of Pennsylvania (West Chester, PA)	Minority status considered as factor	Character & Personal Qualities considered	NR	African American 8%; Hispanic 2%; Asian 2%	10,100
West Liberty State College (West Liberty, WV)	NR	NR	African American 3%; Hispanic 1%	2,449
West Texas A&M University (Canyon, TX)	NR	NR	African American 4%; Hispanic 15%; Native American 1%; Asian 1%	5,861
West Virginia State College (Institute, WV)	NR	NR	African American 15%; Hispanic 1%; Asian 1%	3,318
West Virginia University (Morgantown, WV)	Minority status considered as factor	Alumni relations considered as a factor	NR	African American 4%; Hispanic 1%; Asian 2%	18,653
West Virginia University Institute of Technology (Montgomery, WV)	NR	Alumni relations considered as a factor	Geographic origin/residence, and Character & Personal Qualities considered	African American 8%; Hispanic 1%; Asian 1%	2,001
West Virginia Wesleyan College (Buckhannon, WI)	NR	Alumni relations considered as a factor	Character & Personal Qualities considered important	African American 5%; Hispanic 1%; Asian 1%	1,583

(*continued*)

College	Use of Race in Admission Decisions and Degree Utilized (if at all)	Use of Alumni Relations or Legacies as Factor and Degree Utilized	Use of Other Factors (e.g., geographic origin or religious affiliation) and Degree Utilized	Reported Ethnic/Minority Representation	Total Student Population
Western Baptist College (Salem, OR)	NR	Alumni relations considered as a factor	Religious affiliation and/or commitment and Character & Personal Qualities considered important	African American 1%; Hispanic 3%; Native American 2%; Asian 2%	704
Western Carolina University (Cullowhee, NC)	NR	NR	Geographic origin/residence, and Character & Personal Qualities considered	African American 5%; Hispanic 2%; Asian 1%	6,650
Western Connecticut State University (Danbury, CT)	Minority status considered as factor	Alumni relations considered as a factor	Geographic origin/residence considered	African American 6%; Hispanic 6%; Asian 4%	4,587
Western Illinois University (Macomb, IL)	NR	NR	NR	African American 7%; Hispanic 4%; Asian 1%	11,297
Western Kentucky University (Bowling Green, KY)	NR	NR	NR	African American 9%; Hispanic 1%; Asian 1%	15,211

Western Michigan University (Kalamazoo, MI)	Minority status considered important factor	Alumni relations considered as important factor	Character & Personal Qualities considered	African American 5%; Hispanic 2%; Asian 1%	22,336
Western New England College (Springfield, MA)	Minority status considered as factor	Alumni relations considered as a factor	Character & Personal Qualities considered	African American 3%; Hispanic 3%; Asian 2%	3,020
Western Oregon University (Monmouth, OR)	Minority status considered as factor	Alumni relations considered as a factor	NR	African American 2%; Hispanic 5%; Native American 1%; Asian 3%	4,366
Western State College of Colorado (Gunnison, CO)	NR	Alumni relations considered as a factor	Character & Personal Qualities considered important	African American 1%; Hispanic 5%; Native American 1%; Asian 1%	2,152
Western Washington University (Bellingham, WA)	NR	NR	Geographic origin/residence, and Character & Personal Qualities considered important	African American 2%; Hispanic 3%; Native American 2%; Asian 8%	12,684
Westfield State College (Westfield, MA)	Minority status considered as factor	NR	Character & Personal Qualities considered	African American 3%; Hispanic 2%; Asian 1%	4,122
Westminster College (Salt Lake City, UT)	Minority status considered as factor	Alumni relations considered as a factor	Geographic origin/residence, and Character & Personal Qualities considered	African American 1%; Hispanic 4%; Native American 1%; Asian 3%	1,881

(continued)

College	Use of Race in Admission Decisions and Degree Utilized (if at all)	Use of Alumni Relations or Legacies as Factor and Degree Utilized	Use of Other Factors (e.g., geographic origin or religious affiliation) and Degree Utilized	Reported Ethnic/Minority Representation	Total Student Population
Westminister College (MO) (Fulton, MO)	NR	Alumni relations considered as a factor	Character & Personal Qualities considered very important	African American 4%; Hispanic 1%; Native American 2%; Asian 1%	843
Westminister College (PA) (New Wilmington, PA)	Minority status considered as factor	Alumni relations considered as a factor	Character & Personal Qualities considered	African American 1%; Hispanic 1%	1,261
Westmont College (Santa Barbara, CA)	Minority status considered important factor	Alumni relations considered as a factor	Religious affiliation and/or commitment and Character & Personal Qualities considered important	African American 2%; Hispanic 8%; Native American 2%; Asian 6%	1,351
Westwood College of Technology (Denver, CO)	NR	NR	Character & Personal Qualities considered very important	African American 4%; Hispanic 18%; Native American 3%; Asian 3%	1,363
Wheaton College (IL) (Wheaton, IL)	Minority status considered important factor	Alumni relations considered very important factor	Religious affiliation and/or commitment and Character & Personal Qualities considered important; Geographic origin/residence considered	African American 2%; Hispanic 3%; Asian 7%	2,408

Wheaton College (MA) (Norton, MA)	Minority status considered as factor	Alumni relations considered very important factor	Character & Personal Qualities considered important; Geographic origin/residence considered	African American 3%; Hispanic 4%; Asian 3%	1,524
Wheeling Jesuit University (Wheeling, NJ)	NR	Alumni relations considered as a factor	Religious affiliation and/or commitment and Character & Personal Qualities considered	African American 2%; Hispanic 2%; Asian 1%	1,205
Wheelock College (Boston, MA)	Minority status considered as factor	Alumni relations considered as a factor	Character & Personal Qualities considered important	African American 5%; Hispanic 4%; Native American 1%; Asian 2%	616
Whitman College (Walla Walla, WA)	Minority status considered important factor	Alumni relations considered as a factor	Character & Personal Qualities considered very important; Geographic origin/residence considered	African American 2%; Hispanic 3%; Native American 1%; Asian 9%	1,452
Whittier College (Whittier, CA)	Minority status considered as factor	Alumni relations considered as a factor	Character & Personal Qualities considered very important; Geographic origin/residence considered	African American 3%; Hispanic 25%; Native American 1%; Asian 9%	1,304
Whitworth College (Spokane, WA)	Minority status considered as factor	Alumni relations considered as a factor	Geographic origin/residence, Character & Personal Qualities, and Religious Affiliation/Commitment all considered	African American 2%; Hispanic 2%; Native American 1%; Asian 5%	2,230

(continued)

College	Use of Race in Admission Decisions and Degree Utilized (if at all)	Use of Alumni Relations or Legacies as Factor and Degree Utilized	Use of Other Factors (e.g., geographic origin or religious affiliation) and Degree Utilized	Reported Ethnic/Minority Representation	Total Student Population
Wichita State University (Wichita, KS)	NR	NR	NR	African American 7%; Hispanic 5%; Native American 1%; Asian 7%	10,221
Widener University (Chester, PA)	NR	Alumni relations considered as a factor	Character & Personal Qualities considered	African American 12%; Hispanic 2%; Asian 2%	2,472
Wilberforce University (Wilberforce, OH)	NR	NR	NR	African American 90%; Hispanic 1%	1,180
Wilkes University (Wilkes-Barre, PA)	NR	Alumni relations considered as a factor	Character & Personal Qualities considered	African American 2%; Hispanic 2%; Asian 2%	2,069
Willamette University (Salem, OR)	Minority status considered as factor	Alumni relations considered as a factor	Character & Personal Qualities considered important; Geographic origin/residence considered	African American 2%; Hispanic 5%; Native American 1%; Asian 6%	1,876
William Carey College (Hattiesburg, MS)	NR	Alumni relations considered as a factor	Character & Personal Qualities considered	African American 37%; Hispanic 2%; Native American 1%; Asian 1%	1,239

William Jewell College (Liberty, MO)	Minority status considered as factor	Alumni relations considered as a factor	Character & Personal Qualities considered important	African American 4%; Hispanic 2%; Native American 1%; Asian 1%	1,310
William Paterson University (Wayne, NJ)	Minority status considered as factor	Alumni relations considered as a factor	Character & Personal Qualities considered important	NR	9,418
William Penn University (Oskaloosa, IA)	NR	Alumni relations considered as a factor	Character & Personal Qualities considered important	African American 8%; Hispanic 3%	1,462
William Woods University (Fulton, MO)	NR	NR	Character & Personal Qualities considered	African American 3%; Hispanic 1%	998
William Baptist College (Walnut Ridge, AR)	NR	NR	Character & Personal Qualities considered	African American 2%; Hispanic 1%	504
Williams College (Williamstown, MA)	Minority status considered as factor	Alumni relations considered as a factor	Geographic origin/ residence, and Character & Personal Qualities considered	African American 10%; Hispanic 8%; Asian 9%	1,931
Williston State College (Williston, ND)	NR	NR	NR	African American 1%; Hispanic 1%; Native American 4%	937
Wilmington College (DE) (New Castle, DE)	NR	NR	NR	African American 14%; Hispanic 2%; Asian 1%	4,399

(continued)

College	Use of Race in Admission Decisions and Degree Utilized (if at all)	Use of Alumni Relations or Legacies as Factor and Degree Utilized	Use of Other Factors (e.g., geographic origin or religious affiliation) and Degree Utilized	Reported Ethnic/ Minority Representation	Total Student Population
Wilmington College (OH) (Wilmington, OH)	Minority status considered as factor	Alumni relations considered as important factor	Geographic origin/residence, and Character and Personal Qualities considered important	African American 7%; Hispanic 1%	1,207
Wilson College (Chambersburg, PA)	NR	Alumni relations considered as a factor	Character & Personal Qualities considered	African American 3%; Hispanic 2%; Asian 1%	546
Wingate University (Wingate, NC)	NR	NR	Character & Personal Qualities considered	African American 11%; Hispanic 1%; Asian 1%	1,277
Winona State University (Winona, MN)	NR	NR	NR	African American 1%; Hispanic 1%; Asian 1%	6,996
Winston-Salem State University (Winston-Salem, NC)	NR	Alumni relations considered as a factor	Character & Personal Qualities considered	African American 83%; Hispanic 1%; Asian 1%	2,776
Winthrop University (Rock Hill, SC)	NR	NR	NR	African American 26%; Hispanic 1%; Asian 1%	5,206

Wisconsin Lutheran College (Milwaukee, WI)	Minority status considered as factor	NR	Religious affiliation and/or commitment and Character & Personal Qualities considered important; Geographic origin/residence considered	African American 1%; Hispanic 1%; Asian 1%	687
Wittenberg University (Springfield, OH)	Minority status considered as factor	Alumni relations considered very important factor	Character & Personal Qualities considered important; Religious affiliation and/or commitment and Geographic origin/residence considered	African American 6%; Hispanic 1%; Asian 1%	2,058
Wofford College (Spartanburg, SC)	Minority status considered important factor	Alumni relations considered very important factor	Character & Personal Qualities considered important; Geographic origin/residence considered	African American 7%; Hispanic 1%; Asian 2%	1,158
Woodbury University (Burbank, CA)	NR	NR	Character & Personal Qualities considered important	African American 8%; Hispanic 33%; Asian 14%	1,169
Worcester Polytechnic Institute (Worcester, MA)	Minority status considered as factor	Alumni relations considered as a factor	Geographic origin/residence, and Character & Personal Qualities considered	African American 2%; Hispanic 3%; Native American 1%; Asian 6%	2,805

(continued)

College	Use of Race in Admission Decisions and Degree Utilized (if at all)	Use of Alumni Relations or Legacies as Factor and Degree Utilized	Use of Other Factors (e.g., geographic origin or religious affiliation) and Degree Utilized	Reported Ethnic/Minority Representation	Total Student Population
Worcester State College (Worcester, MA)	Minority status considered as factor	NR	Character & Personal Qualities considered	African American 4%; Hispanic 4%; Asian 3%	3,982
Wright State University (Dayton, OH)	NR	NR	Geographic origin/residence considered	African American 12%; Hispanic 1%; Asian 2%	11,691
Xavier University (Cincinnati, OH)	NR	Alumni relations considered as a factor	Character & Personal Qualities considered important	African American 10%; Hispanic 2%; Asian 2%	3,770
Xavier University of Louisiana (New Orleans, LA)	Minority status considered as factor	Alumni relations considered as a factor	Character & Personal Qualities considered	African American 85%; Asian 4%	3,077
Yale University (New Haven, CT)	Minority status considered as factor	Alumni relations considered as a factor	Character & Personal Qualities considered very important; Geographic origin/residence considered	African American 8%; Hispanic 6%; Native American 1%; Asian 13%	5,294
Yeshiva University (New York, NY)	NR	NR	NR	NR	1,970

| York College of Pennsylvania (York, PA) | NR | NR | Alumni relations considered as a factor | Character & Personal Qualities considered important | African American 2%; Hispanic 2%; Asian 1% | 5,213 |
| Youngstown State University (Youngstown, OH) | NR | NR | NR | NR | African American 10%; Hispanic 2%; Asian 1% | 11,448 |

Appendix B

Department of Education Guidelines on Use of Race in Financial Aid Decisions/Awards

FEDERAL REGISTER

Vol. 59, No. 36

Notices

DEPARTMENT OF EDUCATION

Nondiscrimination in Federally Assisted Programs; Title VI of the Civil Rights Act of 1964

PART VIII

59 FR 8756

DATE: Wednesday, February 23, 1994

ACTION: Notice of final policy guidance.

SUMMARY: The Secretary of Education issues final policy guidance on Title VI of the Civil Rights Act of 1964 and its implementing regulations. The final policy guidance discusses the applicability of the statute's and regulations' nondiscrimination requirement to student financial aid that is awarded, at least in part, on the basis of race or national origin.

EFFECTIVE DATE: This policy guidance takes effect on May 24, 1994, subject to the transition period described in this notice.

FOR FURTHER INFORMATION CONTACT: Jeanette Lim, U.S. Department of Education, 400 Maryland Avenue, SW., room 5036-I Switzer Building, Washington, DC 20202-1174. Telephone (202) 205-8635. Individuals who use a telecommunications device for the deaf (TDD) may call the TDD number at 1-800-358-8247.

SUPPLEMENTARY INFORMATION: On December 10, 1991, the Department published a notice of proposed policy guidance and request for public comment in the **Federal Register** *(56 FR 64548)*. The purpose of the proposed guidance and of this final guidance is to help clarify how colleges can use financial aid to promote campus diversity and access of minority students to postsecondary education without violating Federal anti-discrimination laws. The Secretary of Education encourages continued use of financial aid as a means to provide equal educational opportunity and to provide a diverse educational environment for all students. The Secretary also encourages the use by postsecondary institutions of other efforts to recruit and retain minority students, which are not affected by this policy guidance.

This guidance is designed to promote these purposes in light of Title VI of the Civil Rights Act of 1964 (Title VI), which states that no person in the United States shall, on the ground of race, color, or national origin, be excluded from participation in, be denied the benefits of, or be subjected to discrimination under any program or activity receiving Federal financial assistance.

The Department has completed its review of this issue, taking into account the results of a recent study by the General Accounting Office (GAO) and public comments submitted in response to the proposed policy guidance. The Secretary has determined that the proposed policy guidance interpreted the requirements of Title VI too narrowly in light of existing regulations and case law. While Title VI requires that strong justifications exist before race or national origin is used as a basis for awarding financial aid, many of the rationales for existing race-based financial aid programs described by commenters appear to meet this standard.

The recent report by GAO on current financial aid programs does not indicate the existence of serious problems of noncompliance with the law in postsecondary institutions. That report found that race-targeted scholarships constitute a very small percentage of the scholarships awarded to students at postsecondary institutions. The Secretary anticipates that most existing programs will be able to satisfy the principles set out in this final guidance.

The Department will use the principles described in this final policy guidance in making determinations concerning discrimination based on race or national origin in the award of financial aid. These principles describe the circumstances in which the Department, based on its interpretation of Title VI and relevant case law, believes consideration of race or national origin in the award of financial aid to be permissible. A financial aid program that falls within one or more of these principles will be, in the Department's view, in compliance with Title VI.[n1] This guidance is intended to assist colleges in fashioning legally defensible affirmative action programs to promote the access of minority students

---

[n1] In identifying these principles, the Department is not foreclosing the possibility that there may be other bases on which a college may support its consideration of race or national origin in awarding financial aid. The Department will consider any justifications that are presented during the course of a Title VI investigation on a case-by-case basis.

to postsecondary education. The Department will offer technical assistance to colleges in reexamining their financial aid programs based on this guidance.

This notice consists of five simply stated principles and a section containing a legal analysis for each principle. The legal analysis addresses the major comments received in response to the notice of proposed policy guidance.

SUMMARY OF CHANGES IN THE FINAL POLICY GUIDANCE

Almost 600 written responses were received by the Department in response to the proposed policy guidance, many with detailed suggestions and analysis. Many additional suggestions and concerns were raised in meetings between Department officials and representatives of postsecondary institutions and civil rights groups. The vast majority of comments expressed support for the objective of clarifying the options colleges have to use financial aid to promote student diversity and access of minorities to postsecondary education without violating Title VI. Many comments, however, took issue with specific principles in the proposed policy guidance and questioned whether those principles would be effective in accomplishing this purpose.

As more fully explained in the legal analysis section of this document, after reviewing the public comments and reexamining the legal precedents in light of those comments, the Department has revised the policy guidance in the following respects:

(1) Principle 3—"Financial Aid to Remedy Past Discrimination"—has been amended to permit a college to award financial aid based on race or national origin as part of affirmative action to remedy the effects of its past discrimination without waiting for a finding to be made by the Office for Civil Rights (OCR), a court, or a legislative body, if the college has a strong basis in evidence of discrimination justifying the use of race-targeted scholarships.

(2) Principle 4—"Financial Aid to Create Diversity"—has been amended to permit the award of financial aid on the basis of race or national origin if the aid is a necessary and narrowly tailored means to accomplish a college's goal to have a diverse student body that will enrich its academic environment.

(3) Principle 5—"Private Gifts Restricted by Race or National Origin"—has been amended to clarify that a college can administer financial aid from private donors that is restricted on the basis of race or national origin only if that aid is consistent with the other principles in this policy guidance.

(4) A provision has been added to permit historically black colleges and universities (HBCUs) to participate in race-targeted programs for black students established by third parties if the programs are not limited to students at HBCUs.

(5) Provisions in the proposed policy guidance for a transition period have been revised to provide that, as far as the Department's enforcement efforts are concerned—

(a) Colleges and other recipients of federal financial assistance will have a reasonable period of time—up to two years—to review their financial aid programs and to make any adjustments necessary to come into compliance with the principles in this final policy guidance;

(b) No student who has received or applied for financial aid at the time this guidance becomes effective will lose aid as a result of this guidance. Thus, if an award of financial aid is inconsistent with the principles in this guidance, a college or other recipient of Federal financial assistance may continue to provide the aid to a student during the course of his or her enrollment in the academic program for which the aid was awarded, if the student had either applied for or received the aid prior to the effective date of this policy guidance.

PRINCIPLES

Definitions

For purposes of these principles—

College means any postsecondary institution that receives federal financial assistance from the Department of Education.

Financial aid includes scholarships, grants, loans, work-study, and fellowships that are made available to assist a student to pay for his or her education at a college.

Race-neutral means not based, in whole or in part, on race or national origin.

Race-targeted, race-based, and *awarded on the basis of race or national origin* mean limited to individuals of a particular race or races or national origin or origins.

Principle 1: Financial Aid for Disadvantaged Students

A college may make awards of financial aid to disadvantaged students, without regard to race or national origin, even if that means that these awards go disproportionately to minority students.

Financial aid may be earmarked for students from low-income families. Financial aid also may be earmarked for students from school districts with high dropout rates, or students from single-parent families, or students from families in which few or no members have attended college. None of these or other race-neutral ways of identifying and providing aid to disadvantaged students present Title VI problems. A college may use funds from any source to provide financial aid to disadvantaged students.

Principle 2: Financial Aid Authorized by Congress

A college may award financial aid on the basis of race or national origin if the aid is awarded under a Federal statute that authorizes the use of race or national origin.

Principle 3: Financial Aid To Remedy Past Discrimination

A college may award financial aid on the basis of race or national origin if the aid is necessary to overcome the effects of past discrimination. A finding of discrimination may be made by a court or by an administrative agency—such as the Department's Office for Civil Rights. Such a finding may also be made by a State or local legislative body, as long as the legislature has a strong basis in evidence identifying discrimination within its jurisdiction for which that remedial action is necessary.

In addition, a college may award financial aid on the basis of race or national origin to remedy its past discrimination without a formal finding of discrimination by a court or by an administrative or legislative body. The college must be prepared to demonstrate to a court or administrative agency that there is a strong basis in evidence for concluding that the college's action was necessary to remedy the effects of its past discrimination. If the award of financial aid based on race or national origin is justified as a remedy for past discrimination, the college may use funds from any source, including unrestricted institutional funds and privately donated funds restricted by the donor for aid based on race or national origin.

A State may award financial aid on the basis of race or national origin, under the preceding standards, if the aid is necessary to overcome its own past discrimination or discrimination at colleges in the State.

Principle 4: Financial Aid To Create Diversity

America is unique because it has forged one Nation from many people of a remarkable number of different backgrounds. Many colleges seek to create on campus an intellectual environment that reflects that diversity. A college should have substantial discretion to weigh many factors—including race and national origin—in its efforts to attract and retain a student population of many different experiences, opinions, backgrounds, and cultures—provided that the use of race or national origin is consistent with the constitutional standards reflected in Title VI, *i.e.,* that it is a narrowly tailored means to achieve the goal of a diverse student body.

There are several possible options for a college to promote its First Amendment interest in diversity. First, a college may, of course, use its financial aid program to promote diversity by considering factors other than race or national origin, such as geographic origin, diverse experiences, or socioeconomic background. Second, a college may consider race or national origin with other factors in awarding financial aid if the aid is necessary to further the college's interest in diversity. Third, a college may use race or national origin as a condition of eligibility in awarding financial aid if this use is narrowly tailored, or, in other words, if it is necessary to further its interest in diversity and does not unduly restrict access to financial aid for students who do not meet the race-based eligibility criteria.

Among the considerations that affect a determination of whether awarding race-targeted financial aid is narrowly tailored to the goal of diversity are (1) whether race-neutral means of achieving that goal have been or would be ineffective; (2) whether a less extensive or intrusive use of race or national origin in awarding financial aid as a means of achieving that goal has been or would be ineffective; (3) whether the use of race or national origin is of limited extent and duration and is applied in a flexible manner; (4) whether the institution regularly reexamines its use of race or national origin in awarding financial aid to determine whether it is still necessary to achieve its goal; and (5) whether the effect of the use of race or national origin on students who are not beneficiaries of that use is sufficiently small and diffuse so as not to create an undue burden on their opportunity to receive financial aid.

If the use of race or national origin in awarding financial aid is justified under this principle, the college may use funds from any source.

Principle 5: Private Gifts Restricted by Race or National Origin

Title VI does not prohibit an individual or an organization that is not a recipient of Federal financial assistance from directly giving scholarships or other forms of financial aid to students based on their race or national origin. Title VI simply does not apply.

The provisions of Principles 3 and 4 apply to the use of race-targeted privately donated funds by a college and may justify awarding these funds on the basis of race or national origin if the college is remedying its past discrimination pursuant to Principle 3 or attempting to achieve a diverse student body pursuant to Principle 4. In addition, a college may use privately donated funds that are not restricted by their donor on the basis of race or national origin to make awards to disadvantaged students as described in Principle 1.

ADDITIONAL GUIDANCE

Financial Aid at Historically Black Colleges and Universities

Historically black colleges and universities (HBCUs), as defined in Title III of the Higher Education Act (Title III), *20 U.S.C. 1061,* are unique among institutions of higher education in America because of their role in serving students who were denied access to postsecondary education based on their race.[n2] Congress has made numerous findings reflecting the special role and needs of these institutions in light of the history of discrimination by States and the Federal Government against both the institutions and their students and has required enhancement of these institutions as a remedy for this history of discrimination.

Based upon the extensive congressional findings concerning HBCUs, and consistent with congressional and Executive Branch efforts to enhance and strengthen HBCUs, the Department interprets Title VI to permit these institutions to participate in student aid programs established by third parties that target

---

[n2] Title III states a number of requirements that an institution must meet in order to be considered an historically black college or university, including the requirement that the college or university was established prior to 1964. *20 U.S.C. 1061.* In regulations implementing Title III, the Secretary has identified the institutions that meet these requirements. 34 CFR 608.2(b).

financial aid to black students, if those programs are not limited to students at the HBCUs. These would include programs to which HBCUs contribute their own institutional funds if necessary for participation in the programs. Precluding HBCUs from these programs would have an unintended negative effect on their ability to recruit talented student bodies and would undermine congressional actions aimed at enhancing these institutions. HBCUs may not create their own race-targeted programs using institutional funds, nor may they accept privately donated race-targeted aid limited to students at the HBCUs, unless they satisfy the requirements of any of the other principles in this guidance.[n3]

Transition Period

Although the Department anticipates that most financial aid programs that consider race or national origin in awarding assistance will be found to be consistent with one or more of the principles in this final policy guidance, there will be some programs that require adjustment to comply with Title VI. In order to permit colleges time to assess their programs and to make any necessary adjustments in an orderly manner—and to ensure that students who already have either applied for or received financial aid do not lose their student aid as a result of the issuance of this policy guidance—there will be a transition period during which the Department will work with colleges that require assistance to bring them into compliance.[n4]

The Department will afford colleges up to two academic years to adjust their programs for new students. However, to the extent that a college does not need the full two years to make adjustments to its financial aid programs, the Department expects that the adjustments will be made as soon as practicable.

No student who is currently receiving financial aid, or who has applied for aid prior to the effective date of this policy guidance, should lose aid as a result of this guidance. Thus, if a college determines that a financial aid program is not permissible under this policy guidance, the college may continue to provide assistance awarded on the basis of race or national origin to students during the entire course of their academic program at the college, even if that period extends beyond the two-year transition period, if the students had either applied for or received that assistance prior to the effective date of this policy.

LEGAL ANALYSIS

Introduction

The Department of Education is responsible for enforcing Title VI of the Civil Rights Act of 1964, *42 U.S.C. 2000d et seq.*, at institutions receiving

[n3] For example, an HBCU might award race-targeted aid to Mexican American students or to white students to promote diversity under Principle 4.

[n4] This transition period also applies to recipients of Federal financial assistance that are not colleges, e.g., a nonprofit organization that operates a scholarship program.

Federal education funds. Section 601 of Title VI provides that no person in the United States shall, on the ground of race, color, or national origin, be excluded from participation in, be denied the benefits of, or be subjected to discrimination under any program or activity receiving Federal financial assistance. *42 U.S.C. 2000d.*

The Department has issued regulations implementing Title VI that are applicable to all recipients of financial assistance from the Department. 34 CFR part 100. The regulations prohibit discrimination in the administration of financial aid programs. Specifically, they prohibit a recipient, on the basis of race, color, or national origin, from denying financial aid; providing different aid; subjecting anyone to separate or different treatment in any matter related to financial aid; restricting the enjoyment of any advantage or privilege enjoyed by others receiving financial aid; and treating anyone differently in determining eligibility or other requirements for financial aid. 34 CFR 100.3(b)(1); see also 34 CFR 100.3(b)(2).

In addition to prohibiting discrimination, the Title VI regulations require that a recipient that has previously discriminated "must take affirmative action to overcome the effects of prior discrimination." 34 CFR 100.3(b)(6)(i). The regulations also permit recipients to take voluntary affirmative action "[e]ven in the absence of such prior discrimination * * * to overcome the effects of conditions which resulted in limiting participation by persons of a particular race, color, or national origin" in the recipient's programs. 34 CFR 100.3(b)(6)(ii); see 34 CFR 100.5(i).

The permissibility of awarding student financial aid based, in whole or in part, on a student's race or national origin involves an interpretation of the preceding provisions concerning affirmative action. The Supreme Court has made clear that Title VI prohibits intentional classifications based on race or national origin for the purpose of affirmative action to the same extent and under the same standards as the Equal Protection Clause of the Fourteenth Amendment.[n5] *Guardians Ass'n v. Civil Service Commission of the City of New York, 463 U.S. 582 (1983); Regents of the University of California v. Bakke, 438 U.S. 265 (1978).* Thus, the Department's interpretation of the general language of the Title VI regulations concerning permissible affirmative action is based on case law under both Title VI and the Fourteenth Amendment.

[n5] Some commenters suggested that Native Americans and Native Hawaiians—because of their special relationship with the Federal Government—should be exempt from the restrictions outlined in the policy guidance. The Department has found no legal authority for treating affirmative action by recipients of Federal assistance any differently if the group involved is Native Americans or Native Hawaiians. Thus, the principles in this policy guidance—including Principle 2, which states that a college may award financial aid on the basis of race or national origin if authorized by Federal statute—apply to financial aid that is limited to Native Americans and Native Hawaiians. However, the policy does not address the authority of tribal governments or tribally controlled colleges to restrict aid to members of their tribes.

The following discussion addresses the legal basis for each of the five principles set out in the Department's policy guidance.

1. Financial Aid for Disadvantaged Students

The first principle provides that colleges may award financial aid to disadvantaged students. Colleges are free to define the circumstances under which students will be considered to be disadvantaged, as long as that determination is not based on race or national origin.

As some commenters noted, the Title VI regulations prohibit actions that, while not intentionally discriminatory, have the effect of discriminating on the basis of race or national origin. 34 CFR 100.3(b)(2); see *Guardians Ass'n v. Civil Service Commission of the City of New York, supra; Lau v. Nichols, 414 U.S. 563 (1974)*. However, actions that have a disproportionate effect on students of a particular race or national origin are permissible under Title VI if they bear a "manifest demonstrable relationship" to the recipient's educational mission. *Georgia State Conference of Branches of NAACP v. State of Georgia, 775 F.2d 1403, 1418 11th* Cir. (1985). It is the Department's view that awarding financial aid to disadvantaged students provides a sufficiently strong educational purpose to justify any racially disproportionate effect the use of this criterion may entail. In particular, the Department believes that an applicant's character, motivation, and ability to overcome economic and educational disadvantage are educationally justified considerations in both admission and financial aid decisions. Therefore, the award of financial assistance to disadvantaged students does not violate Title VI.

2. Financial Aid Authorized by Congress

This principle states that a college may award financial aid on the basis of race or national origin if the use of race or national origin in awarding that aid is authorized by Federal statute. This is because financial aid programs for minority students that are authorized by a specific Federal law cannot be considered to violate another Federal law, *i.e.*, Title VI. In the case of the establishment of federally funded financial aid programs, such as the Patricia Roberts Harris Fellowship, the authorization of specific minority scholarships by that legislation prevails over the general prohibition of discrimination in Title VI.[n6] This result also is consistent with the canon of construction under which the specific provisions of

---

[n6] Of course, an individual may challenge the statute under which the aid is provided as violative of the Constitution. The statute would then be evaluated under the constitutional standards for racial classifications authorized by Federal statute that were established in *Metro Broadcasting, Inc. v. FCC, 497 U.S. 547 (1990)* and *Fullilove v. Klutznick, 448 U.S. 448 (1980)*. However, as explained previously, such a suit would not be viable under Title VI, for which the Department has enforcement responsibility.

a statute prevail over the general provisions of the same or a different statute. See 2A N. Singer *Sutherland Statutory Construction* section 46.05 (5th ed. 1992); *Radzanower v. Touche Ross and Co., 426 U.S. 148, 153 (1976); Morton v. Mancari, 417 U.S. 535, 550-51 (1974); Fourco Glass Co. v. Transmira Products Corp., 353 U.S. 225, 228-29 (1957).*

Some commenters argued that the existence of congressionally authorized race-targeted financial aid programs supports the position that all race-targeted financial aid programs are permissible under Title VI. However, the fact that Congress has enacted specific Federal programs for race-targeted financial aid does not serve as an authorization for States or colleges to create their own programs for awarding student financial aid based on race or national origin.

3. Financial Aid To Remedy Past Discrimination

Classifications based on race or national origin, including affirmative action measures, are "suspect" classifications that are subject to strict scrutiny by the courts. *Regents of the University of California v. Bakke, 438 U.S. at 292.* The use of those classifications must be based on a compelling governmental interest and must be narrowly tailored to serve that interest. *Richmond v. J.A. Croson Co., 488 U.S. 469 (1989); Wygant v. Jackson Board of Education, 476 U.S. 267 (1986).*

The Supreme Court has repeatedly held that the Government has a compelling interest in ensuring the elimination of discrimination on the basis of race or national origin. To further this governmental interest, the Supreme Court has sanctioned the use of race-conscious measures to eliminate discrimination. *United States v. Fordice*, _____ U.S. _____ (1992); *United States v. Paradise, 480 U.S. 149, 167 (1987); Swann v. Charlotte-Mecklenburg Board of Education, 402 U.S. 1, 15-16 (1971); McDaniel v. Barresi, 402 U.S. 39 (1971); Green v. County School Board of New Kent County, 391 U.S. 430, 438 (1968).* Most recently, in *United States v. Fordice, supra,* the Court found that States that operated *de jure* systems of higher education have an affirmative obligation to ensure that no vestiges of the de jure system continue to have a discriminatory effect on the basis of race.

The implementing regulations for Title VI provide that a recipient of Federal financial assistance that has previously discriminated in violation of the statute or regulations must take affirmative action to overcome the effects of the past discrimination. 34 CFR 100.3(b)(6)(i). Thus, a college that has been found to have discriminated against students on the basis of race or national origin must take steps to remedy that discrimination. That remedial action may include the awarding of financial aid to students from the racial or national origin groups that have been discriminated against.

The proposed policy guidance provided that a finding of past discrimination could be made by a court or by an administrative agency, such as the Department's Office for Civil Rights. It also could be made by a State or local legislative body, as long as the legislature requiring the affirmative action had a strong basis in evidence identifying discrimination within its jurisdiction for which that remedial action is required.

A number of commenters argued that colleges should be able to take remedial action without waiting for a formal finding by a court, administrative agency, or legislature. The Department agrees. The final policy guidance provides that, even in the absence of a finding by a court, legislature, or administrative agency, a college—in order to remedy its past discrimination—may implement a remedial race-targeted financial aid program. It may do so if it has a strong basis in evidence for concluding that this affirmative action is necessary to remedy the effects of its past discrimination and its financial aid program is narrowly tailored to remedy that discrimination. Permitting colleges to remedy the effects of their past discrimination without waiting for a formal finding is consistent with the approach taken by the Supreme Court in *Wygant v. Jackson Board of Education, supra.* In *Wygant,* the Court clarified that a school district's race-conscious voluntary affirmative action plan could be upheld based on subsequent judicial findings of past discrimination by the district. *Wygant v. Jackson Board of Education, 476 U.S. at 277.*

In the *Wygant* case, teachers challenged their school board's adoption, through a collective bargaining agreement, of a layoff plan that included provisions protecting employees from layoffs on the basis of their race. The school board contended, among other things, that the plan's race-conscious layoff provisions were constitutional because they were adopted to remedy the school board's own prior discrimination. *Id., at 276, 277.* Justice Powell, in a plurality opinion, stated that a public employer must have "convincing evidence" that an affirmative action plan is warranted by past discrimination before undertaking that plan. *Id., at 277.* If the plan is challenged by employees who are harmed by the plan, the court must then make a determination that the employer had a "strong basis in evidence for its conclusion that remedial action was necessary." *Id.*

In a concurring opinion, Justice O'Connor agreed that a "contemporaneous or antecedent finding of past discrimination by a court was not a constitutional prerequisite to a public employer's voluntary agreement to an affirmative action plan." *Id., at 289.* She explained that contemporaneous or antecedent findings were not necessary because "A violation of Federal statutory or constitutional requirements does not arise with the making of findings; it arises when the wrong is committed." Moreover, she explained that important values would be sacrificed if contemporaneous findings were required because "a requirement that public employers make findings that they engaged in illegal discrimination before they engage in affirmative action programs would severely undermine public employers' incentive to meet voluntarily their civil rights obligations." *Id., at 289, 290* (citations omitted).

In *Richmond v. J.A. Croson, supra,* the Court again emphasized that remedial race-conscious action must be based on strong evidence of discrimination. That case involved the constitutionality of a city ordinance establishing a plan to remedy past discrimination by requiring prime contractors awarded city construction contracts to subcontract at least 30% of the dollar amount of each contract to minority-controlled businesses. The Court found that the city council had failed to make sufficient factual findings to demonstrate a "strong basis in evidence" of racial discrimination "by anyone in the Richmond construction industry." *Richmond v. J.A. Croson, 488 U.S. at 500.*

Evidence of past discrimination may, but need not, include documentation of specific incidents of intentional discrimination. Instead, evidence of a statistically significant disparity between the percentage of minority students in a college's student body and the percentage of qualified minorities in the relevant pool of college-bound high school graduates may be sufficient. Such an approach is analogous to cases of employment discrimination where the courts accept statistical evidence to infer intentional discrimination against minority job applicants. See *Hazelwood School District v. United States, 433 U.S. 299 (1977).*

Based on this case law, Principle 3 provides that a college may award race-targeted scholarships to remedy discrimination as found by a court or by an administrative agency, such as the Department's Office for Civil Rights. OCR often has approved race-targeted financial aid programs as part of a Title VI remedial plan to eliminate the vestiges of prior discrimination within a State higher education system that previously was operated as a racially segregated dual system. As indicated by the *Croson* decision, a finding of past discrimination also may be made by a State or local legislative body, as long as the legislature has a strong basis in evidence identifying discrimination within its jurisdiction. The remedial use of race-targeted financial aid must be narrowly tailored to remedy the effects of the discrimination.

As revised, Principle 3 also allows a college to award student aid on the basis of race or national origin as part of affirmative action to remedy the effects of the school's past discrimination without waiting for a finding to be made by OCR, a court, or a legislative body, if the college has convincing evidence of past discrimination justifying the affirmative action. The Department's Title VI regulations, like the Fourteenth Amendment, do not require that antecedent or contemporaneous findings of past discrimination be made before remedial affirmative action is implemented, as long as the college has a strong basis in evidence of its past discrimination. Allowing colleges to implement narrowly tailored remedial affirmative action if there is strong evidentiary support for it—without requiring that it be delayed until a finding is made by OCR, a court, or a legislative body—will assist in ensuring that Title VI's mandate against discrimination based on race or national origin is achieved.

4. Financial Aid To Create Diversity

The Title VI regulations permit a college to take voluntary affirmative action, even in the absence of past discrimination, in response to conditions that have limited the participation at the college of students of a particular race or national origin. 34 CFR 100.3(b)(6)(ii); see 34 CFR 100.5(i). In *Regents of the University of California v. Bakke, supra,* the Supreme Court considered whether the University could take voluntary affirmative action by setting aside places in each medical school class for which only minority students could compete.[n7]

The Court considered four rationales provided by the University of California for taking race and national origin into account in making admissions decisions: (1) To reduce the historic deficit of traditionally disfavored minorities in medical schools and the medical profession. (2) To counter the effects of societal discrimination. (3) To increase the number of physicians who would practice in communities lacking medical services. (4) To obtain the educational benefits of a diverse student body. Similar arguments have been advanced in response to the Department's proposed policy guidance on student financial assistance awarded on the basis of race or national origin.

The Court rejected the first three justifications. The first reason was rejected as facially invalid because setting aside a fixed number of admission spaces only to ensure that members of a specified race are admitted was found to be racial "discrimination for its own sake." *Regents of the University of California v. Bakke,* 438 *U.S. at 307.* In rejecting the second contention that the effects of societal discrimination warranted the racial preferences, the Court recognized that the State had a substantial interest in eliminating the effects of discrimination, but that interest was found to be limited to "redress[ing] the wrongs worked by specific instances of discrimination." *Id.* The third contention, concerning the provision of health care services to underserved communities, was rejected by the *Bakke* Court as an evidentiary matter because the State had "not carried its burden of demonstrating that it must prefer members of particular ethnic groups over all other individuals in order to promote better health-care delivery to deprived citizens." *Id., at 311.*

With respect to the final objective, the "attainment of a diverse student body," Justice Powell found that—

This clearly is a constitutionally permissible goal for an institution of higher education. Academic freedom, though not a specifically enumerated constitutional right, long has been viewed as a special concern of the First Amendment. The freedom of a university to make its own judgments as to education includes the selection of its student body. *Id., at 311, 312.* Thus, colleges have a First Amendment right to seek diversity in admissions to fulfill their academic mission through the "robust exchange of ideas" that flows from a diverse student body. *Id., at 312–313.*[n8] However, the means to achieve this "countervailing constitutional interest" under the First Amendment must comport with the requirements of the

---

[n7] The Court noted that the University "does not purport to have made" a determination that its affirmative action plan was necessary to remedy any past discrimination at the medical school. *Regents of the University of California v. Bakke,* 438 *U.S. at 309.*

[n8] The Secretary believes that a college's academic freedom interest in the "robust exchange of ideas" also includes an interest in the existence of a diverse faculty and, more generally, in diversity of professors nationally, since scholars engage since scholars

Fourteenth Amendment. The Medical School's policy of setting aside a fixed number of admission spaces solely for minorities was found not to pass the Fourteenth Amendment's strict scrutiny test, because the policy's use of race as a condition of eligibility for the slots was not necessary to promote the school's diversity interest. *Id., at 315–316.* Justice Powell found that the Medical School could advance its diversity interest under the First Amendment in a narrowly tailored manner that passed the Fourteenth Amendment's strict scrutiny test by using race or national origin as one of several factors that would be considered as a plus factor for an applicant in the admissions process. *Id., at 317–319.*

Following the *Bakke* decision, the Department reexamined its Title VI regulations to determine whether any changes were necessary. In a policy interpretation published in the **Federal Register** *(44 FR 58509),* the Department concluded that no change was warranted. The Department determined that the Title VI regulatory provision authorizing voluntary affirmative action was consistent with the Court's decision and that the provision would be interpreted to incorporate the limitations on voluntary affirmative action announced by the Court.[n9] Thus, if a college's use of race or national origin in awarding financial aid meets the Supreme Court's test under the Fourteenth Amendment for permissible voluntary affirmative action, it will also meet the requirements of Title VI.

In the Department's proposed policy guidance on financial aid, a principle was included permitting the use of race or national origin as a "plus" factor in awarding student aid. The basis for the principle was the *Bakke* decision and the Department's assessment that using an approach that had been approved by the Supreme Court as narrowly tailored to achieve diversity in the admissions context also would be permissible in awarding financial aid.[n10]

In response to the proposed policy, many colleges submitted comments arguing that the use of race or national origin as a plus factor in awarding financial aid may be inadequate to achieve diversity. They contended that, in some cases, it may be necessary to designate a limited amount of aid for students of a particular race or national origin. According to those commenters, a college's financial aid program can serve a critical role in achieving a diverse student body in at least three respects: First, the availability of financial aid set

---

engage in the interchange of ideas with others in their field, and not merely with faculty at their particular school. A university could contribute to this interest by enrolling graduate students who are committed to becoming professors and who will promote the overall diversity of scholars in their field of study, regardless of the diversity of the students who are admitted to the university's own graduate program.

[n9] The present policy guidance on student financial assistance supplements the 1979 policy interpretation.

[n10] The Department will presume that a college's use of race or national origin as a plus factor, with other factors, is narrowly tailored to further the compelling governmental interest in diversity, as long as the college periodically reexamines whether its use of race or national origin as a plus factor continues to be necessary to achieve a diverse student body.

aside for members of a particular race or national origin serves as a recruitment tool, encouraging applicants to consider the school. Second, it provides a means of encouraging students who are offered admission to accept the offer and enroll at the school. Finally, it assists colleges in retaining students until they complete their program of studies.

The commenters argued that a college—because of its location, its reputation (whether deserved or not) of being inhospitable to minority students, or its number of minority graduates—may be unable to recruit sufficient minority applicants even if race or national origin is considered a positive factor in admissions and the award of aid. That is, the failure to attract a sufficient number of minority applicants who meet the academic requirements of the college will make it impossible for the college to enroll a diverse student body, even if race or national origin is given a competitive "plus" in the admissions process. In addition, a college that has sufficient minority applicants to offer admission to a diverse group of applicants may find that, absent the availability of financial aid set aside for minority students, its offers of admission are disproportionately rejected by minority applicants.

Furthermore, commenters were concerned that, while there may be large amounts of financial aid available for undergraduates at their institutions, there may be insufficient aid for graduate students, almost all of whom are able to demonstrate financial need. Thus, it is possible that a college that is able to achieve a diverse student body in some of its programs using race-neutral financial aid criteria or using race or national origin as a "plus" factor may find it necessary to use race or national origin as a condition of eligibility in awarding limited amounts of financial aid to achieve diversity in some of its other programs, such as its graduate school or particular undergraduate schools.

The Department agrees with the commenters that in the circumstances they have described it may be necessary for a college to set aside financial aid to be awarded on the basis of race or national origin in order to achieve a diverse student body. Whether a college's use of race-targeted financial aid is "narrowly tailored" to achieve this compelling interest involves a case-by-case determination that is based on the particular circumstances involved. The Department has determined, based on the comments, to expand Principle 4 to permit those case-by-case determinations.

The Court in *Bakke* indicated that race or national origin could be used in making admissions decisions to further the compelling interest of a diverse student body even though the effect might be to deny admission to some students who did not receive a competitive "plus" based on race or ethnicity.[n11] However, the use of a set-aside of places in the entering class was impermissible because it

---

[n11] *Bakke* was the Supreme Court's first decision in an affirmative action case. Since that time, the Court has decided a number of affirmative action cases, none of which have invalidated Justice Powell's opinion in *Bakke* that the promotion of diversity in the higher education setting is a compelling interest.

was not necessary to the goal of diversity. In cases since *Bakke,* the Supreme Court has provided additional guidance on the factors to be considered in determining whether a classification based on race or national origin is narrowly tailored to its purpose. These factors will be considered by the Department in assessing whether a college's race-targeted financial aid program meets the requirements of Title VI.

First, it is necessary to determine the efficacy of alternative approaches. *United States v. Paradise, 480 U.S. at 171.* Thus, it is important that consideration has been given to the use of alternative approaches that are less intrusive (*e.g.,* the use of race or national origin as a "plus" factor rather than as a condition of eligibility). *Metro Broadcasting, Inc. v. F.C.C., 497 U.S. at 583; Richmond v. J.A. Croson, 488 U.S. at 507.* Financial aid that is restricted to students of a particular race or national origin should be used only if a college determines that these alternative approaches have not or will not be effective.

Second, the extent, duration, and flexibility of the racial classification must be addressed. *Metro Broadcasting, Inc. v. F.C.C., 497 U.S. at 594; United States v. Paradise, 480 U.S. at 171.* The extent of the use of the classification should be no greater than is necessary to carry out its purpose. *Richmond v. J.A. Croson, 488 U.S. at 507.* That is, the amount of financial aid that is awarded based on race or national origin should be no greater than is necessary to achieve a diverse student body.

The duration of the use of a racial classification should be no longer than is necessary to its purpose, and the classification should be periodically reexamined to determine whether there is a continued need for its use. *Metro Broadcasting, Inc. v. F.C.C., 497 U.S. at 594.* Thus, the use of race-targeted financial aid should continue only while it is necessary to achieve a diverse student body, and an assessment as to whether that continues to be the case should be made on a regular basis.

In addition, the use of the classification should be sufficiently flexible that exceptions can be made if appropriate. For example, the Supreme Court in *United States v. Paradise* found that a race-conscious promotion requirement was flexible in operation because it could be waived if no qualified candidates were available. *480 U.S. at 177.* Similarly, racial restrictions on the award of financial aid could be waived if there were no qualified applicants.

Finally, the burden on those who are excluded from the benefit conferred by the classification based on race or national origin (*i.e.,* non-minority students) must be considered. *Id., at 171.* A use of race or national origin may impose such a severe burden on particular individuals—for example, eliminating scholarships currently received by non-minority students in order to start a scholarship program for minority students—that it is too intrusive to be considered narrowly tailored. See *Wygant v. Jackson Board of Education, 476 U.S. at 283* (use of race in imposing layoffs involves severe disruption to lives of identifiable individuals). Generally, the less severe and more diffuse the impact on non-minority students, the more likely a classification based on race or national origin will address this factor satisfactorily. However, it is not necessary to show that no student's opportunity to receive financial aid has been in any way diminished by the use of the race-targeted aid. Rather, the use of race-targeted financial aid must not place an undue burden on students who are not eligible for that aid.

A number of commenters argued that race-targeted financial aid is a minimally intrusive method to attain a diverse student body, far more limited in its impact on non-minority students, for example, than race-targeted admissions policies. Under this view, and unlike the admissions plan at issue in *Bakke,* a race-targeted financial aid award could be a narrowly tailored means of achieving the compelling interest in diversity.

The Department agrees that there are important differences between admissions and financial aid. The affirmative action admissions program struck down in *Bakke* had the effect of excluding applicants from the university on the basis of their race. The use of race-targeted financial aid, on the other hand, does not, in and of itself, dictate that a student would be foreclosed from attending a college solely on the basis of race. Moreover, in contrast to the number of admissions slots, the amount of financial aid available to students is not necessarily fixed. For example, a college's receipt of privately donated monies restricted to an underrepresented group might increase the total pool of funds for student aid in a situation in which, absent the ability to impose such a limitation, the donor might not provide any aid at all.

Even in the case of a college's own funds, a decision to bar the award of race-targeted financial aid will not necessarily translate into increased resources for students from non-targeted groups. Funds for financial aid restricted by race or national origin that are viewed as a recruitment device might be rechanneled into other methods of recruitment if restricted financial aid is barred. In other words, unlike admission to a class with a fixed number of places, the amount of financial aid may increase or decrease based on the functions it is perceived to promote.

In summary, a college can use its financial aid program to promote diversity by considering factors other than race or national origin, such as geographic origin, diverse experiences, or socioeconomic background. In addition, a college may take race or national origin into account as one factor, with other factors, in awarding financial aid if necessary to promote diversity. Finally, a college may use race or national origin as a condition of eligibility in awarding financial aid if it is narrowly tailored to promote diversity.

5. Private Gifts Restricted by Race or National Origin

The fifth principle sets out the circumstances under which a recipient college can award financial aid provided by private donors that is restricted on the basis of race or national origin.

As noted by many commenters, pursuant to the Civil Rights Restoration Act of 1987, all of the operations of a college are covered by Title VI if the college receives any Federal financial assistance. *42 U.S.C. 2000d-4a(2)(A).* Since a college's award of privately donated financial aid is within the operations of the college, the college must comply with the requirements of Title VI in awarding those funds.[n12]

A college may award privately donated financial aid on the basis of race or national origin if the college is remedying its past discrimination pursuant to Principle 3 or attempting to achieve a diverse student body pursuant to Principle 4. In other words, Principles 3 and 4 apply to the use of privately donated funds and may justify awarding these funds on the basis of race or national origin in accordance with the wishes of the donor. Similarly, under Principle 1, a college may award privately donated financial aid that is restricted to disadvantaged students.

Some commenters were uncertain whether it is permissible under Title VI for a college to solicit private donations of student financial aid that are restricted to students of a particular race or national origin. If the receipt and award of these funds is permitted by Title VI, that is, in the circumstances previously described, it is similarly permissible to solicit the funds from private sources.

Financial Aid at Historically Black Colleges and Universities

To ensure that the principles in this policy guidance do not subvert congressional efforts to enhance historically black colleges and universities (HBCUs), these institutions may participate in student aid programs established by third parties for black students that are not limited to students at the HBCUs and may use their own institutional funds in those programs if necessary for participation.[n13] See *20 U.S.C. 1051,* 1060, and 1132c (congressional findings of past discrimination against HBCUs and of the need for enhancement).

This finding is based upon congressional findings of past discrimination against HBCUs and the students they have traditionally served, as well as the Department's determination that these institutions and their students would be harmed if precluded from participation in programs created by third parties that designate financial aid for black students. That action would have an unintended negative effect on their ability to recruit excellent student bodies and could undermine congressional actions aimed at enhancing these institutions.

Congress has repeatedly made findings that recognize the unique historical mission and important role that HBCUs play in the American system of higher

---

[n12] Similarly, other organizations that receive Federal financial assistance must comply with Title VI in their award of student financial aid. On the other hand, individuals or organizations not receiving Federal funds are not subject to Title VI. They may thus, as far as Title VI is concerned, directly award financial aid to students on the basis of race or national origin.

[n13] This provision is limited to HBCUs as defined in Title III of the Higher Education Act. It does not apply generally to predominantly black institutions of higher education. The reason for this distinction is that Congress has made specific findings concerning the unique status of the HBCUs that serve as the basis for this provision.

education, and particularly in providing equal educational opportunity for black students. *20 U.S.C. 1051,* 1060, and 1132c. Congress has created programs that strengthen and enhance HBCUs in Titles II through VII of the Higher Education Act, as amended by Public Law 99-498, *20 U.S.C. 1021*-1132i-2. It has found that "there is a particular national interest in aiding institutions of higher education that have historically served students who have been denied access to postsecondary education because of race or national origin... so that equality of access and quality of postsecondary education opportunities may be enhanced for all students." *20 U.S.C. 1051.* "A key link to the chain of expanding college opportunity for African American youth is strengthening the Nation's historically Black colleges and universities." House Report No. 102-447, 1992 U.S. Code Cong. and Adm. News p. 353.

Congress has found that "the current state of HBCUs is partly attributable to the discriminatory action of the States and the Federal Government and this discriminatory action requires the remedy of enhancement of Black postsecondary institutions to ensure their continuation and participation in fulfilling the Federal mission of equality of educational opportunity." *20 U.S.C. 1060.* See also, House Report No. 102-447, 1992 U.S. Code Cong. and Adm. News p. 353; House Report No. 99-383, 1986 U.S. Code Cong. and Adm. News 2592-2596. This includes providing access and quality education to low-income and minority students, and improving HBCUs' academic quality. *20 U.S.C. 1051.*

For these same reasons, every Administration in recent years has recognized the special role and contributions of HBCUs and expressed support for their enhancement. See "Revised Criteria Specifying the Ingredients of Acceptable Plans to Desegregate State Systems of Public Higher Education," *43 FR 6658 (1977);* Exec. Orders Nos. 12232, *45 FR 53437 (1980);* 12320, *46 FR 48107 (1981);* 12677, *54 FR 18869 (1989);* and 12876, *58 FR 58735 (1993).* The Department's own data indicate that HBCUs continue to play a vital role in providing higher education for many black students. In 1989 and 1990, more than one in four black bachelor's degree recipients received their degree from an HBCU (26.7%). See, "Historically Black Colleges and Universities, 1976-90" (U.S. Department of Education, Office of Educational Research and Improvement, July 1992).

This policy guidance is not intended to limit the efforts to enhance HBCUs called for by Congress and the President. The Department recognizes, however, that Principle 3 (remedying past discrimination) and Principle 4 (creating diversity) may not provide for HBCUs the same possibility of participating in race-targeted programs of financial aid for black students established by third parties as are provided for other colleges and universities. As some commenters pointed out, HBCUs continue to enroll a disproportionate percentage of black students and need to be able to compete for the most talented black students if they are to improve the quality and prestige of their academic environments and, therefore, enhance their attractiveness to all students regardless of race or national origin.

HBCUs' abilities to recruit, enroll and retain talented students will be undermined unless HBCUs are permitted to attract talented black students by participating in aid programs for black students that are established by third parties in which other colleges, *i.e.,* those that meet Principle 3 or 4, participate. Limiting or precluding HBCUs' participation in private programs, such as the National Achievement Scholarship program, would have an unintended negative effect on their ability to recruit a talented student body. Under this scholarship program, which is restricted to academically excellent black students, one type of National Achievement Scholarship is funded by the institution. If HBCUs were unable to participate in this program, some top black students might be forced to choose between (1) receiving a National Achievement Scholarship to attend a school that met Principle 3 or 4 and (2) attending an HBCU. For these reasons, the Department interprets Title VI to permit HBCUs to participate in certain race-targeted aid programs for black students, such as the National Achievement Scholarship program.

The Department reads Title VI consistent with other statutes and Executive orders addressing the special needs and history of HBCUs. In particular, the Department notes congressional findings of discrimination against black students that are the basis for enhancement efforts at HBCUs. Additionally, the Department interprets Title VI to permit limited use of race to avoid an anomalous and absurd result, *i.e.,* penalizing HBCUs and students who seek admission to HBCUs, and putting HBCUs at a disadvantage with respect to other schools precisely because of the special history and composition of the HBCUs.

The use of race-targeted aid by HBCUs that the Department is interpreting Title VI to permit under this provision is narrowly tailored to further the congressionally recognized purpose of enhancement of HBCUs. HBCUs may not discriminate on the basis of race or national origin in admitting students. They may not create their own race-targeted financial aid programs using their own institutional funds unless they satisfy the requirements of any of the other principles in this guidance. Nor may they accept private donations of race-targeted aid for black students that are limited to students at the institution unless otherwise permitted by the guidance. Because HBCUs have traditionally enrolled black students, it should not subvert the goal of enhancing the institutions to require that they not restrict aid to black students if using their own funds or funds from private donors that wish to set up financial aid programs at these institutions. However, because the applicant pool that is attracted to HBCUs presently consists primarily of black students, HBCUs would be placed at a distinct disadvantage with regard to other colleges in attracting talented students if they could not participate in financial aid programs set up by third parties for black students. Thus, the Department interprets Title VI to permit an HBCU to participate in race-targeted financial aid programs for black students that are created by third parties, if the programs are not restricted to students at HBCUs.

The participation by HBCUs in those race-targeted aid programs will be subject to periodic reassessment by the Department. The Department will regularly review the results of enhancement efforts at HBCUs, including the annual report to the President on the progress achieved in enhancing the role and capabilities of HBCUs required by Section 7 of Executive Order 12876. If an HBCU has been enhanced to the point that the institution is attractive to individuals regardless of their race or national origin to the same extent as a non-HBCU, then that institution may participate in only those race-targeted aid programs that are consistent with the other principles in this policy guidance.

Transition Period

The proposed policy guidance would have provided a four-year transition period for individual students to ensure that they did not lose their financial aid as a result of the guidance. Commenters pointed out that, in some cases, four years may not be a sufficient time for a student to complete his or her academic program at a college. In addition, commenters expressed concern that revising the policies and procedures used in recruiting minority students and in providing student financial assistance would require time to develop and implement. The revisions that have been made to the final policy guidance should result in far fewer instances in which colleges will be required to change their financial aid programs. However, the Department recognizes that colleges may need to conduct extensive reviews of their current programs and that in some cases adjustments to those programs may be necessary. As a result, the Department is expanding the proposed transition period.

The Department is providing colleges a reasonable period of time to review and, if necessary, adjust their financial aid programs in an orderly manner that causes the least possible disruption to their students. Colleges must adjust their financial aid programs to be consistent with the principles previously set out no later than two years after the effective date of the Department's policy guidance. However, colleges may continue to provide financial aid awarded on the basis of race or national origin to students who had either applied for or received that assistance prior to the effective date of this guidance during the full course of those students' academic program at the college, even though, in many cases, this will extend beyond the two-year period and, in some cases, the four-year period identified in the proposed policy.

Although some commenters questioned the Department's authority to create a transition period, such a period for adjustments is consistent with the Department's approach in the past under other civil rights statutes it enforces. See 34 CFR 106.41(d) (transition period to permit recipients to bring their athletic programs into compliance with Title IX of the Education Amendments of 1972); 34 CFR 104.22(e) (transition period to permit recipients to make facilities accessible to individuals with disabilities, as required by Section 504 of the Rehabilitation Act of 1973). It is based on the Department's recognition of the practical difficulties that some colleges may face in making changes to their recruitment and financial aid award processes.

The transition period also is consistent with the Department's policy, in approving plans for the desegregation of State systems of higher education, that students who have been the beneficiaries of past discriminatory conduct not be required to bear the burden of corrective action. For example, while the Department requires State higher education systems to take remedial action to increase the enrollment of previously excluded students, it does not require the expulsion of any student in order to permit admission of those previously excluded. See *Wygant v. Jackson Board of Education, 476 U.S. at 282–85.*

Finally, the transition period is consistent with the Department's obligations under Title VI to seek voluntary compliance by recipients that have been found in violation of the statute. *42 U.S.C. 2000d-1.* During the transition period, the Department will provide colleges with technical assistance to help them make any necessary changes to their financial aid programs in order to achieve compliance with Title VI.

Program Authority: *42 U.S.C. 2000d.*
Dated: February 17, 1994.

Richard W. Riley,
Secretary of Education.

[FR Doc. 94-4010 Filed 2-22-94; 8:45 am]

Appendix C

Recommended Resources and Internet Sites

BOOKS

The following books are recommended as valuable resources in gathering in-depth information about various colleges and universities, as well as the admissions and financial aid processes at different institutions. These books provide comprehensive coverage of institutions from around the United States:

Peterson's *Four-Year Colleges* (Thompson Peterson's, 2006)
Complete Book of Colleges (The Princeton Review, 2006 Edition)
Fiske Guide to Colleges (Sourcebooks, 2006)
The Insider's Guide to the Colleges (St. Martins Griffin, 2004)
The Best 361 Colleges (The Princeton Review, 2006 edition)
Unofficial, Unbiased Guide to the 331 Most Interesting Colleges 2005 (Kaplan, 2004)
America's Best Value Colleges (The Princeton Review, 2006)

The following books are recommended resources in learning more about unique, and sometimes nontraditional, colleges and universities from around the country:

Harvard Schmarvard: Getting Beyond the Ivy League to the College That is Best for You (Three Rivers Press, 2003)
Colleges That Change Lives: 40 Schools You Should Know About Even if You're Not a Straight-A Student (Penguin, 2000)
Cool Colleges: For the Hyper-Intelligent, Self-Directed, Late Blooming, and Just Plain Different (Ten Speed Press, 2000)

The following books are recommended resources in offering broad advice to students and parents about how to prepare and apply for colleges and universities.

> *Black Excel: African American Student's College Guide*, by Isaac Black (John Wiley & Sons, 2000)
> *Fiske What to Do When for College 2005–2006: A Student and Parent's Guide to Deadlines, Planning and the Last Two Years of High School* (Sourcebooks, 2005)
> *Fiske Guide to Getting into the Right College* (Sourcebooks, 2002)
> *Visiting College Campuses* (The Princeton Review, 7th edition)

Finally, the following two books are helpful resources in understanding the basics of financial aid.

> *Paying for College without Going Broke* (The Princeton Review, 2005)
> *8 Steps to Help Black Families Pay for College* (The Princeton Review, 2003)

INTERNET RESOURCES

The following Internet site offers basic information about colleges and universities from around the country, as well as yearly rankings (under "rankings and guide" tab on home page):

> http://www.usnews.com

The following Internet site offers basic information and advice regarding the college admissions process:

> http://www.nacac.com

The following Internet sites offer both good starting information and in-depth information on financial aid and scholarships. (The sites are listed in no particular order.)

> http://tomjoyner.com/foundation
>
> http://www.fastweb.com
>
> http://www.finaid.com
>
> http://www.petersons.com
>
> http://www.sailliemae.com
>
> http://www.collegenet.com
>
> http://www.collegeboard.com

http://www.princetonreview.com/college/finance/articles/scholarships/scholarsearch.asp

http://www.nul.org/scholarships.html

http://www.uncf.org

http://www.gmsp.org

http://www.ronbrown.org

http://www.finaid.org

http://www.ed.gov/offices/OSFAP/Students/

http://www.scholarships.com

http://www.absolutelyscholarships.com

Appendix D

The College Application Checklist

(Reader should make a photocopy of this checklist for each college of interest and organize materials for each college into a separate file. This checklist should be placed at the front of each file.)

Name of College/University:_____
Location (City & State):_____
Federal School Code:_____
Application Deadline:_____

☐ Check box if application is completed, all other steps are completed, and materials have been sent to college or university by or before deadline listed above.

PART I: PRE-APPLICATION

1. Create list of colleges/universities and begin research on each school of interest (including collecting information responsive to Table One in Chapter 5 of this book) ( )

2. Finalize List of Colleges ( )

3. Investigate Institution ( )

4. Request Application ( )

5. Contact Teachers, Coaches, Employers, or Others About Completing Letters of Recommendation on Your Behalf ( )

6. Determine Tests for Admissions that are Required and Last Acceptable Date to Take Test ( )

	Date	Score on Test
ACT:		
SAT:		

7. If you wish to compete in Division I or II athletics and wish to be recruited, register with the NCAA Initial Eligibility Clearinghouse ( )

8. Complete College Visit or Interview (if required)
Date of Visit/Interview: ( )

9. Create (or Revise) Résumé ( )

10. Begin Working on Admissions Essay (with guidance from Chapter 6 in mind) ( )

PART II: APPLICATION

11. Provide Letter of Recommendation Forms and Stamped Envelopes to Individuals Writing Letters ( )

12. Request Transcripts/Grades are Sent to School ( )

13. Complete Admissions Essay ( )

14. Collect Letters of Recommendation ( )

15. Complete Application ( )

16. Make Copies of Application Before Submitting ( )

17. Send in Complete Application as Soon as Possible ( )
If sending the application via U.S. Mail, be sure to get a certificate of mailing (which proves the date it was mailed). If deadline is imminent and based upon date of receipt (as opposed to date of mailing), consider sending in a manner that provides a track number and proof of delivery

18. Contact School and Confirm Receipt of Application if You Do Not Receive Acknowledgment of Receipt Within a Reasonable Period of Time ( )

19. Have Registrar/Guidance Counselor Send Mid-Year Grade Report (if required by school) ( )

20. Complete and Mail in the FAFSA as Soon as Possible ( )

21. Receive (and Note) Decision of College ( )

PART III: POST-APPLICATION

22. In Addition to FAFSA, Complete School-Specific Financial Aid Forms (Contact School or Guidance Counselor for Additional information) ( )

23. If Wait-Listed, Contact School and Update Them on Continued Interest and Spring Grades and Accomplishments ( )

Appendix D • 403

24. Make Final Decision Regarding School ( )
25. Mail Enrollment Form and Deposit Check to Reserve Seat ( )
26. If Competing in College Athletics, Have Final Transcript Sent to the NCAA Initial Eligibility Clearinghouse ( )
27. Finalize Housing at the School ( )
28. Shop for Items Needed for College ( )
29. Sign up for Orientation ( )
30. Make Travel Plans ( )
31. Most Importantly, Resolve to Enjoy This Next Phase of Your Life and Take Advantage of Every Educational Opportunity ( )

Notes

PREFACE

1. Ronald Roach, "Panel Critiques Media Coverage of the Affirmative Action Story," *Black Issues in Higher Education* 15, no. 13 (1998): 26–27.

INTRODUCTION

1. Carol Elam and Gilbert Brown, "The Inclusive University: Helping Minority Students Choose a College and Identify Institutions That Value Diversity," *Journal of College Admissions* (Spring 2005) 187: 14.
2. Ibid.
3. The description of the use of race or minority status in the admissions process as being a "very important factor," an "important factor," or "other factors considered" are categories and terminology employed in the Princeton Review's *Complete Book of Colleges* (New York: Random House, 2005). The description of the use of race or minority status in the admissions process as being of "considerable importance" or "moderate importance" are terminology employed by the National Association for College Admission Counseling, *State of College Admission* (Alexandria, VA, March 2005).
4. National Association for College Admission Counseling, *State of College Admission* (Alexandria, VA, March 2005), p. 39, table 32.
5. Ibid.
6. Ibid.
7. Comment of Arthur L. Coleman, Partner, Holland & Knight, on February 19, 2005, as part of panel discussion on "Experiences after Grutter and Gratz" at the 26th Annual National Law and Higher Education Pre-Conference hosted by Stetson University College of Law in Gulfport, Florida.
8. Ibid.
9. National Association for College Admission Counseling, *State of College Admission*, p. 41.

10. CNBC News transcript, "Brooke Ellison, Harvard Student and Quadriplegic, Graduate with the Highest Honor Possible, Thanks to the Help from Her Mother," *Upfront Tonight*, June 8, 2000.

11. Jeffrey Selingo, "Michigan: Who Really Won? Colleges' Cautious Reaction to the Supreme Court's Affirmative Action Decisions May Have Snatched Defeat from the Jaws of Victory," *Chronicle of Higher Education*, January 14, 2005, p. A21.

12. Vicki Salemi, "Affirmative Action and College Admissions," *CollegeBound Network*, January 2005.

13. Peter Schmidt, "Foes of Affirmative Action Push Colleges to Reveal Policies on Race Conscious Admissions," *Chronicle of Higher Education*, March 23, 2004 (online article in section entitled "Today's News") at http://chronicle.com/daily/2004/03/2004032301n.htm.

14. Any public university or college falls under the Court's ruling under the Fourteenth Amendment. However, the Court made clear in its decision in *Grutter v. Bollinger*, 123 S. Ct. 2323, 2347 (2003), that private colleges are also governed by the decision, by virtue of Title VI of the Civil Rights Act of 1964, which bars public or private discrimination in higher education.

15. Mark R. Killenbeck, *Affirmative Action and Diversity: The Beginning of the End? Or the End of the Beginning?* (Princeton, NJ: Research & Development, Policy Information Center, Educational Testing Service (ETS), 2004), p. 32.

16. Timothy J. O'Neill, "*Regents of the University of California v. Bakke*," in *The Oxford Companion to the Supreme Court of the United States*, edited by Kermit L. Hall (New York: Oxford University Press, 1992), p. 715.

17. Comment of Theodore M. Shaw, on February 19, 2005, as part of panel discussion on "Experiences after Grutter and Gratz" at the 26th Annual National Law and Higher Education Pre-Conference hosted by Stetson University College of Law in Gulfport, Florida.

18. *Regents of the University of California v. Bakke*, 438 U.S. 265, 316 (Powell opinion) (1978).

19. Jack E. White, "Affirmative Action's Alamo," *Time Magazine*, August 23, 1999, p. 48.

20. Michael Nettles, Preface to Killenbeck, *Affirmative Action and Diversity*.

21. Killenbeck, *Affirmative Action and Diversity*, p. 32.

22. The Supreme Court rejected the "role model theory," the theory that affirmative action is needed to foster or promote minority role models, as a compelling government interest in an affirmative action and employment case entitled *Wygant v. Jackson Board of Education*, 476 U.S. 267 (1986). The Supreme Court held, in an affirmative action and contracting case entitled *City of Richmond v. J.A. Croson Co.*, 488 U.S. 469 (1989), that it is not permissible to implement an affirmative action plan in order to improve diversity in society generally. See also, *Wygant v. Jackson Board of Education*, 476 U.S. 267 (1986) and *Taxman v. Piscataway Township Board of Education*, 91 F.3d 1547 (3rd Cir. 1996), *cert. granted*, 117 S. Ct. 2506 (1997), *cert. dismissed*, 118 S. Ct. 595 (1997).

23. Center for Individual Rights, "Supreme Court's 'Mixed Decision' on Racial Preference," press release, June 23, 2003.

24. Rebecca Trounson and Stuart Silverstein, "Bid to Export Prop. 209," *Los Angeles Times*, July 8, 2003, p. B1.

25. Selingo, "Michigan: Who Really Won?" p. A21.

26. Killenbeck, *Affirmative Action and Diversity*, p. 32.

27. Center for Individual Rights, "Supreme Court's 'Mixed Decision.'"

28. Killenbeck, *Affirmative Action and Diversity*, p. 32.

CHAPTER 1

1. Paulina Ruf, "Legacy Preference," in *Affirmative Action: An Encyclopedia*, edited by James A. Beckman (Westport, CT: Greenwood Press, 2004), p. 559.
2. William Bowen and Derek Bok, *The Shape of the River* (Princeton, NJ: Princeton University Press, 1998), p. 1.
3. Ibid., p. 4.
4. Ibid., p. 5.
5. Lyndon B. Johnson, *Public Papers of the Presidents of the United States: Lyndon B. Johnson (1965), 1966*, vol. 2 (Washington, DC: Government Printing Office), pp. 635–640.
6. Bowen and Bok, *Shape of the River*, p. 5.
7. Ibid., p. 6.
8. *Defunis v. Odegaard*, 416 U.S. 312 (1974). For more information on this case, see Ronnie Tucker, "*Defunis v. Odegaard*," in Beckman, *Affirmative Action*, pp. 252–255.
9. James A. Beckman, "*Regents of the University of California v. Bakke*," in Beckman, *Affirmative Action*, pp. 736–737.
10. O'Neill, "*Regents of the University of California v. Bakke*," pp. 713–715.
11. The belief of the "antidiscrimination four" in *Bakke* that race-conscious affirmative action plans could be legitimately utilized to fulfill any important government interest is a noticeably more lenient standard than the Court actually employs. Since 1995 (in *Adarand v. Pena*), the Court made clear that all racially discriminatory practices, even benign discriminatory practices like affirmative action, are subject to the "strict scrutiny" standard. That is, since 1995, in order for a government or public institution to implement an affirmative action plan, the plan must be based upon a "compelling governmental interest," which only allows the most compelling of government interests in justifying the plan. For more information on this topic, see Gregory M. Duhl, "Compelling Governmental Interest," in Beckman, *Affirmative Action*, pp. 219–221.
12. Robert K. Fullinwider, "Civil Rights and Racial Preferences: A Legal History of Affirmative Action," *Philosophy and Public Policy* 17, no. 1/2 (1997): 9–20.
13. Janis Judson, "*Hopwood v. Texas*," in Beckman, *Affirmative Action*, p. 486.
14. Killenbeck, *Affirmative Action and Diversity*, p. 32.
15. Bowen and Bok, *Shape of the River*, p.1.
16. Girardeau A. Spann, *The Law of Affirmative Action: Twenty-Five Years of Supreme Court Decisions on Race and Remedies* (New York: New York University Press, 2000), p. 64.
17. Judson, "*Hopwood v. Texas*," p. 486.
18. Ibid.
19. Maria Beckman, "*Smith v. University of Washington Law School*," in Beckman, *Affirmative Action*, p. 814.

CHAPTER 2

1. Denise O'Neil Green, "*Gratz v. Bollinger and Grutter v. Bollinger*," in Beckman, *Affirmative Action*, p. 456.
2. Adalberto Aguirre, Jr., "Affirmative Action and Education," in Beckman, *Affirmative Action*, p. 312.

3. University of Michigan Expert Witness Report, "The Compelling Need for Diversity in Higher Education," *Gratz & Hamacher v. Bollinger, et al.*, No. 97-75231, and *Grutter v. Bollinger*, No. 97-75928 (E.D. Mich. Filed January 1999), p. 1.

4. *Grutter v. Bollinger*, p. 2340 (quoting the American Educational Research Association's amicus curiae brief in the case).

5. *Grutter v. Bollinger*, p. 2429.

6. Ibid., p. 2337.

7. Ibid., p. 2339, 2340.

8. Ibid., p. 2339.

9. Ibid., p. 2341 (quoting *Richmond v. J.A. Croson Co.*). For more information on the definition and requirements of a narrowly tailored plan, see Mfanya D. Tryman, "Narrowly Tailored Affirmative Action Plans," in Beckman, *Affirmative Action*, pp. 630–632.

10. *Grutter v. Bollinger*, p. 2343.

11. The socialization theory of equality holds that racial stereotypes will break down when individuals from different walks of life work, learn, and live together in close quarters. For more information on this theory, see Kingsley Ufuoma Omoyibo, "Socialization Theory of Equality," in Beckman, *Affirmative Action*, vol. 2, pp. 817–819.

12. *Grutter v. Bollinger*, pp. 2342–2343.

13. Salemi, "Affirmative Action and College Admissions."

14. *Grutter v. Bollinger*, p. 2342.

15. Ibid., pp. 2346–2347.

16. Ibid., p. 2346 (quoting *Croson*).

17. Killenbeck, *Affirmative Action and Diversity*, p. 32.

18. For example, white students at one of the Historically Black Colleges and Universities (often referred to as HBCUs).

19. Ben Gose, "The Chorus Grows Louder for Class-Based Affirmative Action," *Chronicle of Higher Education* (special pullout section entitled Admissions & Student Aid), February 25, 2005, p. B5.

20. Killenbeck, *Affirmative Action and Diversity*, pp. 18, 25–26.

21. Arthur Coleman and Scott Palmer, *Diversity in Higher Education: A Strategic Planning and Policy Manual Regarding Federal Law in Admissions, Financial Aid, and Outreach*, 2nd ed. (New York: The College Board, 2004), p. 22.

CHAPTER 3

1. The signatories to this report were Professor Erwin Chemerinsky (University of Southern California), Professor Drew Days, III (Yale Law School), Professor Richard Fallon (Harvard Law School), Professor Pamela Karlan (Stanford Law School), Professor Kenneth Karst (UCLA School of Law), Professor Frank Michelman (Harvard University), Professor Eric Schnapper (University of Washington School of Law), Professor Laurence Tribe (Harvard Law School), Professor Mark Tushnet (Georgetown University Law School), Professor Angelo Ancheta (Harvard University), and Professor Christopher Edley, Jr. (Harvard Law School).

2. Joint Statement of Constitutional Law Scholars, "Reaffirming Diversity: A Legal Analysis of the University of Michigan Affirmative Action Cases" (Cambridge, MA: The Civil Rights Project at Harvard University, 2003), p. 2.

3. Ibid., p. 19.

4. Ibid., p. 19.

5. Melinda Sadar, "Admissions Process Adjusted to Ensure Diversity: Court Decisions Say Race Still a Factor in University Admissions," *onCampus* (OSU's Newspaper for Faculty & Staff) 34, no. 4, (October 9, 2003), http://www.osu.edu/oncampus/v33n4/thisissue.html (accessed November 14, 2004).

6. Julie Peterson, "New Undergraduate Admissions Policy: Process to Involve More Information, Individual Review," *University Record Online*, September 2, 2003, http://www.umich.edu/~urecord/0203/Sept02_03/00.shtml (accessed September 16, 2004).

7. Peter Schmidt, "New Admissions System at U. of Michigan to Seek Diversity through Essays," *Chronicle of Higher Education*, September 5, 2003, p. A28.

8. See generally, Barry Schwartz, "A Radical Proposal: Top Colleges Should Select Randomly from a Pool of 'Good Enough,'" *Chronicle of Higher Education* (special pullout section entitled Admissions & Student Aid), February 25, 2005, p. B20.

9. Greg Winter, "After Ruling, 3 Universities Maintain Diversity in Admissions," *New York Times*, sec. A, April 13, 2004.

10. Michael Martin, "A Drift toward Elitism by the 'People's Universities,'" *Chronicle of Higher Education* (special pullout section entitled Admissions & Student Aid), February 25, 2005, p. B26.

11. Sadar, "Admissions Process Adjusted to Ensure Diversity."

12. Ibid.

13. Wagoner, Heather, "Black Student Enrollment at Ohio State U. Expected to Increase," *The Lantern*, September 30, 2005.

14. Winter, "3 Universities Maintain Diversity in Admissions."

15. Ibid.

16. Selingo, "Michigan: Who Really Won?" p. A21.

17. Robert Becker, "Black Enrollment at U of I Rebounding from Last Year," *Chicago Tribune*, June 7, 2005, p. 3.

18. Winter, "3 Universities Maintain Diversity in Admissions."

19. Selingo, "Michigan: Who Really Won?" p. A21.

20. Becker, "Black Enrollment at U of I Rebounding," p. 3.

21. Selingo, "Michigan: Who Really Won?" p. A21.

22. Associated Press (Justin Pope), "One Year after Ruling, Colleges Find Affirmative Action Isn't Easy," June 20, 2004.

23. Winter, "3 Universities Maintain Diversity in Admissions."

24. Cyndee-nga Trinh and Tessa Moll, "Race Based Admission Decisions Pass First-Year Mark," *Daily Texan* (University of Texas-Austin), June 23, 2004.

25. Selingo, "Michigan: Who Really Won?" p. A21.

26. Ibid.

27. Zachary Goldstein, "Admittance Rates Differ Drastically by Race for Dartmouth Class of '08," *Dartmouth* (Dartmouth College), May 11, 2004.

28. Becker, "Black Enrollment at U of I Rebounding," p. 3.

29. Ibid.

30. Mark Bauerlein, "Diversity Dropouts: What We Can Learn from Historically Black Colleges," *Weekly Standard*, September 27, 2004.

31. Kelly Simmons, "Fewer Blacks to Start at UGA: School Seeks More in Freshman Class but of 580 Accepted Only 202 May Enroll," *Atlanta Journal-Constitution*, August 11, 2004.

32. Selingo, "Michigan: Who Really Won?" p. A21.

33. Associated Press, "UGA Admissions Will Remain Race-Neutral Another Year," January 6, 2005.

34. Simmons, "Fewer Blacks to Start at UGA."

35. Associated Press, "UGA Admissions Will Remain Race-Neutral."

36. Kelly Simmons, "UGA Effort to Recruit Blacks Pays Off," *Atlanta Journal-Constitution*, May 13, 2005, p. 9D.

37. Larry Faulkner announced in June 2005 his intention to resign as president of the University of Texas at Austin in 2006.

38. Selingo, "Michigan: Who Really Won?" p. A21.

39. Salemi, "Affirmative Action and College Admissions."

40. Ben Gose, "Questions Loom for Applicants and Colleges," *Chronicle of Higher Education* (special pullout section entitled Admissions & Student Aid), February 25, 2005, p. B3.

41. Kevin Miller, "Race Fades as Factor in Academic Community," *Roanoke Times & World News*, sec. Virginia, June 23, 2004.

42. Pope, "Colleges Find Affirmative Action Isn't Easy."

43. Selingo, "Michigan: Who Really Won?" p. A21.

44. Ibid.

45. The seven institutions where enrollment for blacks and Hispanics declined are Carnegie Mellon University, University of Michigan, Ohio State University, State University of New York at Stony Brook, University of California at Berkeley, University of Georgia, and Michigan State University. The eleven institutions that witnessed an increase in enrollment for blacks and Hispanics are the University of Wisconsin at Madison, University of Washington, University of Texas at Austin, University of Maryland at College Park, Texas A&M University at College Station, Pennsylvania State University at University Park, Northwestern University, Harvard University, Georgia Institute of Technology, College of William and Mary, and Clemson University. The eleven institutions that saw an increase in the enrollment in either black freshmen or Hispanic freshmen, with a decline in the other group, are as follows: Brown University, Duke University, Florida State University, Princeton University, University of Colorado at Boulder, University of Florida, University of Illinois at Urbana-Champaign, University of Iowa, University of Massachusetts at Amherst, University of North Carolina at Chapel Hill, and the University of Virginia.

46. Bonnie Miller Rubin, "Family Ties No Longer Buy Ticket to College; More Schools Opt Not to Give Alumni's Children Extra Boost," *Chicago Tribune*, May 3, 2005.

47. Ibid.

48. Ibid.

CHAPTER 4

1. *Grutter v. Bollinger*, pp. 2346–2347.

2. "Presidential Debate: Bush v. Kerry," *Black Collegian*, October 1, 2004.

3. Karin Fischer, "Class-Rank Plan Faces Trouble in Texas," *Chronicle of Higher Education*, April 22, 2005, p. 25.

4. Ibid.

5. Ibid.
6. Karin Fischer, "The Contest to Qualify," *Chronicle of Higher Education*, April 22, 2005, p. A26.
7. Ibid.
8. Melissa Mixon, "Top 10 Percent May Hurt Minorities, Report Says," *Daily Texan* (via University Wire), February 24, 2005.
9. Catherine L. Horn and Stella M. Flores, "Percent Plans in College Admissions: A Comparative Analysis of Three States' Experiences," The Civil Rights Project, Harvard University, http://www.civilrightsproject.harvard.edu/policy/legal_docs/Diversity_%20Reaffirmed.pdf (accessed November 14, 2004).
10. Fischer, "Class-Rank Plan Faces Trouble," p. 25.
11. Fischer, "The Contest to Qualify," p. A26.
12. Ralph K. M. Haurwitz, "Senate Keeps Top 10% Admissions Law," *Austin American Statesman*, May 7, 2005, p. B1.
13. Fischer, "Class-Rank Plan Faces Trouble," p. 25.
14. Trinh and Moll, "Race Based Admission Decisions Pass First-Year Mark."
15. Mixon, "Top 10 Percent May Hurt Minorities."
16. Trinh and Moll, "Race Based Admission Decisions Pass First-Year Mark."
17. Peter Schmidt, "A New Route to Racial Diversity: Texas A&M Raises Minority Enrollment without Race-Conscious Admissions," *Chronicle of Higher Education*, January 28, 2005, p. A23.
18. Pope, "Colleges Find Affirmative Action Isn't Easy."
19. Schmidt, "New Route to Racial Diversity," p. A23.
20. Ibid.
21. Ibid.
22. Lori Rodriguez, "UH Broadens Admissions Rule; Next Fall, the College Will Begin Automatically Accepting Grads in the Top 20 Percent," *Houston Chronicle*, February 19, 2005, p. B1.
23. California Constitution, art. 1, sec. 31.
24. Isaac Black, *Black Excel: African American Student's College Guide* (New York: John Wiley & Sons, 2000), p. 158.
25. Interview of Robert C. Dynes, President, University of California, *San Diego Union-Tribune*, January 30, 2005, p. G-5.
26. Ibid.
27. Ibid.
28. Sara Hebel, "Percent Plans Don't Add Up," *Chronicle of Higher Education*, March 21, 2003, p. A26.
29. Kelly Heyboer, "A Case for Affirmative Action," *Newhouse News Service*, April 12, 2005.
30. Horn and Flores, "Percent Plans in College Admissions."
31. See Horn and Flores, "Percent Plans in College Admissions"; and University Business, "Drop in Diversity: Black Freshman Admissions Are Down at Many Schools, Especially at UC Berkeley," July 2004, http://www.universitybusiness.com (accessed September 2004).
32. Editorial, *San Francisco Chronicle*, April 8, 2005.
33. Charles Burress, "Cal Chancellor Warns of Diversity Crisis; Birgeneau Blames Prop. 209 for Decline," *San Francisco Chronicle*, April 8, 2005, p. B1.

34. Rebecca Trounson, "UC Berkeley Chancellor Inaugurated; Robert J. Birgeneau Says Boosting the Enrollment of Blacks and Latinos, Which Fell after Prop. 209 Was Passed in 1996, Will Be a Priority," *Los Angeles Times*, April 16, 2005, p. 3

35. Heyboer, "A Case for Affirmative Action."

36. Ibid.

37. Burress, "Chancellor Warns of Diversity Crisis," p. B1.

38. Associated Press (Michelle Locke), "Black Admissions Drop 30 Percent at Berkeley," May 29, 2004.

39. Tanya Schevitz, "Admissions of Latinos Rises at UC; Trend Doesn't Extend to Blacks," *The San Francisco Chronicle*, April 20, 2005, p. A1.

40. Eleanor Yang, "Applications to UC for Freshman Rise Nearly 3% for Fall," *Copley News Service*, February 3, 2005.

41. Rebecca Trounson, "UC Shows Rebound in Admissions," *Los Angeles Times*, April 20, 2005, p. 1.

42. Schevitz, "Admissions of Latinos Rises at UC," p. A1.

43. Ibid.

44. Horn and Flores, "Percent Plans in College Admissions."

45. "The Status of Blacks among America's 'Best College Buys,'" *Journal of Blacks in Higher Education* (Spring 1997) Volume 15: 56–58.

46. "CalTech: The Whitest of the Nation's 25 Highest-Ranked Universities," *Journal of Blacks in Higher Education* (Spring 1998) Volume 19: 66–67.

47. Ibid.

48. Black, *Black Excel*, p. 158.

49. Margret Gonzales, "Assembly Approves Use of Race in UC System Admissions," *Guardian* (University of California at San Diego), June 30, 2004. See also Jessica Springgay, "Bill to Reintroduce Consideration of Race in UC, Cal State Admissions," *California Aggie* (via University Wire), July 2, 2004.

50. Charles Nguyen, "California Bill Would Allow Use of Race in University Admissions," *Guardian* (via University Wire), April 21, 2005.

51. Ibid.

52. Charles Burress, "Diversity Is Chancellor's Top Challenge; New UC Leader Uses Inaugural to Push for Greater Inclusion," *San Francisco Chronicle*, April 16, 2005, p. B1.

53. Trounson, "UC Berkeley Chancellor Inaugurated," p. 3.

54. Ibid.

55. Rebecca Trounson, "UC Is Unbiased in Admissions, Analysis Finds," *Los Angeles Times*, July 22, 2005, p. B6.

56. Editorial, *Washington Post*, December 31, 2004.

57. Gary Fineout, "Governor Bush Touts One Florida as Success; Recent Figures Show More Minorities Attending State Universities," *Ledger*, September 3, 2003, p. A1.

58. Editorial, *Washington Post*.

59. Editorial, *Palm Beach Post*, September 26, 2004.

60. Kimberly Miller, "Colleges See Black Enrollment Dropping," *Palm Beach Post*, July 22, 2005, p. 1B.

61. Ibid.

62. David Damron and Jennifer Peltz, "Universities Show Minority Rise; Critics: Bush Plan May Not Be the Reason," *Sun-Sentinel*, September 17, 2004, p. 9B. See also

David Damron, "College Minority Figures Change; Gov. Bush's One-Florida Officials Say Numbers Increase; Others Aren't So Sure," *Orlando Sentinel*, September 16, 2004, p. B5.

63. Damron and Peltz, "Universities Show Minority Rise; Critics: Bush Plan May Not Be the Reason."

64. Editorial, *Palm Beach Post*.

65. Damron and Peltz, "Universities Show Minority Rise; Critics: Bush Plan May Not Be the Reason."

66. Black, *Black Excel*, p. 174, 176.

67. Ibid.

68. Betty Nyangoni, "Bethune, Mary Jane McLeod," in Beckman, *Affirmative Action*, vol. 1, p. 95.

69. Washington State Civil Rights Initiative, c. 49.60 RCW.

70. National Public Radio, "Washington State's Initiative 200," *National Public Radio Broadcast: News & Notes with Ed Gordon*, February 14, 2005.

71. See, e.g., *Louisiana Associated General Contractors v. State of Louisiana*, 95-2105 (La. 3/8/95), 669 So.2nd 1185; and *Lalla v. City of New Orleans*, 1999 WL 138900 (E.D. La. 1999).

72. Amanda Duhon, "LSU Reacts to Supreme Court Admissions Ruling," *Reveille* (via University Wire), July 10, 2003.

73. Americans for a Fair Chance, *Anti-Affirmative Action Threats in the States: 1997–2003*, http://www.fairchance.org (last accessed November 2004).

74. See, e.g., Alyson Kline, "Affirmative Action Opponents Suffer Setbacks in Colorado and Michigan," *Chronicle of Higher Education*, April 9, 2004, p. 23.

75. Karin Fischer, "U. of Colo. to Grant Automatic Admissions," *Chronicle of Higher Education*, January 28, 2005, p. A24.

76. Ibid.

CHAPTER 5

1. Thomas LaVeist and Will LaVeist, *8 Steps to Help Black Families Pay for College* (New York: Random House, 2003).

2. National Association for College Admission Counseling, *State of College Admission*, p. 39.

3. Ibid.

4. Shirley J. Wilcher, "Law School: A Road to Access, Opportunity and Empowerment," *Black Collegian*, October 1, 2004, p. 124.

5. National Association for College Admission Counseling, *State of College Admission*, p. 39.

6. Robin G. Mamlet, "Selectivity Is What Produces the Right Fit," *Chronicle of Higher Education* (special pullout section entitled Admissions & Student Aid), February 25, 2005, p. B24.

7. Elam and Brown, "Inclusive University," p. 16.

8. Trounson, "UC Berkeley Chancellor Inaugurated," p. 3.

9. Mitzi Davis et al., " 'A Fly in the Buttermilk': Descriptions of University Life by Successful Black Undergraduate Students at a Predominately White Southeastern University," *Journal of Higher Education*, July 1, 2004.

10. Tanya Schevitz, "Private Schools Appealing to California's Top Minority Students," *Scripps Howard News Service*, May 8, 2005.

11. Schmidt, "New Route to Racial Diversity," p. A23.

12. National Association for College Admission Counseling, *State of College Admission*, p. 39.

13. Black, *Black Excel*, p. 9.

14. Tom Joyner, foreword to LaVeist and LaVeist, *8 Steps to Help Black Families Pay for College*.

15. Pushap Kapoor, "Affirmative Action in the Twenty-first Century," *Higher Education Digest*, September 2004 Newsletter.

16. William Bowen, Martin Kurzwell, and Eugene Tobin, "From 'Bastions of Privilege' to 'Engines of Opportunity,'" *Chronicle of Higher Education* (special pullout section entitled Admissions & Student Aid), February 25, 2005, p. B18.

17. Ibid.

18. Amicus brief in *Gratz/Grutter*, as quoted in Bowen et al., "From 'Bastions of Privilege,'" p. B18.

19. Randy Cohen, "Affirming Inaction," *New York Times*, March 6, 2005, p. 22.

20. Ibid.

21. Salemi, "Affirmative Action and College Admissions."

22. Ibid.

23. Ibid.

24. LaVeist and LaVeist, *8 Steps to Help Black Families*, p. 24.

25. Salemi, "Affirmative Action and College Admissions."

26. "The College Application Calendar," *College Board*, available online at http://www.collegeboard.com/article/0,3868,5-25-0-23626,00.html.

27. National Association for College Admission Counseling, *State of College Admission*, p. 40.

28. Ibid., p. 39, tables 32 & 33.

29. Interview, "So Many Colleges, So Many Decisions, So Much at Stake," *Post-Standard* (Syracuse, NY), April 3, 2002, p. 9.

30. Bob Laird, "Affirmative Action and Liars," *Chronicle of Higher Education*, May 20, 2005.

31. Carolyn Kleiner and Mary Lord, "The Cheating Game," *U.S. News & World Report*, November 22, 1999, p. 55.

32. Gose, "Questions Loom for Applicants and Colleges," p. B3.

33. National Association for College Admission Counseling, *State of College Admission*, p. 39, table 32.

34. Marty Nemko, "The Admissions Game: Tips for Students and Parents," *Chronicle of Higher Education* (special pullout section entitled Admissions & Student Aid), February 25, 2005, p. B32.

35. Ascribe Newswire, "May 1 Is College Admission Decision Day: News Tips and Sources on Admission Trends and Stories from the National Association for College Admission Counseling," April 29, 2005.

36. Ben Gose, "If at First They Don't Succeed...," *Chronicle of Higher Education*, August 5, 2005, p. A30.

37. Ibid.

CHAPTER 6

1. Laird, "Affirmative Action and Liars."
2. Ibid.

CHAPTER 7

1. James Beckman, "Storer College and African American Home Ownership in Jefferson County," *Magazine of the Jefferson County Historical Association*, vol. 70, December 2004, p. 82.
2. 1965 Higher Education Act, as quoted in "Presidential Debate: Bush v. Kerry," *Black Collegian*, October 1, 2004.
3. Linda Shrieves, "The Popular Kids: They Are Smart, They Are Motivated to Excel, and These Minority Students Are in High Demand," *Orlando Sentinel*, April 3, 2005, p. F1.
4. Editorial, *Baltimore Sun*, March 14, 2005.
5. Ibid.
6. Ibid.
7. Avis Thomas-Lester, "On Black Campuses, Trend Is More White Students," *Virginian-Pilot*, November 10, 2004, p. A1.
8. Black, *Black Excel*, p. 52 (quotation from Norman Francis, a long-time, three-decade president of an HBCU, Xavier University in Louisiana). See also Robert Russ, "Historically Black Colleges and Universities," in Beckman, *Affirmative Action*, p. 478.
9. Shrieves, "Popular Kids," p. F1.
10. Ulysses de la Torre, "Arts Weekly/Books—U.S.: The Struggles of the 'Black Ivy League,'" *IPS-Inter Press Service*, February 26, 2005.
11. Ibid.
12. Schmidt, "New Route to Racial Diversity," p. A23.
13. Shrieves, "Popular Kids," p. F1.
14. Thomas-Lester, "On Black Campuses," p. A1.

CHAPTER 8

1. U.S. General Accounting Office, *Report to Congressional Requesters: Information on Minority Scholarships*, B-251634, January 14, 1994, p. 11.
2. Ibid.
3. Arthur Coleman et al., "Federal Law and Financial Aid: A Foundation and Framework for Evaluating Diversity Related Programs," College Board, 2005, 5n9.
4. LaVeist and LaVeist, *8 Steps to Help Black Families*, p. 5.
5. Ibid.
6. Kevin Miller, "Race Faces as Factor in Academic Community," *Roanoke Times & World News*, June 23, 2004, p. A1.
7. Ibid. See also Susan C. Thomson, "Schools Revamp Restrictive Scholarships: They Cite Court Decision on Race, Admissions," *St. Louis Post-Dispatch*, February 13, 2004, p. A1.
8. Peter Schmidt, "Not Just for Minority Students Anymore," *Chronicle of Higher Education*, March 19, 2004, p. 17.

9. Miller, "Race as Factor in Academic Community," p. A1.

10. Karen Rivedal, "UW Race-Based Grants under Fire; System Officials Say They're Legal and Needed," *Wisconsin State Journal*, January 23, 2005, p. D1.

11. Thomas Dolan, "Keeping the Status Quo Safe in America; Schools Caving In to Foes of Affirmative Action?" *Hispanic Outlook in Higher Education* July 12, 2004, 14, no. 20, p. 18.

12. Seth Peavey, "Group Looks at Legality of Race-Based Awards," *Daily Tar Heel*, April 4, 2005.

13. Peter Schmidt, "U. of Wisconsin Vows to Defend an Aid Program Based on Race," *Chronicle of Higher Education*, April 22, 2005, p. 29.

14. Ibid.

15. Glenn L. Starks, "*Podberesky v. Kirwan*," in Beckman, *Affirmative Action*, vol. 2, p. 678.

16. Leland Ware, "The Details Will Decide Campus Diversity Efforts," *News Journal*, April 27, 2003, p. 11A.

17. Ibid.

18. " 'Educate, Don't Segregate': Twenty Legal and Legislative Milestones in Higher Education," *Black Issues in Higher Education* 21, no. 9 (2004): 96.

19. DOE Press Release, "Department Issues Policy Statement on Race-Exclusive Scholarships," December 18, 1990, as cited in *Washington Legal Foundation v. Alexander*, 984 F.2d 483 (D.D. Cir. 1993), at 485.

20. *Nondiscrimination in Federally Assisted Programs; Title VI of the Civil Rights Act of 1964; Proposed Policy Guidance*, 56 Fed. Reg. 64,548 (1991), as cited in *Washington Legal Foundation v. Alexander*, 984 F.2d 483 (D.D. Cir. 1993), at 485.

21. *Washington Legal Foundation v. Alexander*, 984 F.2d 483, 485 (D.D. Cir. 1993).

22. Dolan, "Keeping Status Quo Safe in America," p. 18.

23. Federal Register, Volume 59, No. 36, Wednesday, February 23, 1994, *Nondiscrimination in Federally Assisted Programs; Title VI of the Civil Rights Act of 1964*, Part VIII, 8756, at 8759.

24. Ibid.

25. Ibid., p. 8760.

26. Ibid., p. 8762.

27. Editorial, *Sun-Sentinel* (Fort Lauderdale, FL), November 19, 1996.

28. Gerrie Ferris, "Around the South; Region in Brief," *Atlantic Journal and Constitution*, November 17, 1996, p. 10A.

29. Dolan, "Keeping Status Quo Safe in America," p. 18.

30. Ibid.

31. Ibid.

32. Ibid.

33. Ibid.

CHAPTER 9

1. Peter L. Platteborze, "GI Bill," in Beckman, *Affirmative Action*, vol. 1, pp. 442–443.

2. James A. Beckman, introduction to Beckman, *Affirmative Action*, vol. 1.

3. Gerry J. Gilmore, "Montgomery GI Bill Goes Unused by Half Who 'Buy,' " *American Forces Press Service*, August 10, 2000.

4. Ibid.
5. Platteborze, "GI Bill," pp. 442–443.
6. Ibid.
7. Ibid.
8. Ibid.
9. According to the VA, if the veteran wishes to use his or her GI Bill benefits for flight training, the student must already have a private pilot certificate and meet any requirements for the certificate.
10. This is not an exhaustive list, and gives only those programs for which there are frequent questions regarding potential GI Bill coverage.

CHAPTER 10

1. Killenbeck, *Affirmative Action and Diversity*, p. 32.
2. *Black's Law Dictionary*, 6th edition, St. Paul, MN: West Publishing Co, 1990, p. 1072.
3. The Administrator Interview: David Ward, "Affirmative Action Won't Matter if We Don't Have Instructions," *Administrator*, January 2004, Volume 23, no. 1, p. 1–7.
4. Paulina Ruf, "Hispanic Americans," in Beckman, *Affirmative Action*, p. 477.

Index

8 Steps to Help Black Families Pay for College, 67
Ability to pay, importance of as admission factor, 61–63
Academic majors, as factor relating to diversity, 79
Admissions, factors considered, 1–3, 33–40, 59–67
Admissions, rules to consider, 59–82
Advising, faculty role in, 80
Affirmative action, alternatives to, 41–58
Affirmative action, beneficiaries to, 3, 15–16, 30
Affirmative action, elimination of, 11, 19, 33–40, 41–58
Affirmative action, frequency in usage since 2003: elimination by states, 41–58; implementation by states since 2003, 33–40; role in admissions decisions since 2003, 59–63; summary of standards for usage, 28–29
Affirmative action, future of, 129–131
Affirmative action, general challenges to, 5–6, 9–11, 20, 105–106
Affirmative action, history of, 6–23
Affirmative action, myths regarding, 3–4
Affirmative action, opposition to, 5, 9–11, 38

Affirmative action, original purposes of, 5, 7, 17–19, 21–22, 108
Affirmative action, Reconstruction Era, 13, 97
Affirmative action, remedy for past discrimination, 17–19, 21–22
Affirmative action, time limitations, 8, 11, 30, 129–131
Affirmative action, usage historically, 1–2
Affirmative action, usage today in admissions: implementation by states since 2003, 33–40; reliance on various factors (gender, race, geography, etc.) today, 59–82; state restrictions, 41–58
Affirmative action, usage today in financial aid, 103–117
Affirmative action plan, 15, 22–23, 29–30, 64–67
African Americans. *See* Affirmative action, beneficiaries to
African American Student's College Guide, 55
Alabama, 22
Alaska, 22
Alaskans. *See* Affirmative action, beneficiaries to
Alexander, Lamar, 109

Alumni relations. *See* Legacy
American Civil Rights Institute, 9, 105
Andrews Sisters, 96
Andrew W. Mellon Foundation, 68
Angelou, Maya, 102
Annapolis. *See* United States Naval Academy
Anti-discrimination four, 18
Anti-Semitism, 14
Application, strategies on effectively completing, 59–82, 83–96
Arizona, 22, 56
Arizona State University, 38
Artistic talent, importance of as factor in admissions, 2, 27, 61–63, 70
Ashe, Arthur, 100
Asian Americans. *See* Affirmative action, beneficiaries to
Athletes, importance of as factor in admissions, 2, 13, 27, 61–63, 70–71
Attendance, minority students, historically, 14–15, 19
Attorneys, blacks as, historically, 14

Bakke, Allan, 16–18
Banneker Scholarship, 107–109
Basically qualified, 3
Beckman, Robert C., 87
Bell, Derrick, 102
Ben R. Lawton Minority Scholarship, 105–106
Bethune, Mary McLeod, 54
Bethune-Cookman College, 54
Binghamton University, 70
Birgeneau, Robert, 49, 52
Black, Isaac, 55, 67
Black flight from HBCUs, 99
Black Issues in Higher Education, 109
Blackmun, Harry, 11
Bluefield State College, 99
Bok, Derek, 14–15, 19
Bookstore, campus visitation to evaluate diversity, 78
Bowen, William, 14–15, 19, 68
Bowie State, 99
Bradley, Ed, 101

Brainstorming, as technique for drafting essays, 88–89
Brown, John, 97
Brown v. Board of Education, 98
Bureau of Refugees, Freedmen, and Abandoned Lands, 13, 97
Bush, George W., 23, 42, 104
Bush, Jeb, 22, 52–54

California: Ninth Circuit, part of, 22; Proposition 209, 10, 20, 29, 41–42, 47–52; *Regents of the University of California v. Bakke*, 17
California Institute of Technology, 50
California Proposition 209. *See* Proposition 209
Caltech. *See* California Institute of Technology
Campus security, 80–81
Campus transportation, 81
Campus visits, 75–78
Carnegie Mellon, 39, 104–105
Catalogue, college, 64, 76
Center for Equal Opportunity, 9, 105, 112
Center for Individual Rights, 9–11, 26, 38
Cheyney University, 97, 101
Choosing a College, 99
Chronicle of Higher Education, 10, 39, 42, 46, 48, 104
City of Richmond v. J.A. Croson, 108
Civil Rights Act of 1866, 113
Civil Rights Act of 1964, 5, 17–18, 20, 22, 27–28
Civil rights movement, 101
Civil Rights Project at Harvard University, 30, 43, 48, 54
Civil War, 13, 97, 99
Class. *See* Socio-economic status
Class based affirmative action, 30. *See also* Socio-economic status
Class rank, importance of, 60–63
Clegg, Roger, 105, 112
Coalition for Economic Equity v. Wilson, 47
College Board, 103, 115
College Democrats, 76
College of William and Mary, 10, 39

College Republicans, 76
College Resource Group, 35
College Scholarship Service, 115
Colorado, 56–58
Community service, role/factor in admissions, 59–63
Compelling governmental interest, 8–9, 18, 21–22, 28–29, 108
Compelling Need for Diversity in Higher Education, The, 26
Connerly, Ward, 10, 57
Coppin State, 99
Cornell University, 77
Counselor. *See* Guidance counselor
Critical mass, 25, 29–30, 103
Crosby, Bing, 97
Curriculum, college, as indication of diversity, 79
Curriculum, high school, importance as admissions factor, 59–63

Dartmouth College, 37
Days of Grace, 100
DeFunis v. Odegaard, 15
Delaware, 108
Demographics, degree considered, 30, 61–63, 65
Demonstrated interest, importance as admissions factor, 61–63, 75–76, 82
Department of Defense, 120
Department of Education, 109–116
Department of Education 1994 Final Policy Guidance, 66, 107–113
Department of Education Office of Civil Rights, 10, 66, 98, 104–111
Department of Veterans Affairs, 119–121, 124–127
A Different World, 97
Disabilities and affirmative action, 2–4, 61–63, 80–81
Dishonesty, on application, 72–73, 83
Diversity: benefits of, 26–30; evaluation of, by applicants, 63–67, 76–77, 79–81; evaluation of, by colleges, 33–40, 64, 123; justification/rationale for affirmative action program, 5–6, 8–9, 17–21, 27–28

Diversity rationale, 9, 18, 22, 28–29, 110–112
DuBois, W.E.B., 131

Eleventh Circuit, 22–23, 37
Ellison, Brooke, 3–4
E-mail, caution in regards to, 76
Engineers, blacks as, historically, 14
Enrollment, minority students, historically, 2, 14–15, 19
Equal Protection Clause, 5, 8–9, 11, 17, 20–22, 26, 28
Essays, importance of, 34–37, 61–63, 71–72, 83
Essays, proper construction of, 83–96
Essays, steps in composing, 84–90
Essays, successful examples of, 90–96
The Ethicist, advice on referencing race on application, 69–70
Extracurricular activities, importance of, as admissions factor, 61–63

Faculty, applicant evaluation of, as indication of commitment to diversity, 76–78
Fair race metaphor, 14–15
Fifth Circuit, 21–23, 44, 55
Financial aid, 10, 80, 103–117
Financial aid, federal guidelines, 109–117
Financial aid, private donors, 113
First generation student, importance of, as admissions factor, 61–63, 72
Flanagan v. Georgetown College, 106–107
Florida: decline in usage of affirmative action, 52–55; Eleventh Circuit, part of, 22; general state law restrictions, 10, 20, 29; One Florida Plan, 41–42, 52–55
Florida A&M, 54–55, 98, 101
Florida Atlantic University, 54, 111–112
Florida International University, 54
Fourteenth Amendment, 5–6, 17–18, 20–22
Fourth Circuit, 107–109
Fraternities, 77, 80

Free Application for Federal Student
    Aid, 114
Freedmen's Bureau, 13, 97
Free-writing, as technique in drafting
    essays, 88–89

Gap year strategy, 81–82
Gates, Henry Louis, 102
Geographic origin of applicant,
    importance as admissions factor, 18,
    61–63, 72, 111
Georgetown University, 77
Georgetown University Law Center, 107
Georgia, 22, 65
Georgia State University, 65
GI Bill, 13–14, 119–127
Grade Point Average, importance of, as
    admissions factor, 2–3, 59–63
Gratz v. Bollinger, 5–10, 17–20, 22–23,
    25–31, 33–40
Grutter v. Bollinger, 5–10, 17, 19–20,
    22–23, 25–31, 33–41
Guam, 22
Guidance counselor, role in process, 34,
    61–62, 64

Hamlet, 73
Hampton University, 67
Harlem Renaissance, 101
Harpers Ferry, West Virginia, 98
Harpers Ferry National Historical Park, 98
Harvard Law School, 15
Harvard Plan, 7, 18, 30
Harvard University, 4, 33, 39, 43, 48, 54,
    77, 98, 102, 104
Hawaii, 22
Higher Education Act of 1965, 97
Hispanic Americans. *See* Affirmative
    action, beneficiaries to
Historically Black Colleges &
    Universities, 3, 66–67, 97–102
History Channel, 87
Holistic review, 25, 28–29, 34–37, 55,
    69–71
Honesty, of applicant and in application,
    72–73, 83
Hopwood v. Texas, 20–22, 37, 42–44, 47

Housing, campus, 80
Howard University, 14–15, 67, 77, 99,
    100–102

Idaho, 22
Illinois, 37
Implementation of affirmative action since
    2003, 33–40
Indiana University, 39, 104
Initiative 200, 55
Interview, importance of, as admissions
    factor, 2, 61–63, 75

Jackson, Jesse, 101
Jazz, 101
Johnson, Lyndon, 14–15
Johnson v. Board of Regents, 22, 37
Journal of Blacks in Higher Education, 50
Journal of College Admissions, 76,
    79–81
Joyner, Tom, 67

Kaplan, 60
Kennedy, Anthony, 28
Kentucky, 23
Killenbeck, Mark, 30–31, 123
King, Martin Luther, Jr., 101

Lee, Spike, 101
Legacy, 13–14, 39–40, 45, 61–63, 71
Legal challenges. *See* Affirmative action,
    opposition to
Letters of recommendation, importance as
    admissions factor, 61–63, 73–75
Life experiences, 2–4, 25, 61–63
Lincoln University, 97, 99, 101
Loans, federally funded, 115–116
Loans, private, 116
Losing Ground, 103
Louisiana, 21, 44, 55–56
Louisiana State University, 56

Marshall, Thurgood, 13, 101
Martin Luther King, Jr., Scholarship,
    111–112
Maryland, 99, 107
Massachusetts, 50, 56, 105

Massachusetts Institute of Technology, 50, 105
Mechanical formula, impermissible use of race by admissions departments, 7, 22, 25, 27–29
Medical students, blacks as, 14, 15–16
Mentoring programs, 64, 79–80, 100–101
Michigan, 23, 56–57
Michigan Civil Rights Initiative, 57
Michigan State University, 57
Military, 119–127
Miracles Happen: One Mother, One Daughter, One Journey, 3–4
Mississippi, 21, 44, 55
Missouri, 56, 99
MIT. *See* Massachusetts Institute of Technology
Montana, 22
Montgomery GI Bill. *See* GI Bill
Morehouse College, 55, 67, 101
Morgan State University, 99
Morrison, Toni, 101–102
Musical ability, importance of, as admissions factor, 2, 13, 27, 61–63, 70–71

Narrowly tailored, 8, 18, 22, 27–30, 108
National Achievement Scholarship, 98
National Association for College Admission Counseling, 38, 59–63, 75, 79–81
National Association for the Advancement of Colored People, 7, 39, 54–55, 112
National Center for Public Policy, 103
Native Americans. *See* Affirmative action, beneficiaries to
Native Hawaiians. *See* Affirmative action, beneficiaries to
Nevada, 22
New Hampshire, 56
New York, 84–85
New York Times, 69–70
New York University, 83–85, 88
Newspapers, college, 78
Ninth Circuit, 22–23, 47
North Carolina A&T, 101–102
North Carolina State University, 10

North Mariana Islands, 22
Northern Virginia Community College, 108–109

O'Connor, Sandra D., 8, 11, 26–29, 41, 129–131
Ohio, 23, 34–37, 72
Ohio State University, 34–37, 72
One Florida Plan, 22, 41, 52–54
Open admissions, 101
Oregon, 22
Outreach. *See* Recruitment

Parents, role in completing application, 73
Pell, Terry, 10–11
Pell Grant, 104, 115
Penn State University, 59
Pepperdine University, 105–106
Percentage plans, 21, 41–52, 58
Percentage plans, criticisms of, 41–43, 47–52
Perkins Loan, 116
Peterson's Guide to Four Year Colleges and Universities, 1
Plus factor, 3, 7, 25, 29, 61–63, 72, 99, 111
Podberesky v. Kirwan, 107–109
Powell, Louis, 7, 9, 18–19, 22, 28–29, 110–112
Prairie View A&M University, 102
Princeton Review Course, 60
Princeton Review's Complete Book of Colleges, 1
Princeton University, 50, 68, 102
Principled affirmative action, 30–31, 123
Proofreading, importance of, on application/essays, 89–90
Proposition 209, 10, 41, 47–52, 55, 57, 66
Proposition 209, negative impact on enrollment, 47–52

Quotas, 6–7, 15, 17–18, 27–29, 41, 66

Reaffirming Diversity: A Legal Analysis, 33
Recommendations. *See* Letters of recommendation

Reconstruction Era, 13, 100–101
Recruitment, 10, 37–38, 45–46, 50
Regents of the University of California v. Bakke, 6–7, 10–11, 15–21, 23, 26–29, 107, 111
Rehnquist, William, 27–28
Reverse discrimination, 9–10, 15, 20, 25–26, 107
Role model theory, 9
Role models, 17, 79–80
Roosevelt, Franklin D., 120
ROTC Scholarship, 122

Safe schools, 81, 99
Sarah Lawrence College, 64
Scalia, Antonin, 9, 28, 130
Scholarships, 11, 39, 104–117
Schwarzenegger, Arnold, 51
Section 1981, 113
Segregation, 14, 21, 97–98
Servicemen's Readjustment Act of 1944. *See* GI Bill
Set asides. *See* Quotas
Shakespeare, 73
Shape of the River, 14, 19, 68
Shaw, Theodore, 7, 39, 47
Sixth Circuit, 23, 26
Smith v. University of Washington Law School, 22–23
Socialization theory of equality, 29
Socio-economic status, 15, 30, 34, 46, 60, 68–69, 104, 130
Soldiers and affirmative action, 119–127
Sororities, 77, 80
Southern Illinois University, 105
Southwest Texas State University, 71
Sowell, Thomas, 100
Space Availability Survey, 81
Spelman College, 55, 67, 99
St. Louis University, 104
Standardized tests, importance of, as admissions factor, 59–63
Stanford, 64, 77, 98
State law limitations, 41–58
State of College Admissions, 59–63, 75
Storer College, 97–98
Student Aid Report, 114

Student organizations, as relating to diversity, 79–80
Swarthmore College, 64

Talented 20 Program. *See* One Florida Plan
Ten Percent Plan, 20, 38, 41–47
Ten Percent Plan, proposed alternatives to, 44–45
Tennessee, 23
Tennessee State University, 101
Texas, 10, 20, 41–47, 55, 58
Texas A&M, 40, 42, 44–46, 102
Textbooks, 78
Thomas, Clarence, 28
Tip factor, 60–61, 71, 75, 99
Title VI, 5, 17–18, 20, 22, 27–28, 47, 99, 106–107, 109–111, 113
Transcript, importance of, as admissions factor, 2, 61–63

UCLA. *See* University of California at Los Angeles
United Negro College Fund, 54, 104, 112–113
United States Air Force Academy, 122
United States Coast Guard Academy, 122
United States Military Academy, 27, 122
United States Naval Academy, 27, 122
University of California at Berkeley, 41, 47–49, 51–52, 66, 83
University of California at Davis, 15–18, 47
University of California at Los Angeles, 47–48, 50–51
University of California at Santa Cruz, 66
University of California System, 47–52
University of Colorado, 57–58
University of Delaware, 108
University of Florida, 52–53, 98, 102
University of Georgia, 22, 37–40
University of Houston, 46–47
University of Illinois, 37
University of Maryland, 10, 99, 107–109
University of Massachusetts, 36–37

University of Michigan, 5–6, 8, 25–31, 34–37, 39, 57, 66, 70, 72
University of Michigan Law School, 6, 8, 23, 25–31
University of Missouri at Columbia, 106
University of North Carolina, 39, 105
University of Notre Dame, 40
University of Pittsburgh, 102
University of Tampa, 34, 69, 75, 89–96
University of Texas at Austin, 37–38, 41–47
University of Texas Law School, 20–21
University of Virginia, 2, 10
University of Wisconsin, 105–106
U.S. News & World Report, 65

Veterans, importance as admissions factor, 2, 13–14, 30, 119–127
Vietnam-era Veterans, 123
Viewbook, college, 64
Virginia, 108
Virginia Tech, 39, 104–105
Vocabulary, applicant usage of, 89

Wake Forest, 102
Washington, 10, 20, 22, 29, 55
Washington Initiative 200. *See* Initiative 200
Washington Post, 52–53
Washington University in St. Louis, 104
Wayne State University, 57
West, Cornel, 102
West Point. *See* United States Military Academy
West Virginia, 97–99, 108
Wilberforce University, 97
Winfrey, Oprah, 101
Wisconsin, 105–106
World War II, 13–14, 120

Yale, 39, 98, 104
Young, Andrew, 101

About the Author

JAMES A. BECKMAN is Associate Professor, Law and Justice, University of Tampa, Florida. He is the editor of the widely acclaimed *Affirmative Action: An Encyclopedia* (Greenwood 2004), which reviewers have called "inspired" and "essential."

REFERENCE
CENTRAL CONNECTICUT STATE UNIVERSITY
NEW BRITAIN, CONNECTICUT